POLITICAL LEADERSHIP & NIHILISM

POLITICAL LEADERSHIP & NIHILISM

A STUDY OF WEBER & NIETZSCHE

ROBERT EDEN

UNIVERSITY PRESSES OF FLORIDA

A University of South Florida Press Book

Tampa

Max Klinger, "Philosopher" (1909). According to Professor Horst Baier, this etching hung in Max Weber's workroom (*Nietzsche-Studien*, 1982, p. 312). Dieter Schubert wrote, "The philosopher stands near the slumbering woman, points questingly beyond 'himself' and 'you,' over river, waterfall and mountain toward heaven. There, however, over the peaks, his mirror image, with a titanic expression on his visage, stretches toward him. That is Zarathustra's vision of the higher man, who appears clearly, brighter than the living, above the peaks in streaming light" ("Nietzsche-Konkretionsformen in der bildenden Kunst," ibid., p. 292). Photograph courtesy of Carus Gallery, New York City.

The following publishers have given permission to quote excerpts from copyrighted material:
Oxford University Press: Max Weber, *From Max Weber: Essays in Sociology*, translated and edited by Hans H. Gerth and C. Wright Mills; New York, 1958.
Random House, Inc., for works by Friedrich Nietzsche: *Beyond Good and Evil*, translated, with Commentary, by Walter Kaufmann; New York: Vintage, 1966; *Ecce Homo*, translated by Walter Kaufmann and R. J. Hollingdale; New York: Vintage, 1967; *The Gay Science*, translated, with Commentary, by Walter Kaufmann; New York: Vintage, 1974; *On the Genealogy of Morals*, translated by Walter Kaufmann and R. J. Hollingdale; New York: Vintage, 1967; *The Will to Power*, edited by Walter Kaufmann, translated by Walter Kaufmann and R. J. Hollingdale; New York: Vintage, 1968.

University Presses of Florida, the agency of the State of Florida's university system for publication of scholarly and creative works, operates under policies adopted by the Board of Regents. Its offices are located at 15 N.W. 15th Street, Gainesville, Florida 32603.

Library of Congress Cataloging in Publication Data

Eden, Robert.
    Political leadership & nihilism.

    "A University of South Florida Book."
    Bibliography: p.
    Includes index.
    1. Authority. 2. Leadership. 3. Nihilism.
4. Weber, Max, 1864–1920—Political science.
5. Nietzsche, Friedrich Wilhelm, 1844–1900—Political
science. I. Title.
JC571.E36   1984   320.2   83–17075
ISBN 0–8130–0758–5

Printed in the U.S.A. on acid-free paper

For Anne;
for my parents, Philip and Rose Eden;
and for hers, Ma and Pa Shotz.

CONTENTS

ACKNOWLEDGMENTS

IN ITS early stages, this inquiry was guided by Samuel H. Beer. For myself and many other graduate students at Harvard, he provided a radiant and productive atmosphere in which to work and teach. We learned through him what the liberal regime of pragmatic tolerance and government by discussion could mean at its best.

A Graduate Prize Fellowship from Harvard University financed two research trips to West Germany, where Johannes Winckelmann generously aided my studies at the Max Weber Archive of the University of Munich. Wolfgang J. Mommsen lent knowledge, moral support, and encouragement and trenchantly criticized a much earlier version of chapters 1 and 2.

Critical readings of parts of the thesis on which this book was based, by Michael Walzer, Barry O'Connell, and Charles Taylor, helped me to see its problems from the perspective of the reasonable left and convinced me that a complete rethinking was necessary. Dalhousie University provided research and travel grants which made it possible.

Without the efforts of many well-wishers, this work would have come to naught. George Armstrong Kelly and Allan Nelson gently kept my eyes on the prize. My colleagues at Dalhousie proved themselves to be not only scholars but gentlemen when it counted. To the faculty judges, referees, and staff of University Presses of Florida go special thanks; I could not have asked for better editors.

The hardest form of gratitude is emulation. It was through Norman Jacobson's essaying and his effort to recover Albert Camus in deed and speech that I first awoke to the problem of nihilism. John H. Schaar did more than anyone to set me thinking about what is noble.

Sheldon S. Wolin introduced me to Weber and to political theory as a vocation, then had the wisdom to send me away.

Mark Blitz led me farther than I had intended to go with Nietzsche and Heidegger and taught me the need for *l'audace*. Most of the questions explored in this study were posed by my mentor and model of the political philosopher, Harvey C. Mansfield, Jr., who kindly kept his counsel about the answers. The skepticism and genial prodding of Hiram Caton raised my adrenalin whenever I teetered on dogmatic slumber. Should this book nevertheless have many faults, they mark my own incorrigible recalcitrance and originality.

ABBREVIATIONS AND TRANSLATIONS

WALTER Kaufmann's remarkable translations have given Nietzsche's writings currency in the English-speaking world. Citations to Nietzsche's works can be consulted by following the table of abbreviations below. Unless otherwise noted, page numbers refer to the Kaufmann translations. I have generally referred, however, to the sections of Nietzsche's work as he numbered them to enable readers of other editions to locate cited passages quickly. Many of the translations are my own, and where I have major disagreements with Kaufmann's translation, I have so indicated in the notes. Many minor corrections have been made to restore Nietzsche's original punctuation and marks of emphasis.

English editions of Weber's works have been similarly cited for the reader's convenience. The quality of these translations varies considerably, and I have therefore relied on the German original, indicating my divergence from the translation on important terms or phrases.

Weber's personal copy of Georg Simmel's *Schopenhauer und Nietzsche* was available for scrutiny at the Max Weber Archive of the University of Munich in 1970, where Johannes Winckelmann kindly helped me to make use of it. I am not an expert on Weber's cryptic handwriting, but after living with his marginal comments for some years, I have come to regard it as a useful source of evidence for gauging what Weber knew about Nietzsche. In the notes to this work, I have attempted to describe Weber's markings and marginal comments and thus to make them more widely available as evidence that Weber was aware of Nietzsche's teaching in considerable depth and held strong views on what Nietzsche did and did not think.

TABLE OF ABBREVIATIONS

Nietzsche's works:

ASZ	*Thus Spoke Zarathustra* (in *The Portable Nietzsche*, edited by Walter Kaufmann)
BGE	*Beyond Good and Evil: A Prelude to the Philosophy of the Future*
BT	*The Birth of Tragedy*
EH	*Ecce Homo*
GM	*The Genealogy of Morals*
GS	*The Gay Science*
KGW	*Kritische Gesamtausgabe* (ed. Colli and Montinari)
TI	*Twilight of the Idols* (in *The Portable Nietzsche*)
WP	*The Will to Power*

Weber's works:

ES	*Economy and Society,* ed. Guenther Roth and Claus Wittich. 3 vols.
From Max Weber	*From Max Weber: Essays in Sociology,* ed. H. H. Gerth and C. Wright Mills
Methodology	*The Methodology of the Social Sciences,* trans. E. A. Shils and H. A. Finch
PE	*The Protestant Ethic and the Spirit of Capitalism,* trans. by Talcott Parsons
PS	*Gesammelte politische Schriften,* 2d ed., 1958
PV	"Politics as a Vocation," in *From Max Weber,* pp. 77–128
RS	*Gesammelte Aufsätze zur Religionssoziologie.* 3 vols., 1963
SV	"Science as a Vocation," in *From Max Weber,* pp. 128–156
WG	*Wirtschaft und Gesellschaft*
Wissenschaftslehre	*Gesammelte Aufsätze zur Wissenschaftslehre.* 3d ed., 1968

INTRODUCTION

"A nihilist," said Nikolai Petrovitch. "That's from the Latin, *nihil,* nothing, as far as I can judge; the word must mean a man who . . . who accepts nothing."

"Say, 'who respects nothing,' " put in Pavel Petrovitch.

"Who regards everything from the critical point of view," observed Arkady.

"Isn't that the same thing?" inquired Pavel Petrovitch.

"No, it's not the same thing. A nihilist is a man who does not bow down before any authority, who does not take any principle on faith, whatever reverence that principle may be enshrined in."

"Well, and is that good?" interrupted Pavel Petrovitch.

"That depends, uncle. Some people it will do good to, but some people will suffer for it."

Turgenev, *Fathers and Sons,* 1862

NIHILISM is familiar to historians from its beginnings in Tsarist Russia, where the term was applied, by liberals and conservatives, to describe and blame the revolutionary anarchists. To philosophers, it is familiar because of its prominence in the thought of Nietzsche and Heidegger. To literary scholars, it is well known from its career over two centuries in European literature.[1] It has been mercifully absent from American politics, however, until recently. As a term of praise and blame, American political scientists have taken little note of it, doubtless because it has been a stranger to American political discourse.[2] Its absence may be traced to the original governmental design. The Founders of the Republic sought to exclude most questions of "ultimate concern" from political controversy. They tried, with notable success, to initiate or secure a moderate politics which would be characterized by conflicts over interests, predominantly economic interests. Relying on a long tradition of political studies, they thought that most issues of high principle could not be settled politically, or that the attempt to do so would exact an intolerable price in human suffering and ill-being. They had ample reason to doubt that a civilization could foster science, commerce, and the productive arts, give great scope to popular passion in free elections, and still seek to settle major spiritual and moral questions in politics. They prized the first goal under the rubric of "progress," resigned themselves to the second under the protections of representative government, and tried to combine these two goals in such a way as to rule out the third. To the American Founders it seemed evident, from the hapless experience of all previous popular regimes, that such questions of principle would inexorably turn democratic politics into a war between fanatics and unleash the most immoderate passions.[3] It was not fortuitous, therefore, but rather a result of their planning and providence, that *nihilism* played an insignificant role in American political discourse long after it had become a standard theme of political conversation in Russia and Europe.[4] For nihilism is a term of praise and blame suited to a politics obsessed with ultimate questions and convulsed by ultimate commitments. This planning and provision has progressively (and with accelerating rapidity) been abandoned by educated opinion in the legal profession, the universities, and the Supreme Court. Hence the Constitution is no longer authoritatively interpreted in American public law as a plan for moderate self-government.[5] The probable future therefore promises all the excitement, intolerance, and intransigence that has in the past made European politics so interesting and so fratricidal. While nihilism remains a relative novelty, Americans have a brief respite before its baneful career is fully under way in the United States. During this respite there is reason to prepare for a new extremism, in which the charge of "nihilist" will become common coin and overbearing factions will have learned to use it for partisan purposes. My hope is that this study will help both to dispel the aura of enticing novelty that surrounds nihilism and to prepare the reader for calm reasoning when this respite ends.

How does nihilism, as a term of blame *or praise,* square with the standards for approving or condemning political leaders that befit a free people? What *is* the standard that befits a free man and a citizen, or better, "a gentleman and a scholar," or, best of all, a good man and citizen? I have addressed these questions through a commentary upon the controversy between Max Weber and Friedrich Nietzsche over the importance of political leadership—a controversy in which their positions on nihilism play a decisive role in determining the standard by which leadership is ranked. The inquiry begins with Weber's earliest formulation of his argument. I consider in chapter 1 the strength and appeal of Weber's argument by comparing it with Woodrow Wilson's more familiar doctrine of leadership. I turn in chapter 2 to the weaknesses of Weber's initial argument, identifying the reasons that led him to revise and reformulate it. The reasons have to do with Nietzsche. The center of the study is a commentary on Nietzsche's nihilistic politics, which I introduce in chapter 2, and on his argument against the kind of political leadership that Weber advocated, an argument discussed in chapters 3 and 4. Weber's final teaching on this theme is subjected to critical scrutiny in chapters 5 and 6. This last formulation was Weber's most comprehensive attempt at a critique of political leadership, posing and answering the questions I have raised concerning standards. Because I find that these questions were not adequately posed or answered by Weber, my commentary culminates in an attempt to surmount the critical shortcomings of his conception of political leadership and to formulate a more adequate standard, in chapter 7.

This study was undertaken before the revised Voting Rights Act was brought before Congress in 1981. Despite the disclaimer in the act's language, there are many reasons to fear that in practice this law will further the cause of proportional representation by race. If I had seen this misfortune on the horizon, I would have devoted more space to Weber's vigorous opposition to proportional representation in Germany.[6] Instead, my attention was focused on what then seemed the most ominous development that a study of Weber might illuminate: the plebiscitary system for selecting presidential candidates in primaries, which governed the campaigns of 1972, 1976, and 1980.[7] It seemed evident that Weber's understanding of plebiscitary political leadership was more rational and more realistic, and hence better prepared for the dangers and opportunities of this selection system, than the conceptions that prevailed in the reform movement. I have tried to explain why in chapter 1. It seemed reasonable to anticipate that the attractions of Weber's conception would be more apparent, to an untutored eye, than its pitfalls. The balance of my study is therefore devoted to these dangers and to a comprehensive assessment of Weber's significance for the future of American politics.

Weber's great virtue was matter-of-factness; his political writings, like his scholarly works, bristle with acutely perceived particulars. But these extraordinary writings on German politics have exercised only minor influence in Anglo-Saxon studies. I should be surprised if more than a few journalists now prominent in England or North America have read Weber's political journalism. (The notable exception was Hans Morgenthau.)[8] One might expect the translation of Wolfgang J. Mommsen's study to alter this situation, but that is most unlikely.[9] For the obstacle to our learning more from Weber's experience lies in the strengths of his political analysis. Its attention to particulars binds it to a distant politics, remote from the concerns that confront serious journalists today. This work attempts to overcome that obstacle by concentrating upon Weber's doctrine of political leadership as it bears on the future of American politics. It is not intended as a substitute for a reading of Weber's *Politische Schriften* but rather an incitement to read them. My intention is to initiate a critical but respectful dialogue with Weber, in which journalists whose concern is not antiquarian can fruitfully engage. Journalism has become an increasingly independent political profession, unfettered by the traditional limits that once restrained its excesses, undisciplined by the constitutional system of checks and balances, and slavishly attentive, on the whole, to intellectual fashion.[10] If there is to be any restraint upon it for the immediate future, the primary source of restraint will have to be a sober intellectual fashion, stabilized by matter-of-fact concentration on enduring political problems. Weber's emphasis upon responsibility and inward restraint may serve American politics well as such a source of sobriety, until something more formidable than "absence of malice" can be brought to the defense of the Republic.[11]

In composing this inquiry, I have been mindful of the expanded range of journalistic activity and of the dynamic vitality of what has been called (by Tom Wolfe and others) *The New Journalism*.[12] As the imperatives of large-scale organization and production came to dominate the newspapers and television, intelligent readers turned away in self-defense, to look elsewhere for their knowledge of "the world of concern to us"—the world of affairs, of the *pragmata*.[13] The new journalism has drawn, with telling effect, on the art of the novel, to bring us into "the world of concern" to its subjects or victims.[14] It is consequently more resourceful than normal journalism in conveying standards of approval and disapproval for evaluating political leadership. At its best, it might aspire to emulate Solzhenitsyn, to become a second, moral government.[15] But the drift of intellectual fashion is not in that direction, and because it has not been for some time, the new journalists are more likely to decide that liberal democratic institutions and the morality of ordinary American citizens are evils from which mankind should be liberated.[16] The forerunner and nonpareil of new journalism in the latter tradition is Nietzsche, and in considering his writings I have not been squeamish about calling attention to their significance as high-brow journalism and "cultural subversion."[17]

There is a reason to be scrupulous, if not squeamish, in this regard. No one who knows Nietzsche—and who is not (as Weber would say) "spiritually dead"—can fail to see that humanity rarely attains such a height. Few have had such gifts or such weapons. In a democratic age, attainment and ability so exceptional are customarily cut down to the scale of more common ambitions and capacities. Drawing Nietzsche down to the level of journalism—however high the brow—surely risks that leveling. The question is whether one can be true to Nietzsche's work without running this risk. I shall argue, on the basis of ample evidence, that Nietzsche himself repeatedly took this risk. He deliberately came down to "journalize." The book on which I shall dwell longest, *Beyond Good and Evil*, is an exercise in which the eye is "forced to focus on what lies nearest, the age, the around-us."[18] Exegesis should not be less circumspect than the original text—or more squeamish.

Nietzsche was an individualist who turned his back on the politics of modern states. He led the solitary philosophic life and was one of its most profound poets. He is a writer's writer and demands a reader's reader. He strove to be an "unpolitical German." To make him political and to treat him as a political theorist or activist, therefore, seems to do violence to his antipolitical individualism. Hence a significant tradition of Nietzsche studies has grown up, under the aegis of Walter Kaufmann, to protect Nietzsche against politics, including his own.[19] I shall consider Nietzsche's individualism in some detail.[20] But my work joins that of many intelligent students in turning away from the hypothesis that has prevailed under Kaufmann's influence for some decades. Our conclusion is that Kaufmann's hypothesis—that Nietzsche's art and philosophy can be understood apart from his politics, by circumventing, "transcending," or sublimating political questions—has exhausted its power to illuminate.[21] From the outset this hypothesis was, in my view, an attempt to sweeten and water down what Nietzsche thought. There was something laughable in an interpretation that allowed us to flirt with nihilism, to enjoy the largess and academic privilege of liberal democratic societies, and to conceal (both from readers and eventually from ourselves) Nietzsche's intention to slay the goose that laid such golden eggs. For Nietzsche meant to make a pâté de foi grasse out of that bourgeois goose. Kaufmann's prettification leads to trivialization, a forgetfulness of the audacity and ruthlessness of Nietzsche's enterprise. To combat this amnesia, we must learn to read Nietzsche again, eyes and minds open with regard to his politics.[22] Still, literary scholars who have come to love Nietzsche's thinking by probing the depths and testing the diamond-brilliant surfaces of his writing should agree with me that the corrective against vulgarity is strict attention to the text and detail of Nietzsche's arguments. In chapters 2–4, I have tried to satisfy the most demanding aficionado by my fidelity in interpretation.

A note on the definition of terms. This is in part a study of opinion leadership. It attempts to attain critical distance on a form of politics which shapes events indirectly by influencing opinion. One of the techniques of shaping opinion, as George Orwell warned us, is to redefine key terms of political discourse. Unfortunately, academics who should know better have participated actively in the technique of creating new realities and making reputations, by redefining crucial words and thereby confounding long-standing traditions of civilized discourse. This has especially been the case with terms such as "liberalism" and "representation," through which we understand the liberal democratic regime and the liberal political tradition. One task of serious political journalism today must be to resist this "newspeak" whenever it threatens to make moderate self-government unintelligible. I have attempted in this book to retain the stable body of meanings that all students of the liberal tradition would recognize, whether they learned from Louis Hartz, Sheldon S. Wolin, Leo Strauss, Raymond Polin, or Eric Voegelin. To retain these stable meanings, I have inducted the reader into extended discussions of The Federalist, Woodrow Wilson, and Weber. I show that the liberal political tradition has undergone several metamorphoses: I argue that part of the accomplishment of Wilsonian opinion leadership was its success in redefining liberalism, just as subsequent "new liberals" have tried to disassociate themselves from Wilson's liberalism. But to understand these vicissitudes, it is necessary to be clear about the original principles of modern liberal politics; there is no substitute for understanding the philosophic founders of that politics.

A similar problem arises with the term *historicism*. I am obliged to adopt this term in order to discuss Wilson's debt to Burke and in order to distinguish Weber from the German Historical School in National Economics and Nietzsche from Hegel. Most informed students of philosophical nihilism would agree that it is impossible to understand Nietzsche and Heidegger if one does not comprehend their use of terms like "historical horizon" and "historicity." [23] To do so one must distinguish their radical, practical historicism from the theoretical historicism of Hegel and the German Historical School. [24] Most social scientists have heard from Karl Popper about the "poverty of historicism" and have disdained Hegel and what Marx retains from Hegel's theoretical historicism. [25] Their attitude is less clear, however, toward practical historicism, which rejects Hegel. In chapters 2–4, I clarify Nietzsche's practical historicism by exhibiting his philosophical politics. I then inquire (in chapters 5 and 6) whether Weber discovered a fundamental alternative.

Social scientists have been inattentive, to say the least, to Weber's dialogue with Nietzsche. In this study I have indicated the price of such neglect and attempted to demonstrate that one can investigate their relation honestly, without in any sense diminishing the greatness of Weber's defense of liberal democratic institutions. [26]

The current view of Weber's limitations is fairly represented by Robert C. Tucker:

> The idea of building a systematic politics upon the foundation of a concept of leadership belongs primarily to the twentieth century. Max Weber pointed the way early in the century. In his essay on "Politics as a Vocation" (1918) he defined politics as "the leadership, or the influencing of the leadership, of a *political* association, hence today, of a state." [27]

But, according to Tucker, "No systematic account of politics in terms of leadership emerged" from Weber's work. [28] The study to follow should raise questions about this assessment. Weber's thought was not only seminal. It was far more coherent and thoughtfully articulated than contemporary political science has recognized. Its intellectual power has yet to be tapped and remains a potential formative influence on American politics. Tucker does not foresee the blind alley into which we may be led by his project of "building a systematic politics upon the foundation of a concept of leadership." This study constitutes a critique of that project.

I have not tried to summarize my argument on political leadership and nihilism in this introduction, because I have presented it as methodically and concisely as I could in the text. The reasoning unfolds by ascending in stages from opinions currently held. This process will at times be disquieting, but perhaps that is unavoidable. It has been wisely said that "it is essential to political philosophy to be set in motion, and to be kept in motion, by the disquieting awareness of the fundamental difference between conviction, or belief, and knowledge." [29] I have tried to convey to the reader enough of that motion to call this a study in political philosophy.

Opinion Leadership and the Liberal Cause

It is a basic fact of the human will that man would rather will annihilation than not will.

Nietzsche, *The Genealogy of Morals*, 3.1

WEBER first formulated his teaching on political leadership in the inaugural lecture he gave upon coming to Freiburg University in 1895. This highly compressed statement of his convictions has deservedly received much attention, but it will reward more. We shall examine it, without repeating earlier studies, in this chapter and the next.[1]

Weber's argument for political leadership is highly controversial because it is the crux both of his attempt to transcend liberalism and of his defense of liberal democratic institutions.[2] That defense is widely regarded as important because of its innovations: new measures appear necessary because liberal democracy is threatened by novel dangers to its effectiveness and legitimacy. The most dramatic threat seems to come from revolutionary mass movements, whose energy must be absorbed and whose passions must be redirected, through mass parties and demagoguery, into the service of liberal democracy. Weber's analysis of politics as a vocation describes how this is done and braces politicians to do it. At a higher level of principle, Weber faced the most formidable critics of liberalism, Marx on the left and Nietzsche on the right, adopting their scientific insights and measuring up to their most penetrating critiques. Weber's position, therefore, does not suffer from the crippling debilities of principled philosophical liberalism. His science announces, and he accepts, an end of ideology, including liberal

1

ideology. Hence the criticisms that have made works like *The Federalist* unworthy of the serious attention of contemporary intellectuals strengthen Weber's claims to it. Furthermore, Weber upholds a heroic standard of responsibility in the way he transcends liberal principles: politics "as a vocation" is not merely a noble alternative to liberalism; it is noble *because* it does without liberalism while defending liberal democracy.[3]

These claims for Weber are in many quarters almost clichés. Like many truisms, however, they conceal serious problems—in this case about the relation between liberal democracy and political leadership.[4] To make some of these problems explicit, in this chapter I will compare Weber's argument for the importance of political leadership with Woodrow Wilson's.

It was principally through Wilson's reinterpretation of the liberal tradition that political leadership first became respectable in American political discourse. It is a tribute to his influence that we have come to think of a liberal as a progressive, for greater democracy and social change; that liberal opinion has come to be synonymous with leading opinion; and that liberal democracy has come to require plebiscitary methods of leadership selection, as in the present system of primary elections—so that to be a liberal now means to be for plebiscitary leader democracy.[5] We have, since Wilson, become addicted to the habit of affirming liberal values by affirming political leadership. Or—to use the language of "popular will" and of Weber and Nietzsche—we have grown used to willing both together. But since it is not clear how the present crisis of liberalism will be resolved, perhaps these habits of will may prove more enduring than allegiance to liberalism. To grasp Weber's potential significance for the future of American politics, it is helpful to recall how we lost our liberal suspicions of political leadership and became attached through our liberal enthusiasms to it. This was especially Wilson's work. By comparing his argument to Weber's, we may attain a clearer view of what it would mean to will political leadership without that remnant of liberalism which Wilson retained.[6]

1. LEADERLESS LIBERALISM

Wilson had reached the conclusion (by a path we cannot here retrace) that private government, the rule of party bosses and special interests, had supplanted public government. This was a consequence, he thought, of the doctrine and system of the Founders of the American Republic—although in contradiction to their intention. To fulfill their intention—to restore authority and energy to the public offices established by the Constitution—Wilson believed it would be necessary to implant a new teaching. The old teaching, the authoritative opinions and legislative science that had so far informed American politics, had proved to be a bulwark of private government.[7] Perhaps no audience that Wilson addressed was more tied, by sentiment and training, to the old teaching than the Bar Association of the State of Virginia, to whom he spoke in 1897. His remarks on this occasion confronted the older liberal tradition with the bold claim that the government of the United States, as constituted by the Founders and defended in *The Federalist,* was leaderless government. However, as we shall see, Wilson tempered boldness with discretion and rather subtly deflected suspicion of political leadership by eclipsing the light of *The Federalist.*[8]

"Leaderless Government" is a critique of "some of the radical features of our constitutional arrangements."[9] Wilson denies that the Constitution need be radical in practice or that a change of the fundamental law is required. What is radical is the direction imparted to American politics by the policies that have accompanied the Constitution; to replace the established public policy, one need only treat the constitutional edifice as a completed work, cleanly separable from the old doctrine.

> But we are now choosing policies, not forms of government. The nation is made—its mode of action is determined: what we want to know is: What is it going to do with its life, its material resources and its spiritual strength? How is it to gain and keep a common purpose in the midst of complex affairs; how is its government to afford it wisdom in action?[10]

Today this no longer sounds like an argument, but only because we have been persuaded so thoroughly by it. Its original purpose was originally no less than to separate the Constitution from the architectural principles on which it was built.[11] The questions raised here by Wilson were not, of course, definitively answered by the Constitution or *The Federalist.* Nonetheless, it was intended that the answers to be worked out in subsequent practice should be profoundly shaped by the understanding of republican government which had informed the Founders, and which they thought were embodied in the fundamental law. When John Marshall later reminded the Court that "it is a Constitution that we are expounding," he surely understood it as guiding statesmen (in and out of Court) on major questions of policy and expected men like Wilson to expound a science of representative government, the "science of politics" referred to in *Federalist* No. 9.[12] The purpose of the classic exposition in *The Federalist* was not merely (perhaps it was not even especially) to insure the ratification of the law; it was also to transmit a practical science, and to light the path of future policy. To make the papers part of the Founding was to secure the liberal teaching firmly in American practice and to imbed the law in a tradition of intelligence. Because the regime set in motion was to be a dynamic, commercial society, in which the arts and sciences would flourish, rational statesmen would require continuing guidance from architectonic principles. For such a regime could not be founded at one stroke.[13] The Convention had made a good beginning; it would be salutary if the Founding were revered; yet from *Federalist* No. 49 we learn the political value of traditionalism on rational, not on traditionalist, grounds.

Wilson overlooked this distinction; he implied that it was merely respect for ancestral ways that bound his conservative audience to the older liberal tradition, and he exhorted them in effect to abandon both. "Our fathers were choosing men, and so must we be. They chose governments to suit their circumstances, not to suit their ancestors; and we must follow the like good rule."[14]

As a disciple of Burke, Wilson was embarrassed by the Lockean character of the American Founding. It is awkward for a Burkean to oppose traditional reverence for the Constitution by an argument for urgency, expediency, or present circumstances. But it is worse to adhere to theoretical principles which had pernicious effects; and the reverence for a Lockean beginning only made Lockean principles more secure. Wilson's rhetoric reflects these dilemmas. He both affirms and denies that "we are now choosing policies, not forms of government."[15] He is apparently seeking a mode of reform in which the revolutionary choice of a new form of government would be accomplished by a choice of men, not by a choice of constitutions, a mode of reforming policy and opinion that would not appear to be a revolution in either. Wilson's emphasis upon the study of facts is in part a resolution of these difficulties or a Burkean means of quieting Locke.[16]

Wilson had to be circumspect about "fact" in order to obscure the possibility that the legislative science of the older liberal tradition could comprehend and master present circumstances. He must finesse the difficulties posed by *The Federalist*'s realistic appraisal of the great facts of human nature that bear upon the choice of policies and forms of government. The liberal enlightenment, prior to Wilson, had combined a prudent (but popular) fear of power with a sober (but universally intelligible) reading of human nature as striving after power. A properly ordered political law would bring these politically relevant facts into sharp focus by instituting a perpetual vigil, a constantly reinvigorated suspicion, against any departure from the strictly limited powers granted to each official.[17] Leadership, as a close look at the language of *The Federalist* will amply confirm, was considered to be precisely such a departure and the one most likely to occur in a democratic republic. Only in a single instance, "the leaders of the Revolution," did *The Federalist* speak favorably of political leadership.[18] This singular, extraordinary reliance upon "leadership" was apparently not to be part of their constitution. Publius generally employed "leader" as a term of opprobrium.[19] Once the republic was placed on a sound footing, the leaders of the Revolution would disappear, to be replaced by (or to reappear transformed into) a chief magistrate, court justices, senators, and so forth. In describing these offices, *The Federalist* used "leader" as a pejorative, with roughly the connotations of the German *Verführer*—"tempter," "seducer," "deceiver."[20] Leadership was so steadily linked to faction that the remedies against faction—perhaps the entire constitutional scheme as a remedy against the dangers of faction—could equally be taken as remedies against political leadership. The only imaginable form in which "independent leadership in action" could appear, once the Constitution was working, would seem to be demagogery, treason, or tyranny.[21] The Founding Fathers went to great lengths to be leaderless. For if one defines policy and leadership as Wilson does, one must conclude that the liberal tradition before him considered it a vice: "Policy means massed opinion, and the forming of the mass is the whole art and mastery of politics. How is this massing done among us? Who chooses our leaders, and by what process?"[22]

Madison had observed that all government was founded upon opinion. But he went on to promote a constitutional piety that would only indirectly form the mass into a law-revering multitude. The great objects of government were to be secured by relying upon reason and institutions rather than upon the popular arts of persuasion or the massing of opinion by leaders. Under this rational and "radical" arrangement, habitual suspicion of leadership did not depend on the temper of statesmen or their "art and mastery." Reason guided passion by attaching the interest of the man to the prerogatives of a place; the rivalry and jealousy of ambitious public men would make them wary of each others' ambitions and suspicious of the slightest encroachment on their jurisdictions. The separation of powers was thus intended to mold the conduct of elected officials, and by indirection to attach the public to the habits and customs appropriate to republican government.[23] Montesquieu had explained this indirection in his maxim "At the birth of societies, it is the heads of republics who make the institution; and it is then the institution which forms the heads of republics."[24] To the Founders, this seemed a reliable substitute for elusive virtues. Wilson concluded that it had become a vicious circle and set himself the task of leading a generation of statesmen out of it.

Wilson discredited liberal suspicion of leadership, then, by obscuring its rationale, by reducing it to mere prejudice, and by diminishing the voice of the Founders in American political discourse. Until recently, Wilsonian liberalism seemed to yield a stable consensus in which *The Federalist* was hardly missed. The Constitution could be left to the courts, and under the new "policy leadership" of the Supreme Court, the older liberal tradition could be excised from the fundamental law. A generation of public-spirited consultants and experts could be educated without *The Federalist* while greatly enhancing the intelligence and competence of personnel in public life. Yet despite Wilson's success, the reader is doubtless aware that suspicion of political officials remains a dominant theme of American politics. And observers like Hugh Heclo have noted that the rise of professional experts in every domain of public policy has made leadership by publicly elected officials almost impossible.[25] To understand how Wilson's argument could have these effects, we must take it a few steps further.

2. OPINION LEADING INDIVIDUALS

Contemporary critics of Wilson, such as Edward Bourne and Lawrence Lowell, perceived that Wilson meant to alter the limits imposed on popular leadership by older liberal suspicions; and they raised roughly the objections of *The Federalist*.[26] In his reply to them,

Wilson indirectly acknowledged that he intended to inaugurate an era of experimentation with leadership that would transform the character of the American experiment with popular government. According to *The Federalist,* the point of that experiment was to prove that popular government could be good government, despite the wretched record of all previous democratic and republican regimes. The United States could overcome the chronic weaknesses of previous democracy and make it choiceworthy before mankind and the tribunal of reason.[27] Wilson's oblique reply to his critics began by making the case for popular government depend upon its ability to govern and legislate without the hindrances of the separation of powers:

> [If] any reform which would tend to give national legislation that uniform, open, intelligent and responsible character which it now lacks would also tend to create that popular interest which would unhinge the Constitution [then] democracy is so delicate a form of government that it must break down if given too great a facility or efficacy of operation.[28]

Wilson relies, then, upon confidence in the firmness and strength of popular government in the United States. His reply seems to presuppose that the initial experiment had entirely and finally succeeded, so that the ground for doubt no longer existed. Against Lowell and Bourne, Wilson took popular opinion about the unquestionable goodness and success of the American experiment as his point of departure. It was as if no challenge to the form of government or, more comprehensively, to the liberal commercial republic, could be entertained. The test was no longer whether democracy could be improved by the discoveries of representative government so as to overcome the strong case for other regimes. The test became whether a popular government entrusted with wide powers, with great facility and efficacy of operation, could be robust and united rather than chronically ill. The new experiment would test the moral constitution of American Democracy, its strength of character and political health. Since this was a higher test and more of a gamble, Wilson had to acknowledge, if only implicitly, the possibility of failure. The new experiment depended heavily upon leaders to elicit what was best in the national character. Accordingly, Wilson replied to his critics that he could not believe democracy "so delicate" and expressed his faith in conservative public opinion in the United States, reminding his critics that, in the last analysis, this opinion was the only support of the Constitution itself.[29] This reply suggests that Wilson intended to rely ordinarily upon what had previously been viewed as a support of last resort. Now that such a conservative public opinion had been formed, it could be tempered and made to bear a constant strain. Confidence and faith in it is consequently the sine qua non of leadership: like an orator, Wilson almost leaves it to public opinion to choose between his confidence and his critics' suspicions. If the argument was not circular, it was ad hominem.

To accept Wilson's argument is to rely directly upon what is best or most robust in the national character and to become accustomed to leadership that draws heavily upon it. The new experiment, as Wilson's reply may indicate, would by turns test the limits of how much power democratic government can wield (or how much "efficacy and facility of operation" it can muster); and if this test brought it to the brink of collapse, it would test how much "character" a democratic people could display in crisis. These are tests of democratic self-confidence and of faith in popular government. Such tests require leaders like Wilson, who are both loyal to the faith and crucial to its success; without leaders to precipitate the testing, the experiment would never be made. The argument is both ad hominem and circular; it is lucidly, consciously circular.[30] But one may doubt whether this lucidity could characterize the rank and file (or even much of the leadership) of Wilsonian liberalism. Perhaps the experiment could not be successful without giving a generation or two as hostage to opinion. However this may be, for Wilson to initiate it, he had to understand the role of faith within it but not be captive to that faith. And to judge the experiment today, we require both detachment from such faith and a clinical eye for the enthusiasms on which Wilson relied.

Wilson's own capacity for such detachment is evident in a remarkable letter on his ambition and intention, written in early manhood.

I have a passion for interpreting great thoughts to the world; I should be complete if I could inspire a great movement of opinion, if I could read the experiences of the past into the practical life of the men of today and so communicate the thought to the minds of the mass of the people as to impel them to great political achievements. Burke was a *very* much greater man than Cobden or Bright; but the work of Cobden and Bright is much nearer to the measure of my powers, it seems to me, than the writing of imperishable thought upon the greatest problems in politics, which was Burke's mission.[31]

The great movement of opinion that Wilson initiated did not rest upon opinion but rather upon "great thoughts," especially of thinkers like Burke; it was to be a movement of translation from political philosophy into public policy, lending the impetus of great thought to democratic politics. At first glance, Wilson might seem to be an advocate of ideology. But at least by intention his experiment was an alternative to liberal enlightenment as the propagation and popularization of liberal political philosophy. Wilson did not accept Lincoln's emphasis upon the Declaration of Independence and modern natural right.[32] Early in his career, Wilson had been highly critical of popular government, but eventually he decided to rely upon faith in it, as a condition of modern statesmanship. He reached the need for such faith as a conclusion, following Burke and Bagehot in their analyses of popular government in Britain.[33] Wilson's experiment was a translation of their formulations of British experience with parties, parliament, and government by discussion. He was confident that the faith in popular opinion so natural to public opinion in the United States was in accordance with a rational understanding of the great problems in politics, or with *imperishable* thought. The sanity of Wilson's position depends upon a continued correspondence between the movement of opinion he initiated in politics and the main tendency of science and political philosophy. If the imperishable thought of the greatest minds were to take another direction, Wilson's position could only be defended by a species of know-nothing liberal fundamentalism. It is therefore not surprising that to attain critical perspective on the problematic relation between political leadership and liberal democracy, we must ascend once again to political philosophy.[34]

Let us return to Wilson's "Leaderless Government" and to his insight into the weak point in Montesquieu's circle for forming statesmen:

We talk of statesmanship and of policy sometimes as if they arose out of institutions; but we know that they do not. They are the children of individual initiative and of individual strength of character. The framers of our Constitution in this country made a great deal of institutions; but after all, institutions only create the condition under which action must be planned: they do not breed action.[35]

To persuade the legal profession of the respectability of political leadership, Wilson had to eclipse *The Federalist;* but he also needed a great and inspiring thought, a new principle or a new object of liberal enthusiasms. This principle was adumbrated, almost unnoticed, in his statement above. Wilson required a statesmanship and policy that were not the progeny of the Founding Fathers; he discovered that both could be fathered by the individual. The independent statesman was not only his own man but his own child; he could adopt as his father the principle of individuality. This paradoxical suggestion should seem odd in a disciple of Burke, since Burke understood the tension between modern individualism and social duty or between individuality and virtue. But perhaps Wilson was not far from Burke in seeking to harmonize individuality and leadership.[36] Tocqueville had suggested that individualism be combated through participation in politics. Wilson took up this suggestion but thought it would be necessary to make higher education support such harmonizing.[37] In the university, Wilson found a place set apart from the Constitution and free from the habits of suspicion it promoted, an institution potentially indifferent to the older liberal tradition.

Wilson had wanted early to be a statesman. The colleges he attended permitted him to exercise his initiative both as a leader in extracurricular activities and in an unconventional study of politics. He knew from experience how individuality formed in college could become the basis of a new education for public life and help provide a way out of the circle of republican education inscribed by Montesquieu. He had developed himself as though he were in Britain preparing for a parliamentary career. Wherever he taught, he left behind a college debating society modeled upon the British House of Commons. As an educator, he intended to breed "a race of men habituated to the methods of public business"; drill in debate could create "a much to be desired class who early make attendance upon public affairs the business of their lives."[38] He did not have to make political education or the breeding of action the main business of college. It was enough if educators respected and then celebrated (as they do now) leading individuals and opinion leaders, enough to establish the principle that "We are not put into this world to sit still and know; we are put into it to act."[39] Wilson was the first American statesman to discover college as the best place to learn liberal enthusiasms without liberal suspicions, in which to lionize ambition, under the aegis of individuality, without inculcating mature distrust. It was part of his genius to have combined the charming playfulness of youth with the presence of mind to exploit it for public purposes. American higher education could be turned to national service by cultivating a circumspect activism and intelligent individuality, while the opportunity college provided for the exercise of initiative would enable the ambitious to form a public character and distinguish themselves as leaders. It was altogether predictable that the political science of *The Federalist* would be replaced, in Wilson's university, by his own.

To elevate the quality of American political life, Wilson sought to bring men of quality into the public service bearing a new stance toward the relation between leadership and liberalism. But the principle of individuality also pointed toward a redefinition of the liberal common good which helped to make leadership more central to American politics. By reinterpreting equality of opportunity as opportunity for self-development, by linking it to a new conception of individual dignity, Wilson made it a principle of innovation and an object of liberal enthusiasm that fairly cried out for popular leadership. Once equality of opportunity ceased to be coordinated with stringent limits on the legitimate objects of governmental action (as had been the case for Locke), it would require the ever renewed exertions of innovative leaders, not only to assert new demands but to coordinate and constrain them. Even without Wilson's exemplary performance, the presidency was bound to become the focus of liberal enthusiasms, as the dynamic point of leadership in the American regime, once individual self-development was accepted as integral to the liberal common good. Thus the principle of individuality could indeed father policy and a new statesmanship.[40]

A parallel analysis could be made of Wilson's teaching on other liberal values, such as accountability and impartiality in government. But let us take the most striking case, his reinterpretation of publicity in government. Clarity had been essential to modern liberal politics from its inception. The liberal common good was emphatically not metaphysical; it did not lend itself to the disputes of theologians or the manipulations of priests; it explicitly did without claims to rule based upon virtue.[41] Still, it was never doubted by the philosophic founders of modern liberal politics, or by *The Federalist,* that the securing of liberty and property would require government and that government would entail confidential deliberations of various kinds.[42] Wilson rein-terpreted clarity and publicity to mean that liberal politics had to be open, all outside and no inside, with nothing secret or confidential.[43] It is thus no surprise that certain suspicions should multiply in Wilson's experiment. After Wilson, public officials are subject to new suspi-cions; to defend secrecy and confidentiality is to risk scandal and to put oneself at the mercy of opinion leaders. When clarity becomes an ob-ject of liberal enthusiasm in Wilson's way, it works against mere mag-istrates to the advantage of leading individuals. General suspicion of ambition or power-hunger, regarded as universal traits of human nature, had worked against popular leadership. This mistrust is transposed by Wilson into a narrower suspicion, of confidential government, that threatens duly elected officials rather than the self-appointed leader of public opinion. It encourages the elected to adopt the methods of popular leadership in bidding for power not conferred by their office. Wilson, one might say, handicapped the haves against the have-nots. This should inflame suspicion, since the haves in ques-tion are the ones who have competed for a public trust and in this re-spect have it, while the have nots have not. Wilson's effort to compel government to be superlatively public thus helps to bring into being a new kind of private government by unelected representatives.[44]

   The Federalist had counseled statesmen in the art or science of bringing citizens to support a constitutional order—first through the operation of the offices it established and, where necessary (as in the ratification campaign), through less formal means.[45] Wilson attempted instead to use established offices and extraconstitutional practices in order to promote public-spirited action through direct leadership of public opinion. Rather than relying upon the competition between branches of government, Wilson sought American equivalents for the opinion-forming debates of the British House of Commons. His cri-tique of leaderless government and of *The Federalist* supports the con-clusion that Wilsonian political leadership was intended to guard and lead an extraconstitutional orthodoxy, a public opinion amassed and directed by popular leaders. That orthodoxy was to be liberal, al-though cut loose from the moorings of earlier liberal doctrine. The bearers of this leading opinion support leadership as the cutting edge of their enthusiasms and come to regard the suspicions of older liberals as a barrier to progress, hence as a species of conservative prejudice to be actively opposed.

   Although this sentence sounds like a truism, which describes characters that are familiar to us all from reform politics, it merits a closer look in the light of subsequent experience.

3. Liberal enthusiasms lost and found

The sentence, until recently, would only have mirrored to liberal opinion leaders an image of themselves. But among the novelties of the 1980 election was the discovery that this description applied as well to the opinion leaders on Governor Reagan's side; it required only slight rewording to suit their view of how they won, what their mandate meant, and why their opponents would resist.[46] This recognition brought reform liberals up short. And it may give us occasion to ponder with them some of the paradoxes of their own success, for this success was nowhere more evident than in the conditions of their defeat.[47]

Under the nominating system that prevailed (by and large) before 1968, Carter would not have been the incumbent in 1980, Reagan would not have been the Republican nominee, and John Anderson could not conceivably have mounted an Independent campaign. Nor would the sequel in Congress have looked as it did, had the House not finally given way to Wilson's critique of congressional government by destroying what remained of the tight discipline and oligarchic control of its legislative business under the old committee system. In tandem, these two major achievements of reform had the immediate effect of making possible the helter-skelter passage of the Reagan Administration's tax program, in a Congress staggered by the rhetorical appeal of a popular president and without means to discipline its own membership.[48] Wilsonian reform politics had made plebiscitary selection through primaries the norm and opinion leadership over the resistance of checks and balances the preferred style. What resulted was a form of plebiscitary leader democracy that gave conservative populism a cutting edge, the appearance of steamroller momentum, and a sudden opportunity to make liberal policies the target of dramatic reform. Perhaps the reversal was necessary and long overdue; arguably it was time the liberals learned (once again) that American populism can be conservative and withhold consent and that electoral justice is a two-edged sword. But the moral of the electoral story is less my concern than the opportunity these events supply, to liberals and the rest of us, to consider Wilson's legacy afresh. What supplied an impetus to do so was the prospect that Reagan and the Conservative wing of the Republican Party might prove to be the inheritors of Wilson's estate.

In retrospect, it is not too surprising that enthusiasm should migrate to the side of counterreform, that brisk and alert conservatives, fresh from the universities, could confidently adopt the Wilsonian style in opinion leadership, or that the Republican Party could be transformed into a vehicle of political movement and innovation. Clearly, the heirs of Wilson in the reform movement had relinquished Wilson's policy of expanding commerce as the basis of political progress throughout the world. And in doing so, they had proudly abandoned the vulgar, material basis of much democratic enthusiasm for liberalism. The new political economy of the Static State could not hold out the promise of prosperity or evoke the support that promise excites. When New Liberals claimed that "conservatism" in 1980 meant a return to bygone days that were gone for good, they meant a return to Wilson's days and Wilson's politics of progress, above all the promise of commercial expansion and prosperity. This gave the Republicans an uncontested claim to be the true Progressives.[49]

Thoughtful observers also knew that a more subtle shift had taken place within reform liberalism, away from enthusiasm and Wilsonian élan. Even when it came to ideals, liberals held themselves skeptically in reserve. This was a shift of greater potential for our theme than the mere replacement of Democrats by Republicans as the Wilsonian avant-garde. What it allows us to reflect upon is the emergence of a new disposition to will leadership without the remnant of liberalism Wilson retained—a remnant the Republicans may have adopted under another name. Such a disposition would require a more radical break with Wilson than libertarian or conservative opinion leaders have propounded, an initiative more likely to be made as a new kind of reform by disillusioned Wilsonians, or perhaps by *nuovi uomini* (new men) without affiliation. This would portend a new relation between leadership and the American regime.

Most liberals had become reluctant by 1980, quite apart from their reservations about Wilson's economic views, to inherit Wilson's legacy on Wilson's terms. Reform liberals might have attacks of nostalgia, as in their response to Senator Kennedy's convention speech in 1980. But on the whole they wanted to recover, or be immunized, from Wilson's infectious enthusiasms. They considered themselves experienced in disillusionment and enthusiasm-worn. Having defeated the older liberal tradition and routed its suspicions of popular leadership, the reform movement seemed to have exhausted its patience with liberal enthusiasms, especially as these no longer promised to hold the electorate to reform leadership. Once Americans had lost their distrust of opinion leaders, the thought was bound to arise that their persuasive powers could be turned against the promises and hopes of liberalism.[50]

The legacy of Wilsonian reform is too substantial to be ignored and cannot be simply disavowed. It has reshaped all avenues to power, as well as the modes in which all power is exercised. To be a serious citizen in the United States, one must stake out some claim to Wilson's estate. The possibility for the future of American politics on which the remainder of this chapter reflects is that of taking Wilson's legacy but on Weber's terms.

4. WEBER AND WILSON'S LEGACY

As a general introduction to Weber's argument, I shall consider first the claim it advances to incorporate and supersede Wilson's argument. The claim in question goes well beyond the observation that Weber anticipated the emergence of a plebiscitary politics that leaves very little scope for the kind of parliamentary leadership of public opinion that Wilson prized in Britain. Weber is better prepared than Wilson for what has become of "the rhetorical presidency" that Wilson and Theodore Roosevelt initiated. He explained why mass persuasion would elevate demagogic skills and irrational appeals, suppressing the modes of sober deliberation and public reasoning which Wilson sought to promote.[51] Weber gives a more comprehensive account of politics as a profession; he is more alert to the imperatives of mass electoral politics and of modern campaign organizations. But while these facts might stagger Wilsonians momentarily, they do not call into question their political principles.[52] The Weberian challenge is more serious. He argues that it is necessary to abandon Wilson's position at the level of principle in order to master opinion leadership, the sorcerer's apprentice that Wilson introduced into American politics. The Weberian charge would be that Wilson promotes Micawberism: instead of making provision for political leadership, marshaling our efforts to prepare a stratum for responsibility, Wilsonian reform politics places us increasingly at the mercy of fortune, undisciplined instincts, sympathies, and antipathies. The Wilsonian dispensation conceals what is problematic in the relation between opinion leadership and liberal democracy; to reveal what is problematic, we must replace Wilson with Weber as the generating architect of reform politics. The future task that Weber adumbrates is nothing less than the reforming of reform politics, root and branch: in its aims, its consequences, its dominant passions, and its drive. To clarify this task, let us begin with Weber's attempt to encompass and supersede liberalism and observe how Weber interpreted the liberals' disenchantment with their former enthusiasm.

When Weber gave his Inaugural Lecture at Freiburg in 1895, German Liberalism was demoralized and seemed a lost cause. By Weber's account, however, the German liberals had merely lost touch with the liberal cause; their disillusionment with liberal ideology served them as an excuse for deserting it. Weber's response was to place the liberal cause before their eyes, in the great migration of German farmworkers away from the Prussian estates:

> In the muffled, half-conscious urge to migrate is hidden a moment of primitive idealism. Whoever is unable to decipher it knows nothing of the charm of freedom. Indeed, its enchantment seldom touches us today in the quiet of the study. The naïve liberal ideals of our early youth have expired, and many of us have become prematurely old and all-too-wise: we believe that one of the most primordial drives in the human breast has been dragged into the grave alongside an expiring political and economic outloook.[53]

Since this passage has been taken to evidence Weber's liberalism, it is worth a close inspection. It describes how one can do without liberalism by learning to separate the liberal cause from ideals, opinions, or ideology. To decipher the cause one must consult passions and primordial drives in the human breast. One must be touched by a spell or sympathize with men who are enchanted. The farmworkers will not tolerate conditions on the Junker estates, where there are only masters and servants. But the liberal cause is not primarily a matter of "freedom from all masters." Weber implies that the German farmworkers could endure servitude.[54] They are driven to migrate by the prospect that their offspring will be condemned, to the latest generation, to labor on someone else's land, moving in herds to the chime of an estate-clock. More is shown in Weber's treatment of their passions than may at first meet the eye. The farmworkers could bear servitude as a struggle for something greater for their descendants. The liberal cause seems to be constituted by responsibility to future generations; it comes to light only against the horizon of a projected future. The horizon of the liberal cause is not ideological but historical. It is constituted by certain drives or passions.[55] Weber gives special stress to the distinction between great and small passions—a distinction the passions themselves seem to assert—"the capacity to hate what is petty" is a capacity for a great passion. The farmers hate the prospect that their descendants will be degraded and diminished. A few pages later, Weber conjures up a loathing of pettiness to rebuke the leaders of the middle class: "Every one of us who retains the capacity to hate what is petty must view the recent doings of the bourgeois politicians as the petty machinations of political epigones."[56] Weber calls upon his audience to disdain this spectacle "with the passion of wrathful sorrow."[57] Great passions create their own horizon; primitive idealism springs from the human breast as spontaneously (if not as routinely) as primitive materialism. These are insights that can survive the dissolution of German Liberalism. Indeed, their significance may only begin to be clear when liberal enthusiasms have been dispelled. Conscious reliance upon the noble necessities, the drives or passions on which the liberal cause depends, may be possible only when it is impossible to rely upon liberalism.

The high contrast between the soberly pessimistic tone of Weber's lecture and Wilson's ebullient hopefulness is therefore necessary. Weber's argument is addressed to those who have inherited a once-enthusiastic liberalism. This is superseded and incorporated as the adolescent is embodied in the mature man. Weber does not simply comment on the evaporation of enthusiasm; the shift toward disillusioned sobriety is a precondition for greater passions. By anticipating the collapse of liberal ideals, Weber makes the travail of disillusionment necessary to devotion in a cause. Only when liberal ideals prove not to be grounded in anything firm or permanent does the real ground of passion for the liberal cause appear. The abandonment of liberalism as an outlook makes possible a more resolute stance toward the liberal cause by making necessary a leap of faith or ultimate choice. The era of naïve belief in liberal ideals is a passing moment in the history of the liberal cause because right beliefs about liberal doctrine are inferior to the conscious assertion of a value-standard or ranking. The historicist premise of Weber's argument is the transience of liberal principles. More generally, "all earthly ideals are transitory and changeable."[58] Weber encompasses Wilson by superseding liberalism.

5. A WILSONIAN OBJECTION

The claim just sketched might be challenged along these lines. Although Wilson relied upon liberal enthusiasms in introducing leadership into American politics, his critique of the American liberal tradition sufficiently anticipates the end of liberal ideology. At a deeper level, therefore, Weber does not reach Wilson's argument. Although Wilsonian opinion leadership has preserved certain liberal practices, Wilson drew a theoretical principle from Burke and the Historical School which subsequently enabled his reform politics to weather the end of ideology. Wilson found a mode of reshaping policy and public opinion that never need appear revolutionary. The Historical School provided Wilson an alternative to liberal enlightenment; the liberal orthodoxy that reform politics requires need not be grounded in any scientific claims. Liberalism could take the benign form of a "public philosophy," a summary of ideals and opinions that would articulate sentiments and projects, without greater pretensions: no one would be so foolish as to think a public philosophy was a public science.[59] To make a first step toward this relativism, Wilson construed the Founders' teaching as the first of many public philosophies, altogether outstripped by historical events. Thus Wilson's claim to have encompassed and superseded *The Federalist* was secured by a doctrine of the Historical School. By virtue of this improvement in doctrine, Wilsonian reform politics has remained dynamic and adaptable to shifts in public opinion, maintaining its lead by shedding liberalisms like snakeskins as it grew from decade to decade. In this respect, the discovery that "our highest and most ultimate earthly ideals are changeable and transient" was already part of Wilson's legacy.[60] And because historicist resignation to the eventual collapse of liberal enthusiasms was implicit in Wilson's original position, Weber's assertion of the liberal cause should require no significant reorientation of reform politics.

To do this objection justice, we must take up Weber's critique of the Historical School in the Freiburg Lecture. The twin pillars of Wilson's political thought, as the objection reminds us, were liberal political economy and the Historical School. Both Wilson and Weber drew upon these two streams of thought, while adding something that was found in neither: an argument for the importance of political leadership. The controversy between Weber and Wilson arises from this agreement. That is why it is not incorrect (though a bit anachronistic) to treat Wilson's argument as if it were before Weber's eyes. The Freiburg Lecture reflected Weber's comprehensive critique of the foundations of Wilson's politics; these were the target of Weber's anti-Wilsonian argument for the importance of political leadership. Wilson's notion of opinion leadership rested upon a unification of liberalism with the doctrines of the Historical School. Weber's counterassertion requires a break with both. From Weber's perspective, the precarious collaboration of liberal dogmatism with theoretical historicism upon which Wilsonian reform politics depended is fecund with confusion; it beclouds the problematic relation between liberal democracy and opinion leadership, indefinitely postponing a reckoning with the real tasks of providing for political leadership.

The objection calls for a closer look at what is constant in the reform movement that has enabled it to shed the Progressivism of Wilson's time, to welcome and then reject the liberal orthodoxy of the New Deal, and, most recently, to adopt the New Liberalism—all without endangering the Wilsonian mold. There must be a constant framework of what might be called Wilsonian customs, transcending the vagaries of political fashion and securing the stable horizon within which the liberal Proteus changes shape. We have suggested that the most interesting of these constants was the Wilsonian leadership convention; and we have highlighted the conventionality of prevailing assumptions by demonstrating that leadership was originally a novelty. Although as a bare phenomenon it was nothing new, as a presentable thing it certainly was. Wilson made leadership respectable, something to be publicly prized, sought, acquired, and willed by a liberal citizenry. The public acceptance of the importance of leadership, which subsequently became customary, formed an unnoticed precondition of reform politics, a hidden premise of American liberalism that has escaped critique and survived the mortality of all things liberal—so far. This Wilsonian custom is secured—as the objection correctly says—by a conjoining of liberal opinion with the insights of Burke or the Historical School. What the objection denies is that Weber attacked these foundations or thereby disclosed the possibility of a radical reorientation of reform politics.

"Political Economy and the National State" drew upon a study undertaken by the Association for Social Policy on the farm labor situation in the German border provinces of East Prussia. The study was conceived as a prelude to recommendations for policy and legislation.[61] Weber provoked a controversy over those recommendations in order to redirect the practical efforts of the association away from its established, predominantly economic inclinations, toward problems Weber regarded as more properly political. Weber called for the closing of the Polish border and the settling of German farmers in the border areas, thus reasserting Bismarck's policy and Bismarckian reason of state. (The primacy of economics and administration over politics was a premise of German political economy that Weber battled for from the Freiburg Lecture to the end of his career; it can be argued that it was a premise of Wilson's politics, but we need not pursue this issue here.)[62] Weber's purpose in asserting Bismarckian demands was to pose more fundamental questions concerning the nature of the German polity and the status of patriotic loyalty in the work of science. Weber approached the border question as a matter of membership or of what constitutes a citizen; and he did so because this is the kind of political question that must be resolved by a political judgment pointing to the constitutive principle of the polity. Weber's evident purpose was to raise the question that Aristotle would have called "constitutional," a question concerning the character of the regime. By forcing dispute onto this plane, Weber set the stage for his wider inquiry into the working constitution of the German polity or into its provision for leadership. The task Weber undertook went beyond his assertion that politics is superordinate to economics. Weber sought to demonstrate that the crisis of the working constitution took priority over all other issues in German public life. By clarifying the "leadership vacuum after Bismarck's fall," Weber showed that no adequate provision had been made for the regular recruitment and training of political leadership.[63]

Weber anticipated almost universal resistance to his public assertion of this issue. Integral to the problem that he outlined was the desire of every major class in Germany to postpone indefinitely any decisive conflict over the constitutional issue. The economically declining Junkers had no interest in bringing the crisis of leadership to a head. The working classes and the Social Democratic Party had none of the "Catilinarian fervor" of a revolutionary class bent on national leadership. The bourgeoisie was wholly apolitical in its traditions and paralyzed by fears of proletarian revolution.[64] Only a determined effort independent of the major classes would force a reckoning or bring the crisis of leadership into German politics. Such an effort was the practical initiative toward which Weber's argument was directed.

> [A]n extraordinary task of political education is to be performed, and no more serious duty lies before us than for each of us, in his small circle, to become conscious of this task: to work together for the political education of our nation, which must be the final goal of precisely our science. The economic changes of the transition period threaten the natural political instincts with destruction. It would be a misfortune if economic science also worked to the same effect, by inculcating a flabby eudaemonism, under however sublimated a form, or under the illusion of a more independent ideal of social policy.[65]

Political economy, however, was a bastion of resistance against any attempt to bring the problem of leadership selection to a head. Weber knew that no practical or legislative initiative would be forthcoming from educated circles unless the authority of the prevailing doctrines in political economy were countermanded. For those doctrines obscured the importance of "the natural political instincts," ignored the consequences of their destruction, and neglected the criteria of political judgment that would have to be shared if such political instincts were to be cultivated. It was precisely the mode of "reform politics" fostered by the Historical School that suppressed ultimate conflicts over the issue of leadership.[66] Because Weber's disagreement with prevailing doctrine was over the ranking of policy questions, he made his central topic the *Wertmasstab,* the criterion or value-measure by which all claims about the ranking of public issues are legitimately adjudicated.[67]

The criterion Weber asserts is inherently disputable and necessarily subjective.[68] It might be said that the question of leadership is implied in the national character of the German state. For it is not evident who acts for the nation or in what nationality consists. The indeterminacy of nationality and the indeterminacy of the form of the state are connected: for only if one knew how to rank citizens according to nationality could one rank the ways and means that make up the state. In particular, arrangements to provide regularly for leadership seem to require a prior determination of ranking. That Germany is a national state settles very little. But it does mean that the primary political problem will be to determine the national way of life. Weber asserts that this was the meaning of national unification: the founding of 1870 would remain incomplete, a childish prank, until the German nation was socially unified.[69] As if to accentuate how open the question of nationality was, Weber made no mention of religion and hardly any of the dynasty. The Conservative understanding of national character is not Weber's understanding: neither throne nor altar is essential to Germany's political being, by Weber's account. Weber and the Junkers assert different standards as the national standard. Weber's is a bourgeois standard that would prove to require liberal democratic institutions. But, like the Junker standard, Weber's *Wertmasstab* asserts a way of life, ranks citizens, and would settle in principle the question of who should rule.[70]

Weber's purpose in asserting his standard was to bring out the latent controversy that the Historical School in German national economics sought to avoid, a controversy over the qualifications of a leadership class. The political economists resisted the notion that politics requires the imposition of a way of life by a leadership class— particularly if that meant that a conflict that might lead to civil war was enucleated in the "national character of the German state." Weber made the controversy impossible to ignore by stating the most powerful case each class in German society could make against the claims to rule advanced by the other classes. He himself gave voice to the critique which the right, or the Junkers, could make of the urban classes. A commercial order and liberal democratic institutions do not generate the strengths of mind and will, or the political instincts, necessary to the governance of a modern state. A bourgeois, liberal Germany would cease to be a nation.[71] There is only one rebuttal that Weber's argument leaves open: the economically rising classes of the new industrial order must generate from their ranks a political class to assert their way of life. They must displace and dominate the economically declining Junkers, dictate new standards of public judgment by upholding their way of life against the Junker way, suppress old habits of deference, and surmount new fears of proletarian revolution. In sum, they must make their standard of qualification for ruling and leading *the* national standard, as Weber does in this speech. This is possible, however, only if they make themselves over by a national standard of responsibility: the liberal cause must be the national cause.[72]

As this summary may indicate, Weber's break with liberalism was most conspicuous in his rejection of the liberal preference for indirect forms of rule. On his interpretation, the liberal cause did not mean the end of domination or rule; it required a frank avowal that a way of life would prevail at the expense of other nations and that certain types of citizens rather than others would rise into ruling positions. The liberal cause is a struggle against other ways of life; the national character of the modern state requires social unification under a dominant way of life. To prevail amid nationalist states, the liberal cause must be asserted nationally. Conversely, it must incorporate the most inclusive reason of state, taking responsibility for "the enduring economic and political power-interests of the nation" and affirming the state as "the worldly power-organization of the nation."[73] Only so can the liberal cause be a national cause.

The Freiburg Lecture also pointed forward to the expanded conception of reason of state that we find in Weber's later studies. The principal theme of the lecture—how politically and culturally leading classes are affected by the development of capitalism—later became a central problem of Weber's social science.[74] The adaptation of reason of state to an "age of popular passion" later required Weber's typology of plebiscitary leader democracy.[75] In Weber's refashioning of modern liberal politics, the liberal cause implies a skeptical view of economic progress and the acceptance of national prejudice and mass emotionality as the givens of political life. The liberal cause must have the support of a tribe even if no tribe is ever fully or primarily liberal. By shaping modes and orders to prevent mass emotionality from damaging the national interest, the liberal cause can invest tribalism with the rationality of modern liberal politics—a modification that a tribe can accept in order to perpetuate itself and enjoy the permanence of a state. Weber's open impatience with traditional liberal squeamishness about domination points forward to his insistence upon domination as a category of his sociology. Weber asserts the liberal cause as a spirited imposition of a ranking of men. The articulation of the political law, or the legal constitution of the state, presupposes a standard of the national way of life. With that standard prominently in view, the defense and creation of political law comes to light as an assertion of "what is humanly great and noble in our nature."[76] On this view, the ranking by which citizens discriminate against what is base in themselves, the standard of national dignity, is an architectonic principle which can guide reason of state, if properly interpreted.[77]

According to Weber's analysis, the conflict between the Junker and the liberal commercial way of life cannot be deferred without stripping Germany of national leadership. He argued against the Historical School that it supplied an excuse for indefinitely postponing a public conflict over the working constitution. "The disciples of the Historical School are prey to a specific illusion: that we can refrain from asserting a conscious judgment of value." [78] This illusion puts us "at the mercy of uncontrolled instincts, sympathies, and antipathies." [79] It prevents us from holding ourselves firmly by reasoning to "an adequate project." [80] In the absence of an independent *Wertmasstab,* scholars and citizens will inevitably allow their political judgments to be shaped by the claims advanced by powerful groups, to whom they are bound only by "uncontrolled instincts, sympathies and antipathies." When the contending partisans desire to put off any major conflict over the provisions for leadership selection, or to keep the question of their own qualifications from becoming a public issue, the disciples of the Historical School will invariably supply some rationale for deferring to their will. Political economy will slavishly mirror the outcome of the struggle for power or provide reasons for submitting to the result. But since the necessity for leadership to assert a way of life is never visible without a prior value-judgment, the Historical School cannot envision any such necessity. An "adequate project" would connect reason of state to a prior ranking of ways of life. In the absence of any such criterion of political judgment, reason of state is impossible: one cannot rationally determine ways and means without a prior determination of ends. [81]

In arguing that national prejudice and reason could mutually support each other in political economic work, Weber's emphasis fell heavily upon patriotism as a motive for scholarship. In part this stress was due to the doctrinal bias against regime questions in the training of political economists. Weber found nothing in classical liberal political economy, or in the Historical School, to support the enterprise of political education he thought was necessary. Their participation would have to be elicited by national sentiments until reason and science could be brought around. The country could not wait for the revolution in political economy that Weber subsequently tried to carry through. But it is Weber's prolonged effort to encompass and supersede the Historical School and classical political economics which secures his critique of Wilson's position. The objection we have been considering is therefore untenable.

6. The end of public philosophies

Weber's critique, then, goes to the foundation of Wilsonian reform politics. This means that one cannot stay at the level of legislation and rules in comparing Weber's alternative. It would surely produce a different diagnosis of the present plebiscitary selection system, of the weakness of political parties, and of the problems of leadership in Congress. Different remedies would also flow from Weber's argument. But to see where the issues are joined, one must pursue the opposition to a further plane. Once it is recognized that public acceptance of leadership is conventional and was an achievement of Wilson's statesmanship, it becomes conceivable that the convention could be contested politically and that a challenge could be launched against the unseen agenda of Wilson's politics. Weber's initiative strikes at Wilsonian customs and norms, which are more basic than the rules governing party nominating procedures or the laws on campaign financing. To assess what Weber's challenge would mean for the future of American politics, this conflict over fundamental leadership conventions must be understood. Weber's alternative should not be construed as a project for a new public philosophy. That would presuppose the acceptance of the Wilsonian convention, in which the notion of "the public philosophy" has a place of honor.[82] The same may be said of "the rhetorical presidency," that conception of presidential leadership which leads one to expect inspiring eloquence and moral suasion from White House speechwriters.[83] The rationale often advanced by the Progressives for primary elections—that they would be a means to educate the public on issues—is likewise bound to the Wilsonian leadership convention.[84] Difficult as it may be to dissociate political leadership from Wilson's legacy of opinion leadership, that is what is required in order to take Weber's measure and assess the challenge he poses to reform politics. Weber's new "reform politics" would not promote a new liberal orthodoxy; nor would success in creating a public philosophy be a proper measure for assessing the political leaders Weber attempts to promote. Weber's critique of the theoretical basis of Wilsonian opinion leadership prepares the way for a practical effort, an effort to break the hold of those customs and habits on which opinion leadership depends. Partisan politics is a battlefield in which words are weapons; the Weberian words for Wilson's alternative, opinion leadership, would have to be *political evil*. Because the norms of Wilsonian leadership are presently thought to be innocuous or benign, that charge is (for the time being) difficult to imagine. To a degree, one may catch sight of what is radical in Weber by conceiving his argument on political leadership as a revaluation of liberal values: what has been devalued as "reactionary" by the reform movement is celebrated by Weber as essential to the struggle against reaction. For example, the desire to disguise leaders as mere populists or to ignore the politically relevant differences between men makes it impossible to defend the liberal cause forthrightly as a cause worthy of "what is humanly great and noble in our nature." [85]

Politics is not made more responsible and accountable when all arenas of government become like theaters open to all viewers. The effects are reactionary because public men are made prisoner to the appearances of the moment, aggressively manipulated by opinion leaders. The most important witnesses to whom politicians must be responsible are not yet born: reform politics, preoccupied with visibility, serves the present and the past, not the future. The doctrine that elitism and domination are crimes for which political leaders should mortify their flesh provides an excuse for them to "collapse inwardly" rather than defend liberal democratic institutions with fortitude and vigor against the Right and the Left. According to Weber, liberals who do not want to be puppets jerked by the Right or the Left must learn that, in politics, domination is the name of the game and take their maxim (as Weber does) from the Junkers: *Landgraf werde hart!*—"a politician must become hard." [86] These Weberian reassessments are not merely verbal inversions of the tenets of liberal reform. The practical meaning of Weber's attempt to end ideology would be the termination of opinion leadership, the end of the regime of public philosophies in American politics. These are remnants of liberalism that Weberian political leadership would attempt to do without.

Weber would not, of course, encourage political leaders to ignore the importance of opinion in politics. His Freiburg Lecture was a defense of national prejudices against academic doctrines that disdained such opinions and blinded political economists to their practical significance. [87] Rather than try to refine popular opinions through reason of state and constitutional reform, German political economists would have relied on administrative solutions managed by educated guardians like themselves. Opinion leadership does not necessarily reflect a regard for opinion in politics. Weber's critique of the Historical School can be applied, ceteris paribus, to reformers proud of the most advanced liberal orthodoxy and willing to do without the consent of the

less advanced, underdeveloped majority.[88] One can elevate the importance of opinion and vigorously deny that Wilsonian leadership is the
best form of politics for the defense and perfection of liberal democracy. To clarify this point, and to illustrate what in American political
experience might conform to Weber's notion of the liberal cause, let us
turn briefly to an example.

To clarify his notion of political leadership as an assertion of a
national standard of values (an assertion that would constrain, and
eventually extinguish, a contested way of life, by excluding its spokesmen from national leadership), Weber might have chosen Lincoln's initiative against the repeal of the Missouri Compromise, the Dred Scott
decision, and Stephen Douglas's doctrine of popular sovereignty.[89]
Lincoln based his statesmanship on the moral limits of a republican way of life propounded in the Declaration of Independence and on
the Constitution as the organic law securing that way of life. His image
for this union was the Constitution as a silver frame around the golden
apples of the Declaration.[90] The Republican victory in the election
of 1860 was rightly considered a victory for that union. It meant that
slavery, and all that slavery implied as a way of life, would henceforth
be confined to the existing slave states. Majority leadership in the national government was bound to pass to the free states as an inevitable
result of this confinement, for their numbers would increase while the
number of slave states would remain constant. It was equally clear to
both Lincoln and the secessionists that the decision of 1860, if left to
stand, would doom slavery and the prevailing way of life in the southern states to extinction. Prior to the election, the question had been
whether the United States could remain "a house divided," whether
two ways of life, based on slavery and free labor, could coexist under
the Constitution.[91] In Weber's terms, the question was whether "the
meaning of the founding of the nation" had been that the nation should
be "socially unified" in a single way of life.[92] Lincoln's reasoning articulated a standard independent of "undisciplined instincts, sympathies and antipathies" by which to adjudicate this question. He concluded that a political decision over the ultimate national standard was
unavoidable. The Constitution could not, and would not, be construed
to embrace both of two irreconcilable moral/legal alternatives. The
Dred Scott decision merely made this clear. The Constitution would be
made consistent either with slavery or with the Declaration. The choice
that Chief Justice Taney precipitated was between two national leadership classes, standing for opposed ways of life, only one of which

could prevail if the United States was to remain one under the Constitution.[93]

Wilson and the Historical School subsequently discovered a third possibility: Lincoln's reasoning was a public philosophy. His opposition to the public philosophies of Calhoun and Douglas was perhaps justified but certainly not for the reasons Lincoln had given. Without going into the debate started by the American Historical School as to whether the Civil War was necessary or as to whether a choice between two ways of life had to be made, one can see why the Wilsonian view of Lincoln's statesmanship as opinion leadership renders it unintelligible. Wilson's premise strikes at the reasoning by which Lincoln bound the Constitution, through the Declaration, to truths not amenable to transmutation by opinion leaders.[94]

It is also doubtful whether Lincoln's statesmanship would be supportable within the now dominant conventions of Wilsonian reform. Wilson required a divorce between leading liberal opinion and the original constitutional scheme.[95] Lincoln had instead deepened Madison's concern to entrench the parchment Constitution in ancestral prejudice to make it a firm bulwark of liberal reason of state in an age of popular passion. Rational statesmanship would have to rely upon firm constitutional prejudice, on what Lincoln termed "political religion," or resign itself to ineffectiveness.[96] Political religion would accompany and thus transform the constraints of the law, by bringing the mind into conformity with them. Its claims upon the mind would curb the claims of individuality whenever the necessities of republican government and the free unfolding of individuality did not harmonize. Political religion would be the voice of a *res publica,* the public thing or republican way of life, against the claim to "your thing." It would secure the meeting ground where Lincoln's reasoning and popular prejudice could come together to judge the claims of opinion leaders and would-be public philosophies. Once the Constitution's effect in curbing political behavior became merely behavioral, conveying no deeper moral habits or claims upon the mind, Lincoln thought certain forms of statesmanship would become impractical. He considered but rejected the divorce between traditional constitutional prejudice and liberal orthodoxy which Wilson promoted.[97]

These observations may prepare us for Weber's argument that a break with Wilson's position is necessary in order to recover reason of state and the legislative science of modern liberal politics. The argument suggests that rationality depends upon a traditional prejudice,

which cannot be shaken without depriving liberal politics of its footing. The disregard for popular opinion that finds expression in reform
without consent results in elitism without the power to govern, because
the bonds between governing science and ancestral prejudice or loyalty
have been severed. The weakening of confidence in the rationality of
liberal legislative science seems paradoxically to result from a weakening of prejudice. Weber's recourse to national prejudice was accordingly coordinated with an attempt to bind it to reason of state: without
strengthening one, the other could not be secured. Since Wilson believed he was accomplishing both, a closer look at what went wrong is
in order.[98]

7. POWER TO THE PIECES

The crux of the rational plans of the founders of modern liberal
politics had been a method of bringing individuality under the constraints of a common order. Liberal confidence in the possibility of
progress had originally been based on the motive power to be drawn
from energetic individuality released from the limits of the old regime.
Liberal legislative science supplied a new method of governing and ordering, which would not curb the powers of the individual as the old
regime had done. The necessities of government could be met without
much direct restraint on the passions, by means of a supple constitutional order that could reframe and regenerate itself to surmount all the
contingencies of political life.[99]
    Although this picture was clouded for Wilson by Burke's critique
of the rationalist principles of the politics of progress, Wilson did believe that he was making American politics conform as closely as possible to the highest models of modern liberal rationality in practice.
Wilson thought the electorate could be led to more rationally concerted
action if a parliamentary cadre along British lines, rather than a separation of powers, were made the mainstay of reason in politics. He fostered a cleavage between the constitutional scheme and liberal orthodoxy because he thought the existing scheme could not impart reason
to democratic deliberations. The promised result of the new opinion
leadership was a greater concentration of authority and power in public
offices, a withering of private government, and a more clearly etched
public awareness of the liberal regime as a distinctive common enterprise.[100] Although it generated several "new classes," however, Wil-

son's project failed to generate a national leadership class, much less a coherent regime.

This failure points to an unsolved problem that has bedeviled all modern political thought: the problem of establishing a principle of order by which individuality could be constrained without depriving modern man of all humanity. After the American Founders had put the older liberal solution into effect, the problem was reopened by Rousseau's powerful writings, and Wilson's vacillations reflect, without resolving, the subsequent crisis of liberalism.[101] If Weber's critique is correct, submission to "undisciplined instincts, sympathies and antipathies" was implied in Wilson's argument—and therefore a loss of constitutional rationality was predictable—from the outset. We may restate this by saying that Weber acknowledged the necessity to curb individuality. His assertion of a ranking of ways of life means constraint exercised by leadership. It does not mean the free unfolding of individuality. Because a comparable principle of restraint is difficult to discern in Wilsonian liberalism, reform politics has trouble in justifying the most obvious fact about the liberal commercial republic. Like all regimes, it imposes constraint upon individuality, constraint which comes to light in the plain fact that when we look at the citizenry we see a restricted range of most common types. This constraint bears down on everyone, albeit not equally. When it is widely regarded as unjustified, illegitimate, or unconstitutional, the regime or way of life is in question, the whole ensemble of customs and institutions which constrain individuality into certain forms. While "the power to govern" may be the most obvious casualty of reform politics, as a recent study from the Academy of Political Science suggests, and while this may provide a first reason for "assessing reform politics in the United States," reform has also promoted illegitimate power in government by making it difficult for citizens to assert or fashion a common way of life apart from govermental compulsion.[102] The agenda of expectations that political leaders must satisfy has grown geometrically as reform has singled out seriatim the constraints upon individuality that had in the past restricted Americans to a few dominant or most common human types. Counterreform has then raised the opposed claim that elected officials should strengthen those restraints, again seriatim. Once this process is set in motion, it leads inexorably to intense and highly public disagreement about the existence of any common principle to which political leaders can appeal and on which they can base their policies. *Is there* an order to which the many conflicting parties can appeal to curb the unjust assertions of selfish individuals, on the matter, say, of abortion? Can the alternative ways of life now open to Americans be brought under a single moral and legal order in the Constitution?[103] Wilsonian leadership seems to presuppose such an order rather than to assert it. Therefore reform liberalism lacks an answer to Weber's criticism of "the specific illusion" of the Historical School: that under its doctrine no conscious assertion of an independent value-standard is necessary.

Despite Wilson's concern with national leadership, in practice his directives require leaders to seek out distinctive constituencies whose separate claims call for articulate leadership. Without a leader these constituencies might not perceive their shared "individuality" or assert it in concert; without a collectivity, united by some common principle of individuality, opinion leaders would have no firm base of electoral support. The Wilsonian conventions of rhetorical, opinion-leading politics lend themselves to the assertion of individuality in concert with an aggressively opinionated group and to the defense of a group that has been (or can be persuaded that it has been) victimized by opinion. Such assertion and defense is promoted, by Wilson's argument against private government, as a politics morally superior to Madisonian interest group representation. The Madisonian multitude or plurality had been connected to the Constitution through institutions that promoted compromise; whereas the link to the Constitution that is most useful to leaders of identity-constituencies is the link that compels public recognition of their individuality as a source of constitutionally protected rights. To reap the benefits of that constitutional imprimatur, the leaders of such groups are almost *compelled* to hold themselves aloof from the kinds of compromise and persuasion that Madison's scheme was designed to foster.[104] Why undertake the arduous task of persuading a majority if one can gain his goal, without their consent, by "hanging tough" when a campaign manager, a congressional staff member, or a White House aide comes to court support? Thus the chief beneficiaries of the issue-oriented opinion leadership that Wilson strove to institute have turned out to be uncompromising and narrow- or single-minded individuals, whose constituents are firmly committed on a single issue. Instead of generating a parliamentary leadership class at the national level, Wilson's reform politics has fostered a multiplicity of intransigent constituencies. Quitting the founding theory did not promote public government, contrary to Wilson's hopes. But it gave private government loftier justifications, and claims that are quite independent of the legislative principles of republican government, despite the pro forma curtsey always made toward the Constitution. The result is a flourishing of reputedly liberal claims, each engendering its own leadership and lobby, seeking its niche in legislation and court-mandated rights, producing its distinct administrative agencies, its professional issue-networks, its congressional subcommittees and staffs, its distinctive journalists and media-tenders.[105] Wilsonian "common counsel" had been bound to popular consent. But the necessities of opinion leadership in the arenas of American politics seem to require a turn away from consent toward constitutional compulsion, a turn that militates against any sustained effort to compose a working regime and coherent leadership class. Government by discussion, which Wilson prized, must give way to a kind of serial subjection to ritual self-expression, in which each constituency asserts its claim in turn and suffers, without listening, while the others speak out for themselves. This is a disaster for Wilson's project but one that his reasoning and example did much to bring about. Such contradictions between Wilson's argument and its outcome lend weight to Weber's judgment that we must reject Wilsonian reform to recover the rationality of liberal democratic constitutionalism.

But Weber's critique of the Historical School and its theoretical historicism suggests a further problem. Does Wilson concede too much to the principle of individuality or too little? One might say "too much," because Wilson weakened the capacity of republican government to constrain or answer claims advanced by narrow factions on the basis of their distinctive individuality or way of life. But Weber could hardly criticize Wilson for the crisis of representative government or the loss of confidence in liberal principles of order. Weber held that science could not disclose an order or standard of value to which appeal could be made in curbing the claims of individuality. It could not because no common order was there to be disclosed.[106] For Weber, the principles of natural right articulated in the Declaration of Independence were even less than they were for Wilson; Weber did not look back upon them as a public philosophy.[107] Weber goes beyond Wilson in frankly asserting that no order is immanent in historical development and that the liberal commercial regime cannot, therefore, be secured in such a hypothetical order. There is as little in History as in Nature to constrain individuality. The foundation of a common order can only be created by a self-imposed constraint, in which the qualities or passions are ranked, or in which the self chooses its individuality by limiting itself. From that ranking alone can a polity derive the authority to constrain the claims of individuality.[108] Thus Weber's criticism of Wilson must be that he gave too little scope to individuality. Wilson perpetuated the illusion that the liberal cause could be stretched indefinitely to accommodate the claims of many small tribes; he did not see that the claim of individuality had to be asserted against such tribes to make them into a liberal tribe. Wilson gave no priority of rank to leaders whose individuality is bound to the liberal cause as the national cause. Weber's movement away from the Historical School toward an understanding of the liberal cause on the plane of practical historicism was an attempt to establish this priority.[109]

8. NIHILISM AND THE LIBERAL CAUSE

There is no need to identify Wilson with the fragmentation of leadership that we have discussed, but no reason to deny that so long as his project governs reform politics, this fragmentation is bound to accelerate. Nor is Weber's conclusion unwarranted, that Wilson's argument is unlikely to promote a reckoning with the comprehensive problem of leadership to which this fragmentation points. Despite his jeremiads about leaderless government, Wilson cannot, I think, satisfactorily respond to Weber's charge that his reasoning promotes Micawberism.

Yet Wilson is not without all defense, or at least a counterattack. Perhaps his best rejoinder would be to question Weber's position on its own ground, raising doubts about its internal cogency in theory and hence its stability in practice. The study to follow pursues this possibility. To develop a rebuttal along these lines, Wilson might call attention to Nietzsche's writing on the liberal cause in passages that clearly presaged Weber's argument.[110] These anticipated Weber's attempt to surpass liberalism by discovering a liberal cause more attuned to "what is humanly great and noble in our nature." They show why the collapse of liberal ideology need not affect our judgment that the struggle for liberal institutions was a cause worthy of man as man. The problem for Weber's position is that Nietzsche had developed these themes in opposition to liberal democracy. His interpretation of the nobility of the liberal cause was part of a rationale for abandoning or subverting the liberal commercial regime. In Nietzsche's account, the struggle for republican government pointed beyond liberal democracy to a new politics; his retrospective "Yes" applied to the past but negated any defense of liberal institutions in the present.[111] In his account as in Weber's, the liberal cause came to light historically; it required no reference to natural right. But Nietzsche's account brings us face to face once again with issues the American Civil War appeared to have settled: it moves us toward an aristocratic politics and a rehabilitation of slavery and tyranny.[112] This would not have surprised Lincoln, for if doing without liberalism meant doing without the Declaration, no defense of liberal democracy would have been conceivable to Lincoln. Nor is it accidental that Nietzsche's argument reopens issues that have long been considered closed for American political discourse and public morality. To affirm the liberal cause, according to Nietzsche, is to discover *his* concept of freedom, which is freedom both from public morality and from the limits of political discourse.[113] Nietzsche propounds a version of the liberal cause that is aggressively nihilistic. Nihilism is his answer to a paralysis of the will caused by morality: "Man would rather will annihilation than not will." [114] Nietzsche prescribes active nihilism, directed against morality, as the salvation of will. He teaches a devotion to freedom that would hold us devotedly to the tiller as we sail right over morality, destroying the remnants of our moral nature.[115] If Nietzsche is correct, therefore, willing leadership in the liberal cause, without those remnants of liberalism that Wilson retained, is merely the overture to a willing of leadership without the remnants of morality that Weber retained. What is at stake, according to these passages from Nietzsche's work, is a larger struggle between morality and nihilism, of which the matter of leadership is only a part. Nietzsche claims that once it is agreed that individuality must curb itself, the liberal cause must become the cause of nihilism.

The possibility that the arguments of Weber and Nietzsche run parallel, and may converge here, compels one to question whether there is a momentum in Weber's initiative that his argument cannot keep in rein. Does Weber's responsible sobriety and political moderation, so prized by his admirers in social science, rest on firm principles of resistance against the nihilism that Nietzsche proclaimed? In the study to follow we shall try to measure the distances that divide them and to judge whether these parallels point to an inexorable convergence. To be aware of such parallels is to understand why we must insist that Weber submit to certain questions. How is his reconfiguration of reform politics, and his attempt to reframe the liberal commercial republic as a regime without liberalism, different from Nietzsche's avowedly nihilistic experiment? What becomes of liberal politics if we abandon the plane of theoretical understanding as Weber and Nietzsche do, to reconstitute the liberal cause on the plane of practical historicism? Is Weber's defense of liberal institutions, then, anything more than an atavism, a mere residue of the struggles in which his "historical individuality" was formed? Must not Weber show that such a defense is necessary and possible as a defense against nihilism?

The difficulty of finding an answer to these questions within the circle of Weber's thought justifies sustained study of his relation to Nietzsche and makes one doubt that Weber's victory over Wilsonian reform politics, if it should come, would be more than Pyrrhic for the friends of liberal democracy.

2. PHILOSOPHY AND THE LIBERAL CAUSE

". . . the devil is old, grow old to understand him." This . . .
means that if one wishes to settle with this devil, one must not take
flight before him as so many like to do nowadays. First of all, one
has to see the devil's ways to the end in order to realize his power
and his limitations.

Weber, *Science as a Vocation*

WE have shown that opinion leadership is a more
problematic addition to liberal democracy than liberals in the Wilsonian tradition have been prepared to admit. We will see that it is even
more problematic when we consider Nietzsche's transformation of
"leading opinion" over the course of the next few chapters. But the
case for Weber's alternative is also far more questionable and controversial than social scientists in the Weberian tradition have recognized.
In both instances the lack of clarity can be traced, I believe, to the
same general cause. For neither reform liberals, nor Weberian scholars, have given the crisis of liberalism the attention it deserves; and
consequently, they have not shown the vigilance it demands. Both
groups have too readily assumed that liberal democracy could subsist
without liberalism in its classical or traditional formulation. In Wilson,
we have seen that assumption in a benign form. But more recently,
enthusiasts of reform have moved with hardly a blink from John Stuart
Mill to Nietzsche, or from a liberal defense of individuality against
majority tyranny toward a radical assertion of individuality which does
not include a liberal regard for consent and majority rule.[1] A similar
disregard for distinctions on which republican government depends
was displayed in social science. Once plebiscitary leader democracy

36

had become a fact of American political life on Wilson's terms, scholars began to adopt Weber's terms as a matter of routine, without pausing to wonder whether changing the terms might not eventually change the facts. Weber's doctrine of political leadership is truly perplexing and ought to give us pause. It becomes more evidently perplexing as one becomes aware that it contains Weber's response to the crisis of liberalism, reflecting both the gravity of that crisis and a sense of its exhilarating possibilities. It becomes a cause for philosophic wonder, finally, when one recognizes that the opportunities this crisis provides for extraordinary leadership are opportunities in which science and philosophy have a stake, in which, indeed, they may be at stake. As I shall try to demonstrate, these are reasons for taking Nietzsche as the foil for Weber's enterprise.[2]

Weber and Nietzsche both attempt to transcend liberalism. Up to a point, their attempts are parallel rather than at cross-purposes. The parallels support the prevailing view in Weber's scholarship: Weber adopted Nietzsche's scientific insights and measured up to his most penetrating criticism of liberalism; hence it is unnecessary to consider the matter more closely; one knows in advance that Nietzsche's reasons for disdaining liberal statesmanship, or for dismissing *The Federalist,* would only strengthen Weber's claim to serious attention. In this chapter, some of these parallels will be explored. Our effort to distinguish Nietzsche's interpretation of the liberal cause from Weber's account is designed to identify the sources of forward motion in Nietzsche's politics and thereby to indicate why Weber's initial argument on political leadership (in his Freiburg Lecture of 1895) was inadequate to restrain the potential momentum of hypermodern nihilism.[3]

Weber and Nietzsche ultimately diverge in their interpretations of the history of liberalism and of the struggle for liberal institutions—most conspicuously, modern capitalism. The divergence is most evident in Nietzsche's insistence upon the philosophic impetus of the scientific and political revolution with which the modern era began. The philosophic roots of that distinctively modern motion, the politics of progress based upon the scientific mastery of nature, are strangely ignored by Weber.[4] Nietzsche interprets what is most powerful and still vital in the liberal cause as integral to the cause of philosophy, engaging us to study the original coordination between modern liberal politics and the struggle of modern philosophy against the authorities of the old regime. Weber diverts attention from this entire problem, explaining the origins of the liberal commercial republic without reference to philosophy and chiefly (though not exclusively) by reference to the Protestant Ethic. This contrast is not, I think, merely a matter of historiographic significance. In this chapter, I will begin to show that it was integral to Nietzsche's attack upon liberal democratic institutions, and therefore to Weber's defense of them. For those "free spirits" who joined Nietzsche, liberal democracy was bound to seem unworthy of a thinking man's defense, and Weber's attempted marriage of the liberal and national causes was bound to be a matter for ridicule. Once it is severed from the cause of science and philosophy, the liberal cause becomes indefensible. And so it has, according to Nietzsche: except, perhaps, as a purgative or Mardi Gras, to exhaust rabble-rousers, nationalist Tartuffes, and moral fanatics. Light-hearted as these accusations may appear, they adumbrate the problems that called forth Weber's final formulation of his teaching on political leadership.[5]

1. WEBER AND NIETZSCHE'S LEGACY

In surveying the problems that Nietzsche posed for Weber, our eyes naturally alight first on Nietzsche's most conspicuous projects for scientific research, since Weber's reputation for coming to terms with Nietzsche rests chiefly on his scholarly works.

Nietzsche argued that scholarly rigor and probity demanded the application of the most advanced methods of empirical inquiry to the domain of moral phenomena.

> The project is to traverse with quite novel questions, and as though with new eyes, the enormous, distant, and so well hidden land of morality—of morality that has actually existed, actually been lived; and does this not mean virtually to discover this land for the first time?[6]

Having conceived this project, Nietzsche needed "scholarly, bold, and industrious comrades."[7] He sought to point them "in the direction of an actual *history of morality,* which would investigate "what is documented, what can actually be confirmed and has actually existed, in short, the entire long hieroglyphic record, so hard to decipher, of the moral past of mankind."[8] Only a strict, empirical, and historical inquiry, hostile to the traditions of moral philosophy and profoundly suspicious of every vestige of metaphysical speculation, would disclose morality in its truly problematic, questionable character.

> In all "science of morals" so far one thing was *lacking*, strange as it may sound: the problem of morality itself; what was lacking was any suspicion that there was something problematic here.[9]
> I see nobody who ventured a critique of moral valuations; I miss even the slightest attempts of scientific curiosity, of the refined, experimental imagination of psychologists and historians that readily anticipates a problem and catches it in flight without knowing what it has caught. . . . I have scarcely detected a few meagre preliminary efforts to explore *the history of the origins* of these feelings and valuations (which is something quite different from a critique and again different from a history of ethical systems). . . . Thus nobody up to now has examined the value of that most famous of all medicines which is called morality; and the first step would be—for once to *question* it. Well then, precisely this is our task.[10]

Methodic imperatives required a disrobing of the moral past and an anatomical postmortem to ascertain the effects of morality as "medicine." These imperatives would seem to be binding for all scholars. In this respect the new moral history is open to all who submit to the discipline of science. But Nietzsche seems at the same time to need a principle of selection or restriction, because it matters how and by whom the domain of morality is laid bare. Science can divest mankind of illusions and deprive it of ideals. Its power has already been demonstrated on religious ideals. But if science can slay morality as well it may degrade mankind: what is risked in unleashing science upon the moral past and present is a diminution of Man. Without discipline, spirit, or purpose, men would be worthy of neither respect nor love.[11] Nietzsche had no intention of recruiting a plodding army of mediocrities moving in blind obedience to the rules of rigorous science. Such an army might be irresistible, but it would also be undiscriminating and unmanageable for Nietzsche's delicate enterprise. Nietzsche therefore scorns the average scholars and seeks warlike princes of science to captain his dangerous exploit. He appeals to what Descartes called *generosité:*

> All problems demand great love, and of that only strong, round, secure spirits who have a firm grip on themselves are capable. It makes the most telling difference whether a thinker has a personal relationship to his problems and finds in them his destiny, his distress, and his greatest happiness, or an "impersonal" one, meaning that he can do no better than to touch them and grasp them with the antennae of cold, curious thought. In the latter case nothing will come of it . . . for even if great problems should allow themselves to be *grasped* by them they would not permit frogs and weaklings to *hold on* to them.[12]

Yet Nietzsche's literary presentation of his projects for science is not without irony. In posing assignments for bold scholars, he mimics the *Académie* of the Enlightenment: his projects are imitations of Bacon and Descartes or of the founding projects of the modern scientific revolution. But they are also mocking parodies of the modern "conquest by method."[13] Nietzsche's ironic mockery reflects the character of the problem of morality as a problem for science: the dangers it poses are not only social. Consistency demands that science dissect the morality that "has actually been lived" by men of science, the morality of truth-seeking. Once in pursuit of its moral quarry on Nietzsche's "great hunt," the scientific hunting party is bound to find itself at bay in its own cave.[14] Science too is a moral phenomenon. Having shaken the ground of moral conduct and of commitment to moral ideals, science is unable to provide a theoretical foundation for practical ethics and is compelled to admit that it cannot ground itself.[15] The consequence of the rigorous application of science to the problem of morality is therefore a comprehensive crisis:

> As the will to truth thus gains self-consciousness—there can be no doubt of that—morality will gradually *perish* now: this is the great spectacle in a hundred acts reserved for the next two centuries in Europe— the most terrible, most questionable, and perhaps also the most hopeful of all spectacles.[16]

The reflexive questioning of science by science is properly the task of philosophy. Yet this questioning, according to Nietzsche, can proceed only if recourse to all previous philosophy and science is ruled out. For, taken as an empirical project, the advancement of science into the study of morality exposes, and thus subverts, the presuppositions of philosophy as it has been. When subjected to strict historical inspection, even the most scientific philosophy of the past proves to have taken certain moral values (above all, the value of truth) as unshakable.[17] But nothing can be taken as established and unshakeable by a strict historical inquiry: it must find out how these givens were established or created.

Nietzsche's treatise on these themes, *On the Genealogy of Morals,* was prominent and controversial as a "brilliant essay" on the historical study of practical ethics, when Weber began his inquiries into the economic ethics of the world religions. Weber accordingly devoted most of his theoretical "Introduction" to these studies to a dialogue with Nietzsche, at times referring explicitly to the *Genealogy,* at other times wrestling with Nietzsche's themes. Weber began the introduction by dismissing a dim and rather vulgar version of Nietzsche's argument on *ressentiment.* The major part of his analysis, however, was given over to what he calls a "proper understanding" of Nietzsche's argument. This commentary on Nietzschean themes made a fitting preface. For Weber's studies on the economic ethics of the world religions, together with parts of *Economy and Society,* constituted his comprehensive response to Nietzsche's project for an empirical science of moral phenomena.[18] They amply reflected Weber's intensive study (and attempted mastery) of Nietzsche's thought on the problem of morality. In Weber's terminology, Nietzsche's demand that science conquer the hidden land of morality was a demand to bring "the disenchantment of the world by science" to its culmination. Weber strove vigorously to fulfill this requirement, according to his lights. For these reasons, the claims made by Bendix and Roth are securely founded: Weber's scholarly work is indisputably the greatest and most complete attempt to execute Nietzsche's project within the limits of a "strictly empirical" science.[19]

Weber's Freiburg Lecture did not give much warning of these things to come. Weber's remarks did point to a refashioning of the science of political economy, as we have noted. But no necessity for such a sustained squaring off with Nietzsche's projects for science was evident. And such an *Auseinandersetzung* with Nietzsche would appear to have been a grandiose distraction from the pressing tasks of political education that gripped Weber. The element of truth in this first impression is that Weber's politics required that he resist Nietzsche. But for that very reason, he could not dismiss Nietzsche's questioning as a distraction. After the Freiburg Lecture, Weber's understanding of Nietzsche deepened, as all interpreters agree. To this consensus, we will try to add a more precise knowledge both of the problems Nietzsche posed for Weber's own enterprise and of Weber's effort to solve them. Most readers would concur that Weber distinguished himself more carefully from Nietzsche in the later formulation of his teaching on political leadership. The Freiburg Lecture was on its face the most warlike and Nietzschean of Weber's formulations. Previous debate on Weber's intellectual development has focused, in part, on the question of why Weber changed his tone and distanced himself from Nietzsche.[20] *Politics as a Vocation* is clearly less offensive to liberals, because it is far less abrasive of their moral sensibilities. The same might be said of morally acute readers on every side of the political spectrum. Even observers who judge Weber to be a nihilist, destructive of all transcendent values, have seen in his later studies a remnant of piety, a link to the Hebrew prophets, that distinguishes him from Nietzsche.[21] Most students of Weber's politics would also agree that he managed to accomplish this change of tone and emphasis without any significant retreat from his attempt to unite the liberal cause with the national cause. Weber's predominating concern for national greatness remained constant; the crisis of leadership was never resolved and never ceased to vex him. But Weber's later solicitude for a certain moral approval represented a rhetorical advance (or, Nietzsche would say, retreat) that reflected his heightened awareness of Nietzsche's significance.[22] In the remainder of this chapter, we shall expand our sketch of Nietzsche's interpretation of the liberal cause, survey his philosophic politics, and try to understand why it was necessary for Weber to resist Nietzsche more deliberately and resourcefully in his later writings. Weber was not unacquainted with the questions raised at the end of the last chapter. The study to follow does not consider problems of which Weber was unaware. Instead, it attempts to assess his tenacious effort to meet difficulties that he knew he could not ignore. Weber was compelled to reformulate his Freiburg argument in order to counter Nietzsche's influence. His defense of leadership became a "moral" assertion; his assertion and defense of liberal democratic institutions became a defense of "moral forces" against Nietzsche's nihilistic politics.[23]

2. DECADENCE AND THE CRISIS OF LIBERALISM

Nietzsche's philosophic politics is an interpretation of decadence and a policy toward this "fatality." As he presents it, the crisis of liberalism must be understood as a dimension of the "problem" of decadence. "Decadent" is obviously a term of rhetoric, but to understand its force as a term of criticism directed at liberal democracy and liberalism, one should first consider what Nietzsche's analysis of decadence as a problem for philosophy implies for them at the level of science and philosophy. Modern liberal politics is linked in some manner, as everyone is aware, to modern progress. At the origins of the modern project, confidence in the possibility of progress somehow replaced resignation in the face of the cyclic decay of all things human. All the "problems" of ancient political philosophy were reinforced by the transience of human accomplishment. Against the background of the never-ending pageant of growth and decay, human excellence and nobility shone forth brightly, as approximations or intimations of eternity. In the classical perspective, the great and abiding problems for thought were independent of what man could construct or fortune tear down. To take decadence seriously or make of it a problem for philosophy was to distract the soul from its exalted destiny and vocation. The discovery of progress entailed at least the transformation of growth and decay into philosophic problems, and probably more: a reorientation of philosophy toward another destiny for the human soul.[24] Since decadence and progress are aspects of the same problem, Nietzsche's announcement that decadence is (once again) *the* problem for a philosopher means a return to the discovery with which modern philosophy began its quest for progress. The undeniable success of modern liberal politics in acquiring or building a world in which its mode of progress could be implemented ought to have removed "decadence" from the agenda. Instead (as Nietzsche anticipated) the charge that "bourgeois society is decadent" is heard on every hand, not least from "liberals." If the problem of decadence recurs, it is because the possibility of progress must once again be in doubt. The crisis of liberalism is inseparable from the doubt that the means available to liberals, the means supplied by liberal legislative science, liberal reason of state, and liberal philosophy, can continue to secure the possibility of progress. Confidence in that possibility has been inseparable from liberalism; the accusation of "decadence" is not one that it can leave unanswered. If liberal philosophy cannot defend the principal institutions of liberal democracy as means for dealing with the problem of decadence, the philosopher must return to the origins of progress and think again.[25]

Nietzsche prided himself in being the opposite of a decadent: "I have always instinctively chosen the right means against wretched states."[26] Such pride in correct instinctive choice has a philosophic side because the problem of decadence (as Nietzsche presents it) is essentially a problem of interpreting the instincts. "To have to fight the instincts—that is the formula for decadence: as long as life is ascending, happiness equals instinct."[27] Decadence is "instinctively to choose what is harmful for oneself, to feel attracted by 'disinterested' motives."[28] The possibility of progress is a matter of instinct, because man is distinguished from the other animals by the indeterminacy of his interpretation of his instincts. Man alone is able to choose the wrong methods for coping with decay, because man alone can disregard or redirect instinct. "Such a total aberration of mankind from its basic instincts, such a total decadence of value judgments—that is the question-mark par excellence, the real riddle that the animal 'man' poses for the philosopher."[29] Since all ages have mere growth and decay, what is problematic for philosophy is not decadence as such.

> Decadence itself is nothing *to be fought*: it is absolutely necessary and belongs to every age and every people. What should be fought vigorously is the contagion of the healthy parts of the organism.
> Is this being done? The *opposite* is done. Precisely that is attempted in the name of *humanity*.[30]

For Nietzsche, *decadence* is a term of criticism directed against policies toward decay. He can therefore accuse of decadence those who attempt to fight decay in the name of "humanity."

"Decadent" is a plausible accusation against modern liberal politics because the ideal of liberalism is humanitarian. The institutions framed in the light of that ideal limit the legitimate use of force to a few purposes on which all men can agree. Used for any other purpose, the exercise of power is a priori "cruel and unusual," that is, *inhumane*. With the exception of those forms of decay (and growth) which endanger "life, liberty, and property," limited government has no mandate to "fight vigorously the contagion of the healthy parts of the organism."[31] It must therefore be very difficult to combine Nietzsche's terms of criticism with a defense of liberal democratic institutions, but this is nevertheless what Weber sets out to do. His attempt makes us wonder whether the liberal cause can be divorced from the ideal that made liberalism charitable and accommodating to human frailty and imperfection.

One of the pronounced characteristics of Weber's Freiburg Lecture is his hardness and demand for sacrifice; with regard to what is declining, Weber is unyielding about the Nietzschean principle: let what is perishing perish. The Junkers are a declining class incapable of willing the national interest; they will no longer trust their natural political instincts because their economic position is increasingly untenable. By turning the political instincts of the Junkers toward mere economic survival, the development of capitalism in Germany "threatens the natural political instincts with destruction." [32] If Weber's policy were adopted, the Junker decline would not be arrested. Instead, national economics would be concerned to prepare the economically ascending classes to assume responsibility for "the enduring economic and political power interests of the nation." [33] The Freiburg Lecture is a polemic against the Caprivi policy of protective legislation to ameliorate the economic decline of the Junkers. In later political writings, Weber argued vigorously (although not in these words) that what should be fought was "the contagion of the healthy parts of the organism." National economic policy should encourage the commercial and working classes to spurn the Junker way of life rather than bind themselves culturally to a dying landed class. [34] In sum, Weber's analyses of the declining and ascending classes, and his recommendations for policy, turn Nietzsche's terms of criticism to the purpose of Weber's assertion of the liberal cause; the Freiburg Lecture is a Nietzschean argument for political "modernization."

Weber further identified himself with Nietzsche in 1895 by combining this affirmation of power-instincts with a harsh stance toward "disinterested" motives. Weber spoke of his lecture as "a good swift kick" at "ethical culture," that is, at the Ethical Culture movement in which Ferdinand Tönnies played a vocal part. Tönnies had conducted a pamphlet war against "the Nietzsche cult." [35] The choice that Weber frames is between disinterested motives and "the great passions with which nature has endowed us" or between ethical culture and great power politics. [36] Bismarckian policy does not provide a precedent (as Weber later emphasized) for the necessary affirmation of the power-instincts of the ascending classes.[37] The critique of ethics in the Freiburg Lecture is carried on Nietzsche's terms, not on Bismarck's. Weber sided with Nietzsche against Tönnies.

A difficulty in thus adapting Nietzsche's rhetoric is evident in Weber's ambivalence toward the bourgeoisie. The problem is that even a militant middle class inspired with "Catilinarian fervor" would still be carried toward a more relaxed and pacific way of life, by the inherent "humanity" of commerce. Montesquieu and Rousseau had argued this point, from opposed perspectives, as Weber was probably aware.[38] The "flabby eudaemonism" that characterized "the economy of the transition period" of German industrialization would seem to be a characteristic of the bourgeois way of life in the liberal commercial republic in every period. In opposing the indulgent "humanity" of modern liberal politics on Nietzsche's grounds, Weber is in danger of dividing himself from the main classes whose moral and political support he needs to unite the liberal cause with that of the nation. The terms of criticism that Weber adopted would seem to propel him toward a direct attack on morality, as a hindrance to the affirmation of healthy instinct.

> "Good and evil" is merely a variation of [the problem of decadence]. Once one has developed a keen eye for the symptoms of decline, one understands morality too—one understands what is hiding under its most sacred names and value formulas: impoverished life, the will to the end, the great weariness.[39]

Weber is quite firm in his disdain for the liberal "humanity" which he identifies with "flabby eudaemonism."[40] It is not clear that he could similarly condemn morality while uniting the liberal cause with the national cause. The consequences of such a Nietzschean attack for Weber's politics are uncertain, but it would seem that Weber and Tönnies needed each other more than the Freiburg Lecture allowed.

In calling for a leadership class that would affirm the state as "the worldly power organization of the nation" and assume responsibility toward future generations, Weber seems to be in agreement with Nietzsche. Nietzsche's policy toward decadence is necessarily a choice of institutions and modes of rule. Domination is not in contradiction to instinct but is rather an affirmation of certain instincts.

The whole of the West no longer possesses the instincts out of which institutions grow, out of which a *future* grows: perhaps nothing antagonizes its "modern spirit" so much. One lives for the day, one lives very fast, one lives irresponsibly: precisely this is called "freedom." [41]

According to Nietzsche, the surrender of responsibility for the future and hostility toward the institution-fostering instincts find their logical political expression in democracy. "Once we have lost all the instincts out of which institutions grow, we lose institutions altogether because we are no longer good enough for them. Democracy has ever been the form of decline in organizing power." [42] "The peoples who had some value, attained some value, never attained it under liberal institutions. It was great danger that made something of them that merits respect." [43] Democracy favors humaneness instead of cultivating men who command respect. The root of democratic hostility toward institutions lies in the potential for cruelty or inhumanity which the people apprehend in human beings who inspire fear and respect. By glorifying the social virtues, work and moral goodness, "modern ideas" promote tamer, less threatening men. Democracy in its modern, liberal form is therefore partial to the decay and diminution of man, making men mediocre and lowering their worth.

What today constitutes our antipathy toward "man"? *Not* fear; rather, that we no longer have anything left to fear in man; that the maggot "man" is swarming in the foreground; that the "tame man," the hopelessly mediocre and insipid man, has already learned to feel himself as the goal and the zenith. For this is how things are: the diminution and levelling of European man constitutes *our* greatest danger, for the sight of him makes us weary.—We can see nothing today that wants to grow greater, we suspect that things will continue to go down—together with the fear of man we have also lost our love of him, our reverence for him, our hopes for him, even the will to him. The sight of man now makes us weary—what is nihilism today if it is not *that*?—We are weary *of man*. [44]

Weber's Freiburg Lecture draws much of its rhetorical power from its articulation of similar themes. Weber holds out the prospect of a future generation capable of "great politics." The present generation should acknowledge their wretched situation, as epigones of the founding of 1870, but the spectacle of mediocrity and insipidity should not make them weary. They should work as forerunners to a greater generation.[45] Like Nietzsche's critique, Weber's argument is directed against the weak pessimism, disillusionment, and world-weariness fostered by fin de siècle "historical consciousness." As a tonic against that mood, Weber prescribes definite work to pave the way for a future generation of national politicians worthy of fear and respect.

> It is not age that makes a man senile: he remains young, so long as he is able to experience the *great* passions with which nature has endowed us. And it is not the yoke of centuries of renowned history that ages a great nation. It remains young, if it has the ability and the courage to recognize itself and the great instincts which are given to it, and if its leading strata can raise themselves into the hard and clear air, in which the sober work of German politics flourishes, and in which the grave majesty of national feeling resonates.[46]

There is also more than an echo of Nietzsche's maxim, that it is great danger that makes a people merit respect. The antidote to Micawberism put forward in the Freiburg Lecture is great power politics and heightened awareness of the danger that accompanies the responsibilities of great power status. Weber welcomes those responsibilities as a trial of "what is humanly great and noble in our nature."[47] Weber's essay is an experiment in harnessing the great, potentially revolutionary passions that Nietzsche had elicited.

It is an unstable experiment, however, because the institutions toward which Weber tries to direct those passions are the modern state and (as became clearer in Weber's later political writings) parliamentary government, the very institutions that Nietzsche had attacked as means to diminish and level European man. The noble indignation that Weber tries to transpose from Nietzsche's rhetoric into his own politics is not easily bonded to the disciplines of the modern state, the factory, and liberal democratic politics. The task that Fascist interpreters set themselves—of adapting Nietzsche's writings to their project for the destruction of bourgeois civilization—was a more straightforward task than the one that Weber set for himself.[48]

Nietzsche's critique of the modern instrumentalities of political organization is coordinated with what seems to be an arcane attempt to resuscitate aristocratic institutions. Despite the vivid counterevidence of modern Fascism, until recently Nietzschean scholarship had systematically neglected his politics. Quite apart from the moral and political reasons for taking Nietzsche's politics with the utmost concentration—Doctor Johnson's remark on the wonderful effects of hanging is appropriate here—there are compelling philosophical reasons for resisting this intellectual fashion. Nietzsche's rediscovery of hierarchy has nothing to do with King Arthur's Court. If one assumes that the Connecticut Yankees of the modern liberal state and capitalism have explosives and means of power superior to Nietzsche's, Weber's difficulties will appear to be chimeras, and the nature of the conflict over Nietzsche's initiative in the liberal democracies of the West will never be posed with the starkness and clarity that Nietzsche himself sought with all his powers. The order of rank Nietzsche sought to impose was not feudal. It was designed to release more powerful explosives than liberal democratic politics could handle by destroying the obstacles liberal institutions set up against the further expansion of human power through philosophy and science. The modern means of political organization, and the doctrines of political economy that go with them, are such obstacles. Nietzsche's critical path passed through political economy in order to jettison the weakness of Romanticism. The critique began in 1874 with Nietzsche's seminal essay *On the Advantage and Disadvantage of History for Life,* an attack upon the specific illusions of the German Historical School.[49] In subsequent books, Nietzsche purged his political and economic thinking of Romanticism by a critical return to the spirit of Descartes and Voltaire, seeking the best that could be said for modern institutions. His final conception of hierarchy—if one can speak of anything in Nietzsche's thought as "final"—reflected a principled determination not to sacrifice any element of power that could be generated by modern methods. He reached the conclusion that a novel aristocratic politics, a practical assertion of hierarchy, was necessary precisely because of "the nihilistic consequences of the [current] ways of thinking in politics and economics."[50] Since it is by no means self-evident that the appropriate remedy for a "way of thinking" is a way of acting (spirited self-assertion), the steps by which Nietzsche reached his conclusion deserve some scrutiny.

Nietzsche's grasp of the history of political economy was sufficient on the essential point: that the modern representative state, and civil society with its corporations, are artifacts that have enabled modern societies to govern themselves without much reliance upon direct rule, or upon the open domination of man by man.[51] Routine administration and commerce are methods for doing without Coriolanus and Cato, the *condottieri,* godfathers, and Galahads: they make ruling virtue dispensable. The modern inventions of political science concentrate power and generate productivity by relying in the main upon intelligence and the labors of ordinary men. Intelligence is not incidental: It is by means of the intelligence of modern political economy that civil society renders the political activity of ruling obsolete. As Weber put it, the modern bureaucracy and the factory are "mind objectified."[52] "Ways of thinking in politics and economics" are inseparable from these instrumentalities and reinforce the principle of their operation, a principle which requires a devaluation of the masterful virtues or a refusal to rely upon them. Its doctrine rests upon the discovery that the ruling political virtues, the qualities required to assert a ranking of values or a way of life, are quite unnecessary. Marvels of power are possible without such human strengths. The drives and instincts of princely men need not be destroyed altogether. What the ascendancy of political economy means is that great intelligence and artfulness will be directed toward administration and commerce. Incomparably less attention will be devoted to perfecting the drives and powers of princely men for political assertion or to concerting and orchestrating them into ever greater concentrations of political ability. The result is untempered, ill-disciplined, haphazard willfulness. Powers are squandered because the politically relevant gifts are left to grow wild. The resources of civilization are devoted to other purposes. No modern society bids for princes in the way it bids for gifted athletes or coaches them with comparable prudence and imagination. Nietzsche's concern is not to promote spirited self-assertiveness that will exhaust itself in random jabs and fits of pique. It is rather to establish a principle of rule that can be sustained and enforced in the face of the modern state and civil society, taking into account all the intelligence that is "objectified" in these institutions and devoted to their defense. Thus Nietzsche must not only absorb the lessons of modern political economy. He must find a way to neutralize its influence over the potential *virtuosi* of domination. Spiritedness or will-to-power must be brought under the guidance of a doctrine more suited to the task of sustained assertion, one that accepts direct rule or domination and treats the necessities of mastery with the same respect that a great coach would treat the needs of gifted athletes. Nietzsche cannot be neutral toward "ways of thinking in politics and economics" that divert princely men into ruinous training programs and occupations that will destroy their political coordination and physique. He must expose "the nihilistic consequences." A vigorous projection of the new possibilities is required to capture the attention and imagination of "the higher men." Doctrines that ignore the necessities of men whose talent is for assertion and rule must be exposed and discredited. Any teaching that defers or demotes the tasks that require the exercise of masterful virtues must be pilloried as Micawberism. Nietzsche's reasoning thus lays the groundwork for Weber's parallel critique of the German Historical School by showing why a practical initiative is the necessary and proper remedy against modern political economics.[53]

There are spurious reasons for dismissing Nietzsche's aristocratic politics, but the analogy to athletics may help to separate them from more substantive reasons. It is a vanity that democracies cannot safely indulge to deny that aristocracy can generate great power both for good and for evil. It is precisely because the hierarchic argument may generate an "unbeatable team" that Weber must take Nietzsche seriously. The substantive reasons should frankly be stated for what they are: moral objections and prudent reservations about keeping the unbeatable team on our side. We have an arrangement, under limited government, that keeps our political athletes teamed against each other, so that we can stand back while they crush one another. The ideal of "humanity" and its constitutional implementation insure that we who are not princes cannot be crushed. Virtuosos of domination would overleap these limits to create a way of life out of our bodies. One might well object that this is unnatural: our bodies are separate for weighty reasons.[54] One might argue that it is immoral. But in the Freiburg Lecture, Weber acknowledges no such grounds for objecting to an aristocratic politics. The experiment he initiates would combine the Nietzschean principle that leadership is the assertion of a ranking of ways of life with a defense and assertion of liberal democratic institutions. Joining national loyalty with liberal reason of state, Weber must defend the *Rechtsstaat,* individual rights, the liberties of subjects, and a commercial way of life. But the genius of the liberal commercial republic, and of the modern state, lies in the principle of indirect rule. Citizens are subject to natural necessity and must make a living. But they are not and cannot be compelled to acknowledge any authoritative ranking of values or men.[55] Weber's conception of political leadership stands in a problematic relation to the liberal institutions it is intended to defend. Ultimately, Weber cannot dismiss Nietzschean politics on the spurious grounds that it is impractical or too weak to stand against modern economy and society. Weber must find substantive grounds for affirming institutions of indirect rule. It is this logical necessity that led him subsequently to modify his argument on political leadership.[56]

The most challenging dimension of the accusation that "bourgeois democracy is decadence," or that the modern bureaucratic state and the corporate economy no longer serve progress, is the claim that they are means to prevent the further enhancement and assertion of human power. The constraints that limited government imposes upon self-assertiveness, according to this Nietzschean interpretation, are constraints that keep us in premodern impotence. Bourgeois democracy coopts our natural leaders and princes, diverting them into administration and commerce, relaxing their natural political drives, and preventing us from asserting our distinctive way of life or our ranking of human qualities. Bourgeois "legitimacy" is a disguised warfare against concentrated self-assertion. Weber's attempt to adapt Nietzsche's terms of criticism to the needs of German nationalism, against Anglo-Saxon colonialism and imperialism (as well as against Junker domination), sounds a familiar note, for these charges have since become the lingua franca of the new nations in international forums.[57] The Freiburg Lecture shows that these accusations may be turned to the advantage of the liberal cause: the critique of decadence can be turned against the alternatives to bourgeois democracy, making the will-to-power of the alternative ruling classes the axis of controversy. This spirited counterthrust presupposes a militancy and firmness of purpose, however, which the leadership strata of liberal democracies have not often shown, and which the German bourgeoisie had never shown in Weber's memory. Perhaps the most significant thought in Weber's 1895 lecture is his solution to this problem of morale. He attempts to resolve the crisis of German liberalism by introducing Nietzsche's argument as a self-criticism of bourgeois democracy by the bourgeoisie itself. Weber's political leadership class serves liberal democracy by turning Nietzschean rhetoric against its critics. But Weber also upholds a Nietzschean standard against the bourgeoisie. He tries to fashion a weapon for national liberal leaders out of Nietzsche's aggressive critique of bourgeois decadence. He wields this weapon as a class-conscious member of the middle class.[58] In his hands it becomes a noble defense of the liberal cause against liberalism; Weber's partisan assertion calling for "a national party of bourgeois freedom" concludes with the slogan *Landgraf werde hart!*—a baron must become hard.[59]

If the liberal cause is to be defended on these Nietzschean terms, however, such a militant nobility within the bourgeoisie must advance a plausible claim to be the standard-bearer of the liberal political and economic tradition. Weber's resolution of the crisis of liberalism requires that the history of the liberal cause be interpreted from a standpoint alien to liberalism; it entails a break with Whig historiography and the earlier self-interpretation of bourgeois democracy. To meet and deflect Nietzsche's critique of bourgeois decadence, Weber found it necessary to rediscover or invent "the heroic age of the European bourgeoisie," an age in which its guiding ideal was hard, ascetic, disciplined, and cruel, not least toward the bourgeoisie itself. The founding era of the liberal commercial republic, in this Weberian account, was not vulnerable to Nietzsche's critique of modern "ways of thinking in politics and economics." His history of the struggle for liberal institutions and the origin of modern capitalism would show the bourgeoisie its true self, its individuality, its natural political instincts. A hard school of asceticism would form the most precious, noblest part of the heritage of the liberal cause.[60] Weber's New Model Army would then be led by a political class worthy of this heritage, a leadership stratum that is within and of liberal democracy. But is its noble self-assertion truly *with* and *for* the liberal commercial republic? Is Weber's reconstruction of the ascetic heroism of the liberal cause a true history, or is it a noble lie about the mettle of the middle class? In these questions what is at stake is not only historical verisimilitude but also the stability of Weber's attempt to draw strength for his own politics from Nietzsche's attack. Weber's reconfiguration of the liberal commercial republic as a regime without liberalism requires a new historiography to show that the regime never really required liberalism. The problem, for this history of the liberal cause, is the originating power that caused the modern commercial republic to be born. The key to that power lies in the human soul, as Weber and Nietzsche agree.[61]

3. RANK ORDER AND THE LIBERAL CAUSE

The liberal commercial republic invites the charge of "decadence." It is a regime that combines unprecedented power with flabby hedonism. The remarkable achievements of its concentrated intelligence and skill seem to serve the least memorable human needs and human beings. Great genius and sacrifice were required to create liberal institutions, yet only to house and feed a petty and mediocre breed, addicted to self-indulgence and disinclined to make sacrifices. This result seems to mock the effort. Little vision is needed to imagine that more disciplined and demanding men could turn this vast productive and formative power to better purposes than "mass consumption." It is difficult to believe that such discrepancies were invisible during the long genesis of the modern liberal regime. Every account of the history of the liberal cause must explain why such discrepancies did not deter extraordinary men from giving their best for what is so much less than the best.[62]

Weber's explanation, crudely restated, is that the new political and economic orders were brought into being primarily by entrepreneurs whose souls craved certainty of their salvation but were denied sacramental, ritual, or doctrinal reassurance by Calvinist theology. They created colossal productive enterprises because their souls could not rest or concede the slightest indulgence to flabby eudaemonism.[63] Since their efforts were determined by a spiritual compulsion, rather than by a considered plan, they entrusted the outcome to Providence. They had no anticipation that the result would be a civilization of "specialists without spirit, sensualists without heart."[64] Weber admits that the result mocks the effort, but he denies that it could be foreseen by the entrepreneurs who were chiefly responsible for bringing it about.

Nietzsche's explanation is so much less familiar, and so intellectually challenging, that it will take several pages to summarize. What is the connection between the "flabby eudaemonism" of modern commercial nations and the unprecedented expansion of human power in which the liberal commercial republics of Europe and America have played such a prominent part? According to Nietzsche, we must approach this question in the perspective of a philosophically self-centered history of the philosophic cause. The touchstone of our summary will be the Preface to *Beyond Good and Evil,* one of Nietzsche's most succinct presentations of his renegade history of philosophy.

In this Preface, Nietzsche describes his philosophy as a reinvigoration of the struggle against Plato's errors of "the pure mind" and "the good as such."[65] It is also a continuation of "the fight against the Christian-ecclesiastical pressure of millenia."[66] These are not separate

campaigns against unrelated enemies, because Christianity is the popular form of Plato's errors, and it provided the massive support to impose those errors for millenia. The attack of scientists and philosophers upon Plato, and upon Aristotleian scholasticism, was connected with the struggle for new political arrangements to break "the
Christian-ecclesiastical pressure of millenia." This battle against the
authorities of the old regime "has created in Europe a magnificent tension of the mind, the like of which had never yet existed on earth: with
so tense a bow we can now shoot for the most distant goals."[67] Prior to
this battle, philosophy had supported the moral and political limits of
"the old regime" or of "traditional society." The "imaginary republics
and principalities" of ancient political philosophy were regimes of virtue ruling over the body and the passions; modern philosophy turned
away from regimes of virtue and proposed a method of governing the
body and passions without elevating "the pure mind and the good as
such" to rule over them.[68] Governance without saints or priests, and
hence without "Christian-ecclesiastical pressure," became possible
through the implementation of these "new modes and orders."[69] The
body and the passions did not have to be mortified and subjected to
direct rule. They could be given greater scope and yet be brought within
limits. Indeed they could be brought to enforce limits.[70] Nietzsche's
philosophic politics is a return to the modern philosophical affirmation
of the body and the passions and a reinvigoration of the modern emphasis upon the enforceability of law and moral limits. Nietzsche's attack upon Platonic nihilism, his disclosure that transcendent values
"devalue themselves," is a reinvigoration of Machiavelli's contempt
for any law or ethical standard that does not carry with it the power or
virtú to enforce compliance. The truth about values that Nietzsche requires is a *verità effetuale,* an efficacious truth.[71] His attack on the
highest values is conducted in the spirit of Machiavelli's question:
"How may the strength of any rule be assayed?" The Machiavellian
answer is "Attack it."[72] Nietzsche's purpose in making "man stand before man as even today, hardened in the discipline of science, he stands
before the *rest* of nature" is to discover the elements of an enforceable
hierarchy of values, enforceable because they are deeply rooted in the
body and the passions.[73] Although he assaults Socrates and Plato,
Nietzsche seeks an order of rank as aloof and unyielding as Plato's hierarchy. His task requires him to preserve the conflict which "has created in Europe a magnificent tension of the mind the like of which had
never yet existed on earth." That conflict, it would seem, is between

principles aloof from man and attentive to his suffering, between principles cruel toward man or accommodating to him. If no principle of excellence can be secured in the body and the passions, Nietzsche thought the modern affirmation of human nature would become wormwood. If it means that we must affirm a world of bodies that inspire neither reverence nor love, the modern project will become inseparable from world-weariness and despair.[74] Nietzsche scrutinizes the history of moral codes and ideals in order to learn what it was in human nature, in the body and the passions, that enabled mankind to uphold transcendental standards for millenia. How were the Platonic errors enforced? How did Socrates establish the rule of the pure mind and the good as such? To answer these questions, Nietzsche initiated an empirical history of the highest values in their integral connection to the natural powers upon which all worldly enforcement depends. The higher things must exercise their compulsion upon men through men. Within men, the higher problems must have great passions, drives, and instincts on their side in the struggle to establish order in the soul. The scientific conquest of the hitherto hidden land of morality must yield Nietzsche a "natural history of morals" that will disclose a history of how values became embodied in men.[75] In principle, Nietzsche's method acknowledges no order independent of contingent individuals, by which the excesses of men could be curbed or their deficiencies supplemented. Values and moralities must therefore come to light in their dependence upon the drives and instincts of mortal men. It follows inexorably that "the solution to the problem of the rank order of values," when it is reached, must be one in which what is highest is embodied in a contingent highest individual and is wholly dependent for enforcement upon this mortal's strength.[76] Nietzsche's principle of excellence is an alternative to the classical ascent toward pure, bodiless intelligibles; it is also an alternative to the prophetic vision of man's ascent under divine guidance. It is philosophy as the most spiritual will to power, the tyrannical drive to "create the world," to become the prima causa or first cause. The highest values that are "embodied" in such a philosopher are inseparable from his tyrannical drive to enforce them.[77]

Let us return to the "historiographical" problem that Nietzsche poses in the Preface: to understand the struggle of modern science and philosophy against the Platonic errors of the "pure mind" and "the good as such." The pure mind would be the faculty of man by virtue of which philosophy is possible as contemplation. The life devoted to the pure mind is the *vita contemplativa* or *bios theoretikos*. To have grasped the error of Socrates or Plato is to have discovered that philosophy, so understood, is impossible. There is no pure mind of which the human mind is an imperfect approximation; no such life is knowable to man; philosophy was in error about the conditions of its own possibility. It was in error merely to think that the conditions of its own possibility could be disclosed to contemplation.[78] The other Platonic error envisioned a first cause, the Good, toward which the pure mind could ascend. Nietzsche equates the modern awakening from this error with the discovery that philosophy is the prima causa or, more exactly, the will to become the first cause.[79] What is its own "first cause" is not determined or defined by causes that transcend it. The philosopher in particular is not limited or determined by anything transcending his contingent individuality. When Nietzsche says that what makes us weary of man, what chills our love of man, what makes it impossible to will man, is *nihilism,* he reinvigorates a principle that necessarily arises in the struggle against Platonic error. The modern affirmation is a negation of first causes intelligible to pure mind: both the Good and the pure mind are errors. Our self-affirmation of man is linked to the "discovery" that no authoritative order determines and defines ourselves. A self that recognizes the error of pure mind knows no limits disclosed to contemplation. It knows no limitations save those that it discovers in its own character as first cause. The unveiling of Socratic error is inseparable, on Nietzsche's interpretation, from the discovery of modern individuality.[80] The original principle of the modern philosophical project is the assertion of the undetermined, independent, self-legislating philosopher. The need for self-definition through practice, by means of legislation, is a deduction from the discovery that the pure mind was an error. For if there are no limits disclosed through contemplation, the first cause must experiment to arrive at the limitations that are required for its philosophic life. Integral to the discovery of oneself as first cause is the necessity for a regime of one's own legislating. The original regime in which radical individuality set out to define and curb itself, creating laws with the authority to enforce their commands upon the autonomous individual, was the regime legislated for himself by the first philosopher who awakened to the truth that Plato was in error. The philosopher who is prima causa begins from his radical contingency and sets forth to determine his own limits. Philosophy cannot know through contemplation the conditions of its own possibility; hence it is essentially experimental, essaying the power of the (noncontemplative and impure) mind, and particularly its power to determine its own limits.[81]

One can understand why the struggle against Plato generates such "a magnificent tension of the spirit," if this Nietzschean account is close to the truth about the philosophical origins of the modern scientific revolution. Philosophy stands in an experimental, probing stance toward all claims that might be made upon the philosopher in the name of revealed religion, natural justice or natural law, or any moral code. This probing is no mere raised eyebrow: the eye of the philosopher is steadily set on self-determination and self-rule. His question regarding limits is whether he should nullify them or become their source. Philosophy so conceived is in constant tension with every power in the world that does not subserve its sovereign purposes, its tyrannical drive to "create the world." Devotion to the cause of philosophy has nothing in common with devotion to something greater than and separate from oneself, devotion that is haunted by "the curse of the creature's worthlessness."[82] It is rather greatness of soul or *generosité*.

The history of an essentially experimental philosophy should disclose this legislating of limits in which philosophy determines itself. To understand the "causal" role of philosophy, the historian would have to understand its discovery of a radical individuality knowing no limits that are not self-legislated. History must perceive ruling magnanimity in the perspective of the philosopher. Such history is the test of the magnanimity of the historian; it is perhaps indistinguishable from philosophy itself. Nietzsche introduces his remarks on the origins of the liberal cause, to which we now turn, by distinguishing his historiographical task from that of theoretical understanding. What is needed is not Hegelian history of philosophy, "which secures and formulates established truths, making everything that has so far happened and been prized surveyable, graspable, intelligible, ready to hand, abbreviating everything long, including Time itself, overpowering the whole past."[83] Such theoretical understanding will not disclose authentic philosophy.

> *Genuine philosophers . . . are commanders and legislators*: they say, "thus it *shall* be!" They first determine the Whither and For What of man, and in so doing have at their disposal the preliminary labor of all philosophical laborers, all who have overcome the past. With a creative hand they reach for

the future, and all that is and has been becomes a means for them, an instrument, a hammer. Their "knowing" is *creating*, their creating is a legislation, their will to truth is—*will to power*." [84]

Nietzsche's history of the liberal cause is a philosophical history that discloses the original relation between philosophy and the liberal cause. But it is not simply retrospective; there seems to Nietzsche to be no way to separate the questions "Are there such philosophers today? Have there been such philosophers yet? *Must* there not be such philosophers?" [85] In Nietzsche's history, "all that is and has been" comes to light as "an instrument, a hammer." His history of the origins of the liberal cause is inseparable from his explanation of why philosophy must at present, and for the future, turn against liberal institutions.

Having sharply distinguished Hegel's merely theoretical philosophy of history from his own horizon-forming perspective, Nietzsche turns in the next aphorism (*Beyond Good and Evil*, no. 212) to our theme. His cryptic portrayal of the struggle against Platonic error in the sixteenth century, and of the overture to the struggle for bourgeois institutions, is one of three examples that Nietzsche elaborates of the philosopher "as a necessitous man of tomorrow and the day after tomorrow," who "has always found himself, and *had* to find himself, in contradiction to his today: his enemy was ever the ideal of today."

So far all these extraordinary furtherers of man whom one calls philosophers, though they themselves rarely felt like friends of wisdom but rather like disagreeable fools and dangerous question marks, have found their task, their hard, unwanted, inescapable task, but eventually also the greatness of their task in being the bad conscience of their time. [86]

The sixteenth century "suffered from its accumulated energy of will and from the most savage floods and tidal waves of selfishness." What philosophy initiated, acting as the bad conscience of the age, was "the ideal of a timid, abjuring, submissive, disinterested, frail humanity." [87] At first glance, this description is perplexing. It does not seem an apt illustration of the point, for Nietzsche had introduced his philosophic lawgiver with the remark "Precisely when he takes the knife to the breast of the virtues of the age to vivisect them, he betrays his own secret: to know a new greatness for man, a new untrodden way to make man greater." [88] One should be puzzled by the discrepancy between the end, to make man *greater* by legislating new virtues, and the means adopted, which is evidently a puny, enfeebled ideal of humanity. Nietzsche engages us to look closely at the origin of the ideal of "humanity," the ideal from which the modern state, representative government in the modern form, and liberal institutions received their steadiest impetus and sanction. His observations refer to the era in which the centralizing monarchies, in France and England, neutralized the aristocracy as an independent military force, disbanded their armed retinues, and consolidated a "monopoly of legitimate violence" within their territories. [89] The new ideal, which Nietzsche deftly sums up in a few bold strokes, persuaded significant elements of the aristocracy to support these state-building efforts. It was an ideal of gentlemanliness attentive to human frailty, prepared to abjure rather than throw down the gauntlet, disengaged from religious warfare rather than committed in it, willing to accept peace and self-preservation as the end of the state rather than virtue or the glory of God. Considered in this context, the appearance of paradox dissolves. The unassertive ideal led swiftly and surely to a dramatic expansion of human power through the creation of the modern state. The humble ideal persuaded subtle and farsighted aristocrats to serve concentrated power and to withdraw from the spirited aristocratic factions of the sixteenth century. It was a weapon in "the struggle against the Christian-ecclesiastical pressure of millenia," compelling thoughtful men to seek out a new mode of governance in which the state would be independent of the church and sovereign over churchmen. The ideal of "humanity" also provided a powerful rhetorical alternative to prophetic politics: it showed men how to measure religious claims against the incentives to cruelty they provided and against the terrible costs, in human suffering, of religious civil wars. [90]

The unnamed modern Socrates, to whom Nietzsche refers in this aphorism, can only be Montaigne, the most eloquent of the *Politiques* and the creator of the archetypal *bourgeois gentilhomme*. [91] To comprehend why a philosopher initiated the liberal cause, one must learn to connect Montaigne's indulgent benevolence toward human frailties (beginning with his own) to an intrepid search for "a new greatness for man, a new untrodden way to make men greater." [92] Montaigne vivisected chivalric honor and heroic virtue and advanced a new civility and sensibility. What seemed a humility almost Christian (and sounds in Nietzsche's summary like abnegation if not self-mortification before

God) was an instrument for extending the range and precision of human power. Montaigne's personal "secret" was the quest for a "new, untrodden way" to acquire greatness for man. Who would suspect a plan to raise man to new heights in "a timid, abjuring, humble, disinterested, humanity"?[93] With such hints, Nietzsche adumbrates the link between the "bourgeois" ideal of "humaneness" and a philosophical revolution for which the "will to truth" was "will to power." Montaigne was a "necessitous" man; the liberal cause was subordinate to his necessity, to philosophy as a cause, the prima causa of the modern project.[94]

Nietzsche's account makes Montaigne the founder of liberalism, though with no fanfare, and certainly no concern to enter a dispute between academics over who deserves that honor. His point has not been taken by historians, who have been more open to Weber's hypotheses. Yet it results in a far less mysterious, not to say less obscurantist, interpretation of the link between "flabby eudaemonism" and the expansive power of the liberal commercial republic. Nietzsche treats the liberal cause as something great; he speaks of it as he says one should speak of great things: cynically and with innocence.[95] Cynically, because he presents ideals as means. (Aphorism 212 implies that Nietzsche is no more devoted to nobility than Montaigne was to soft humaneness; if the liberal ideal was provisional, an instrument for the expansion of human power under the guidance of philosophy, so is Nietzsche's ideal.) Ideals are means to determine the path along which mankind will travel to a new greatness. Nietzsche's "innocence" is most evident in contrast with Weber's history of commercial liberalism: Nietzsche's account is devoid of guilt or shame. There is no anguish about our decline from heroic militancy, no nostalgia for the obstinacy of dogmatic faith, no remorse, no indignation about bourgeois ignobility, no yearning for an iron theology, a hairshirt, a soul-flogging. Nietzsche has no need to postulate the Protestant Ethic as psychic cause because the necessities of philosophy suffice, once philosophy awakens from its Socratic spellboundness. No new tension in the soul of the commercial middle class is required to explain the modern *Griff nach der Weltmacht*. The original dynamism of the modern regime in acquiring world power can be traced to the same causes that make it powerful once established. The passions of the body are harnessed by intelligence to a division of labor and to methods of production guided by science and philosophy. Properly organized, the needs of the body can be indulged and given greater scope. Nietzsche does not need to turn away from Whig historiography as radically as Weber does. His interpretation does not require one to forget what liberal enthusiasts of progress saw in the victory of modern liberalism over superstition and religion. His account merely deepens the perspective and probes further into the shadows. The paradox that comes to light in comparing Weber and Nietzsche as "historians" of the liberal cause is that Nietzsche, despite his enigmatic style, is more forthright and empirical. Weber is famous for his remark on ideas as empirical causes:

> Not ideas, but material and spiritual interests, directly govern men's conduct. Yet very frequently the "world images" that have been created by "ideas" have, like switchmen, determined the tracks along which action has been pushed by the dynamic of interest.[96]

Yet Weber's work is devoid of any account of this idea itself. He ignores how modern philosophy sought to determine the tracks along which history would be pushed by accepting "the dynamic of interest," by affirming the body and the passions, by formulating "world images" that would release "the dynamic of interest." Weber speaks of the "rosy blush" of the Enlightenment but not of the steely gaze of its founding fathers. In Weber's history, philosophy and its marriage of knowledge with power play no part in the ancestry of the liberal cause.[97]

In the Freiburg Lecture, Weber accepted Nietzsche's critique of decadence. He attempted to unite an assertion of parliamentary institutions and bourgeois freedom with a rejection of the bourgeois ideal of "humanity." Weber adopted Nietzsche's noble ideal of greatness and treated Montaigne's ideal with contempt. Doing without liberalism means doing without the *bourgeois gentilhomme;* it promises a pessimism of strength that is hard rather than indulgent toward human frailty.[98] This is rhetorically appealing because it makes the defense or assertion of liberal institutions "noble." But if such a marriage between Nietzschean ideals and liberal democracy is possible, it is most unlikely to succeed on the terms of the Freiburg Lecture. Weber's argument was a more or less violent attack on the Ethical Culture movement—a "good swift kick."[99] Distancing himself from the strain of Kantian moralism in German education, Weber paid a high price for the noble grandeur of his rhetoric, which threatened to burst the moral limits of "bourgeois freedom." Weber's reliance on Nietzsche promised to alienate him from the principle groups he needed in order to join the liberal cause and the national cause together. In part the problem was one of respect for moral sensibilities. But inseparable from this was the unsolved problem of the Freiburg Lecture: how to combine Nietzsche's assertive ideal with the modern state and representative institutions; how to reject Nietzsche's aristocratic politics and yet cultivate a leadership class capable of asserting a *Wertmaßtab,* a ranking of ways of life. Weber drew deeply upon Nietzsche's rhetorical discoveries, in his affirmation of "the natural political instincts," in his spirited critique of the Historical School, and in his stance toward the declining Junker oligarchy.[100]The momentum of Nietzsche's rhetoric, however, carries one toward a forthright assertion of institutions that would make direct rule, domination, and slavery possible once again. Weber's commitment to the liberal cause (as he understands it) requires him to retain the institutions which prevent such self-assertion. Weber is at once constrained to make any assertion of a common way of life by governmental means impossible, while elevating political leadership because it wills a ranking of values. It is not easy to be a Nietzschean individualist and an aristocratic liberal.[101] Furthermore, Weber's early formulation would seem to promote a splinter faction within the middle class, a faction that propagates Nietzschean contempt for the hedonistic bourgeoisie but cannot reasonably hope to become a majority even within the commercial middle class. Unable to bring a majority to the national liberal cause or to provide a common ground for the friends of liberal democracy at the center of the political spectrum, Weber's faction would strengthen the enemies of constitutional democracy by adding its voice to their attacks on the flaccid bourgeoisie.

Weber could not, therefore, remain with his earliest formulation. He had to work out a principled defense that would enable him to affirm the modern state, indirect rule or representative government, and the capitalist division of labor. A bourgeois Odysseus who had opened his ears to the Nietzschean call to greatness, Weber had to find a stratagem for muting its Siren song while steering the liberal democratic ship of state.

4. NIETZSCHE'S "YET UNTRODDEN WAY TO GREATNESS"

Philosophy was the first cause of the liberal cause but must now supersede it. The same need for the highest problems that once led

Montaigne to the humane ideal now dictates a philosophic politics aloof from the modern state and liberal institutions.

> Today, conversely, when only the herd animal receives and dispenses honors in Europe, when "equality of rights" could all too easily be changed into equality in violating rights—I mean, into a common war on all that is rare, strange, privileged, the higher man, the higher soul, the higher duty, the higher responsibility, and the abundance of creative power and masterfulness—today the concept of greatness entails being noble, wanting to be by oneself, being able to be different, standing alone and having to live independently.[102]

Nietzsche's quest for power to enforce a ranking of values is necessarily an attempt to estrange "the higher men" from any ideal of "humanity" or social responsibility that would prevent them from imposing the necessities of a higher way of life. But liberal principles of equal justice are in Nietzsche's view "Christianity made natural" or placed on a naturalistic footing. They stand or fall with the universal moral law of the Bible. Hence Nietzsche is compelled to promote moral nihilism.

> A declaration of war on the masses by the higher men is needed! Everywhere the mediocre are combining in order to make themselves master! . . . But we should take reprisal and bring this whole affair (which in Europe commenced with Christianity) to light and to the bar of judgment.[103]

The revolutionary justice of Nietzsche's new European order would sweep away the ancient moral law of Europe, the biblical morality, just as the French Revolution swept away the "ancient common law of Europe," the feudal land law.[104] Instead of a universal moral law, justice requires moral diversity. "What is fair for one cannot by any means—for that reason alone—also be fair for others; the demand of 'one morality for all' is detrimental to the higher men."[105] Nietzschean justice would uphold an order of rank between different moralities. At the peak of Nietzsche's "long ladder of rank" are men of a "high spirituality" subsuming all the moral virtues of other men:

It is a synthesis of all those states which are attributed to "merely moral" men, after they have been acquired singly through long discipline and exercise, perhaps through whole chains of generations: that high spirituality [which is] the spiritualization of justice and of that gracious severity which knows that it is its mission to maintain the *order of rank* in the world, among things themselves—and not only among men.[106]

An order of rank among things as well as men must reflect the diversity of "problems."

Ultimately there is an order of rank among states of the soul, and the order of rank of problems accords with this. The highest problems repulse everyone mercilessly who dares approach them without being predestined for their solution by the height and power of his spirituality.[107]

The converse of Nietzsche's project for science— to disclose how values had been enforced and embodied in the history of morals—is that science could provide a negative index of rank, by laying bare the limits of human endurance.

[O]ne could measure the strength of a spirit according to how much truth one could still barely endure— or to put it more clearly, to what degree one would *require* it to be thinned down, shrouded, sweetened, blunted, falsified.[108]

For each mind there is a potential moment of truth in which would be disclosed the limits beyond which experience would be "just too much." The existence of a hierarchy of problems that men may or must confront is due to the natures of men, not just to the things in the world. Each being has limits beyond which it cannot countenance reality; beyond those limits it cannot enforce values or assume responsibility. This understanding of human limitation does not, however, lead Nietzsche to counsel moderation, because the circle is not drawn permanently. Nietzsche's maxim is "will nothing beyond your capacity."[109] But he belittles any "prudence" that does not drive men to the limits of their capacity.[110] And the key to rank is the comprehensiveness of one's capacity for responsibility. The highest man is "predestined" for the greatest responsibilities; he not only understands the limits of other men but can assume the responsibility for leading them beyond these limits. The philosopher "has the conscience for the overall development of man." [111] "Order of rank: he who *determines* values and directs the will of millenia by giving direction to the highest natures is the *highest* man." [112] The highest man weighs policies that lesser men would consider presumptuous because their capacity for responsibility could not possibly extend to such decisions. "Put in its crudest form," the choice weighed by the highest man is "how could one sacrifice the development of mankind to help a higher species than man come into existence?" [113] To have the conscience for the overall development of man means to have a crime on one's conscience against the development of mankind as a whole. Mankind cannot make the great leap forward. To impose an order of rank means that some must be sacrificed. Those who can endure higher responsibilities must therefore be hardened in "that unshakeable faith that to beings such as we are, other beings must be subordinate by nature and have to sacrifice themselves." [114]

As one would expect from the preceding analysis, Nietzsche's order of rank is to be backed with the sword and enforced by men of powerful will.

> The most powerful man, the creator, would have to be the most evil, in as much as he carries his ideal against the ideals of other men and remakes them in his own image. Evil here means: hard, painful, enforced. [115]
>
> Such men as Napoleon must come again and again and confirm the belief in the autocracy of the individual: but he himself was corrupted by the means he *had* to employ and lost noblesse of character. If he had had to prevail among a different kind of man he could have employed other means; and it would thus not seem to be a necessity for a Caesar to become bad. [116]

Nietzsche arrives at the necessity for aristocracy as a means to enable the philosopher to rule without stooping to base and degrading actions. To prevent Caesars from turning bad, to make possible a new kind of Napoleon, "a Caesar with Christ's soul," an entourage of nobles is indispensable.[117] Hence "the new philosopher can arise only in conjunction with a ruling caste, as its highest spiritualization."[118] The central political question, upon which the creation of Nietzsche's new man and world would seem to depend, is therefore "What is noble?"[119] This is to ask what rank order is, since in German *Vornehm* means "first in rank" or "of high rank." A ruling caste for Europe is the precondition of the future philosophy, but only if such a caste permits the highest man to prevail without loss of noblesse. In order to forge this new ruling caste, Nietzsche requires a new conception of politics, a great and philosophic politics.

> The *greatest* struggle: for that a new *weapon* is needed. The hammer: to conjure up a terrible decision, to confront Europe with the final choice whether its will "wills" its own destruction. Prevention of the decline into mediocrity. Rather even destruction.[120]

To precipitate a decision, Nietzsche requires a philosophic teaching. Its function is, in effect, psychological warfare to strengthen morale and fighting spirit on one side: "A doctrine is needed powerful enough to work as a breeding agent: strengthening the strong, paralyzing and destructive for the weak."[121] The stage for psychological warfare is set because a period of great political upheavals is in the making. Nietzsche seems to have foreseen not only the great suffering of the victims of modern warfare but also the pathos of mass combat, in which men who are unprepared, psychologically and physically, must share the responsibility and guilt for terrible events. The crucial weapon is the one that makes men hard; the promise of Nietzsche's doctrine is that it will reverse Christ's prophecy: not the meek but those who can endure the terrible wars of the future will inherit the earth:

> That new party of life which would tackle the greatest of all tasks, the attempt to raise humanity higher, including the relentless destruction of everything that was degenerating and parasitical, would again make possible that excess of life on earth from which the Dionysian state, too, would have to awaken again. I promise a tragic age: the highest art in saying Yes to life, tragedy, will be reborn when humanity has

weathered the consciousness of the hardest but most necessary wars *without suffering from it*.[122]

By all indications, Nietzsche's new weapon is the doctrine of the
eternal recurrence of the same.[123] It will be the experience of this doctrine that creates the conscience upon which the comprehensive responsibilities of the higher men will rest.[124]

5. THE VULGATE NIETZSCHE

The project we have adumbrated from Nietzsche's sketches is
resolutely in defiance of common sense.[125] But it would be foolhardy to
assume that it is therefore neglectful of the exigencies of communal
life or of the more plebian side of political life. Thus far our survey of
Nietzsche's politics has mirrored his bias toward "the higher men." It
would, however, distort Nietzsche's thought to ignore his attention to
the democratic or vulgar problems of politics. Nietzsche did not consider the news that "God is dead" to be politically irrelevant. Religion,
as he understood it, was first and foremost a means of governing the
people. The assertion that Christianity is Plato for the people compels
us to consider how popular religion can be useful to philosophy, enforcing a philosopher's ranking of values over millenia. The Preface to
Beyond Good and Evil reflects Nietzsche's preoccupation with the
problem, that is, the task, of vulgarization. The death of God is of the
utmost consequence for popular government. Limited government is
greatly strengthened when it can presuppose the existence of moral
limits supported by settled opinion; once the religious agreement that
had secured trust and mutual faith is eroded, limited government can
become a framework for criminality. It is not intended to govern the
soul. The opportunity that Nietzsche discerns in the death of God is an
opportunity to reach beyond the limits of liberal politics to reorder the
soul. That does not mean the souls of the higher men alone; it is an
opportunity to reorder democratic selves as well. Nietzsche's reflections on religion in Part 3 of *Beyond Good and Evil* point to the conclusion that the "essence" of religion is philosophic rule.[126] One must
therefore anticipate a "Nietzsche for the people," to replace the vulgarization of Plato. The Preface accordingly warns against the danger

to philosophic politics arising from alternative methods of organizing, indoctrinating, and leading the people.

> [W]ith so tense a bow we can now shoot for the most distant goals. To be sure, European man experiences this tension as need and distress; twice already attempts have been made in the grand style to unbend the bow—once by means of Jesuitism, the second time by means of the democratic enlightenment which, with the aid of freedom of the press and newspaper-reading, might indeed bring it about that the spirit would no longer experience itself so easily as a "need."[127]

Nietzsche's concern with the methods of the Jesuits and the propagandists of democratic enlightenment reflects his determination not to ignore his own vulgarization. Although Nietzsche wrote many difficult and obscure passages, one must bear in mind that his books are not uniformly obscure. He is not always reserved and austere; he can be piercingly eloquent and insultingly clear. Nietzsche was a genius in the arts of propaganda, a vulgar trade; his writings lend themselves to modern political warfare. They are full of passages that fit Weber's account of political speech:

> When speaking in a political meeting about democracy, one does not hide one's personal standpoint; indeed, to come out clearly and take a stand is one's damned duty. The words one uses in such a meeting are not means of scientific analysis but means of canvassing votes and winning over others. They are not plowshares to loosen the soil of contemplative thought; they are swords against the enemies: such words are weapons.[128]

In the later parts of *Beyond Good and Evil,* Nietzsche's preoccupation with demagogy is reflected in his treatment of European nationalism.[129] The most recent "counterpart of Jesuitism" is *Vaterlanderei.* Weber is antithetical to Nietzsche in continuing the struggle for liberal institutions, and in unifying the liberal cause with the national cause. Weber joins the democratic enlightenment with *Vaterlanderei.* This conflict is not between "the court" and "the country" or between an effete Nietzsche diddling with the literati and a Weber who scuffles in the marketplace. Nietzsche and Weber disagree about demagogy and the role of nations because they both have policies that require peoples and demagogues. Weber's political writings conjure with Nietzsche's influence because Nietzsche's writings constituted a kind of political journalism, albeit much more than that as well. When the Fascists came to Nietzsche they did not have to translate him into political speech: the "vulgar" formulations were waiting to be seized. Nietzsche published an armory of antidemocratic words. Even more significant was Nietzsche's replacement for "the Christian-ecclesiastical pressure of millenia." In place of the Platonic errors of the pure mind and the Good, Nietzsche fashioned a doctrine of the self which lent itself to vulgarization in a multitude of forms.[130] This vulgate Nietzsche has been largely ignored by Nietzsche scholars, in part because Nietzsche's association with Nazism in Germany (and Fascism everywhere else, from England to Argentina) had already ruined their digestion, as far as his politics were concerned.[131] Nietzsche's doctrine of the self provides a bridge between the vulgar side of politics and the more refined heights of Nietzsche's psychagogy. To use Hannah Arendt's insightful terms: it provides a bridge between the mob and the intellectuals.[132] It makes Weberian political leadership difficult not only by winning politically talented (and otherwise gifted) men away from Weber's cause but also by influencing the followers or the mass. Nietzsche's politics has nothing to do with rural idiocy or medieval torpor. It is a politics of motion as dynamic and tumultuous as the mass movements and revolutions of the twentieth century. To understand its power and its limitations we will have to consider both its absorption or sublimation of modern science (in chapter 3) and its explosive interpretation of the self (in chapter 4).

In Nietzsche's perspective, Weber's reinterpretation of the liberal project comes to light as an attempt to arrest the momentum of what is vital and powerful in the liberal cause. The momentum of the struggle for liberal institutions is intelligible, according to Nietzsche, only when we perceive it as a dimension of the scientific and philosophical revolution of the Renaissance and the seventeenth century. Liberal institutions arose from the philosophic struggle against Platonic error; they were instrumentalities to liberate science and philosophy from the constraints of the old regime or, more particularly, from the Church and from scholasticism. They were necessary to promote a "new greatness for man." Weber's defense of liberal democracy binds the liberal cause to the national cause, placing the power of nationalism in the service of liberal reason of state. By giving strength and staying power to the regime of the liberal commercial republic, Weber's defense severs the liberal cause from the larger philosophic and scientific struggle of most concern to Nietzsche. Because science is so essential to Nietzsche's opposition to Weber's policy, and because Nietzsche argues that the continuation of the scientific revolution requires science to be resolutely nihilistic, our next topic will be Nietzsche's conquest or courtship of modern scholarship.

3. LEADING SCIENCE: *BEYOND GOOD AND EVIL*, PART 6: "WE SCHOLARS"

THE crisis of liberalism is reflected in the strength of that growing movement of opinion which claims that the progress promoted by liberal democracy is not inherently benevolent, or that the motion in which the Western democracies are caught up is neither essentially humane nor moral. This new "leading opinion" does not deny the reality of progress but rather argues that we must choose between its continuation and "humanity" or "the relief of man's estate." The conditions of scientific and technical advance are apparently not quite what Bacon and Descartes originally "promised," for progress based upon the mastery of nature through modern science is as cruel and dangerous as it is benevolent for mankind.[1] The necessity for choice arises as a political issue because the method of democracy is unquestionably humanitarian, giving a sovereign voice to the necessity for self-preservation in all men. Science, however, is not similarly committed to preserving mankind; the progress of modern science may endanger the human race, but this consequence does not for a moment call into question the validity of the scientific method or its findings. The crisis of liberalism thus reflects and clarifies the tension—or worse yet, the disharmony and contradiction—between the method of democracy and the method of science.[2] Weber and Nietzsche anticipated this new climate of opinion and contributed to it in different ways. Both were certain that the crisis could only be interpreted and shaped but could not be arrested; both recognized in it an opportunity for extraordinary leadership. They agreed that there was no ground to be confident that science would continue to enjoy the security and standing within modern regimes that it had come to take for granted in Europe and America.[3] Neither Weber nor Nietzsche fundamentally doubted the viability of modern scientific methods or thought they could be greatly altered. Both regarded intellectual probity as the virtue par excellence for men of science; they expected science to be refined and perfected without changing its essential character. What would have to be changed as the crisis of liberalism came to a head was the relation between science and society, theory and practice, or philosophy and politics.[4] In particular, Weber and Nietzsche agreed that the status of leadership and the importance attached to it by science would have to be changed. Since the method of science was essentially unalterable, the method of democracy would either be transformed, as in Weber's policy, or abandoned, as in Nietzsche's.

Although Weber did not challenge the method of science, his policy was to alter its horizon or its conception of the vocation of science within the total ethical economy of human life.[5] This redrawing of horizons was reflected in Weber's new rhetoric for science and in his abandonment of the promises or hopes that had originally helped to justify modern science and have continued to do so until recently. Weber scorned the charitable and beneficent pretensions of Baconian propaganda. He abandoned "the dream of peace and human happiness"; above the portals of the future, science must chisel Dante's infernal greeting, *lasciate ogni speranza*.[6] Weber renounces the rosy blush of the Enlightenment and its enthusiasm for eudaemonistic progress: only "a few big children," who hold academic chairs, still believe that modern science can be Santa Claus.[7] Weber inculcated a new prudent modesty for science and its proponents. Integral to the humbler stance was a new civility to reconcile science to the rather irrational conditions of public deliberation. Weber taught science to drop its arrogance or at least its claim to hold a standpoint superior to mere partisans and ordinary citizens. His doctrine, that science could not rank the highest values, was explicitly advanced to defend the conditions of political debate, compelling scholars to respect the limits of a democratic arena in which partisans advanced their claims against opponents no less intransigent in their convictions and no more willing to respect an authority above their convictions.[8] Weber's doctrine required science to surrender the implicit and explicit claims to leadership that it had steadily advanced through modern liberal politics and the Idealist interpretations of the modern *Rechtsstaat*. The converse was that science need not take much responsibility for the progress it was bound to generate. Since this progress was no longer evidently humane or beneficial, it was prudent for science to keep its distance. Under Weber's policy, science could claim to be skeptical of the value of progress and morally concerned about its regrettable consequences. Scientists could join their fellow citizens in urging responsible leaders to meet "the demands of the day" and could be especially useful in clarifying those demands where they resulted from scientific progress.[9] Weber's plan held out the promise of a harmonious relation between science and liberal democracy, though it was a harmony to be worked out in practice since it did not obtain in theory.[10]

Weber's plan seems impressively circumspect and has accordingly won many adherents. It accommodates the new dimension of controversy over the consequences of science by placing the quarrel squarely within the political realm and by teaching scientists to respect the limits of reasonable discourse within that arena. Upon sustained analysis, however, it proves to be far less circumspect. The question that Weber begs, or leaves darkling, is of such paramount importance as to cast doubt on his entire plan: *Who leads science?* As Nietzsche insists (in the text we shall presently consider), this is the chief question posed for philosophy by the crisis of liberalism. In taking it up, we begin our attempt to gauge the distance between Weber and Nietzsche in Weber's final formulation of his teaching on political leadership. Our initial topic is the most obvious difference between their alternatives: Nietzsche's philosophic politics is, in the first instance, leadership of science; Weberian political leadership most emphatically is not.[11]

1. LEADERLESS SCIENCE

In the last chapter, we considered the parallels between Weber's initial argument for leadership and Nietzsche's critique of decadence. Those parallels lend a certain plausibility to Karl Jaspers's assertion:

When in 1918 Max Weber conceived of a democracy with a strong leader, he saw that there were no leaders. Leaders can develop only on a political proving ground, which today is provided only by a genuine democracy. They cannot appear spontaneously, when the need for them arises. Max Weber might have said, with Nietzsche, "The necessity for such leaders, the frightening danger that they may not appear, or that they may warp or degenerate—these are our real anxieties and our grounds for gloom." [12]

This passage is apropos and will reward our attention. But Jaspers's analogy is unsound, to say the least. The necessity Nietzsche describes is for philosophic leaders, and in the sequence of aphorisms that follows, his theme is the rule of philosophy over science. Why does scholarship need leaders? Who are the antagonists, the party of darkness and reaction, against which science must be led?

In answering these questions, Nietzsche attempts to revive the warlike spirit of independence in which early modern philosophy attacked the authorities of the old regime. One must, however, emphasize that those old enemies of science are, for all practical purposes, no enemies at all. Nietzsche's intention was to prevent Micawberism in science by clarifying the need for philosophic leaders. While appropriating the spirited rhetoric of modern rationalism and enlightened progress, the current analytic orthodoxy in philosophy places science in a cozy and comforting relation with liberal democracy. The dominant orthodoxy portrays science and its literary defenders as champions in the continuing struggle against the forces of dogmatism and obscurantism. According to Nietzsche, this is in fact a vast relaxation from the vigilance of science. Far from carrying forward the high tradition of philosophic warfare launched in the Renaissance (and reignited in the seventeenth century), it is a great retreat. The powers that be are nations organized in modern states, led by parties and opinion leaders. The source of the power of such half-educated opinion leaders as Woodrow Wilson is the people; and what matters most to the people, according to Nietzsche, is *morality*. The intellectual power to which science today bends its knee, the new queen that stands in theology's place demanding that science do her will, is public opinion, democratic opinion, or, in more formal dress, "moral intuition."[13] The source of danger to the formation of scientific intelligence and to the conduct of inquiry comes from the guardians of morality and from the shepherds of the people; it comes from fashionable opinion-leadership. Science requires philosophic leadership in order to withstand power in its present forms; it needs philosophy to pose the questions which the people and opinion leaders do not want to hear, but above all to protect its will to truth from the "Minotaurs" of morality and conscience.[14] Scientific progress is threatened by collapse from within, as scholars prostrate themselves before the new *vox dei*. The most powerful accusation that opinion leaders can make to intimidate science and to warp the conduct of inquiry is that science is morally nihilistic, that scientific progress is neither humane nor moral. It is this charge that Nietzsche meets head-on; he knows that beating dead horses and mouthing the old rhetoric of enlightenment will not disarm the enemies of science.

From Nietzsche's standpoint, it would be charitable, but wrong, to say that science headed by the present scholasticism in academic philosophy is leaderless. It is more like an army commanded by the enemy, except that science wisely ignores its self-appointed spokesmen. Nietzsche begins "We Scholars" with a survey of the opinions held by scientists about philosophy, a survey that would undoubtedly yield the same results today. But while justifiably disdaining the leadership of academic philosophers, science is in danger of yielding its governance and its leadership to even less qualified bellwethers. The difficulty of science is profound because the philosophic leadership that modern science requires is entirely without precedent, according to Nietzsche. While he insists, from the beginning of Part 6, that the ancient philosophers were capable of leadership and command, Nietzsche knows that ancient political philosophy made no effort to lead or defend anything like modern science in its imperious conquest of nature and man's estate.[15] For all its attention to democracy, to the authority of opinion in the city, and to the opinion-leading poets and sophists, ancient political philosophy is not concerned with the problems of leadership that Nietzsche considers; its philosopher-kings are the very embodiment of Platonic error.[16] The philosophic leaders who originated modern science, on the other hand, did not and perhaps could not anticipate the dangers that the success of their project would pose for science. They did not have to contend with democracy in its modern form or with the moral antagonism that modern science provokes once the old authorities no longer serve as a common enemy against which science and the people can unite.[17] It is by no means clear what constitutes the task of leading science when it is subject to the charge of moral nihilism.

2. WE SCHOLARS

Nietzsche's treatment of science in *Beyond Good and Evil* does not, of course, begin with Part 6. The subjects of every preceding thematic part are of obvious concern for science. Part 1 develops the problem of the value of truth; Part 2 considers the connections between the will to knowledge and the will to ignorance; Part 3 raises the project of "a history of the problem of science and conscience in the soul of the *homines religiosi*"; Part 5 begins with a critique of the present "science of morals."[18] We will try to be mindful of these problems, although we cannot hope to do justice to them here; we will have to be content to discuss the immediate overture to Part 6, the aphorism from which Jaspers quoted. We will try to do justice to the integrity of Nietzsche's argument in Part 6, to find the center of gravity of the section as a whole, and to decide what is marginal. Our hypothesis is that what gives each remark in the part its specific gravity is its bearing upon the task for philosophy posed by "we scholars." The part is not a loose anthology but rather an ordered whole. Since it begins as an attack upon scholars, upon more than usually scrupulous readers, "the conscientious in spirit," I will assume that Nietzsche expected his criticism to be read with scientific alertness and precision, even with a Jesuitical suspicion.[19]

The argument begins as a brusque assertion: the scholar is a dependent type, a tool, a slave, a technically perfect mirror meant to be used by a more powerful type.[20] But this brusqueness is part of a larger, and considerably more subtle, argument for the dependence of the scientist upon the philosopher. This dependence is in the first instance a matter of rank order in the mundane sense: it is a political relation that must be created by initiative and maintained by assertion. Nietzsche enacts enough of this imposition to clarify the psychological preconditions and political framework of a relation of dominance over science.[21] The enactment shows what Nietzsche knew, or thought he knew, about the problem of leading science; the aphorisms of Part 6 present a sequence of stances which constitute a dramatic case for dependence. The stances evidence Nietzsche's knowledge; in his argument, the relation between reasoning and such "evidence" is necessarily reflexive. We will try to learn to think about the leadership of science by studying Nietzsche's example. He insisted that philosophic leadership would be unintelligible to German scientists because the German universities did not teach them how to see, how to think, how to speak, and how to write.[22] Nietzsche's writings are a qualified attempt to teach these things—qualified by his economy of effort, which led him, much of the time, simply to hold out and hold back for readers who already knew them. In any event, Nietzsche teaches how to speak by demonstration. His assertion of philosophical leadership is literary

but indicates how an order of rank must come into being and be maintained.[23] The practical task may be subtle, but it can save us from the
curse of arbitrary interpretivism that condemns much Nietzsche scholarship to trivialization. The task is one that calls for a gentlemanly
reader tough and worldly enough to resist distraction.

Part 6 consists of ten aphorisms. Nos. 204–7 describe the opinions and inclinations of the average scholar; Nos. 208–9 are about the
skeptical climate of fin de siècle opinion in Europe, its causes, its consequences, and what might replace it; Nos. 210–13 describe the distinctive tasks of the philosopher. One can also discern two coherent
halves. The first five aphorisms are on present conditions; they are "in
all essentials a *critique of modernity.*"[24] The last five are about what is
not modern; they provide "pointers to a contrary type that is as little
modern as possible—a noble Yes-saying type."[25]

The title indicates that Nietzsche will speak about and on behalf
of "we scholars." Who has the right to speak for science? Nietzsche's
standpoint is at once within and beyond scholarship; he claims to comprehend science without being bound or limited by it. "We scholars"
have particular, specialized problems, but together we constitute a unified problem for the philosopher, a political problem of rank order.
Nietzsche reminds us of the contradiction between the method of science and the method of democracy by acknowledging that the right to
speak about science and philosophy is reserved for those who know, on
the basis of experience. "Science," as Weber said, "is the affair of an
intellectual aristocracy."[26] Yet the complexity of the problem of governance within science is suggested by Nietzsche's dictum that "Science
is fundamentally democratic and anti-oligarchic."[27] What kind of regime does science require for the realization of its integral purposes
and for the continuation of its progress? The specialist has an interest
in the politics of science, as indicated by his "declaration of independence" from philosophy.[28] But what kind of leadership does it take to
satisfy his legitimate interests? Is there an ordering of rank implicit in
science? Can science hope to be governed by those who have shared
the experience of science? The question of the regime required for the
continued unfolding of the modern scientific enterprise within the
world is implicit in Part 6 and yet is curiously never answered within
it.[29]

Rank order is a political notion. Because Nietzsche begins by as-
sociating modern scholars with democracy, he leads one to view the

problem, of his title to speak, as a political problem. Nietzsche seems to adopt the tactic that Aristotle, counseling moderation, had recommended to prevent class warfare:

> [A] mistake is made both in democracies and in oligarchies—in democracies by the demagogues, where the multitude is supreme over the laws; for they always divide the city into two by fighting with the well-to-do, but they ought on the contrary always to pretend to be speaking on behalf of men that are well-to-do, while in democracies the oligarchical statesmen ought to pretend to be speaking on behalf of the people, and the oligarchics ought to take oath in terms exactly opposite to those they use now, for at present in some oligarchies they swear, "And I will be hostile to the people, and will plan whatever evil I can against them," but they ought to hold, and to act the part of holding, the opposite notion, declaring in their oaths, "I will not wrong the people." [30]

Nietzsche's philosopher is like an Aristotelian statesman who speaks on behalf of the popular party—or pretends to. "We philosophers" are of necessity scholars; by speaking for scholars, we can lead them. Aristotle's remark points to an obvious difficulty. Nietzsche cannot conceal his distinction from democratic scholars any more than a wealthy man can conceal his privileges; but he must win their trust and the right to speak for them. It is not self-evident that Nietzsche solves this problem. At first glance, he seems to defy Aristotle's counsel: instead of moderating conflict, he exhorts the factions to extremes, driving a wedge between the "rich" and the "poor." He cannot have taken an oath not to wrong the scholars, for he promptly sets to browbeating them.[31] In the first aphorism of Part 6, Nietzsche "moralizes" in a spirit of intransigence that might recall Gobineau: like an aristocrat who refuses to surrender to the French Revolution, he denies the victorious democracy the only thing he can withhold, their moral title to prevail by right. As a spokesman for what appears to be a lost cause, Nietzsche runs a risk of "showing his wounds," since to do so is to remind his opponents of their power to do damage. Nietzsche runs that risk and makes *montrer ses plaies* his theme, because the harm that science and philosophy can do each other in fratricidal civil war points to the lasting problem of philosophic politics. The potential for civil war is significant. The old conflict between theology and science has ended in a resounding practical victory for philosophy and science.[32] Unable to discern a common enemy or to submit to leadership, the victors have now set to squabbling amid the spoils. Nietzsche must run the risk and moralize. But rather than do so impotently, philosophy should "take reprisal" and reopen the possibility of alliances against science with the enemies of democracy.[33] Rather than strengthen the morale of the plebian party by showing philosophy's wounds, it is better to remind the democratic party of theirs: even in its current, contemptible state, philosophy creates a shambles in the ranks of science.[34]

Nietzsche ventures "to speak out against an unseemly and harmful shift in the respective ranks of science and philosophy."[35] He ridicules "the Declaration of Independence of the scientific man, his emancipation from philosophy."[36] One is bound to be amazed by Nietzsche's tone. Despite the fact that science was celebrating an unprecedented sequence of practical triumphs, as invention after invention stunned even the most dedicated opponents of scientific progress, Nietzsche spoke with magisterial calm about the weakness and even the decay of science. His confidence in ridiculing the apparently irreversible trend toward the emancipation of science, particularly from the authority of philosophy, seems to be a groundless confidence. Although he accuses science of democratic proclivities, Nietzsche's unstated premise seems to be that science is inherently hierarchical. When philosophers take hold of their proper tasks, scholars will have no trouble understanding the priority of those tasks. But the difference becomes less imposing and can be assaulted by rebels in the name of scientific autonomy, when philosophy abdicates responsibility for the highest problems. If this is so, Nietzsche can only disclose the proper relation between philosophy and science by raising the problems of philosophy again to their proper location in human affairs or by shouldering the responsibilities that philosophy has sloughed off. A parallel interpretation of the French Revolution had been advanced by Tocqueville: if the aristocracy had performed its tasks, there would have been no uprising, no effort to eliminate the aristocracy or to deny the importance of the tasks it performed.[37] Nietzsche portrays the philosopher who breaks ranks to lead science in its democratic revolt against philosophy in more or less the "moralistic" terms an aristocrat would use against a member of his class who broke ranks to lead the plebs. In turning to the commoners, he shows himself incapable of living by the higher standard of an aristocratic code.[38] Thus Nietzsche judges the positivists:

> They are all losers who have been *brought back* under the hegemony of science, after having desired *more* of themselves at some time, without having the right to this "more" and its responsibilities—and who now represent, in word and deed, honorably, resentfully, and vengefully, the *unbelief* in the masterly task and masterfulness of philosophy.[39]

If the philosopher does not dominate science, the result is a slave revolt, a release of the *ressentiment* of those who yearn for "freedom from all masters." Yet it seems symptomatic of the dependence of science that the scholar alone would not know how to lead an attack against philosophy. He lacks the Catilinarian fervor that would drive men either to philosophic or antiphilosophic politics. Nietzsche adopts the principle that the responsibility for misgovernment in science must lie with philosophy; the dissolution of the rule of philosophy must be due to its omissions or mistakes.

3. MORALLY RESPECTABLE SCIENCE

Science resists the emergence of leadership from within its ranks. Its resistance is inseparable from its moral discipline and difficult to overcome because the moral claims of scientific discipline are just. The philosopher cannot ignore them but must determine their limits, for the claims of specialized science upon the seeker of knowledge are limitless. "The scope and the tower-building of the sciences has grown to be enormous."[40] The sensitivity of the philosopher in matters of intellectual conscience may deter him from imposing such necessary limits:

> [H]e is afraid of the seduction to become a dilettante . . . he knows too well that whoever has lost his self-respect cannot command or *lead* in the realm of knowledge—unless he would like to become a great actor, a philosophical Cagliostro and pied piper, in short, a seducer.[41]

The difficulty is however also the source of an interdependence that makes science open to leadership, including the seductions of opinion leaders and Cagliostros. If the experiences of science and philosophy did not overlap, science would enjoy a relatively complete autonomy from philosophy. This would hold even if philosophy were the master and science its slave, as Hegel's discussion suggests: the autonomy of the slave's activity enables him to create a world that stands apart from and ultimately replaces the world of the master.[42] Philosophy must subsume science in order to lead it; the experience of philosophy must be a sublimation of the scientific experience.

Although the philosopher is endangered by the moral hazards of science, overcoming those hazards seems to be a necessity for science itself if the values of science are to be enforced. Unlike the scholar, the philosopher demands a value judgment of himself; his problems require him to create and rank values. The philosopher looks down upon the moral horizon of the scientist insofar as the value of science becomes a problem for him.[43] For Nietzsche, as we have seen, values are not primarily objects of theory; they are embodied in men. Both the scholar and the philosopher embody the morality of truth-seeking; this morality is problematic for the philosopher. Science is surrounded by a humanity for whom this morality is problematic (if they understand it at all). The weakness of the scientific morality is that it does not provide for the governance and leadership of science or come to terms with the dependence of science upon the world outside of science. The conditions for the possibility of science are in part political. Freedom from philosophic leadership cannot mean "freedom from all masters." It means dependence upon men who have lost their self-respect and become Cagliostros, or, worse, dependence upon public opinion, the *Diktat* of politicians or the leaders of various moral majorities.

In aphorisms Nos. 206 and 207, Nietzsche describes the average scholar. The traits he selects are not accidental; they reflect a moral and psychological necessity: Nietzsche's scholar, to paraphrase Hobbes, is not any particular scientist but Science-kind.[44] Science is democratic; it has the moral characteristics that make majority tyranny a problem in democracies. The price of moral respectability is high. On the one hand, the average scholar depends on "the sunshine of a good name" to offset his "inner mistrust." On the other hand,

> The worst and most dangerous thing of which scholars are
> capable comes from their sense of the mediocrity of their

own type—from that Jesuitism of mediocrity which instinctively works at the annihilation of the uncommon man and
tries to break every bent bow, or preferably, to unbend
it. Unbending, considerately, of course, with a solicitous
hand—*unbending* with familiar pity, that is the characteristic
art of Jesuitism which has always known how to introduce
itself as a religion of pity.[45]

As these allusions to the Preface indicate, science is in danger of relaxation, of succumbing to a new scholarly Jesuitism of mediocrity within
its ranks.[46] The dynamism of scientific advance depends upon excellence, but the moral discipline of science favors a type that is deeply
opposed to excellence. By favoring democratic modes of governance
within science, morally respectable science seems to endanger its own
sources of power. Moreover, a science preoccupied with the sunshine
of its good name seems extraordinarily vulnerable to the tyranny of the
majority so long as science is environed by a liberal democratic
regime.

According to Nietzsche's account, the average scholar has nothing
in common with the noble type of man. To follow the progress of his
argument, however, one must stress that Nietzsche anticipates many
exceptions. Not every scholar lacks commanding qualities; an individual may bring to science the traits of another breeding or surmount the
limitations of the average scholar by force of character. Because there
are exceptions, one must consider the bearing of Nietzsche's assertions
on men of different mettle. Having denied that there is anything noble
or manly about scholars, Nietzsche goes on in aphorism No. 207 to
call the scholar a mere tool and to question his virility: scholars are like
old maids who have nothing to cling to but their respectability.[47] One
may take this as effrontery, intimidation, or good-humored ribbing. A
timid and slavish scholar is bound to be stung. But what of the scholar
whom Nietzsche describes in the *Genealogy of Morals*": fundamentally brave, proud, and magnanimous animals who know how to keep
their hearts as well as their sufferings in bounds and have trained themselves to sacrifice all desirability to truth"?[48] To call such magnanimous animals eunuchs and old maids or slaves is unjust, but the insult
challenges the pride if it is there. Nietzsche is deliberately unjust in
order to create a bond—initially a bond of enmity—between the philosopher and a certain atypical class of scholars. Nietzsche takes on the
responsibility and guilt for an offense in order to intensify the nobler

scholar's pride in his distinction from the scholarly herd. Nietzsche elicits anger. Having a severe philosophic antagonist is an experience that isolates and elevates.[49] Scholars of commanding character can be divided from the mass by selective attacks that strengthen their pride while provoking their wrath. The solution to the problem of scientific governance toward which Nietzsche is leading would require a nobility within science.

4. A SKEPTICAL RIPOSTE

Aficionados may find the foregoing interpretation too crude, too political, too preoccupied with pecking orders. Let us put this line of objection in the form of an alternative reading.

Consider the delicacy of the philosophic task adumbrated in Nietzsche's overture to Part 6. As aphorism No. 203 indicates, Nietzsche cannot have much doubt about the vulnerability of philosophy. He stresses the pain, worry, and anxiety that afflict anyone who hopes for philosophic leadership, and this anxiety is evident throughout the first half of Part 6. Nietzsche is spirited, he speaks up for philosophy, he even moralizes. But he does not conduct himself as if he were in a position to rule. If one can identify a distinctive voice in Part 6, it comes close to Pascal's in the *Lettres provinciales*.[50] It is the voice of a polemicist who does not have a position of power and must rely on reason against the many and against the mighty. When Nietzsche reviews the opinions commonly held about philosophy in aphorism No. 204, he turns the critical standards of scholars against the lax habits they fall into when judging philosophy. His "moralizing" amounts to an assertion of scientific canons of evidence against a lapse into prejudice and hearsay.

It is, moreover, a fallacy to assume that Nietzsche's attempt to counter the democratic prejudices of scholars requires a counter-prejudice in favor of aristocratic rule. Nietzsche reinforces an anti-democratic, Hobbist prejudice common in European science, when he accuses democracy as a decline of the form of organizing power: it was a decline from the standard established by the modern Leviathan. From the outset, the rise of European science had been accompanied by an unprecedented growth of political, military, and commercial power. Nietzsche trades heavily upon the historical memories of European science. In Part 6, his philosopher-leader appears as a successor to the enlightened despots who fostered the progress of science; Nietzsche gives a prominent place to Frederick the Great and highlights the scientific spirit he promoted.[51] Although Nietzsche objects to the democratic tendencies of modern science, he does not try to separate it from its deeply rooted alliance with the modern state. He understands the fears and insecurities of modern scholars, their need for the protective shield of state power, their readiness to leave politics to the princes and to vote as Hobbists for any power that would create the conditions of public peace and prosperity required for their specialized work. In addition to his appeals to canons of evidence (No. 204) and to the Hobbist prejudices of scholars (No. 209), Nietzsche reawakens some of the idealism of Baconian propaganda. Like Bacon, he makes his initial themes (in No. 203) faith and hope; he conveys the promise of philosophic leaders of a benevolence that will dwarf all precedents. The possibility he holds out is a science confident of its benevolence, drawing steadily upon its accumulated force and its cumulative tasks. But this is merely to revitalize the Baconian project and its well-established habits of mind.[52] Furthermore, the pathos of responsibility for mankind that Nietzsche conjures up appeals to a certain moral sensibility, a noble idealism in men of science. In sum, Nietzsche is both more attentive to the ordinary fears and needs of scientists than the preceding interpretation seems to allow and more concerned to win their trust. The philosophic leader must persuade and reason. Like Rousseau's legislator, his authority rests less on assertion than on his capacity to forge a bond of trust.[53]

In reply to this objection, we may grant that in No. 203 Nietzsche is cautious and anxious. But his criticism of democracy is not merely that it is a decline from the Hobbist Leviathan. The "faith" of Nietzsche's party is that democracy is also "a form of the decay, namely the diminution, of man, making him mediocre and lowering his value."[54] That is equally a critique of the modern state and would apply as well to Alexander Hamilton's "administrative republic," despite its modifications of democracy. If one takes Frederick the Great with Machiavelli, who is the ultimate source of the "skepticism of audacious manliness" discussed in No. 209, one is left with a modern state fully suited to the "degeneration and diminution of man into the perfect herd animal . . . this animalization of man into the dwarf animal of equal rights and claims."[55] As they understood it, the modern state was not a means "to prepare great ventures and over-all attempts of discipline and cultivation by way of putting an end to that gruesome dominion of nonsense and accident that has so far been called 'history.'"[56] Nietzsche did not think it possible to preserve the full momentum of scientific progress without overcoming the inevitable resistance of the people. In his writings there is no continuation of the Baconian posture of benevolence and humanitarian concern. Nietzsche does harken to enlightened despotism as a kind of precedent, but the Machiavellian plotters he conjures up are not simply benevolent: "whatever has existed on earth of concealed, terrible, and benevolent spirits will look pale and dwarfed by comparison."[57] Admittedly, aphorism No. 209 is a parable open to many readings, but it hardly points to a continuation of the alliance with the modern state that had aided modern European science in its first flights. Nietzsche's parable awakens men of science to the possibility of breeding a future generation of knowers. The modern state is not suited to the task of cultivating definite types of men, for reasons we have previously considered.[58] As Nietzsche presents them, the policies of Frederick were not an exception to "the gruesome dominion of nonsense and accident that has so far been called 'history.'"[59] Frederick did not set out to conquer European thought through German historical science. The parable is put forward to show that heightened military and political tensions, in particular a greater likelihood of war with Russia, could promote the cause of European science. Just as Frederick Wilhelm I set in motion a chain of events that strengthened science, when he began to build the Prussian armies, Nietzsche indicates that by building a European ruling caste, he could deliberately create a new breed of scientists ready for "dangerous journeys of exploration and spiritualized North Pole expeditions under desolate and dangerous skies."[60] But as the term *ruling caste* indicates, the policy Nietzsche adumbrates points beyond the modern state.

It is true that Nietzsche caters to the idealism of scholars when he speaks of responsibility for the future of mankind. In accentuating the pathos of his responsibilities, he is less than candid about the fact that his philosophic legislators will approach their tasks in a spirit of childlike play and insouciance.[61] The dimension of great criminality and moral nihilism which he emphasizes elsewhere is obscured in No. 203 and perhaps in Part 6 as a whole.[62] On an essential point, however, Nietzsche is quite frank: there is nothing humanitarian about "*cet esprit fataliste, ironique, mephistophélique.*"[63] And there is "a new explosive being tried somewhere, a dynamite of the spirit . . . that does not merely say No, want No, but—horrible thought!—*does* No."[64]

The necessity for moral nihilism in the leadership of science will become evident as we move through the second half of "We Scholars."

5. CRITICS AND PHILOSOPHIC LABORERS

As the case of Frederick the Great proves, the strong skeptic is capable of great acts of practical will. His activism does not presuppose the value of truth, and thus he stands outside the moral horizon of the scholar. But his own horizon is problematic. One may act powerfully while remaining a skeptic, but one's capacity for action remains a mysterious quantum, apparently resting upon the mute facts of courage and health or the state of one's body—which is all that seems to separate strong skepticism from weak.[65] According to Nietzsche it is possible to transcend the skeptic's limited horizon, for his capacity to suspend judgment implicitly presupposes fixed values, of which the skeptic is hardly aware. The philosopher is a critic and conductor of experiments; he may consider Machiavellian *virtú* as a subject of genesis and decay. The strong skeptic—in Machiavelli's famous example from *The Prince*, Cesare Borgia—may fall sick.[66] But he does not conduct his illness as an experiment in order to explore the boundary conditions and value horizons of his healthy experience. The Nietzschean philosopher does.[67] The problem of decadence comes to light for him, and discloses a problem of ranking values, as it does not for the skeptic, who is repulsed by the "higher problems" because—unlike the "critic"—he cannot raise his experience to the level of an experiment.[68]

While the skeptic understands that truth is problematic and its value questionable, he does not take the will to truth seriously as a philosophical problem. His will to power is less comprehensive than the philosopher's: it never takes the form of a passionate will to truth. The critic is superior in demanding that his experience be subjected to critique and experiment. For the problem of rank order to become an object of experience, the horizon of skepticism must be transcended. The skeptic cannot raise man higher by deliberate policy; he cannot articulate a standard by which to perfect himself or other men. The situation described in Nietzsche's parable on Frederick is therefore typical: the skeptic is unable to foresee the import of his actions for the future of science, and problems of breeding for the will to truth fall beyond his horizon. The critic demands an explication of the a priori

conditions within which an experience is possible; he insists upon definite value standards. But critics and philosophical laborers like Kant
and Hegel are also more comprehensive, conscientiously embracing a
wider range of experience than the robust skeptic will pause to contemplate. Such endeavors constitute the apex of science and the most
comprehensive horizon of scholarly work. Kant and Hegel represent
the highest men of science, and in Nietzsche's treatment of them we
can study his policy for consolidating the rule of the philosopher over
the sciences.

At the beginning of Part 6, science appeared as an obstacle, a
source of distractions and dangers; it was a rebellious instrument. But
in the latter aphorisms (Nos. 210–13) Nietzsche considers a higher
type of scientist, and his stance is promising rather than imperious.
Kant and Hegel are not accused of being out of touch with their true
needs, of being unsubtle, slovenly, or grossly mistaken about themselves.[69] Nor do they share the average scholar's Jesuitical hostility toward greatness. Earlier, Nietzsche tried to wound and challenge the
pride of the nobler scholar; toward the end of his argument he attempts
to win over such men by showing them tasks of a difficulty "in whose
service every subtle pride, every tough will can certainly find satisfaction."[70] This enables us to understand why Nietzsche did not pause to
advocate a revanche against positivism and the independence movement in science. Rather than make much of such opinion leaders by
combating them, Nietzsche's policy is to remove the motives for rebellion and the incentive to it by undermining their credibility in the
eyes of normal scholars. Specialists and novices rely upon hearsay and
authority in such matters. The situation described in No. 204 is not
apparently subject to much alteration, for Nietzsche accepts it in concluding his argument in No. 213.[71] Because first-hand acquaintance
with the problem of rank order in science is impossible for specialists,
the important case is the unusual scholar who has the ambition and capacity for wider responsibilities. Philosophy need not deal directly
with rebels leading the cause of scientific autonomy; the highest men
of science can be marshaled to deal with them. Nietzsche's project
therefore turns on the needs, the pride, and the sense of shame of these
higher men; he must consolidate an aristocracy within science to enforce his policy. In order to meet the challenge of plebian princes
within science, Nietzsche must strengthen the highest men in their
pride of rank and adherence to the unwritten constitution of science.[72]

For these reasons, a doctrine of conscience is introduced toward the end of his argument in Part 6.

6. THE INTENTION WITH REGARD TO THE WHOLE

The highest problem of philosophic leadership within science is portrayed, in aphorisms Nos. 211–13, as a restructuring of common sense through the reformation or recreation of conscience. Critique, experiment, and the most wide-ranging philosophic labor culminate in this highest problem. It would be hard to overestimate the subsequent importance of Nietzsche's formulation for the history of philosophical nihilism. After Nietzsche, noble nihilism in German thought centered upon the task of reinterpreting conscience; it was undertaken in *Being and Time*, and Weber was almost obsessed with it.[73] Nietzsche compressed the task enigmatically in an unpublished note: "Science—the transformation of nature into concepts for the purpose of mastering nature—belongs under the rubric 'means.' But the purpose and will of man must grow in the same way, the intention in regard to the whole."[74] The enigma lies in Nietzsche's phrase "in the same way," since it implies—contrary to one's first impression—that the Baconian project with respect to nature is not fundamentally at odds with the cultivation of a certain moral attitude of affirmation. Not to rebel against the Baconian conquest of nature, but rather to extend it, seems to be the task:

> To translate man back into nature; to become master over the many vain and overly enthusiastic interpretations and connotations that have so far been scrawled and painted over that terrifying basic text of *homo natura*; to see to it that man henceforth stands before man as even today, hardened in the discipline of science, he stands before the *rest* of nature, with intrepid Œdipus eyes and sealed Odysseus ears . . . that may be a strange and insane task, but it is a *task*—who would deny that? Why did we choose this insane task? Or, putting it differently, "why have knowledge at all?"[75]

This passage implies the extension of the most complete determinism to the human and moral phenomena.[76] Whether it leads to a revision of

the Baconian understanding of nature is a vexed question, in part because that understanding is itself a question. In particular, it is uncertain whether the nature disclosed by modern science is hostile and indifferent to man or partial toward the greatness of man, and Nietzsche
perpetuates and elaborates this ambiguity.[77] What is clear is that subsequently the reinterpretation of nature and the reinterpretation of conscience are closely linked, as in Heidegger's engagement with *physis*
(the Greek word for "nature").[78] Heidegger and Weber were in accord
with Nietzsche in joining science with the task of cultivating the intention in regard to the whole. The connection is perhaps clearest in a
passage from Weber's *Economy and Society* that bears quoting at
length, as it is never quoted or discussed. In it, Weber elaborates a
comparison he had briefly explored in *The Protestant Ethic*, his most
sustained work on conscience.[79] The comparison was there drawn explicitly between Calvin and Nietzsche and between the doctrines of
predestination and eternal recurrence; here Nietzsche is unmentioned
but unmistakably present.

> Under all circumstances, the determinism of predestination
> remained an instrument for the greatest possible systema-
> tization and centralization of the ethic of intentions. The
> "total personality," as we would say today, has been pro-
> vided with the accent of eternal value by "God's election,"
> and not by any individual action of the person in question.
> There is a non-religious counterpart of this religious evalua-
> tion, one based on a mundane determinism. It is that distinc-
> tive type of "shame" and, so to speak, godless feeling of sin
> which characterizes modern secular man precisely because
> of his own ethic of intentions, regardless of its metaphysical
> basis. Not that he has *done* a particular deed, but that by vir-
> tue of his unalterable qualities, acquired without his cooper-
> ation, he "*is*" such that he *could* commit the deed—this is
> the secret anguish borne by modern man, and this is also
> what the others, in their "pharisaism" (now turned determin-
> ism) blame him for. It is a "merciless" attitude, because
> there is no significant possibility of "forgiveness," "contri-
> tion," or "restitution"—in much the same way that the reli-
> gious belief in predestination was merciless, but at least it
> could conceive of some impenetrable divine rationality.[80]

In order to understand the distinctively philosophical or scientific impetus to carry through the nihilistic critique of morality, one must appreciate the conviction, which Nietzsche did much to inculcate, that conscience in the forms known to Western civilization—forms derived from biblical morality—both could not and should not survive the disenchantment of the world by modern science. The necessity to see moral nihilism through to the bitter end becomes almost unspeakably serious, an ethical imperative too weighty to admit of "ethics": an imperative to forge a new conscience to take the place of the old.[81] This imperative imparts to science and philosophy an animus they had lacked prior to Nietzsche, an animus one is tempted to characterize as a "Catilinarian fervor."[82] Somehow, the lightness and playfulness that Nietzsche thought were inseparable from the new task got lost in the transition to Weber and Heidegger. For these reasons, the passage of Nietzsche's argument on science that treats of conscience merits special attention.

We have already devoted considerable commentary to aphorisms Nos. 211–12. [83] On the Seventh Day of his philosophic labors, the whole domain surveyable by science lies open to the view of the critic and philosophic laborer. What has been comprehended is the totality of the common sense of mankind as it is intelligible to the human mind; there is no more comprehensive "common sense."[84] What the highest scientist, "after the noble model of Kant and Hegel," has accomplished, is

> to determine and press into formulas, whether in the realm
> of *logic* or *political* (moral) thought or *art*, some great data
> of valuations—that is, former *positings* of values, creations
> of value which have become dominant and are for a time
> called "truths."[85]

Philosophic labor makes intelligible "everything that has happened and been esteemed so far." It exhibits the entirety of "the world of concern to us," or the world of common sense, as a world unfolding in time, which it makes intelligible through a philosophical history.[86] The issue for such history is the relation between what has happened and what has been esteemed so far, or between creations of value (such as the objectivity of the scientist, the freedom and justice of the citizen of the Hegelian *Rechtsstaat*, or the sublime rapture of tragic artistry)

and the history of contingency in which they are enmeshed.[87] What
Nietzsche's critique of Hegel's retrospective theoretical understanding
implies is that Hegelian reason must be the object of a solicitude oriented toward the future; it must be encompassed by a more comprehensive form of philosophic conscience that takes practical responsibility for the future of man. The history laid bare by Hegelian
philosophic labor is evidence for Nietzsche's interpretation of philosophy as a "cause," for it discloses "that gruesome dominion of nonsense and accident that has so far been called 'history,'" or "the mon-
strous fortuity that has so far had its way and play regarding the future
of man—a game in which no hand, and not even a finger, of God took
part as a player."[88] In the creation of the world of concern to us, God
did not lift a hand. It was always the responsibility of the philosopher,
although philosophy did not always undertake it; *faute de mieux* it was
usurped by prophets, moral legislators, and "the improvers of mankind."[89] The establishment of tables of virtue, the creation of conscience, the determining of human nature, have therefore been a mon-
strous fortuity. The whole of this history must be reconquered in order

> To teach man the future of man as his *will*, as dependent on a
> human will, and to prepare great ventures and over-all at-
> tempts of discipline and cultivation by way of *putting an end*
> to that gruesome dominion of nonsense and accident that has
> so far been called "history."[90]

This new end of history is brought about by the creation of a new conscience, a new intention and will in regard to the whole. That conscience enables man to see his future as dependent upon a human will.
To inculcate it requires a most comprehensive philosophic conscience
informed by, but not bound by, the common sense of mankind made
intelligible by the labors of the highest men of science, whose labors in
turn are the culmination of the "tower-building" of the specialized sciences.[91] Thus Nietzsche forms a bond between the philosophic legislator and the highest men of science.

7. RIGHT OPINION ON THE RANKING OF SCIENCE

Nietzsche's argument ends on a playful note. In a sublime sense,
science is the creature of philosophy; the dependence of the creature

upon the creator is reflected in the *distance* that Nietzsche upholds in the last aphorism of Part 6. He imposes this distance much as one might underscore social distance between two classes: what separates science from philosophy is prejudice or the difference between their respective positions, which in a ranked society must appear to reflect the primeval law of things. Nietzsche opens No. 213 by linking pride to minding one's own business. The highest scholar should take pride in his limits: "What a philosopher is, that is hard to learn because it cannot be taught: one must 'know' it from experience—or one should have the pride *not* to know it." [92] Nietzsche's motto for the higher men, "Will nothing beyond your capacity," would provide some support for this pride; it is a remedy against the most damaging forms of ambition and resentment—men who desire too much of themselves and fall short endanger the world; they have in the past usually become its opinion leaders. [93] But there is a difficulty in persuading men of great critical intelligence to take pride in what they do not know firsthand. However salutary a right opinion about the tasks of philosophic leadership might be, such opinions tend to migrate insensibly into their opposites unless they are reinforced by something firmer than mere belief. Nietzsche therefore gives this belief the appearance of an order of nature. The authority of the philosopher rests upon a "primeval law of things."

> Ultimately, there is an order of rank among states of the soul, and the order of rank of problems accords with this. The highest problems repulse everyone mercilessly who dares approach them without being predestined for their solution by the height and power of his spirituality. What does it avail when nimble smarties or clumsy solid mechanics and empiricists push near them, as is common today, trying with their plebian ambition to enter the "court of courts." Upon such carpets coarse feet may never step: the primeval law of things takes care of that; the doors remain closed to such obtrusiveness, even if they crash and crush their heads against them. [94]

Nietzsche speaks as if the distance between philosophers and scholars were no different from that between nobles and plebians: he gives birth, breeding, cultivation, and inherited qualities almost as much emphasis as experience. This language suggests that the problem of the regime of science is not resolved in Part 6 but merges with the problem of Nietzsche's aristocratic politics. As we shall see, there is a promise or possibility of intimacy between the philosopher and the Nietzschean nobility, which is denied to the scientist. Perhaps what the nobility knows, by nature and experience, is that the primeval law of things does not take care of itself.

8. THE SCIENCE OF ENDANGERED SPECIES

Nietzsche welcomes and indeed fosters the climate of opinion that doubts the humanitarian and moral character of progress based upon science. He sees in modern science what its originators promised: the power to remake the human condition from top to bottom.[95] He also sees that the official propaganda for science cannot withstand the disclosure of what that promise entails. That power is now apparent both in the capacity to destroy peoples and to merge them, to breed castes and kinds and to terminate them; more generally, science makes the human condition more precarious and dangerous, compelling humanity to face situations that call for new virtues, a new conscience, and the destruction of old moral codes. These compulsions are admitted and affirmed in Nietzsche's affirmation of "we scholars."[96] In part because of the timidity of scholars, science is bound to sense the profound threat to itself in the dissolution of popular faith in the benevolence of modern progress. Scholars are also well positioned to know from their daily experience that there is a profound contradiction between the method of democracy and the method of science. Perhaps for these reasons, Nietzsche begins his discussion of philosophic politics in *Beyond Good and Evil* with an account of science. His endeavor in leading science is to restore confidence and a horizon of great promise for the future of science and to recover that skepticism of audacious manliness with which the modern scientific revolution began. Nietzsche attempts to combine intellectual rapture at the discovery of intelligible order with passionate self-affirmation and pride. Properly combined, pride in individuality does not threaten the hierarchical discipline of science: it permits a recognition of limits and giving what is beyond one's limits its due. The politics of science unfolded in Part 6 is based upon the modern discovery of individuality. Its task is to reconcile individuality to an order, to curb individuality and attach the individual to limits; the scientist must take pride in his own limits. In Part

6, as throughout his writings, Nietzsche abandons the modern state and liberal institutions as methods of reconciling individuality to the requirements of a common order. But he pursues a politics to accomplish a similar purpose, releasing the fullest powers of the individual while chaining him up to a comprehensive order. Nietzsche releases science from the restraints of limited government in order to create a new conscience or intention with regard to the whole that enchains individuality to "the world of concern to us."[97] In the domain of science, this curbing of individuality means that the discipline of common sense is retained against mere solipsistic interpretation and arbitrariness: the philosopher subsumes the labors of the critic and philosophic laborer.

Yet when the philosopher makes himself the "first cause" of this most comprehensive common sense of mankind, he weighs it in the scales of his own "justice." There is a (recurrent) moment in which the sanity of mankind as a whole and the future form of its common sense is determined.[98] If Nietzsche's philosopher understands his task, enforcement must follow inexorably, almost fatalistically, upon this determination. There is no appeal against the Nietzschean philosopher, no sense in which he could be said to have made a mistake, no standard by which one could demand that he repent.[99] Nietzsche inherits the arrogance of the modern project from Machiavelli and Montaigne and raises it to an incandescent flame. The philosopher as first cause excuses himself. He knows no repentance. He plays the dangerous game and makes life an experiment of the knower, in which we are all players and victims, whether we will or no. Nietzsche abandons the exhausted promises of Bacon and Descartes as though they could only confuse men of science. He draws new courage and confidence for science from a resolute acknowledgment of the danger and the uncertainty of scientific progress. The tasks into which Nietzsche leads science are bound to be "insane." From the viewpoint of the highest scientist, it is evident that the world of common sense is ultimately created and subject to recreation by the philosopher, insofar as it is more than a product of accident and nonsense. The abyss that divides democratic politics from science is a moral cleavage because science is embarked on an enterprise of destroying and reforming common sense and the moral standards that democratic politics takes for granted. Rather than create the false expectation that the truth about science could win the hearts or votes of the people, Nietzsche banks upon their resistance and sets science upon the road to an antidemocratic politics to defeat that resistance. To the charge that this affirmation of science is insane, Nietzsche's reply might well be Marx's immortal insight into the human comedy: "There ain't no Sanity Clause." [100]

Heightened conflict between moral common sense, on the one hand, and the dominant drives of science and philosophy on the other, creates precisely that "magnificent tension of the mind" which the original assault upon Platonic error generated. Science cannot expect to be at home in the moral world of the people and their opinion leaders once it joins philosophy in making life an experiment of the knowers. [101] The gravest charge that can be brought against science by popular opinion leaders is true: science is morally nihilistic. No effort to enlighten mankind, or to popularize science, will dispel the opposition on this count; its foundation is not superstition but knowledge. [102] To combat such accusations science must become Machiavellian and employ fraud. Nietzsche's understanding of the disenchantment of the moral world by science points to the necessity for a political defense of science. When scientists think themselves back to their true necessities, they discover their dependence upon philosophic leaders to perform political tasks. To combat the accusers of science, Nietzsche creates a new kind of opinion leader whose task is to divide the shepherds of democratic opinion against each other, and to forge science a protective shield of popular beliefs. The promises of prosperity and longevity held out at the beginning of the modern project by Bacon and Descartes no longer suffice. They must be supplanted by more credible illusions. [103]

Thus Nietzsche reintroduces irony and a form of the "double doctrine" into the education of scholars. Science and philosophy must comport themselves politically in relation to the people. Because science endangers mankind, it is a precarious enterprise so long as democracy prevails: to survive, it must behave like an endangered species. This grim prospect gives way, however, when science faces away from the people, toward the highest problems and philosophy. Nietzsche reawakens the beauty, the promise of rapture, which makes science high-spirited and cheerful in spite of its danger. One cannot form a sound estimate of the dynamism and vitality of Nietzsche's politics if one fails to see that it draws to itself the passions of scientific men. It restores that remarkable enthusiasm for science as an adventure and romance for knights of knowledge that has made the last several centuries so remarkable for good and evil. Nietzsche promises to protect timid scholars with a forceful politics. But he also gives science a clear conscience once again, and attaches bad conscience to what inhibits the quest for knowledge.[104] Beyond assuaging moral qualms, or removing them, Nietzsche promises that what is revealed to the knowers will again be ravishingly graceful and elegant, that the spectacle of the highest and noblest problems will be profoundly gratifying to the spirit. The scholar may be limited, as Aphorism No. 213 implies, to seeing the philosopher's solutions: the higher problems themselves are not fully visible to science.[105] But science may not need more to maintain its interest in Nietzsche's experiment: to come this close to looking into the mind of a god may suffice.

The requirements of Nietzsche's politics inevitably appear contradictory because of this irony. The task of Nietzschean opinion leadership must be to obscure the conflict between the method of science and the method of democracy and to make the charge that science is nihilistic seem implausible or confused. On the other hand, to wean men of science away from the principles of modern liberal politics, its legislative science, and its reason of state, Nietzsche must clarify and sharpen that conflict. The political tasks mentioned in "We Scholars"—the breeding of a ruling caste—are not the stuff of liberal politics. More striking is the effect of Nietzsche's critique of Kant and Hegel in Aphorism Nos. 211 and 212: philosophic politics will transcend the *Rechtsstaat* and legislate political means suited to Nietzsche's new ideal of greatness, the antithesis of Montaigne's humane ideal.[106] These observations lead the reader to expect a "new politics" in the later parts of Nietzsche's book, for Nietzsche needs a leadership that will exploit the media of opinion and culture for his illiberal purposes. He must also address the problem of discipline for the higher men. It is not enough to win them away from the doctrines of modern political economy and the *Rechtsstaat*. A new source of cultivation for the spirited man is necessary if self-assertiveness is to gain constancy, poise, and address. If the gifted are not to be distracted by the rewards of bourgeois decadence, or tempted into administration and commerce, they will require coaching, a regimen, a structure of tasks and cues. These are the concerns of *Beyond Good and Evil* in its final Part.[107]

4. ENNOBLING NIHILISM: *BEYOND GOOD AND EVIL*, PART 9: "WHAT IS NOBLE"

> [S]ince Nietzsche, we realize that something can be beautiful, not
> only in spite of the aspect in which it is not good, but rather in that
> very aspect.
>
> Weber, *Science as a Vocation*

To the extent that the threat to liberal democracy
comes from revolutionary mass movements, Weber's task of defense is
relatively straightforward but also essentially repetitive, since Machiavelli covered this ground quite thoroughly before him.[1] In this
chapter, I shall give reasons for considering Weber's distinctive argument as a response to a somewhat different problem, one that is both
less tractable and more likely to dominate the future of American politics. It is evident from *Politics as a Vocation* that revolutionary mass
movements played a major role in Weber's reflections; his 1919 lecture
shrewdly anticipated the path by which Hitler subsequently came to
power in Germany.[2] No one should minimize the dangers of revolutionary Caesarism.[3] But an incentive for studying Nietzsche's philosophic politics is that "the revolution of nihilism" (Rauschning's famous label for the Nazi phenomenon) is not reducible to Nazism or to
Hitler's Caesarist methods; the threat it poses for liberal democracy
can take forms less manageable, harder to discern, and therefore much
less convenient. It should be remembered that even the Weimar Republic, with weak, untried, and superficially rooted liberal democratic
institutions, very nearly defeated Hitler's attempt to seize power
through elections.[4] The strengths of the liberal commercial republic in
meeting revolutionary Caesarism are considerable, as Tocqueville's
chapter on "why great revolutions will become more rare" made

clear.[5] That analysis provides no grounds for complacency or lack of vigilance, but it may help us to focus on the less dramatic but more immediate threat that nihilism poses. Taking my cue from Tocqueville, I shall suggest that Weber's argument for leadership is directed at the danger of a new individualism. Nietzsche's philosophic politics intensified and transformed individualism through a new interpretation of the self. That interpretation lent itself to a multitude of vulgarizations, but the chief features of the individualism that Nietzsche promoted and reinforced can be identified clearly enough. After delineating these features, we shall go on in the balance of this chapter to study the most subtle and beautiful exposition of Nietzsche's politics, the concluding part of *Beyond Good and Evil*. Our purpose is to gauge the distance between Weber's reconfiguration of liberal democracy as a regime without liberalism and Nietzsche's frankly nihilistic experiment. To do so, we need to see Nietzsche's regime in its most refined articulation, in which its cutting edges stand out most harshly and in which its difference from liberal democracy is most perspicuous. Once we understand Nietzsche's regime at its best, we will see why it is unlikely even to be attempted, much less attained. It is therefore doubly appropriate to begin by looking at Nietzsche's politics in the vulgar form it usually takes, the form it has indeed already taken in the United States.[6]

1. INDIVIDUALISM RECONSIDERED

One of the more puzzling failures of reform politics, despite its temporary success in transforming the political agenda during the last two decades, was its inability to ameliorate the political evil of individualism, despite a preoccupation with this evil and despite a long experiment with increased political participation to remedy it. Weber's potential to provide an alternative to Wilsonian reform liberalism must be considered in the context of this failure. For Weber, the political dangers of individualism were not at all the dangers that Wilson and the subsequent reform movement addressed. Weber's perspective leads one to anticipate that the remedies advanced against individualism during the last decades, particularly those intended to make political participation more attractive and accessible, would intensify rather than ameliorate the threat posed by individualism to constitutional democracy.[7]

In reassessing individualism, the most illuminating text is Tocqueville's. Despite my admiration for it, I shall have to argue that it contributed to confusion on this issue. Through Tocqueville's influence, individualism came to be regarded as an evil of liberal regimes so serious that liberals let down their guard to unite with almost any group of opinion leaders if they were willing to support quasi-Tocquevillean remedies against it. According to Tocqueville, individualism is profoundly antipolitical, and the remedies for it are greater participation in civic life, in political associations and decision-making. Tocqueville's persuasive diagnosis of privative individualism, and his wonderful portrait of the participatory remedies, greatly facilitated the absorption of "the new politics" into the mainstream of respectable liberal opinion. Tocqueville's stamp had also been imprinted upon reform politics at an earlier point, for prior to the discovery of participatory democracy and Rousseau, Wilson had taken account of Tocqueville's warnings against individualism.[8] As we observed in chapter 1, opinion leadership was Wilson's remedy against it. Wilson's own arguments against Madisonian interest politics gain depth and a coloration of prudence when they are combined with Tocqueville's analysis, for the Madisonian plan obviously promotes the individualism that Tocqueville described.[9] Unfortunately, the Tocquevillean remedies promote the individualism that Nietzsche described, and this individualism is arguably much more dangerous for liberal democracy in America. As Machiavelli wrote, "Men resemble certain little birds of prey in whom so strong is the desire to catch the prey which nature incites them to pursue, that they do not notice another and greater bird of prey which hovers over them ready to pounce and kill." The new individualism is more predatory than the old and thrives upon the remedies provided against the old.[10]

Tocqueville apparently did not contemplate an individualism that would draw men out of themselves and into entanglements with the world. Intrinsic to his analysis was the implied assumption that in democratic ages, egoism would remain more or less what it had always been: a self-destructive and solipsistic passion:

> Our fathers were only acquainted with egoism (selfishness). Selfishness is a passionate and exaggerated love of self, which leads a man to connect everything with himself and to prefer himself to everything else in the world. Individualism is a mature and calm feeling, which disposes each member of the community to sever himself from the mass of his fel-

lows, and to draw apart with his family and his friends, so that after he has thus formed a little circle of his own, he willingly leaves society at large to itself. Selfishness originates in blind instinct; individualism proceeds from erroneous judgment more than from depraved feelings; it originates as much in deficiencies of mind as in perversity of heart.[11]

The new individualism, by contrast, was a product of mind deliberately affirming instinct; it emerged from Nietzsche's analysis of instinct and the passions needed for the embodiment and enforcement of values. It does not, therefore, leave instinct at the level of blind egoism; it projects the individual outward to "connect" with the world and to value "involvement" in it. It affirms the world and does not evidently lead to a simple egoistic preference for oneself. Though passionate, it is neither solipsistic nor indeliberate. It seeks constancy, a kind of maturity, and a steadiness in purposeful willing. It is actively hostile to the old individualism; it considers "the little circle" of family and friends as a potential curse and confinement; it has no intention of leaving society at large to itself. It regards withdrawal into privacy as privation and a surrender of individuality, insofar as the self requires assertion and mastery to realize itself. The older individualism was devoid of such imperatives for self-assertion. Its place was not naturally in politics or the pursuit of power; it was neither drawn to other men "at large" nor aware of a need in itself for giving laws, commanding, or reshaping society. The "deficiencies of mind" that Tocqueville strove to correct by means of "the science of association" was an astigmatism of social and political vision: the older individualism failed to grasp the opportunities for self-aggrandizement and self-expression in collective endeavor. It had to be seduced into the discovery that "Feelings and opinions are recruited, the heart is enlarged, and the human mind is developed only by the reciprocal influence of men upon one another."[12] The new egoism is attuned to this truth and alert for opportunity to exercise its full powers. When lucid (as it seldom is), this individualism sees that what it needs requires tension with a world of others: it wants lovers, slaves, and enemies but, above all, a "goal" beyond its present limitations. The remedies against the old individualism must therefore fuel the passions of the new. It wants resistance, activity, and exercise for its strengths; it is predisposed to recruit its feelings and opinions, enlarge its heart, expand its mind.[13]

This disposition bears a certain resemblance to the old, because it is "calm and mature," in exploiting the modern state and liberal institutions for its purposes, without giving its loyalty to the political community. But in contrast to the old, it is forearmed against the seductions of the moral life, and consequently its individualistic bent is more apt to be fortified than to be corrected by Tocquevillean remedies. For Tocqueville the art of association was meant to introduce the self to procedures, customs, and the social forms prerequisite to civil deliberations. But his real objective in drawing men toward associations was to bind their hearts to a humanitarian ideal and habituate them to its delights: "[B]y dint of working for the good of one's fellow citizens, the habit and the taste for serving them are at last acquired." [14] Nietzsche discovered antidotes to every charm of the moral life and precautions to insure that the habit of serving others would never be acquired. The new individualism cannot be won over to the bourgeois freedoms with their corresponding rights by Tocquevillean remedies because it is immune to the blandishments of civility. The fortified individualist knows that liberal institutions will prevent his self-assertion and self-realization; he smells "decay" in the moral life. Moreover, in contrast to the old, the new individualism seeks to express itself by imposing a new order and a new law. It is an individualism of creativity, of form-giving potency that needs matter to work upon. Knowing intuitively that it needs to form a world or tyrannize one, its prejudice is for positions of command. Demanding self-expression, it propels itself toward a world that it can manipulate and mold. To hold out opportunities for political participation and cultural authority to this individualism is not to redirect but, on the contrary, to ignite it.

For reasons that I will elaborate in this chapter, I shall call this new antithesis to liberal democratic citizenship *demonic individualism*. It rests upon a Nietzschean doctrine of the self. Nietzsche was not the first to appreciate the destructive and creative power of demonic individualism or its capacity to overwhelm all the moral powers of this world; Goethe's writings attest to that. [15] But he was the first philosopher to conceive the possibility that philosophy could bring down an established civilization, and erect one more suited to philosophy on its ruins, by unleashing and fortifying this demonic potency of "the terrifying basic text of *homo natura*." [16] Nietzsche was the first to give philosophy the future task of coordinating, orchestrating, and disciplining demonic individualism in order to create on a world scale a new civilization, law, and man. No philosopher before had taught that morality should be allowed to perish; no one had discovered that to do so was noble precisely because it was devilishly difficult; no one had placed nihilism ahead of mankind as a great task or taught that it should be embraced as a noble necessity. Although we will resist the vulgarization of Nietzsche in this chapter, by attending to one of his most sublime and subtle writings, the better part of valor is to begin from the Nietzschean phenomena that are before our eyes, from the world of individualists breaking passionately with morality in all its traditional, authoritatively limiting forms, seeking to define themselves through self-assertion and expression. Rather than turn one's gaze away from that world, as Nietzschean scholarship is inclined to do, one should take one's cue from Tom Wolfe and the other Balzacs of this world. For it is precisely such a world that the philosophic leader wills as the necessary expression of his tyrannical drive to "create the world," his most spiritual will to power.[17] To scale the heights of his "new greatness for man," Nietzsche needed a new poetics of the assertive self, a comprehensive affirmation of spirited self-expression. His "great politics, philosophic politics" was intended to precipitate war throughout "the total ethical economy of human life" by challenging morality with nihilism in every quarter.[18] The final result, as we shall presently see, was meant to be unprecedented discipline. But Nietzsche understood that discipline was impossible, in medias res, over the "jungle growth" of vulgarizations to which his initiative would inevitably lead.[19]

Weber concluded *Science as a Vocation* with the enigmatic moral imperative that each must find and obey the demon who holds the fibers of his very life.[20] To understand Weber's intention, I will argue, one must consider his politics as a response to the demonic potentialities latent in the modern project. These are best studied where they are articulated most fully and most brilliantly, in Nietzsche's exposition of his philosophic politics.[21]

2. NIETZSCHE'S THOUGHTS ON MACHIAVELLI

In a previous chapter we noted an inherent instability in Weber's early attempt to combine a Nietzschean ideal of a hard and noble manliness with a defense of liberal democratic institutions. Our study of "What is noble" will elaborate this difficulty by showing what is entailed in a consistent break with the liberal ideal of "humanity" from which liberal institutions (and subsequently many socialist or social democratic ones) were derived.[22] In Part 9 of *Beyond Good and Evil*, Nietzsche refines a noble ideal of the assertive self; he ascends, by stages, well beyond the political realm as it is delimited by the modern state and looks down with contempt upon the politics of this realm. But he is preoccupied throughout his argument with the enforcement of values and with the necessity for force and fraud. Even at the most refined heights of the loftiest man, Nietzsche is emphatically a Machiavellian:

> No philosopher will be in any doubt as to the type of perfection in politics; that is Machiavellianism. But Machiavellianism *pur, sans mélange, cru, vert, dans toute sa force, dans toute son àpreté*, is superhuman, divine, transcendental, it will never be achieved by man, at most approximated.[23]

"What is Noble," I believe, is Nietzsche's poetics of such an approximation. By considering Nietzsche's politics in its unachievable Machiavellian perfection, one can establish, beyond any reasonable doubt, that it is thoroughly inimical to "political leadership" as a defense of liberal democratic institutions. Such leadership seeks the perpetuation of limited government; it is devoted to the concentration of the means of force and fraud in the modern state and political parties and to the narrowing of the purposes for which such means may be employed.[24] Nietzsche teaches that the unprecedented powers released by the modern affirmation of the body and the passions could be united with a surgical, disciplinary cruelty reminiscent of ancient virtue and classical regimes. What the moderns had unchained could be made yet more powerful by chaining it up in new hierarchies. The liberal cause had initially heightened the power of mankind by liberating human energies and needs, but to continue that heightening great constraints will be necessary to exercise and perfect man's powers. Thus the liberal cause points forward to its sublimation in a nonliberal, commanding, philosophic politics, which will supply those constraints and do so without contradicting the philosophic insights that had led philosophers at the very origin of modernity to overthrow the dominion of ancient constraints. Nietzsche returns to the Machiavellian first principles of modern politics in order to transcend the liberal humanitarianism that absorbed Machiavelli and watered him down. In so doing he releases a force for the rebirth of that "pious cruelty" which Machiavelli had done his best to banish from the earth.[25]

3. THE STUDY OF *VORNEHMHEIT*

Part 9 is introduced by an aphorism in which Nietzsche provides the guiding thread of his argument, as he often does, at the beginning of an aphoristic sequence. According to this proem, the subject of Part 9 is the mysterious growth of the philosophic "pathos" out of the aristocratic "pathos." [26] The next thirty-eight aphorisms (nos. 258–95) fall into four main groups. The aristocratic "pathos of distance" is the subject of an initial group of five (nos. 258–62), encompassing the rise and fall of an aristocratic regime. The last eighteen (nos. 278–95) are introduced by a dialogue between Nietzsche's "wanderer" and his "shadow" and are devoted to the philosophic "pathos of distance" mentioned in the proem. Thus aristocracy is the acorn, philosophy the oak. Between the aristocratic seed and its full maturity in philosophy, we find fifteen aphorisms devoted to two subjects. The first five (nos. 263–67) are on breeding. The other ten are given to the higher men and greatness or to the problem of pity for the higher man. This pity seems to be the problem for which the philosopher most needs distance. The decade on pity begins with a thematic question, "What, in the end, is common?" A matching thematic question, taken from the title, introduces the last half of the group on philosophy (nos. 287–95): "What is Noble?" Part 9 thus ascends through four major stages:

    1. The rise and fall of aristocracy (five aphorisms, nos. 258–62)
    2. Breeding (five aphorisms, nos. 263–67)
    3. The higher men (ten aphorisms, nos. 268–77); Question: "What, in the end, is common?"
    4. Philosophy (eighteen aphorisms, nos. 278–95); Question: "What is Noble?"

This quaternary form recalls an early aphorism on *Vornehmheit* which may assist in digesting Part 9. In "The Wanderer and His Shadow," Nietzsche gave the following ladder of rank:

The noblest [vornehmste] virtue.—In the first era of higher
humanity, courage is prized as the noblest virtue; in the second, justice; in the third, restraint; in the fourth, wisdom. In
which era do we live? In which era do you live?[27]

Taking our cue from this ranking, we might surmise that the four parts
of Nietzsche's later argument correspond to these four virtues; or, if he
changed his mind, perhaps to four other virtues. Turning to aphorism
no. 284, a series of vows, we find that Nietzsche exhorts the reader to
vow "to remain master of one's four virtues: of courage, insight, sympathy and solitude."[28] We will take this hint and tentatively associate
stage 1 with courage (nos. 258–62); stage 2 with insight and justice
(nos. 263–67); stage 3 with restraint and sympathy (nos. 268–77);
and stage 4 with solitude and wisdom (nos. 278–95). Our hypothesis
is that Nietzsche's argument discloses four ranks, at each of which one
virtue "is prized as the noblest virtue."[29]

At the outset, however, Nietzsche speaks not of virtues but of a
pathos of distance. And in contrast to his earlier aphorism, in no. 284
Nietzsche makes a vow not to *have* virtues but rather to remain master
over them. Is there a link between mastery over virtues and "pathos of
distance"? We know that for Nietzsche, the will to power is a pathos.[30]
And it is reasonable to expect that his argument will disclose four
stages in the development of the will to power, with philosophy as its
highest form.[31] We might therefore guess that in stage 1, *Vornehmheit*
will be courage; in stage 2, it will be a justice that remains master over
insight; in stage 3, it will be a restraint that remains master over sympathy; and in stage 4 it will be a wisdom that remains master over solitude.[32] Nobility would then initially be unidimensional, but in all subsequent stages or ranks one virtue would tyrannize over other virtues,
and there would be a pathos of distance within the soul between the
tyrant-virtue and the subject-virtues.[33]

These hypotheses may disclose some of the subjects that Nietzsche treats. But in order to study Nietzsche's text with precision, we
must know what kind of argument it is and what modes of study it
requires. Let us therefore try to characterize the argument as a whole
and to place it beside roughly comparable arguments.

Both the manner and the matter of Nietzsche's argument on politics seem to be indicated in the proem by the emphasis upon pathos, in
implicit contrast to ethos. Aristotle's account of the good citizen and
the good man was an "ethics." Broadly speaking, Nietzsche seems to

present his political teaching as a "pathics."[34] This contrast may be extended, for Nietzsche drew it out in *Ecce Homo*. There, Nietzsche located himself within and against a specific tradition of political philosophy, by claiming that *Beyond Good and Evil* was "a school for the *gentilhomme*, taking this concept in a more spiritual and radical sense than has ever been done."[35] As a classicist, Nietzsche no doubt meant his claim to originality as a critique of Aristotle's *less* spiritual and radical ethics, and of his teaching on the rule of gentlemen in the *Politics*.[36] The claim must rest preeminently upon Part 9. "What is Noble" is an alternative to the Aristotelian schooling of gentlemen; it presents a "more spiritual and radical" concept of *kalokagathia* than the *Nichomachean Ethics*.[37] Such claims lead us to study the contrast with Aristotle as a way of distinguishing Nietzsche's mode of argument.

Nietzsche's radicalism is immediately obvious in the order of topics and the style of his argument. He begins with the most brutal and necessitous side of aristocracy; slavery confronts us in the very first sentence of Part 9, and the proem ends starkly on the brutal founding of aristocratic rule by military conquest. Our attention is fixed upon exploitation, slavery, force, and violence.[38] The contrast with Aristotle is striking. He indeed began his *Politics* with a discussion of slavery, but his education of the gentleman opened on a gentler theme. Aristotle postponed the study of politics, arguing that a grasp of even the first problem of his *Politics* required a certain maturity of character: knowledge of political science would only be of great benefit to "those who regulate their desires and actions by a rational principle."[39] The education of a gentleman therefore begins with ethics, but while ethics is sufficient for rational persuasion, it is insufficient for political life:

> [W]hile words evidently do have the power to encourage and
> stimulate young men of generous mind, and while they cause
> a character well-born and truly enamoured of what is noble
> to be possessed of virtue, they do not have the capacity to
> turn the common run of people to goodness and nobility.[40]

Politics is a necessitous alternative to ethics, appropriate for those whose emotions can be curbed by only law or force. Aristotle's argument on gentlemanliness thus progresses from persuasive speech to deeds of domination and slavery. It also moves from a most perspicuous and apparently "common-sensical" account of a subtle subject, ethics, toward a dense account of a much less subtle subject, politics.[41] These contrasts are supported by an explicit rationale. Aristotle troubles to create an optical illusion: he makes the pursuit of virtue appear as accessible as possible while making the approach to politics correspondingly tortuous. No doubt one could learn from Aristotle to be a skillful tyrant. It is hard to learn only that, however, because the form of his books resists it.

Nietzsche, by contrast, begins with what is simple, obvious, and brutal, becoming more obscure as he progresses. He reverses Aristotle, ascending from force to persuasion, or from the barbarian man of prey to the "genius of the heart." [42] The brutality of conquest is bluntly asserted, and the seductions of philosophy are enigmatically beautiful and hard to penetrate.[43] No optical illusion masks the reality of slavery from Nietzsche's ephebe. This reversal of Aristotle is deliberate; a remark in *The Gay Science* provides Nietzsche's rationale for it.[44] But this remark alone does not explain Nietzsche's intention. Aristotle had given reasons for making ethics more exoteric, and politics more esoteric, than they are as they meet the eye; it would be useful to know Nietzsche's reasons for his exotericism and esotericism in Part 9. Aristotle's approach reflected his view that to be a gentleman meant to have a certain habituation in virtue; ethical precepts and the teaching of *kalokagathia* would bear fruit in the attainment of virtue as firmly fixed habit, the *habitus* of "those who regulate their desires and actions by a rational principle." [45] Nietzsche's style follows similarly from his more radical or more spiritual—that is, more corporeal—interpretation of habituation. Attained *Vornehmheit* is the embodiment (*Einverleibung*) of a pathos. To incorporate a pathos is to discharge the will in a certain way over time, until the body or the instincts learn to accomplish what initially required the exercise of will. To undergo an experience that demands will and exhausts it is to suffer a pathos; through such an experiment the instincts may acquire the power to endure and eventually to master the experience.[46] Given this view of incorporation, it is not surprising that Nietzsche's argument is little concerned with rational principles and precepts. It serves the need of gentlemen who are to regulate their desires and actions not by a *logos* but initially by will and ultimately by instinct. What is noble is just this embodying of a pathos. To be *Vornehm*—distinguished, superior, higher in rank—means to embody a pathos.[47]

Yet if all life is will to power, as Nietzsche asserts, it is the embodying of pathos in instinct; does it follow that all life is noble? How can nobility serve as a term of distinction, if everything is noble? Aristotle establishes a distinction between the beasts and man by relying upon reason, thus distinguishing his task of habituation from the task, say, of breeding racehorses. Nietzsche's reliance upon instinct makes the boundary between lower and higher forms of life problematic. Whereas an argument in ethics is proper only to man, an argument in pathics extends to all life that wills; according to Nietzsche, that means all life *tout court*.[48] Thus "what is noble" is a long ladder of rank indeed: it extends from the lowest forms of life to the highest. But how does it distinguish ranks?

When Nietzsche opens Part 9 with the problem of aristocratic domination, he is not beginning at the theoretical origin of what is noble. His starting point is a deliberate practical intervention for a practical legislative purpose. He begins with aristocracy because "Every enhancement of the type 'man' has so far been the work of an aristocratic society—and it will be so again and again."[49] This is why the lower forms of life and also the other regimes are excluded from Part 9. Democracy may be *Vornehm* with respect to lower forms of life and may embody the pathos of man's struggle to elevate himself above them. But it leaves "man" where he is and prevents his further enhancement.[50] Nietzsche's intention is to teach the embodiment of the pathos of a praeterdemocratic politics, the politics of the enhancement of man.

Comparison with Aristotle tells us that Nietzsche's argument is not an ethics. But are there other works on the gentleman, which are more oriented to pathos than to ethos, that might illuminate Nietzsche's argument and help us to get a firmer grasp upon it? When Nietzsche asserts that the purpose of style is "to communicate a state, an inward tension of pathos, by means of signs, including the tempo of these signs," he emphasizes that such style presupposes "that there are those capable and worthy of the same pathos, that there is no lack of those to whom one *may* communicate oneself."[51] This is a conception of style eminently suitable to the performing arts, and Nietzsche was especially concerned with the politically relevant performing arts: as aphorism no. 247 indicates, Nietzsche's style, with its emphasis upon "long periods," is to be understood in terms of the art of rhetoric, not literary but rather oratorical rhetoric.[52] Because the orator's art of style must rest upon a sound practical understanding of the audiences and occasions to which he must speak, the great works on the art of rhetoric are necessarily concerned with the connection between speech and statesmanship, for in oratory the solution to a problem of style is inseparable from the solution to a practical problem. Works on rhetoric are a schooling for gentlemen that teaches the connection between speeches and deed, between the art of moving men to action and the science of judging men and polities in motion.[53]

4. ARCHAEOLOGY OF THE GREATEST *KINESIS*

The first great works of this kind to become a school for gentlemen in the West were Homer's epics, which captured the movement of the expedition against Troy and the return to Hellas, conveying the words and deeds of the heroes in song.[54] Both epics centered upon a pathos: the anger of Achilles, in *The Iliad,* and the suffering of Odysseus, in *The Odyssey.* Moreover, Nietzsche recognized in Homer a pathos comparable to his own:

> This was the *happiness of Homer!* The state of him that gave the Greeks their gods—no, who invented his own gods for himself! But we should not overlook this: with this Homeric happiness in one's soul one is also more capable of suffering than any other creature under the sun.[55]

Nietzschean nobility is more radical and spiritual than Homer's. Socratic political philosophy had displaced Homeric poetry with inquiry into virtue; Nietzsche stands closer to Homer insofar as he returns to pathos and poetry. Another rival of Homer deserves closer consideration. Thucydides began his history with a critique of Homer: he claimed that the Peloponnesian War was a greater motion (*kinesis*) than the expedition to Troy and the recovery from it.[56] Thucydides taught the art of rhetoric by presenting speeches in the context of deeds but without adornment or magnification and without misrepresenting the true stature of the events.[57] Thucydides claimed to surpass Homer in understanding and laying bare the necessities that underlay the speeches and deeds of the war between Athens and Sparta and of the Trojan War as well.[58] According to his critique, Thucydides brought to light the noble and the just in their true relation to necessity, whereas Homer allowed the fabulous to obscure the precarious status of nobility and justice within the whole.[59] The fabulous style of Homer, like the arms that the piratical peoples still wore in Thucydides' day, covered over the beauty and nobility of human nature, making this nobility seem less precarious than it truly is; Thucydides shows man exposed to necessity, like the naked athletes at the Olympic games.[60] The contest, and the true motion, are more starkly delineated, and the speeches and deeds of the heroes are more nakedly visible. Hence Thucydides' *War,* though "less pleasing to the ear," is a superior account of what is noble and a superior school for the gentleman; it provides a critique or measure of the political art "for all time."[61]

Thucydides' problem of style was to give the speeches in the language in which the several speakers would express the sentiments most befitting the occasion on the subjects under consideration.[62] Unlike Homer, Thucydides allowed necessity to speak urgently and directly, to show how forcefully necessity limits what is noble. His account therefore provided a clearer view of the causes that produce the occasion for noble acts. Nietzsche was well attuned to that account, with its emphasis upon power.[63] Thucydides' political problem was coextensive with "the greatest motion" or the war itself, and he gave an archaeology of the origin of this motion as the prelude to his work. As a comprehensive school for gentlemen, his *War* was as encompassing as the war and the preceding peace that made it possible.[64] Nietzsche's claim that his school for the *gentilhomme* was without precedent in its radicalism and spirituality seems to require that his politics encompass a greater movement and indeed a greater war than Thucydides' work. It must be an enterprise that involves all mankind and shows human nature more perspicuously than the Peloponnesian war. It must rest upon an analysis of the long accumulation of resources, experiences, and energies that make this greatest motion possible, and it must fit speeches to occasions in such a way that what is noble will be visible in its true character. If Nietzsche is not to be put to shame by Thucydides' criticism of Homer, of poetry and the fabulous, his school for the *gentilhomme* must allow necessity to speak and become visible. The great motion he articulates must display what is noble in its true relation to necessity. Only thus could Nietzsche rival Thucydides in providing a critique or ranking of the political art "for all time." The pathos of the enhancement of the type "man" must incorporate and surpass the pathos of the Thucydidean war.[65] Nietzsche must supply a critique of politics that embraces the subject completely, but to be truly "more radical and more spiritual" it must also be more comprehensive. It must embrace the modes of political action to be found in *The Peloponnesian War* and an additional range of more spiritual politics as well. As we shall see, Nietzsche's argument on "What is Noble" displays a ranking of politics in which the pathos of Thucydides' war is ranked beneath that of a higher philosophic politics. Nietzsche ranks the occasions for action and speech in accordance with the kind of men these occasions require. His problem of style is akin to Thucydides': to create speeches that befit the pathos of the men at each rank and to allow the necessities of each rank to become visible through these speeches. If Nietzsche solves this problem, his aphorisms will embody a criterion of ranking men and values; they will constitute a noble *Wertmaßstab* comparable to Weber's.[66] The ranking will be reflected in the speeches given at each level.

The boasts in *Ecce Homo* are frequently taken to be an index of imminent insanity. Nietzsche's claims for *Beyond Good and Evil* in *Ecce Homo* (if I have interpreted them correctly) seem to provoke such a judgment. No doubt there is a good deal of buffoonery in *Ecce Homo*.[67] But even in jest, how could a sane man claim to supersede Thucydides in a chapter of forty aphorisms, a scant thirty-five pages? I cannot settle the question of Nietzsche's mental illness, but I contend that if Nietzsche can affect our own sanity, for good and ill, it is because his writings constitute a psychagogy of unprecedented beauty and breathtaking lucidity about matters of undeniable importance to the sanest and soberest among us—precisely those readers who (in every age) have been nourished by Thucydides. To gauge Nietzsche's power over grave men like Max Weber, and to assess the resistance mounted by Weber against him, it may be necessary to risk overestimating Nietzsche's sanity and to take seriously what may be only jests. In this chapter, I shall pursue the questions one would ask if one assumed that Nietzsche was perfectly sane when he made such grandiose claims: (1) Does Nietzsche present an analysis comparable to Thucydides' famous archaeology to justify his assertion that the motion, to which his philosophic politics is devoted, will be the greatest *kinesis*? (2) Does Nietzsche give a reasonable justification of the brevity and compression of his argument on what is noble? (3) Does he provide a perspicuous account of the relation between nobility and necessity, as his claim seems to require?

The first question need not detain us long, although a complete description of Nietzsche's archaeology could go on for volumes, paralleling Thucydides point for point by disclosing the accumulation of military, industrial, commercial, and organizational might that made the global wars of the twentieth century so destructive. To see it, however, one needs only to read Nietzsche's writings and the preceding parts of *Beyond Good and Evil* without the illusion that Nietzsche was a romantic who rejected modern science. For it is evident on almost every page that he was a revolutionary in sympathy with the expansion of human power accomplished by modern science and determined to incorporate it into his philosophic politics. If the illusion that he was a romantic can survive my arguments in the last two chapters, nothing I can say in this one will dislodge it. It requires us to believe that Nietzsche was blind to what was perfectly obvious to anyone reading Thucydides after the American Civil War: that if a world war broke out, it would unleash a revolution in power-relations and productive and destructive power that would dwarf the Peloponnesian War. Thucydides wrote that he had believed from the very outset, before the *kinesis* was under way, "that it would be great and noteworthy above all the wars that had gone before." [68] Nietzsche's books are peppered with similar statements. [69] But his anticipations of a warlike age about to break upon Europe and the world are not merely inspired prophecies. Thucydides had given the grounds for his belief in the archaeology of power in Book 1 of his *War*. Nietzsche's writings abound in comparable analyses of the unprecedented power released by modern science. [70] Like Thucydides' schooling, Nietzsche's is intended for men who must dwell with the realities of war. The context of his training of gentlemen is war and revolutionary politics: "One has to have guts merely to endure it; one must never have learned how to be afraid." [71] Nietzsche teaches men to incorporate an experience on the scale of the pathos of Thucydides' war. He did not have to foment such a war: the world was doing that without his prompting. The task he set himself was to teach men to endure and to grow noble through it.

5. THE GENEALOGY OF NOBLE NIHILISM

In addition to an archaeology of the forms of power analyzed by Thucydides, Nietzsche presents an archaeology of the means of spiritual warfare. The motion Nietzsche anticipated was not merely grandiose in conventional military terms. The foundation for his claim that his teaching prepares a more radical and more spiritual nobleman is his analysis of the "accumulation of forces and tasks" for a new politics to enhance man and raise him to a new pinnacle of power and creativity. Such an analysis is enucleated in the remarks of the Preface. When Nietzsche asserts that "with so tense a bow we can now shoot for the most distant goals," [72] he is referring to a spiritual or intellectual tension created by the impact of modern philosophy and science upon moral and religious authority. That remark is expanded by *On the Genealogy of Morals*. The great motion that Nietzsche anticipated "is the great spectacle in a hundred acts reserved for the next two centuries in Europe—the most terrible, most questionable, and perhaps also the most hopeful of all spectacles," for "as the will to truth thus gains self-consciousness—there can be no doubt of that—morality will gradually *perish* now." [73] The political tasks for which Nietzsche prepares his new nobility arise from this nihilistic motion of moral disintegration. We cannot examine the *Genealogy* here, but it may help with my second question. It is an expansion of *Beyond Good and Evil* and thus sheds light on Nietzsche's brevity: "What is Noble" is in a sense a breviary of the later work. [74]

Nietzsche justified his brevity in a long aphorism published just after *Beyond Good and Evil*. There he justified his deliberate suppression of scholarship in his writings, his practice of touching briefly upon matters that would require massive scholarship for authoritative treatment. That justification makes clear that Nietzsche abbreviates by presupposing scholarship, not ignoring but rather implicating it:

> We *are* something different from scholars, although it is unavoidable for us to be also, among other things, scholarly. We have different needs. . . . It is not fat but the greatest possible suppleness and strength that a good dancer desires from his nourishment—and I do not know what the spirit of a philosopher might wish more to be than a good dancer. [75]

This passage means that in order to understand Nietzsche's arguments, one must become knowledgeable in the scholarship that he compresses. In the *Genealogy*, Nietzsche shows by example what this would entail. There he provides a more scholarly but fatter and lengthier treatment of the subjects treated in *Beyond Good and Evil*. The first comparison that leaps to the eye is that the First Essay, "Good and Evil, Good and Bad," is obviously a completion and clarification of aphorism no. 260—the central aphorism of stage 1, on the rise and fall of aristocracy. [76] That hint leads quickly to the observation that the *Genealogy* supplies a lengthier and more scholarly account of the first three sections of Part 9: breeding, the subject of aphorisms nos. 263–67, is the subject of the Second Essay, which begins on this theme ("To breed an animal with the right to make promises"); [77] the higher men, the subject of aphorisms nos. 268–77, are also the subject of the Third Essay, which is a survey of the meaning of ascetic ideals to the higher men. [78] This correspondence is also reflected in quantitative proportions. In Part 9, the third topic receives roughly twice as much attention as the preceding topics; this is also true in the *Genealogy*. [79] It is apparent that in teaching what is noble, Nietzsche treats the subjects of the *Genealogy* from the viewpoint of the *gentilhomme* rather than the scholar. He achieves a concentration, by means of abbreviation, that he cannot attain in the more scholarly treatise. This leanness permits his argument to conform more precisely to the needs of the philosopher and to the character of his activity as motion and dance. It remains poised over problems of great scope, which in a more scholarly, historical account would bridge decades, if not millennia. [80] The latent connection to these problems is articulated at length in the *Genealogy*. Nietzsche subsumes Thucydides by implicating, abbreviating, and subsuming him. It has been said of Thucydides' work that it conveys a ranking of men, an attempt "to assess every human type at its worth." [81] This "clearsighted giving to every man his due" makes Thucydides' experience of the war a proof of lion-like strength. [82] Nietzsche's rivalry with Thucydides is centered upon this ranking: it should be enough if his account makes his own ranking fully perspicuous.

Thucydides wrote of the emergence of a kind of moral nihilism in his account of the revolution at Corcyra. [83] But it would be difficult to argue that he perceived in nihilism a potential for the release of human powers for a higher, spiritual politics. The speeches of "What is Noble" constitute a rehearsal of Nietzsche's task for the philosophic leader, the task of the enhancement of man. Its subject is what must be said and taught by the philosopher in guiding mankind through an extended enterprise reaching beyond the limits of Thucydidean politics. As a compendium of speeches, Part 9 indicates the reminders that must be spoken, or the deeds that must be performed, if this enterprise is to be realized. But like the speeches in Thucydides, Nietzsche's are to be understood in the context of stages or occasions in the unfolding of this encompassing motion. The *Genealogy* is useful in clarifying our view of these occasions. [84]

These stages fall into four ranks or four levels of politics. The first concerns the politics of class domination or the maintenance of slavery (Nos. 258–62). This is primarily a politics of the sword, and its principle is that the underclass must be kept in fear; there must be no doubt that the masters will use their strength with a clear conscience. Nietzsche argues for direct government: an aristocracy is to rule in its own right, without appealing to a common good, to the traditional legitimacy of a dynasty, to natural law, or to divine right.[85] Direct rule is precarious and engenders the causes of its own downfall; it also generates tensions and opportunities that cannot be turned to advantage by aristocratic rulers. Despite these limitations, it is a recurrent, indispensable necessity for higher politics and must be affirmed by the philosopher.[86] The highest civilization requires not only slavery but almost every form of exploitation.[87] Moreover, it is indispensable to embody courage in a whole class of men, the long courage required for enterprises beyond the creation and maintenance of an aristocratic polity. All the higher forms of politics call for courage; the philosopher must carry courage into the most refined and delicate psychological tasks.[88] The masters create values by giving vent to their courage in saying Yes and No; they legislate language; the philosopher's task of revaluating values requires this elementary courage in refined forms.[89] There is also a connection between courage and the absence of vanity. All the higher forms of politics demand strict control over vanity; this control would be unthinkable if courage were not brought in its fullest strength to the most delicate enterprises. These enterprises require a subtler hierarchy and a recognition of less visible distinctions between men: what is *Vornehm* may be made clear in rather gross terms in a class society, but Nietzsche seeks to create a far longer ladder of rank. In it the less visible differences between men must be recognized, and the distances between them enforced, as unequivocally as the difference between master and slave. Vanity would prevent men from acknowledging these distinctions. The distinctive absence of vanity that Nietzsche praises in courageous men—they have no need for it—must become instinctive for men of higher rank.[90]

The cyclic rise and fall of class rule is a time-worn subject; Nietzsche does not have to describe it elaborately to make us fully aware that he is propounding a new interpretation of an ancient theme.[91] Rather than portraying the cycle of a regime systematically and scientifically, he gives us a series of perspectives illuminating crucial aspects of this cycle. The trajectory is evident without an extended account; the work of his aphorisms is to school us in correct judgments about a familiar history.[92] Nietzsche describes enough to bring the old story to mind. Yet he is so forceful in his judgments that the cycle remains in the background. We must ourselves supply pages of illustrations to flesh out Nietzsche's account of the political cycle, but this is an exercise that establishes a pattern and enables Nietzsche to abbreviate without losing the alert reader.[93]

The second group of occasions concerns the politics of the domestication of men, of the breeding of a certain kind of man over generations. It is the politics of Rousseau's Legislator, whose task was to deprive men of their original nature and replace it with a second, moral nature.[94] The familiar instance, to which Nietzsche alludes, is the historical accomplishment of Christianity; the first aphorism in this section (nos. 263–67) draws attention to the Bible. This is, however, only an instance: Nietzsche sees Christianity as an adjunct of law, tyrannical means, and the state.[95] It displays to Nietzsche what can be accomplished by a single book accompanied by "some external tyranny of authority for [its] protection."[96] A firm framework of law is required to reshape human nature over generations through education, religion, and manners. In this politics, men are punished systematically for their original nature—a form of cruelty as bizarre, and as difficult to justify, as slavery.[97] Every attempt to remake man has been a long, painful tragedy. Creating new distances within the human soul, this politics of virtue is essentially a long war against the instincts.[98] In the Second Essay of the *Genealogy*, Nietzsche recapitulates the steps of this history; that essay is cast on the scale of millennia. For the European case, it spans at least the consolidation of Roman civilization and the long emergence of Christian Europe through the formation of the territorial states.[99]

According to Nietzsche, this history too is a cycle that brings us back inexorably to the beginning of the entire transformation. It is a cycle of the will, just as the rise and fall of aristocracy is a cycle. Nietzsche portrays aristocracy as a collective willing by a master class, a discharge of its will to survive and to overcome external enemies. It requires external resistance and danger: a class of slaves that threaten it from below and foreign powers against which it can exercise its courage and maintain its will to fight. With the consolidation of its power and the defeat of its immediate enemies, the collective discipline of an aristocracy is bound to disintegrate. What necessitates its decline is the absence of an appropriate object for the collective willing of the aristocrats.[100] In a more subtle fashion, the politics of virtue is a mode of willing that bears the causes of its own disintegration within itself. The justice that remakes men through force and fraud requires an internal resistance, a discrepancy between human nature and an authoritative

ideal. The exercise of such justice, against others and oneself, becomes impossible just to the extent that it is arguably successful. When
men become predictable, and instinctively command themselves to do
what had been exacted from them by punishments and fear and authoritative persuasion, *will* ceases to be necessary. Instinct accom-
plishes the enforcement. The end of this long tragedy is therefore great
confusion: having willed the subordination of man's original nature,
the legislators and the virtuous lack an object of the will.

In no. 266, Nietzsche presents a strikingly brief aphorism. It exemplifies the egoistic faith mentioned in the previous aphorism and the
psychological differences that result from generations of breeding,
mentioned in no. 264. It also implies a criticism of Goethe's policy.
Goethe's aloof nobility illustrates the contempt that helped to keep the
lower orders in European society "thinking small." But this moderate
contempt provides no policy for the day when Goethe, and other men
of breeding, experience nausea at what European man has become.[101]
(This use of a very brief aphorism to call attention to a problem or to
set in play somewhat speculative reasoning is a characteristic feature
of the later sections of Nietzsche's argument on politics.)[102]

The question "What, in the end, is common?" introduces the
third rank of Nietzsche's politics; it also introduces a new kind of brevity. Its origin lies in the limitations of exoteric communication, or communication based upon a common language and common experiences.
It is not an accident that this should become a problem just after
Nietzsche's remarks on the politics of remaking men through law and
institutions. The standing objection to the rule of law has always been
that it does not take unique situations sufficiently into account.[103] The
virtue of the rule of law is that it establishes a constant pressure that
brooks no exceptions, but that is a vice in matters in which the exception is what counts. The third group of occasions is concerned with the
discipline of men of truly exceptional natures. The higher men are
unique and stand in a perpetual tension with what is common: not only
what is common to other men but what is common in themselves.
Their inescapable task is to create their own rules and laws; they must
determine what is to be common, regular, lawlike in their natures and
what is to remain untouched by the rules. This is the problem of giving
style to one's character.[104] Politics at this level is not concerned with
eradicating an original nature and imposing upon a group of men a
second artificial nature. Its task is to find a moving balance between a

unique original nature and an artificial or cultural nature, which enables this original nature to exercise its multifarious powers without creating contradictions that would destroy the individual. What is in question is the possibility of a common style that supports the exception, making it possible for the higher men to disclose and conceal their powers. Nietzsche had adumbrated the problems of such a style in Part 8 of *Beyond Good and Evil*. In Part 9, he tries to solve them. In the *Genealogy,* Nietzsche presents an account of the meaning of ascetic ideals for the higher men: the artist, the philosopher, the saint, the priest, and the scientist. This Third Essay exhibits the disproportion between the incommensurable needs of these higher men and the common ascetic ideal, which had hitherto provided the common standard of the higher man in Europe. Nietzsche finds the attempt to reconcile such divergent needs by a crude common ideal to be comic.[105] What the higher men have in common is the need for a task, a goal for their will. But when looked at in detail, this common need fragments into essentially unique needs for unique tasks. The common horizon of ascetic ideals is a disguised attempt to subordinate the higher men to more common men and to common morality.[106]

The courage of the aristocrats and the justice of men of breeding is intrinsically collective. Even the faith of aristocratic "egoists" is not really individualistic: it is expressed in terms of who "*we* are." [107] Who they are is determined by the group and by a common standard; their needs are expressed directly in that standard. But the needs and identity of the higher man cannot be predicated in such a standard. He himself must find them, and the search is so unlikely to succeed that it is almost bound to result in ruin.[108] However, the possibility of any enhancement of the type "man" beyond the mere creation of "an animal capable of making promises" depends upon these higher men. While the exceptions can never become the rule, they are the key to the progress of mankind beyond the moral plane. When they do turn out right, they create a style in which man's original nature and a second cultural nature can live in coordination and harmony. The higher men create the forms in which a noble life is possible for a species of (common) men who are not exceptions. If the cycle in which merely moral man is brought into being is not to become a catagenesis toward a premoral humanity incapable of even keeping promises, the higher men must succeed in creating a new, more difficult style for common life: a style that is postmoral, or "beyond good and evil" in the Christian sense.

Such a style would ultimately be fairly exoteric and common, but it could only be the fruit of a long experiment in the esoteric, during which "What is common" would be truly problematic.[109]

If such a style is to be achieved, the higher men must risk themselves, hazarding their ruin, again and again. No enterprise is less likely to succeed. Nothing is harder to behold than the ruin of a truly gifted individual. But Nietzsche conceives this creation of style to be a higher political task deserving the greatest statesmanship and holding the greatest promise for man. The initial task is negative: the true precariousness of the higher men must be unequivocally displayed, and a nihilistic attack must be launched against the teachings that obscure this harsh vulnerability of the noble. In the *Genealogy,* this takes the form of a critique of ascetic ideals. In Part 9, Jesus is singled out, instead, as the archetypal misleader of the higher men.[110] The negative task is also carried out in a series of aphorisms on the necessary suffering and precariousness of the higher men. Like the unpublished fourth part of *Thus Spake Zarathustra,* nos. 268–77 are concerned with overcoming the temptation of pity for the higher men.[111] These aphorisms adumbrate the politics of the psychologist and psychagogue whose task is to lead the higher men to risk their own ruin. The higher men are primarily endangered by their inability to grasp their true needs. What they require cannot be distinguished by any common standard; it is essentially an imperative of their own becoming, the need to discharge their full powers, upon the right task, at the right time. Failing that, Nietzsche seems to be certain that their powers and virtues will destroy each other. The higher men have a multitude of strengths which must be fused into a living, organic unity; such a fusion can occur only on meeting a task, in an ecstasy of problem-confrontation.[112] The psychagogy of the philosophic leader is thus a matter of attuning men to the difficulty of seizing their task when it is at hand. The occasions in question in nos. 268–77 are occasions in the becoming of the higher man.[113]

The fourth and highest level of Nietzsche's philosophic politics concerns the ordering of the soul of the highest man; it is a politics of force and fraud exercised against the self. The philosopher seems to order his soul by rehearsing his highest task as if it were play. This task is not adumbrated in the *Genealogy;* it may be considered the primary theme of Zarathustra's quest. We will imitate Nietzsche's brevity and not enter upon the difficulties of this fourth part. A few comments must suffice. What is noble provides a bridge, articulated in style, between the aristocrat and the philosopher. But there is an abyss between them as regards their experiences, and Nietzsche shows us why this must be so. The link between aristocracy and philosophy seems to be formal rather than substantive, except perhaps for their sharing in the virtue of courage. At a formal level, the men of an ordinary oligarchy, being accustomed to rule, are familiar with force and fraud. The formal art of the philosopher, however, seems to be a deception practiced upon the masters and the tyrants; they too must be deceived into becoming "tools in the hand of one more powerful." [114] That this may be a further, and unspoken, reason for Nietzsche's brevity is suggested in *The Gay Science*:

> The Greek philosophers went through life feeling secretly that there were far more slaves than one might think—meaning that everybody who was not a philosopher was a slave. Their pride overflowed at the thought that even the most powerful men on earth belonged among their slaves. [115]

The leanness of Part 9 serves the purpose of our study by presenting a succinct account of Nietzsche's argument for philosophic politics and against Weberian political leadership. But its brevity is also a substantive concern and inseparable from the political problem as he understands it. The task of the enhancement of the human species, which is the political problem for Nietzsche, requires the progressive abbreviation we have just outlined. A lengthier account would falsify the character of Nietzsche's philosophic politics and misrepresent his criterion for ranking the forms of politics. Since politics at its upper limit becomes increasingly a matter of style, the highest form of power must find expression in the greatest style; the greatest motion or war must be conveyed by the truly *grosse Stil*. [116] And the power to compress great matters into a few words is inseparable from the greatest style.

6. RANKING THUCYDIDES

We have seen that Nietzsche provides a reasonable justification of his brevity; we must still examine whether Nietzsche's claim to surpass Thucydides as a teacher of gentlemen, and as a thinker, has substance. The claim is not a light one, for Thucydides stood very high in Nietzsche's esteem. He spoke of him as

[T]he great sum, the last revelation of that strong, hard, severe factuality which was instinctive with the older Hellenes.
In the end it is *courage* in the face of reality that distinguishes a man like Thucydides from Plato: Plato is a coward
before reality, consequently he flees into the ideal; Thucydides has control of *himself,* consequently he also maintains
control of things.[117]

Nietzsche also admired Thucydides as a thoughtful stylist, a *Men-
schen-Denker* whose style made his work immortal: "One must follow
him line by line and read no less clearly between the lines: there are
few thinkers who say so much between the lines."[118] If we are correct
in treating Part 9 as Nietzsche's *Wettkampf* or contest with Thucydides,
Nietzsche would measure himself against the resolute realism, the
tragic vision, the density of thought, and the greatness of style of
Thucydides. Let us then consider what Nietzsche's ranking of Thucydides may tell about the substance of what is noble.

The ranking we have sketched suggests that Nietzsche's claim to
have superseded Thucydides may be a variant upon the theme, familiar
in political philosophy since Marsilius of Padua, that the Roman *eccle-
sia* had introduced a new form of politics, to which classical, Aristotelian political science had not addressed itself.[119] Nietzsche would
have replied negatively to Karl Löwith's question "Can there be a
Christian gentleman?"[120] But his own, more spiritual and radical conception of the *gentilhomme* is inconceivable without Christianity. Like
Machiavelli, who treats Christianity as "the present religion," Nietzsche considers the Christian religion as a mortal institution, subject to
the cyclic rise and fall of all earthly things.[121] But its history discloses
the possibility of a philosophic and spiritual politics, a politics for the
reshaping of human nature, which is above and beyond the politics re-
counted by Thucydides. The problems of instinct and breeding, and of
the determining of the self, can come to light only in the private life of
the individual, which does not concern Thucydides. His limitation as a
teacher of gentlemen lies in his failure to portray the soul and the relations between gentlemen within the city; he gives us neither a portrait
of a regime of gentlemen nor a portrait of the soul of the noble.[122]

This means that Thucydides could not combat Plato and Socrates
on the plane of philosophic politics: "the height attained in the way of
thinking of a Democritus, Hippocrates, and Thucydides was not attained a second time."[123] Platonic error succeeded in imposing a tyr-

anny of thought upon European civilization, a tyranny that triumphed through Christianity.[124] One might therefore compare Nietzsche's contest with Thucydides to Themistocles' *Wettkampf* with Miltiades: Nietzsche attempts a greater strategy, to win greater glory but ultimately in the service of the same cause—philosophy as a cause, the height of a way of thinking attained by Thucydides.[125] However, this means that Thucydides was wrong in his policy toward the great war which he studied and in judging its character as a "motion." He failed to grasp the true sources of motion and rest in his own age; he did not see the greater cycles that would be released by the war: the cycle set in motion by Socrates and brought to a close by Nietzsche.[126] Thucydides' ranking of men was superior to Plato's:

> What do I love in Thucydides, what makes me honor him more highly than Plato? He has the most comprehensive and unprejudiced joy in all types of men and events and discovers that a quantum of sound reason belongs to every type; this he seeks to disclose. He has a greater practical justice than Plato; he is no maligner and denigrator of the men who do not please him, or who in life have caused him grief. On the contrary, he sees something great within all things and persons, and perceives it in seeing them only as types.[127]

Yet his ranking was eclipsed by Plato's. What Thucydides perceived in Alcibiades, for example, and the greatness that the type Alcibiades would receive from Thucydides as his due, was obscured by Plato, who calumniated Alcibiades and belittled him.[128] It was Alcibiades' wounded praise of Socrates in the *Symposium* of Plato, not a Thucydidean speech of what Alcibiades would have said, or should have said, on such an occasion that rang down through the centuries.[129] According to Plato, Socrates, the moralist who considered life a disease, was higher in rank than Alcibiades. And with true genius, he had Alcibiades himself testify to Socrates' superiority.[130] Thucydides was defeated because he did not comprehend the true necessities of his own vision, the necessity for a philosophic politics.

  If this was Nietzsche's view, it suggests that Nietzsche must display a Thucydidean understanding of the relation between what is noble and necessary but transpose this understanding to the higher philosophic politics that Thucydides did not encompass. Whether this implies a fundamental break with Thucydides, or a misunderstanding of his notion of justice and necessity, is a question we cannot pursue here.[131] Remaining within the limitations of Nietzsche's picture of Thucydides, taking his version of what Thucydides implies about nobility and necessity "between the lines," we will try to measure Nietzsche's accomplishment by his own Thucydidean ranking.

7. THE NOBLE AND THE NECESSARY

The highest feeling of power and sureness finds expression in what has *great* style. The power which no longer needs any proof, which spurns pleasing, which does not answer lightly, which feels no witness near, which lives oblivious of all opposition to it, which reposes within itself, fatalistically, a law among laws—that speaks of itself as a great style.[132]

Nietzsche envisions his philosophical politics in a world-historical framework; the context of his school for the *gentilhomme* is one of crisis and motion, not rest. Anticipating a period of world wars, a contest for rule over the globe, and a release of the long-accumulated energies of the European peoples, Nietzsche's politics is intended to master the greatest motion in the history of mankind, a cycle of destruction and creation that will include and surpass every previous cycle.[133] He anticipates not only the shattering of polities, the emergence of new states and power-constellations, and a period of ideological politics but, as we have seen, the shattering of the moral foundation of European civilization as well. The work of the great prophets and legislators who created morality, beginning from Zoroaster, must be undertaken once again.[134] To imagine the scope of Nietzsche's politics, one might compare the myth of the cycles in Plato's *Statesman*. Like Plato, Nietzsche assigns a long but finite career to the cycle of human generation and nurture: the biological and erotic foundations of human life can be shaken by great cataclysms. Such a cataclysm appears to Nietzsche to be at hand: the physiological basis of civilization is deranged and must be reordered from the beginning on correct first principles.[135] The task of philosophic leadership is to seize the opportunity of a most comprehensive crisis. At the moment in Plato's myth when the *demiourgos* releases the helm and allows the world to reverse its cyclic motion, Nietzsche's philosopher must seize the helm, take advantage of the most unprecedented interplay of contingency and necessity, and swing the world and man into its most beautiful motion.[136] This noblest, most dangerous Eighteenth Brumaire would release the mightiest concentration of human power and creativity, setting into action all the resources of experience, knowledge, and wealth, built up over millennia in Europe. The consequent Renaissance would be an ineffaceable event, demonstrating for all time what the type "man" can be.[137] To understand the character of this monument to man, one may refer to Pericles' speech on Athenian glory, a speech Nietzsche particularly remarked:

> Many are the proofs which we have given of our power, and assuredly it does not lack witnesses, and therefore we shall be the wonder not only of the men of today but of aftertimes; we shall need no Homer to sing our praises nor any other poet whose verses may perhaps delight for the moment but whose presentation of the facts will be discredited by the truth.[138]

Nietzsche translated the remainder of the passage thus: "[O]ur boldness has gained access to every land and sea, everywhere raising imperishable monuments to its goodness *and wickedness.*"[139] It is such an "imperishable monument" that Nietzsche seeks to create or set in motion by seizing the opportunity presented by a tragic age of terrible war. Consider this formulation:

> Let us look ahead a century; let us suppose that my attempt to assassinate two millennia of anti-nature and desecration of man were to succeed. That new party of life which would tackle the greatest of all tasks, the attempt to raise humanity higher, including the relentless destruction of everything that was degenerating and parasitical, would again make possible that excess of life on earth from which the Dionysian state, too, would have to awaken again. I promise a tragic age: the highest art in saying Yes to life, tragedy, will be reborn when humanity has weathered the consciousness of the hardest but most necessary wars *without suffering from it.*[140]

Thucydides did not teach this. Nietzsche claims that his teaching on necessity and nobility will permit or enable not only the exceptional, lion-like Thucydides but humanity itself to bear such consciousness. Can this kind of *virtú* be taught?

We may approach this problem through Nietzsche's reading of Thucydides' Melian dialogue. Nietzsche's teaching on justice can be traced to the Athenians' position in this dialogue.[141] The Melians were given a choice between submission or destruction; they chose resistance and their own destruction. The dialogue was followed by the slaughter of the Melians and the enslavement of their women and children.[142] The Athenians posed this choice to the Melians and then carried it through: Melos was an everlasting monument to the *tolma,* the boldness of Athens and Alcibiades, forcing itself down into a place— Thucydides' word is *katanankasantes,* from *ananke,* "compulsion" or "necessity"—in all its goodness and badness.[143] In the dialogue it is shown that the alternative to submission would not be ignoble for the Melians: bowing to necessity or compulsion in such a case involves no disgrace.[144] Both the Melians and the Athenians are "realists" in Nietzsche's sense: the dialogue is the most unadorned and naked statement of power-political realities in Thucydides' work. But after seeing the naked truth about their situation, the Melians choose destruction: they commit suicide. Instead of bowing to necessity while bearing the tragedy of their city with noble dignity, they gamble upon unfounded hopes in their allies and in Providence.[145] The Athenians carried through their policy without flinching and apparently without suffering from the consciousness of what it cost the Melians. Ignoring what this may have meant to Thucydides, let us take it to illustrate what Nietzsche thought was possible. Humanity will not suffer from the consciousness of the most terrible and necessary wars—this is Nietzsche's thought—because that portion of mankind which is susceptible to such suffering will perish.[146] Those who can be inured to face such wars without suffering will be those who prevail. The Melians of the future will seek their own destruction; Nietzsche's future Alcibiades and his new party of life will remain resolute.

Nietzsche propounded a teaching that he believed would make this outcome inescapable. The idea of the eternal recurrence of the same is "a selective principle, in the service of strength (and barbarism!)."[147] "It is the great cultivating idea: the races that cannot bear it stand condemned; those who find it the greatest benefit are chosen to rule."[148] It is "the idea that gives many the right to erase themselves."[149] Nietzsche's policy might be said to assert that the doctrine expounded in the course of the Melian debate was the essential cause precipitating the Melians' self-destructive choice. Nietzsche asks: "Does one reproach Thucydides for the words he put into the mouths of the Athenian ambassadors when they negotiated with the Melians on the question of destruction or submission?"[150] His teaching of the eternal recurrence, a doctrine that propounds a higher realism like that of Thucydides and the Sophists, is a comprehensive publication of the terrible truth spoken by the Athenians. Perhaps Part 9 begins with slavery, exploitation, and conquest because it is a presentation of the eternal recurrence.[151]

The problem with the Athenian position is that it does not support a sound regime in Athens: what the Athenians say seems to erode the foundations of the Periclean polity and to make united, disciplined action impossible.[152] One may doubt that things could be otherwise, so long as the doctrine remains limited to deliberations on war and peace between cities. Nietzsche's remedy for the failure of the Athenian position is to argue that the position requires a more radical and more spiritual philosophical politics for its success. The relation between *ananke* and the noble must be comprehensively thought through. Part 9 therefore takes the form of a graduated teaching on the relation between compulsion and nobility, in an attempt to think men back to their true necessities.[153] The four parts of Nietzsche's argument disclose the true needs of four types of men.

Stage 1 (nos. 258–62).—"[T]he straight line, the grand style in action rediscovered; the most powerful instinct, that of life itself, the lust to rule, affirmed."[154] Nietzsche was aware that most conquerers have been unable to act upon the Athenian doctrine with a good conscience; it will take philosophy to affirm the lust to rule and endow it with a clear conscience.[155] But the cyclic rise and fall of regimes seems to mock the lust to rule by rendering it meaningless. What is noble in barbarian courage and strength of will seems to be precarious. Courage enforces values, but this enforcement appears to lead nowhere, given the Sisyphean rise and fall of power-constellations. Courage seems to be impossible to sustain without a goal beyond this cycle: that is its necessity. Nietzsche redeems the compulsion of politics and the nobility of courage, by exhibiting this pathos as the precondition of the highest creativity. The lust for rule in its naïve expression is the creation of values. But it is indirectly a cause for the emergence of higher men. What would appear meaningless to a naïve aristocracy—the disintegration of their caste into a jungle-growth of geniuses and individualists—presents the opportunity for the creation of a higher type. Aristocratic rule must "go under" for the enhancement of the type "man" to become possible.[156]

Stage 2 (nos. 263–67).—If the most powerful instinct of life it-self is the lust for rule, the *instinct for rank* is the great "institution-building instinct." [157] It is a need that reshapes men through long disci-pline by supporting reverence and tradition; it finds its natural expres-sion in preserving social distinctions and "the primordial law of things." [158] But its rule is a tyranny over human nature; an insightful man can see that it not only inflicts punishment upon innocents but also makes the lower orders small while it makes the great arrogant. [159] One is punished for being born as another is rewarded for the accident of his birth; the diminution of many is the nauseating price for the elevation of a few. If the relation between what is noble and what is necessary is to be affirmed, therefore, insight must be suppressed. So Nietzsche "proposes" that

> [E]goism belongs to the nature of a noble soul—I mean that unshakeable faith that to a being such as "we are" other be-ings must be subordinate by nature and have to sacrifice themselves. The noble soul accepts this fact of its egoism without any question mark. [160]

This belief is a matter of faith and is unquestionable because it is a myth, but Nietzsche recommends that we say "it is justice itself." [161] This conception of justice must "remain master" over every insight to the contrary: Nietzsche believed that this was what the Athenians as-serted on Melos. [162]

Stage 3 (nos. 268–77).—In Part 9, *Vornehmheit* becomes pro-gressively more refined: it comes to mean "distinguished" in the sense of "fully individuated." We have indicated how compulsion and no-bility are related in this third stage of Nietzsche's argument. [163] The teacher of the higher men must have the hard and cheerful resolute-ness, the unflinching firmness of policy, that the Athenians displayed at Melos. That many of the higher men will perish under such a policy, indeed at their own hands, must be no objection. The growth of the higher men is natural and precariously subject to the laws of decay; nature is a squanderer. But the risk of numberless failures must be taken, for a new "man" and for the realization of the highest man. Nietzsche interprets the origin of Christianity as the result of one man's inability to submit to the harsh compulsion that rules the higher men. Jesus was unable to withstand the knowledge that he had not turned out well; his terrible need for love was based upon the illusion that love could mend his shattered greatness. When he learned the truth about love, that is, the Thucydidean truth about other men, he sought death.[164] This hard and cheerful account of the Passion indicates how Nietzsche's relentless teaching on the nature of love precipitates (or is intended to promote) the perishing of certain types of men. Greatness requires that the *kairos* be seized, that the right moment be taken in its flood. For this to be possible, the higher man must habituate himself to hardness, must impose laws upon himself, and must utterly abandon dependence upon other men or common rules.[165]

At this stage, what is noble means embracing suffering as a means to individuation: "To *endure* the idea of the recurrence one needs . . . new means against the fact of *pain* (pain considered as a tool . . . the enjoyment of all kinds of uncertainty, experimentalism, as a counter-weight to this extreme fatalism)."[166] The higher man must believe there is no support in the universe as will to power for what is noble:

> In all kinds of injury and loss the lower and coarser soul is
> better off than the nobler one: the dangers for the latter must
> be greater; the probability that it will come to grief and per-
> ish is actually, in view of the multiplicity of the conditions of
> its life, tremendous.[167]

What is noble is therefore more dependent upon artificial compul-sion: upon the hardness and cheerfulness of other men, insofar as they provoke him, and upon his own laws of style.

Stage 4 (nos. 278–95).—Facing his situation candidly, the high-est man must see that he is the least likely being in the universe. The philosopher is a *summum bonum,* also a *summum malum.* He is aware of his character as a fortuity, his dependence on continued will to en-force his existence. "The sublime man has the highest value, even if he is terribly delicate and fragile, because an abundance of very difficult and rare things has been bred and preserved together through many generations."[168] He is also aware of his mortality and the contingent character of all the conditions that have made him possible: he will per-ish, and another like him will not come into existence for centuries, perhaps millennia. From this, Nietzsche derives his necessities, his "categorical imperative": as the meridian of life, the philosopher must affirm the whole as the necessary precondition of his being. A strict and almost logical rigor requires him to be the teacher of the eternal recurrence; as the greatest accident, he is under the highest compulsion to affirm all accident. His imperative is to master chance by loving it: affirming chance means releasing it again and again so that it may be repeatedly conquered.[169] Ultimately, the reasons that lead Nietzsche to live the philosophic life as a "dance" may be traced to these imperatives: the modern project for the conquest of nature through the mastery of accident does not result in a static tyranny of man over nature, like the static tyrannies that led nowhere prior to the Peloponnesian War; it leads to the release of chance, to a more dynamic and constantly reinvigorated contest with nature that can never be relaxed and becomes ever more dangerous for mankind and the highest man. The philosopher must be a dancer to affirm his mastery and enforce his most tyrannical drive, his will to create precisely such a world of dynamic will to power.[170] The dependence of the highest man upon the conditions of his own possibility, and his need to affirm these conditions, is reflected in the character of his pathos. In his body and self he must embody all the instincts, all the forms of the will to power, that are present in the lower men; his pathos must subsume the pathos of every lower rank in the long ladder described in Part 9. Nietzsche's first sketch of the philosophic task of teaching the eternal recurrence reflects this: "We teach the doctrine—it is the strongest means for us *to incorporate* it ourselves."[171] The pathos of the philosopher, then, is not simply the subject of the final eighteen aphorisms (nos. 278–95): his pathos is reflected in the character of the argument as a whole. The philosopher is a dancer whose dance rehearses and recapitulates the entire politics that makes him possible. The necessity to create a style and give form to his character holds for the highest as well as the higher man: his power to create and recreate a style is a test of his attained mastery and his rank. The task that he must recurrently set himself, and seize, is the task that exercises the entire range of his powers and consolidates his strengths in a great style. He must pose such a task in play whether or not the *kairos* is there; or perhaps one should say, the *kairos,* the critical moment, is precisely whenever his powers require consolidation.[172] For these reasons, the Nietzschean philosopher must constantly practice upon himself a dancer's discipline, working by strict artistic laws, and these will in turn be reflected in the music of his style: the necessitous character of his task and his need for laws is transparent in the musical mathematics of his style.[173] But the formal laws of Nietzsche's style also serve philosophic purposes that musical forms do not serve. They create and help to solve *riddles* and are thus a means of guiding the mind, conveying a pathos of inquiry, the pathos of the will to power as the will to truth. The formal and mathematical relationships between the aphorisms of Part 9 are means to draw our attention to connections and proportions within Nietzsche's argument. Let us consider, as an instance, the exercise in style with which Nietzsche brings his argument to an end in no. 295. The stylistic, formal riddle, as Walter Kaufmann observed, is that "some of the features" of the portrait of Dionysus in no. 295 "bring to mind Socrates." [174] That alone is a paradox because the book began as an attack upon Platonic-Socratic error. But Kaufmann's observation does not go far enough. The entirety of the long speech in this aphorism is modeled upon a speech from Plato's *Symposium,* in which Alcibiades describes Socrates. All the features of Socrates are transformed: the philosopher-god Dionysus is emphatically different from Socrates. The speech is a *verkehrte Welt* inverting the world of Plato's symposium: its subject is the seduction of Alcibiades *by Dionysus* and thus the inversion of Plato's evaluation of Alcibiades or the defiance of Socratic error. [175] Nietzsche's argument culminates in the speech that Thucydides' Alcibiades should have spoken and would have spoken if Thucydides and Alcibiades had been fully aware of the truth of the noble necessities. It is a fitting finale for Nietzsche's *agon* with Thucydides: philosophic psychagogy is a politics to perfect and spiritualize tyranny. But it also bespeaks the Homeric pathos, which Thucydides did not share with the highest man, the pathos of "him that gave the Greeks their gods—no, who invented his own gods for himself!" [176]

8. NIETZSCHE'S REGIME

It is possible to discern some of the features of the regime of the philosophic leader in the criterion of rank that Nietzsche articulates in "What is Noble." Because Nietzsche's ranking is attuned to the necessities of rule, his critique of politics stands very close to the standard by which Nietzsche's regime would be governed. In the course of Part 9, Nietzsche shows how an initially social tension between classes, reflected in the pathos of distance of the ruling class, could be transmuted by stages into the widest psychological distances within the soul. [177] Hence his critique of politics is a gauge of the souls of men and of the psychological distances within men. It may indicate how the men on the different levels of Nietzsche's hierarchy would perceive themselves and (to an extent) each other. How Nietzsche's regime would appear from within, through the eyes of those who govern and lead it, is adumbrated in "What is Noble." The argument describes the philosopher in his relations with the staff that radiates from him. It exhibits a possibility, approximating a superhuman Machiavellianism, a highest man combining the qualities of Caesar and the soul of Christ while leading a Napoleonic enterprise "without loss of *noblesse*." [178] It is a ladder from "base means" toward forms of psychic coercion and fraud that do not threaten the highest man with the loss of his nobility. The prize to be attained by the victory over vanity and unjust self-esteem is the subordination of base means to higher forms of leadership capable of effectuating an elevation of man. [179]

Given the tendency of Nietzsche scholarship, which is at present dominated by literary concerns and aesthetic fashions, and by Heidegger's treatment of politics as the unmentionable, it is necessary to underscore the practical, political dimension of Nietzsche's style. Nietzsche's criterion of nobility must be capable of the most subtle but law-like refinement in order to give a firm and exacting standard by which to govern a regime. He articulates a criterion of nobility in style, a criterion that permits the finest calibration, from the most exoteric to the most esoteric. If Nietzsche's measure, which is essentially an "art of style" or a poetics, is not to degenerate into the effete mannerisms of a politically sterile elite, and thereby to lose touch entirely with Nietzsche's intention, it must be unmistakably a style of action. Nietzsche strove to attain such a style, taking his model from the political historians Sallust and Tacitus and competing for realism with the least "literary" of the Greek authors, Thucydides. [180] Where Nietzsche departs from classical models, impatient with their contemplative calm, he seeks out the power-artists of the Renaissance and finds his rivals in Machiavelli and Napoleon. How an art of style may find expression in politics is indicated by a remark on Napoleon that Nietzsche copied out from Taine in one of his notebooks:

> "Suddenly the *faculté maîtresse* unfolds: the artist enclosed in the politician emerges *de sa gaine;* he creates *dans l'idéal et l'impossible*. He is once more recognized for what he is: the posthumous brother of Dante and Michelangelo: and in truth, in view of the firm contours of his vision, the intensity, coherence, and inner logic of his dream, the profundity of his meditation, the superhuman grandeur of his conception, he is like them *et leur égal: son génie à la même taille et la*

même structure; il est une des trois esprits souverains de la renaissance italienne." Nota bene—Dante, Michelangelo, Napoleon.[181]

Nietzsche sought a criterion of style attuned to the true laws of power and leadership, a style equal to the task of governing the greatest motion in the history of man and capable of imparting the pathos of this motion to a regime. Anticipating the most terrible wars, Nietzsche seeks to impose upon "a warlike age" the necessities of the enhancement of the type "man." In the horizons of these necessities, the most terrible wars would be seen as necessary wars. Nietzsche attempts to convert the dance of death into a warrior's dance of life, created by and creating the man of the highest courage, whose will to power is will to truth. Judged by the standard Nietzsche found in Pericles' Funeral Oration, his standard is the noblest and most comprehensive that could be imagined:

[T]he man who is most justly accounted courageous is he who best knows the meaning of what is sweet in life and what is terrible, and then goes out undeterred to meet what is to come.[182]

5. SERVING MORAL FORCES: SCIENCE AS A VOCATION

> [I]f all of us who come from Nietzscheism, from nihilism, or from historical realism said in public that we were wrong and that there are moral values and that in the future we shall do the necessary to establish and illustrate them, don't you believe this would be the beginnng of a hope?
>
> Camus, *Notebooks 1942–1951*

WEBER'S teaching on political leadership is necessarily a critique and delimitation of science. His writings bring science to the fore as a practical force that has transformed the conditions of political action and will continue to transform them into the indefinite future. The politician cannot ignore this force, and the observer must understand it in order to judge political men. Bureaucracy and factory are mind objectified. The organizational imperatives of administration and commerce create an agenda for public business, determining the consequences of most public initiatives in modern states. Even when these imperatives cannot be traced back to scientific discoveries and the application of scientific knowledge (as many of them can), the guiding roles in administration are taken by managers attuned to the progressive mastery of the world through science. The execution of policy in such organizations is often supervised by technicians conversant with some branch of science. The continuous revolution in the external conditions of life that goes forward under modern capitalism, and within the modern rationalized state, is a revolution made possible by modern science and intelligible only through its focused lenses.[1] This perpetual revolution is reflected in the conduct of public business and in the recruitment of the staffs that surround political leaders.[2]

134

It is no accident, then, that Weber's writings have become a routine part of the curriculum of public administration, political science, and sociology as the most trenchant and succinct introduction to these facts of modern social life. But because Weber occupies the status of a standard authority today, it is necessary to correct the optical illusion that makes one identify the tour guide with the tour. The tour antedates Weber. He was by no means the first to recognize and plot the disenchantment of the world by science and the rationalization of administration and commerce. These had been the themes of most philosophic and scientific discourses about political society for more than three centuries. What one interpreter has dubbed "the politics of progress" had also been a favorite subject of salon and parlor conversation in an ever-widening circle of enlightened publics in Europe and America for at least a century.[3] Weber's turgid, cramped, and gloomy accounts replaced a lively and brilliant dialogue that had engaged good minds for most of the modern era.[4] Weber was not alone, of course, in crashing this party, but he was among the most successful in disrupting the dialogue and transforming it into a more serious and somber one. Weber's writing consolidated the new model of professional gravity; he divided the discussion of these topics between science and politics, sought to professionalize both, and insisted throughout upon the same intransigent principles of ultimate conflict. When one studies those principles, it is difficult to avoid the conclusion that what Weber introduced to this well-established tradition of discourse was a fresh and candidly political perspective—not the perspective of a specific party, program, or political ideology but what Weber regarded as the perspective of political man as such. His critique and delimitation was in the channel cut by Rousseau and subsequently by Kant, insofar as it was a defense of morals and the virtuous citizen against the encroachments of science, the arts, and the republic of letters.[5] But he greatly modified that channel. Weber was more radical than Rousseau and Kant in adopting the perspective of political life. He took the standpoint of the politically mature citizen and gave it remarkable formulation in *Science as a Vocation*. According to Weber, this was the perspective of the ancient *politikos*—a prephilosophic, prescientific, and prebiblical understanding of the world of concern to man:

> We live as did the ancients when their world was not yet disenchanted of its gods and demons, only we live in a different sense. As Hellenic man at times sacrificed to Aphrodite and

at other times to Apollo, and, above all, as everybody sacrificed to the gods of his city, so do we still nowadays, only the bearing of man has been disenchanted and denuded of its mystical but inwardly genuine plasticity. Fate, and certainly not "science," holds sway over these gods and their struggles.[6]

Weber's politically mature man "knows" that there is no appeal beyond this world of irreconcilable gods locked in eternal combat. The moral maturity of Hellenic man consisted in affirming a world of antagonists drawn to different gods and serving opposed moral forces. The ancient *politikos* knew that the moral claims he would inevitably offend, the values or gods he would have to rebuff, would be asserted against him by men and women worthy of respect. There would inevitably be heroes devoted to the cause opposed to one's own: Creon would respect Antigone or suffer for it.[7] The mature, serious citizen is capable of letting such realities work upon him with inner concentration and calm.[8] The spectacle of tragic conflict moves him, but it does not bewilder him or reduce him to a confused relativism. Ignoble indifference, based on the false belief that ultimate values do not matter (or that the gods do not exist), is foreign to him: he still fights for his own gods.[9] His perspective or horizon does not acknowledge the possibility of an end to this conflict. It is unthinkable for him that the values could be ranked or that one god could finally set the heavens in order. This perspective informs his code of combat. Having no hope that his most defiant enemies would betray their gods to worship his own, he does not expect them to acknowledge the justice of his cause. But knowing that he cannot destroy their gods or terminate the conflict, their refusal does not drive him to extremes. The antithesis of his perspective (which is inherently an affirmation) is the grandiose claim that "the world is base and stupid, not I."[10] Hence the mature man has no need to see his opponents as degraded or subhuman. He is not compelled by his passions to assassinate their character. If he does so, it is for a calculated purpose, not because he is subject to "undisciplined sympathies and antipathies."[11]

According to Weber, this standpoint precedes science and the triumph of biblical morality. It is anterior to the discovery of political philosophy by Socrates. But the transformation of human affairs that science and Christianity brought about eventually restores us to this original perspective, albeit in a modified form:

Today the routines of everyday life challenge religion. Many old gods ascend from their graves; they are disenchanted and hence take the form of impersonal forces. They strive to gain power over our lives and again they resume their eternal struggle with one another.[12]

Weber's perspective is not identical, then, to the standpoint of the ancients. It stands at the end of a prolonged scientific and religious development. Unlike the standpoint of the *politikos,* the perspective of Weber's politically mature man looks out upon powerful organizations striving for power and embodying the struggle between the gods as a conflict between routine impersonal forces. Statistical science is required to bring the struggle to light, and sober men of business are called for to fight it out in public forums. Weber's delimitation and critique of science thus points in two directions. On the one hand, it anticipates the invasion of the public realm by scholars, scientifically educated specialists, and professional experts. It exhibits science as a practical force with which politicians must contend. On the other hand, the critique is the basis of Weber's claim to have initiated a critical advance *within* science. His rediscovery of the prescientific perspective of "the ancients" is, according to Weber, a scientific discovery pregnant with new projects and imperatives for research. With it "the light of the great cultural problems moves on" into new domains that science must learn to chart and negotiate.[13] This discovery is enucleated in Weber's doctrine of values and their irreconcilable conflict. It requires a new interpretation of social action and of the relations between the diverse "spheres" of human activity. Implied in the perspective of the ancient citizen is a new exegesis of "the total ethical economy of human life." [14] It would be only a slight exaggeration to say that all of the problems that Weber introduced for scholarly inquiry, the new horizon he delineated for political economy, his refinement of the fact/value dichotomy, and his interpretation of the logic of the cultural sciences are implications or deductions from this rediscovery of the standpoint of the Thucydidean *politikos.*[15]

The rediscovery requires science to transcend liberalism. By carrying it through consistently, Weber leads science away from the principles of modern liberal politics, resolving the crisis of liberalism as it affects science by divesting science of its former connections to the liberal cause. In particular, Weber breaks the ties that bound social science to its heritage in modern liberal politics. He cancels all debts to

Kantian liberalism and modern Natural Right: the former because it is irrelevant to an "age of popular passion," the latter because it is bound to illusions about the beneficence of modern progress.[16] The tragic outlook of "the ancients" enables Weber to invest science with a skeptical empiricism that claims not to be shakeable by the realization that scientific technique has made the human future problematic and uncertain as never before. By abandoning liberalism, Weberian science surmounts the discovery that modern scientific progress has become "the great pain-bringer" or that technological humanitarianism is in actuality profoundly inhumane.[17]

Because Weber invested a life-long effort in teaching social science to transcend liberalism, Weberians have justifiably denied that Weber's teaching is merely liberalism in disguise or that his methodological principles are part of an ideological justification of liberal institutions. But we would diminish Weber's stature if we were silent about the indirect ways in which his attempt to divide science from liberal principles constituted a strategy in his defense of the liberal commercial republic. There is substance to the controversy between Weber's proponents and his critics over Weber's liberalism, but the debate would shed more light on the future of liberal democratic regimes if it were conducted with greater attention to the precise character of Weber's innovations or of his departures from the liberal tradition.[18]

In this chapter, I shall argue that Weber mounts a defense of liberal democratic institutions within science by interpreting scientific activity as service to moral forces. This defense is not, properly understood, an ideological or narrowly political one. It is a defense of morality against nihilism. Its practical significance should be accentuated rather than underplayed. The question is not whether Weber's defense would help to secure the liberal commercial republic if it were successful, but *how* it would do so. Not everything that is relevant to the health of liberal democracy is subject to the smear of *Ideologiekritik*. The truly troubling questions are whether the defense is sound or based upon intelligible principles and whether its price is one that can be paid, especially by science.

These problems become sharply visible in the light of Nietzsche's politics. We have shown that Nietzsche expands the scope of "politics" by undermining the authority of the political doctrines that support the modern state and liberal institutions. He undermines the limits within which limited government is necessary and possible. Those are, on Nietzsche's interpretation, chiefly moral limits.[19] The guiding question of this chapter and the next will be whether Weber's critique and delimitation of science raise any firm, principled obstacles against Nietzschean nihilism.

Science as a Vocation is Weber's most eloquent statement on his devotion to the cause of philosophy and science. It is a vigorous rebuttal of Nietzsche's claim that liberal democracy ceases to be worthy of a thinking man's defense when the liberal cause is severed from the cause of philosophy.[20] Weber's principle—that science cannot rank values and that this ranking does not constitute a problem for philosophy—undermines the claims to leadership that modern science had advanced through modern liberal politics with its promise of progress. But Weber's principle is no less forcefully opposed to Nietzschean philosophic leadership. By adopting the perspective of the Thucydidean *politikos* as his standard, Weber insulates science against Nietzsche's leadership. If the horizon of "the ancients" cannot be transcended by science or philosophy, and if no higher authority can be consolidated above that ceiling, then the political leader becomes the only one to bear comprehensive practical responsibilities. He is the only candidate to rank values in practice, to institute law. Weber's principle bestows an importance and dignity upon political leadership that is paralleled only in the ancient cities.[21] A science that adopts Weber's perspective will be too preoccupied with political leadership to entertain Nietzsche's "anxieties and grounds for gloom" about philosophic leaders. And, as I shall show, the moral anxiety that Weber elicits and cultivates can be expected to blunt Nietzsche's subtler appeal to many men of science.

I have commented upon the inadequacies of Weber's attempt in the Freiburg Lecture to unite the liberal cause with the national cause. Without recapitulating the steps by which Weber reformulated his position, I shall concentrate upon the final result of his prolonged encounter with Nietzsche.[22]

Weber's *Science as a Vocation* was frankly confessional. By serving "moral" forces in scientific work, Weber claimed to have found and obeyed the demon who held the fibres of his very life.[23] In this confessional mode, he framed the conflict between morality and nihilism as a struggle over the meaning of one's vocation and pointed the way toward a resolution of this conflict *within* science "as a calling." This way of coming to terms with nihilism has broad significance for Weber's regime as a whole. Science is only a part of the modern division of labor. But the conflict between morality and nihilism within science necessarily illuminates that conflict in every sphere of human activity. As Weber understands liberal democracy, it stands or falls with its division of labor. Science and capitalism are integral to that division of labor.[24] The problem Weber had not solved in the Freiburg Lecture was that while he prized political leadership for asserting a national way of life, liberal democratic institutions seemed to disallow any such assertion.[25] This difficulty of making the liberal commercial republic a coherent regime asserting a common way of life reappears in a new form in his lectures on the vocations. It becomes the problem of forging a working unity among the professions. Politics is one of several callings. As we will see in considering the case of scholarship, the conflict between morality and nihilism takes different forms in the various professions. It is not a single problem but several. The struggle with nihilism is not primarily an "affair of state." Professional politicians cannot assume comprehensive responsibility for the entire moral fabric of a liberal democratic regime. If their work is to be a defense of limited government, they must accept severe constraints in moral matters. Their "service to moral forces," in the first instance, lies in upholding the restraints of limited government. Consequently, the political profession must insist that government is not the primary line of defense against nihilism and that it is intrinsically a very limited mode of defense. In Weber's final argument, the limitations of the political profession come to light by contrast to the moral tasks of science.

Weber forms science by his example. I shall begin my commentary with a portrait of the moral stance that Weber brought to science and held up for emulation.

1. THE MORAL PROFILE OF WEBERIAN SCIENCE: BAD CONSCIENCE FOR A NIETZSCHEAN AGE

The nemesis of Weberian scholarship—the "worst devil" against which it pits its efforts—is "intellectualism."[26] The first way in which science serves moral forces is to prevent the deification or idolization of the intellectual powers. The abasement of man before mere intellect is the bête noire of genuine scholarship. In particular, Weber sets science against those who profit by making intellect a power in society—who accrue wealth, status, and authority through the glorification of the intellect. Weberian scholarship is the bad conscience of an age that looks to the academically educated for leadership and lionizes (as "the

best and the brightest") those who combine the will to truth with will
to power. Weber's moral fervor is directed against opinion leaders who
base their appeal and influence upon claims to education and knowledge. His scholarship is intended as a counterweight to the modern republic of letters—the "literati" and the "intelligentsia."[27] The opportunity to mold character that scholars have in teaching should be used,
according to Weber, to encourage and inculcate the virtues antithetical
to intellectualism and the dominant vices of the literati. For Weber,
"the one thing needful" is matter-of-factness or *Sachlichkeit*.[28] In science, *Sachlichkeit* means above all intellectual probity or *Redlichkeit*.
Those virtues are essential in shaping scholars and professors. Weber
is also concerned to convey them to a wider public of educated professionals. His moralism in matters of method, his strictures about vanity,
his explosive contempt for the literati all reflect one of Weber's great
passions: a hatred of the worship of power in its modern form, worship
of knowledge-power or "brilliance." The Weberian ethic is the antithesis of self-aggrandizing *esprit*.[29] It is profoundly suspicious, therefore, of Cartesian *generosité* and of the Nietzschean conception of
philosophic magnanimity which we have considered earlier. The philosopher as "first cause," whose contingent individuality is the *prin-
cipio* of a new world and a new greatness for man, is the very paragon
of self-aggrandizing animals.[30]

The vulgarization of Nietzsche into the common coin of the intelligentsia was well under way by 1917. Toward the end of the First
World War, the most common form of popular Nietzscheism was
Lebensphilosophie.[31] Weber's friend Heinrich Rickert wrote a critique
of life-philosophy directed at Nietzsche's unwholesome influence.[32]
Science as a Vocation was obviously directed at it as well; one prominent target of Weber's moral indignation is what Thomas Mann called
"the deformation of irrationalism," that is, the vulgarizing of irra-
tionalist philosophy.[33] Weber speaks of "idols whose cult occupies a
broad place on all street corners and all periodicals. These idols are
'personality' and 'personal experience'—for that befits a personality,
conscious of its rank and station."[34] Weber initiated a tradition within
science, a tradition of "serving moral forces" by combating such currents of opinion. This is a protean enterprise because it is dictated by
the course of popular educated opinion. It is "reactive." But while the
vulgate Nietzsche is a thing of fashion, behind the popularization lies
the constant force of Nietzsche's thought. The foundation of Weber's
conscientious opposition is a steady antagonism toward the doctrine of

the self which fortifies (and indeed generates) these varieties of Nietzschean individualism. Weber was not original in prizing scientific training as an antidote to subjectivism and irrationality; the novel result of his prolonged *Auseinandersetzung* with Nietzsche was more, however, than that traditional antidote. Weber found a new mission for science in combating the socially relevant forms of Nietzschean psychagogy.

Following Weber, the "moral" scholar has a new resource as well as a new antagonist. Weber teaches scientists how to turn the tougher, sterner Nietzsche against the Nietzsche adolescents are most likely to adore. To combat the cult of personality and experience, Weber arms science with Nietzschean terms of criticism: "What is hard for modern man, and especially for the younger generation, is to measure up to *workaday* existence. The ubiquitous chase for 'experience' stems from this weakness; for it is weakness not to be able to countenance the stern seriousness of our fateful times." [35] Weber also turned Nietzschean contempt for weakness and disdain for those who lacked *amor fati* against Nietzsche's attempt to join science with philosophy. Neither science nor philosophy can be "the gift of grace of seers and prophets dispensing sacred values and revelations." [36] They must no longer "partake of the contemplation of sages and philosophers." [37] This too becomes an imperative of *amor fati*. It is "the inescapable condition of our historical situation. We cannot evade it as long as we remain true to ourselves." [38] Weber dismisses Nietzsche's meditation on future philosophic leaders and his portrait of Zarathustra—again, as signs of weakness—with a blunt reply: "the prophet for whom so many of our younger generation yearn simply does not exist." [39] Tarrying for new philosophers and prophets is worse than mere time-serving. The Nietzschean promise of a new civilization beyond liberal commerce and the modern state is merely fancified escapism. [40] These moral assertions are not sufficiently secured by the virtues of *Sachlichkeit* and *Redlichkeit*. They point beyond such minimal virtues toward a more predatory moralism that will hunt down Nietzschean individualism "on all street corners and in all periodicals." [41]

The "moral" ideal by which Weber measures scholars in *Science as a Vocation* thus has an aggressive, even intrepid dimension. Although Weber's mirror for scholars recalls certain traits of the ascetic ideal discussed in Nietzsche's *Genealogy,* it shows something else that is absent from Nietzsche's portrait: a combative and spirited science endowed with enough noble strength to affirm itself and attack its enemies. Weber attempts to fuse scholarly probity to a passionate animus against Nietzschean immoralism. He was reported to have made the following remark in a conversation on one of those "street corners":

> The probity of a scholar today, and above all of a philosopher today, can be measured by how he stands toward Nietzsche and Marx. Whoever does not admit that he could not conduct the most weighty part of his own work without the work these two have done, swindles himself and others. Intellectually, the world in which we ourselves exist is to an exceptional degree a world formed by Marx and Nietzsche." [42]

In his lectures on the vocations, Weber went beyond such acknowledgments. His moral stance anticipated a "world of the intellect" dominated for the foreseeable future by Nietzsche and Marx. That stance was meant to fortify scholars against the primary vices of such a "world" and to motivate scholars as the bad conscience for a Nietzschean age.

The moral imperative of the Weberian ethic is directed toward participation within the rationalized institutions of the modern division of labor. Weber opposes the tendency that both Marx and Nietzsche promoted in the liberal commercial republic: the tendency toward polarization, into a world of "specialists without spirit or vision" on the one hand and movements for "liberation," or countercultures, on the other. [43] To combat that polarization, Weber sought to elicit a commitment that would reach far beyond the mere performance of the duties of a professional position. Weberian leadership stands for devotion to a problem and task, to an activity as one's cause. Against the Marxian doctrine of alienation, and against Nietzsche's teaching on decadence, Weber counterposes the maxim "nothing is worthy of man as man unless he can pursue it with passionate devotion." [44] The professions are testing grounds for that devotion. This implies a new moral vigilance. The older liberal tendency had been not to look deeply into the soul, to rest content with outward conformity to the standards of a profession. Weber does not, to be sure, mount a new witch hunt or attempt to ferret out Nietzscheans in the academic profession. Instead, his answer to alienation is mastery of the division of labor through professional work. Weber's intention is to compel men to prove their nobility and greatness, above all to themselves, by the character of their performance *within* the "iron cage." [45] The task for psychagogy within science that is adumbrated by *Science as a Vocation* is the moral service of turning demonic individualism around—particularly when it seeks to exploit a professional niche for its own "sovereign" purposes.

Before we examine Weber's attempt in *Science as a Vocation* to counter Nietzsche's psychagogy, let us step back to consider its bearing upon our larger theme of political leadership and nihilism.

2. LIMITED GOVERNMENT, LIMITLESS MEN

Liberal democracy draws most of its vitality and dynamism from science, commerce, and the arts. Its productivity and power are generated, in the main, by activities that are "private" rather than "public" according to the liberal scheme. In this respect the "public" is dependent. But the delimited sphere of government or politics is also dependent (upon activities above and below it) in a more subtle respect. In defining the public sphere, liberal democracy excludes certain activities that were previously regarded as highly political. It delegates to private initiative, or to institutions distinctly set apart from government, the tasks of forming character, of education, moral suasion and exhortation, of evoking politically significant sentiments such as patriotism, and of tempering politically relevant passions such as ambition. Therefore moral limits were traditionally upheld in the liberal order by the family, the churches, "society" in the old and mannerly sense, voluntary associations, intellectual clubs, universities and professional schools, sects, cults, and fraternities of various kinds. These bodies inculcated moral and religious norms and helped to attach citizens to moral limits. Government was categorically prevented from asserting those norms directly by political means.[46] These delegated tasks have an inherent nobility. If they are removed from "politics," the rank and stature of politics is necessarily diminished. The original intention of limited government was to keep politics down and circumscribed. When the liberal democratic solution worked, as it did for several centuries in the United States, it reinforced this original intention.[47] It also kept the harsher side of politics, the use of force and fraud, out of many domains of human activity. While that exclusion was always incomplete, it was remarkably successful in creating bourgeois tranquility—or, as one could also say, dullness and mediocrity.[48] This tranquility was what the humane ideal required, as Montaigne's formulation clearly indicated.[49] And to the extent that Americans can still discern themselves in Tocqueville's portrait, they can appreciate how much of what is best in themselves they owe to this solution.[50]

What we have witnessed since Tocqueville wrote—and with increasing intensity in the last few decades—is the erosion, and perhaps the collapse, of this solution. Opinion leadership in the United States no longer accepts the separation of private from public activities that was originally thought essential to the success of limited government. On the contrary, "leading opinion" is now a force for the redefinition of the relation between private and public. Symptomatic of this new situation is the redefinition of the public powers of the nominally private media and the entry of public broadcasting into the fertile domain of propaganda and "political education."[51] In addition to the liberal forms of opinion leadership favored by Wilson, new "styles" of opinion leadership have emerged that are self-consciously antagonistic to the "bourgeois way of life." In this respect, Americans can join Weber in saying that "the world in which we exist is to an exceptional degree a world formed by Marx and Nietzsche," especially as that world is a media world shaped by intellectually "leading opinion."[52] The Nietzschean strain in the new opinion leadership is discernible in the scope given to the self-assertive and self-expressive individualism earlier discussed.[53] It elevates the full unfolding of individuality above the requirements of consent and majority rule—although rarely with candor, since those requirements cannot be frontally attacked *yet*. In the professional schools and universities, this Nietzschean style in opinion leadership is evident in a new politics that accepts the formal procedures of liberal democratic institutions in order to undermine the authority of traditional moral limits, and, it is hoped, in the fullness of time, to raise up a new civilization on the ruins of bourgeois society. *Crescit interea Roma Alba ruinis.*[54]

Nietzsche anticipated that the democratization and equalization of social conditions could become a breeding ground for tyrants, particularly tyrants of a new, more radical and spiritual kind.[55] He foresaw the emergence of actors like Cagliostro and geniuses of many media, like Richard Wagner, who would take up the tasks of liberating the mind from bourgeois moral limits, raising consciousness above the liberal horizon and weaning citizens away from the forms necessary for democratic self-government. Nietzsche alerts such opinion leaders to the potential power lying untapped in nongovernmental institutions. By politicizing the family, the churches, and voluntary associations, creative and destructive power can be released. These nongovernmental institutions can help to undermine the limits upon which liberal democratic government depends and form the nucleus of a new order beyond liberal limits.[56]

What the probing of the former boundaries between political and private action means in practice may be one of two things. Either the public sphere may be left to itself, while a profession or church is brought to foster the arts of self-assertion and the free unfolding of individuality, or formerly apolitical associations may become embroiled with the instrumentalities of politics. Although American churches do not yet have their own private armies, some have become sufficiently involved in military struggles abroad to make Machiavelli's analyses of the bizarre interpenetration of religion and politics a useful primer on the activities of American divines.[57] The Sierra Club, once the preserve of sedate recreationists, has become a power-conscious lobby modeling itself upon mass movements. This transformation of private associations is so reminiscent of Tocqueville's beguiling account of the traditional American remedies against individualism that one is hesitant to call it pernicious. But one consequence of the shift has been that private associations have in many cases lost their former patina of *noblesse*. They share avidly in politics; in the process they surrender some of their former functions and lose what was previously a great strength: the quiet power to establish limits, through acts of reverence, love, and repentance. Because questions of partisan morale and political solidarity occupy their energies, they cannot give wholehearted attention to violations of moral limits that would at one time have galvanized them. Such associations must now make provision for ambition and spiritedness on a continuous basis, because they need a steady supply for political combat. Once they have crossed the line into politics, the development of new moral habits appropriate to their struggle, the definition of a politically effective identity, the generation of a politically powerful membership, and the invention of techniques for collective self-assertion become vital issues for such organizations.[58] However one judges the political achievements that this new participation has made possible, in any extended survey one's evaluations are almost certain to cancel each other out. If one favors the transformation of the Sierra Club, the issue in point may be raised by noting that a similar transformation leads to the Moral Majority. The influence of private associations upon character and their capacity to reinforce moral limits are bound to change with this new relation to the means of force and fraud. It is inevitable that adversaries will be defined politically and that moral indignation will take a political bent: opposed opinion leaders, hostile congressional staffs, and uncooperative government agencies become the proximate moral evil. The primordial laws of partisan conflict come into play: political friends become immune from serious moral critique.[59] This declension should be familiar to every reader of Thucydides' description of the revolution on Corcyra.[60]

Under the classical liberal delimitation of government, nihilism and radical individualism were steadily and effectively opposed in the daily life of associations. When the internal transformation of private associations that has been sketched erodes this liberal delimitation, nihilism cannot be directly challenged in them without jeopardizing political commitments or endangering electoral and legislative prospects. Through such a transformation, liberal democracy loses its hidden lines of defense against nihilism, if only because they cease to be hidden. Nietzsche saw the beginning of a new development when the morning paper replaced the Bible at the breakfast table. Today, we open the morning paper and read that the Bible is a matter of political controversy, with spirited opinion leaders raising funds for either side with computerized mailing techniques. If a family, a university, or a church were to take a serious stand in upholding moral limits it thought inviolable, our first knowledge of it would probably come in reports of a legal case, brought by some single-issue constituency offended by the attempt. These constituencies are so opposed that if one of them is not offended by a given moral initiative, another surely will be. Or the initiative will provide a handy opportunity to strengthen the flagging interest of the membership, embarrass a hostile congressman, or unite a bickering staff against a common enemy. Unless one is willing to go to court, then one will take no moral initiative.[61]

It is my suggestion that Weber's significance for the future of American politics lies in his attempt to defend limited government and liberal democratic institutions within a setting comparable to this new context of unlimited politics. In this context, the limits of the traditional liberal solution are no longer respected in the normal course of associational life.[62] Limited government depended heavily upon nongovernmental institutions to form limited men and women. Weber's point of departure was shaped by his understanding of Nietzsche and the crisis of liberalism in Germany; he could not assume that liberal democracy in the Weimar Republic would be secured against nihilism by the steady action of private associations. Weber set himself the task of restoring the line that circumscribes the political sphere in the liberal democratic order. In order to accomplish this, in the new context of Nietzschean opinion leadership, it was necessary to find a way to make nonpolitical associations once again the first line of defense against nihilism, for limited government precludes the use of governmental means to promote a morality or to attack nihilism.[63]

3. SELF-DELIMITATION IN THE PROFESSION OF SCIENCE

My commentary on *Science as a Vocation* will concentrate upon Weber's defense of the autonomy of science. Autonomy means that in the most important matters, science delimits itself through the self-delimitation of scholars. It also means that science is under no necessity to prepare the way for the solution to the problem of the rank order of values. Since the ranking of values, or the solution of that problem, was Nietzsche's response to nihilism, the autonomy of science means that science does not need philosophic leadership to come to terms with nihilism. In delimiting himself, the scholar is ranking values, affirming values, and combating nihilism. Weber's principle that the ultimate values cannot be ranked by philosophy or science is a declaration of independence from philosophy; it proclaims that Weber's inquiry into the moral phenomena is not a propaedeutic for philosophic leadership. The purpose of my analysis will be to identify the reasoning on which the putative autonomy of science rests. Why is such autonomy a good thing? What makes it possible and necessary? Having identified Weber's answers to these questions, I shall proceed in later sections to assess whether those answers establish any firm principles of resistance against Nietzschean nihilism.[64]

In describing both the political calling and the profession of science, Weber adopts the same unwavering and methodical approach. He begins with an account of the external conditions that circumscribe each calling as a routine occupation. This account is comparative in both instances, and it is designed to lay bare the major developmental tendencies determining the routine or average conditions under which the profession is practiced throughout the modern West.[65] Weber goes on to describe the internal premiums and psychological demands of each profession, sketching the type of man who is suited to work of this character or under these conditions.[66] His inquiry then broadens to establish the ethical locus of each calling within the total ethical economy of human life, insofar as it is possible to do so while respecting the limits of science.[67] Both lectures conclude by holding up a standard derived from the earlier analysis; by this standard, Weber measures his audience. His final word, in each lecture, is what the man who has the calling in question will say to himself and others: if he is a scientist, "find and obey your demon!"— if he is a politician, "In spite of all!"[68]

Science as a Vocation consists of a series of inquiries organized under (or gathered around) a sequence of questions. Weber establishes this pattern with the first few sentences: the lecture begins with the question "What are the conditions of science as a vocation in the material sense of the term?" After six pages he terminates this inquiry with the remark "This much I deem necessary to say about the external conditions of the academic man's vocation."[69] The pattern is not always made so explicit; the guiding question is at times provided at the conclusion of an inquiry. Elsewhere, a question is opened, but the endpoint of the inquiry is not so clear.[70] One can also discern a distinction between the questions: some are clearly of a different order of rank. The lecture is governed by two cardinal questions and ten thematic questions:

1. What are the conditions of science as a vocation in the material sense of the term? What are the prospects of a graduate student who is resolved to dedicate himself professionally to science in university life?

Cardinal question A. What does science mean to its devoted disciples?

2. What does the specialist hope to accomplish by his works, which are bound to be superseded?

3. What is the practical meaning of the progress generated by science and scientific technology?

4. Does this progress have any meanings that go beyond the purely practical and technical?

Cardinal question B. What is the vocation of science within the total life of humanity? What is the value of science?

5. What is the meaning of science after all these former illusions have been dispelled?

6. Is there such a thing as science free from presuppositions?

7. Has the contribution of science no meaning at all for a man who does not care to know facts as such and to whom only the practical viewpoint matters?

8. What then does science actually and positively contribute to practical and personal life?

9. Which of the warring gods should we serve? Or should we perhaps serve an entirely different god, and who is he?

10. Which stand does one take toward the factual existence of "theology: and its claim to be a "science"?

Weber begins by comparing the conditions of academic work in Germany and America. The impression he creates by this first discussion is that he will uphold the limits of his professional expertise as a political economist; that he will rigidly assert the rules of academic instruction throughout his talk; and that the necessary first step of any rational orientation toward science is to know the typical circumstances under which the modern scholar must work. Weber deliberately antagonized his audience by adopting this approach.[71] For them it was by no means obvious that science, properly understood, had a place as a profession in the modern division of labor. Their doubts that thought could be an occupation or profession without violating its intrinsic requirements were intensified by Nietzsche and Marx. Modern, vocationally ordered civilization, according to these doubts, creates no space for individuals who are inwardly called to science as a spiritual calling: the logic of specialization is to select those who have no such intractable, passionate need and to eliminate those who do. To articulate the true meaning of science or philosophy, along the paths laid out by Nietzsche and Marx, would be to mount a fundamental critique and indictment of modernity: it would yield "critical theory."[72] Such a critique would fortify the belief that the world of modern occupational work, including scientific work, is base and stupid.[73] Weber's initial inquiry intensifies these doubts by forcing his listeners to face the rather inauspicious conditions in which the modern scholar must make his way. Weber postpones the topics his audience expected in order to bring their doubts to the forefront. These doubts are worth mentioning because they raise the question of the autonomy and rank of science. Weber implicitly denies that there is a standard of thought external to science by which the profession of science can be judged and found wanting. The denial is implied in his resolute adherence to the method of political economy. Later, Weber will provide more explicit arguments to satisfy the demand for an explanation which his own denial provokes.

Weber's first inquiry sets out his credentials, dramatizes his viewpoint or attitude, and sketches an example of his craft as a professor of political economy. It demonstrates how a specialist transposes a topic into the terms appropriate for treatment within his field of competence.[74] It makes one painfully aware that political economy, following its regular method, is inadequate to the urgent and important questions posed by this dubious audience.[75] Weber prefers to let these questions emerge from the facts, as questions that a particular graduate student must answer. He does not claim to know whether science, constituted as he describes it, has a place for individuals who feel compelled by a higher or inward calling to practice science. He acknowledges that it is normal for academic routine to eliminate or ruin those who have a calling for thought:

> [A]cademic life is a mad hazard. If the young scholar asks for my advice with regard to habilitation, the responsibility for encouraging him can hardly be borne. If he is a Jew, of course one says *lasciate ogni speranza*. But one must ask every other man: Do you in all conscience believe that you can stand seeing mediocrity after mediocrity, year after year, climb beyond you, without becoming embittered and without coming to grief? Naturally, one always receives the answer, "Of course, I live only for my 'calling.'" Yet I have found that only a few men could endure this situation without coming to grief.[76]

The existing order in science imposes a criterion, but it is palpably mediocre. Only a few individuals of exceptional character can surmount the severe testing of the occupational setting. Not only do novices underestimate the force of established orders, they also misjudge their own commitments. To comprehend science as a calling one must have a correct assessment of the external conditions and of one's own ultimate tenacity. Young scholars are thus challenged by the doubt Weber raises about themselves to look upon science as a proving ground. Weber effaces himself in order to bring the student before this problem.

After this lead inquiry, the main body of Weber's talk is divided into two parts. The first is devoted to the cardinal question "What does science mean to its devoted disciples?" Weber discusses the calling *for* science in three steps. He begins with the inward calling for specialized research; then he treats the practical results of modern science and thereby adumbrates a practical motive for pursuing science; finally, he explores the connection between science and cultural progress, thus exhibiting a cultural or nontechnical reason for devoting one's life to science. These three inquiries show that science makes strenuous demands upon its devotees; it imposes a morality upon them, a morality implied in the criteria that define perfect or good work. The contrast that Weber brings out is between this morality and the passionate character of science. The standards of science are not self-evidently meaningful, yet those who devote themselves to science give their all to meet its perfectionist standard. To attain perspective on the frenzy or psychic compulsion that drives the scholar, Weber digresses into an account of the disenchantment of the world by science. The passion for science might be explicable to some degree by reference to the practical and cultural meanings of science. Despite the fact that every effort, however perfect, is bound to be superseded, the practical mastery of the world that results for man may be sufficient reward for some.[77] For others, the spectacle of the human spirit disporting itself in endless works of culture may justify a life devoted to specialized science.[78] But Weber does not believe that these motives explain the frenzy or mania of the scientific man; his description of that enigmatic, indeed demonic, drive that dominates the authentic scientific man remains a riddle throughout these inquiries. Weber places the inspired and passionate scholar at the very center of modern specialized science, as its norm.

> [W]hoever lacks the capacity to put on blinders, so to speak, and to come up to the idea that the fate of his soul depends upon whether or not he makes the correct conjecture at this passage of this manuscript may as well stay from science. He will never have what one may call the "personal experience" of science. Without this strange intoxication, ridiculed by every outsider; without this passion, this "thousands of years must pass before you enter into life and thousands more wait in silence"— according to whether or not you succeed in making this conjecture; without this, you have *no* calling for science and you should do something else. For nothing is worthy of man as man unless he can pursue it with passionate devotion.[79]

Weber is content that those who lack this mysterious drive should never come near science. This is an attribute of contingent beings, a value or "god" that they embody. It is what sets them apart, not by their doing or choice but as a fatality; it is, *in nuce,* their "individuality."[80]

The difficulty in these first inquiries (questions 2–4) seems to be this: if the scholar affirms technical progress and the endless, inexhaustible spectacle of the human spirit disporting itself in cultural accomplishments, he is merely affirming himself and his own passions. Weber does not deny that possibility: the scholar may be a demonic individualist who views these processes as the condition for the exercise of his natural powers, regardless of the consequences for mankind. He may be "beyond good and evil" or merely "before it," like a "big child," but one who does not need any illusions about the happy results for the rest of the world.[81] He may enter science because his will to power takes the form of the will to truth and accepts the process of science (as a motion in the world) as his natural milieu.[82] What brings this unsettling possibility to the surface in *Science as a Vocation*—if we approach it as a speech and hear it as its audience was bound to hear it—is the pain and destruction caused by modern scientific weaponry in the Great War. The capacity for butchery on a world scale, which results from the headlong progress of science, is the specter that haunts *Science as a Vocation*. Weber's studied effort to force it into the background by not treating it explicitly may be taken as an index of the intensity of the feelings this slaughter provoked, feelings that threatened to make any reasonable discussion of science impossible.[83] If the scholar is a berserker of the intellect, who embraces the modern conquest of nature and the unfolding of man's cultural works as the condition for his continued willing, then he must come to terms with the moral resistance of the rest of mankind and with any residues of "our moral nature" that remain in him; he must come to terms with what others may do when faced with a science that is manifestly "the great pain-bringer" to mankind.[84] Weber had no reason to expect that anyone in his audience would face this prospect "with inner concentration and calm."[85] It was precisely what filled them with urgent and insistent questions about science. By deferring them in order to dwell on the peculiar nature of the scholarly animal, Weber adds a new, reflexive twist to those questions. In his first inquiry, he had raised doubts about the strength and staying power of his hearers' commitments to a calling in science. They are now prompted to reflect on the source of that strength and staying power, to consider it as an irrational and demonic thing, and to wonder what it means to be possessed by such an obsession. Science is a natural phenomenon, inseparable from the contingent individuality, the peculiar idiosyncrasy, of a certain type of being. For both those who are thrown into the world with this passion and those who are not, the question is what stand does one take toward it, how does one live with it? The problem of science is thus one instance of the general difficulty of Weberian politics: the foundation of a common order can be created only by a self-imposed constraint in which the passions are ranked and in which the self chooses its individuality by limiting itself. From that ranking alone can a polity derive the authority to constrain the claims of individuality. Thus the general issue of how the division of labor constrains individuality arises within science. Science can claim autonomy within the liberal democratic regime only if it can curb its berserking passions by its own effort. This implies that science must make provision for scholars whose dominant passion cannot be described by Weber's portrait in these early inquiries. It must make ample provision for men like Weber whose dominant passion is hatred of intellectualism, or men who enter science because they want to dominate the berserkers of the intellect. The autonomy of science implies a moral government within science, over the passions with which Weber begins *Science as a Vocation*.[86]

Weber has elucidated the calling for science as a possible object of ultimate commitment. With the aid of Weber's inquiries, the student is to clarify for himself whether he has the calling for science and what stand he is to take toward those who make science their work. Weber frames this issue by pointing the way toward a criterion by which the individual may judge. But this is not primarily a route to be traced in thought: his inquiries pose a series of challenges or tests that must be surmounted if one is to win through to an autonomous criterion. We have seen how he poses the difficulty of affirming an academic vocation as one's personal fate, as the first of these tests. The test is made severe by Weber's insistence that it must be comprehensive: the progressive rationalization of science as an enterprise is what must be affirmed.[87] The first thus leads to the second, the trial of affirming or rejecting science as a whole, from an ultimate standpoint toward life as a whole. Weber equates this with the decision to reject or affirm the disenchantment of the world by science.[88] The remainder of *Science as a Vocation* is a quest for a criterion by which to make this judgment. The quest is conducted in two major stages. In the first (questions 5–8) Weber presents what purports to be an objectively valid doctrine of science, his *Wissenschaftslehre* in summary. In the second (questions 9 and 10) Weber takes a stand, asserting his own criterion and ultimate commitment. In this last part, Weber's path ceases to be authorized by science and becomes a personal quest, hence a matter of faith.[89]

The scientifically authorized quest is conducted in four stages. Weber surveys the previous answers to the question of the meaning and value of science, establishing the superiority of present to past approaches (question 5). Having disposed of the earlier quest for meaning in ancient and modern science, Weber considers the presuppositions of the various disciplines of scholarship (question 6). He devotes an inquiry to the education of the practical man, for whom nothing matters but action and for whom knowledge of fact is either irrelevant or relevant only within a context of practice (question 7). Finally, he reaches the outer limit of the scientifically authorized quest for meaning by showing how scientific clarity can serve moral forces and a sense of responsibility.[90]

Weber begins his quest with a pageant of defeated heroes in the pursuit of truth. His parade of outmoded scientific fashions displays and discredits the forgotten hopes of four major traditions: classical political philosophy (Plato and Socrates); Renaissance science and natural philosophy (Da Vinci and Bacon); anti-Aristotelian Christian science (Swammerdam); and the Enlightenment tradition of utilitarian progress.[91] In these traditions, science as a whole was unified by a common horizon. Despite the differentiation into fields, all scholars shared a common illusion about their work and its meaning in the total life of humanity. Because the truth (about Being, Nature, God's works, or the conditions for human progress) was "the one thing needful," science, as the way to this truth, was valuable.[92] According to Weber, science was therefore always instrumental; he does not consider the possibility that science or philosophy was a way of life constituting an end in itself. Rather it was an activity employing certain distinctive means, the concept and the experiment, toward extraneous purposes. (Only by this interpretation can he arrive at his bizarre view of Plato's *Republic*, according to which Socrates knew no ascent beyond the cave of politics to higher concerns: he was merely "Hellenic man, whose thinking was political throughout.")[93] Weber dismisses these traditions because they do not bear any necessary relation to modern science and the civilization it generates. The question is what contemporary science thinks of itself, for it is this unique science, and its vocation within the total life of humanity, that must be affirmed or negated. The autonomy (or the dependence) of modern science, so long as it remains "true to itself," must rest upon a new basis.[94] The classical argument for the autonomy of science had rested upon the autonomy of the intelligibles, the highest objects of knowledge, but these had also served to limit science, for reasons we have adumbrated in treating Nietzsche's attack on Platonic Error.[95] Nietzsche's argument for the dependence of science rests upon the comprehensive responsibility and creativity of the philosopher. Science cannot be independent, because there are no intelligibles beyond the becoming, the endless creation and destruction, of the world as will to power. The philosopher's affirmation is superior to the highest theory, because it is a ranking of values consonant with an eternally recurring world.[96] Weber rejects Plato but continues to seek a basis for the autonomy of science against Nietzsche.

What the new basis might be seems to be revealed in the fact that science can survive the collapse of these former illusions. The new foundation of scientific autonomy would take account of what is permanent, the distinctive means of scientific work: science would have to generate a critique of itself that could comprehend all the means of scientific work. But it would also have to account for the experience of disillusionment, as Weber does. Weber's survey adumbrates a historicist explanation of disillusionment. In his survey it is evident that scholarly thought, in each period of the history of science, was determined by the prevailing or ascending ideals of the age. Socrates reflects the ascendancy of Hellenic civic idealism, Bacon the artistic aspiration of the Renaissance, Swammerdam the religious quest of the Reformation, and so forth.[97] The sequence culminates in the uniqueness of the present age. "We live in a godless and prophetless time" but also a time in which these former philosophical and political ideals no longer move science.[98] An imperative of intellectual honesty and authenticity seems to demand not only that we recognize what is unique in our historical predicament but that we affirm it as our own:

> Science today is a "vocation" organized in special disciplines in the service of self-clarification and knowledge of interrelated facts. It is not the gift of grace of seers and prophets dispensing sacred values and revelations, nor does it partake of the contemplation of sages and philosophers about the meaning of the universe. This, to be sure, is the inescapable condition of our historical situation. We cannot evade it so long as we remain true to ourselves.[99]

Weber seems to think that his science inherits the great tradition that began with Socrates' assertion that an unexamined life was not human. The highest task of Weberian science is self-clarification. Only in Weber's time does science emerge into a clearing from which the enterprise of science as a whole is fully perspicuous. But Weber's historicism is not theoretical: the uniqueness of the predicament is practical and moral. Today, according to Weber's claim, we are compelled to make a practical choice in full view of what the scientific enterprise entails. Weberian scholarship is unprecedentedly aware that science is deeply implicated in the generation of creative and destructive power. Its potential moral superiority as fully contemporary science lies in the unique difficulty of measuring up to the dreadful consequences of science without the excuses or hopes that had clouded all prior philosophy and science, including Nietzsche's.[100] But this is only potential: the task of conducting science and of affirming it in this new clarity is practical.

To comprehend what this task of practical historicism entails, it may be useful to recall our earlier formulations.[101] The self-delimitation of science is an instance of the more general problem of how the modern self can determine itself. What authenticity (holding true to one's individuality, or becoming what one is) would require is not primarily a matter of doctrine or right belief. In the case of science, self-determination would entail affirming the full means of science and the articulation of science as an enterprise in the world with a specialized division of labor. More generally, this instantiates the requirement that the self affirm the conditions of its own autonomous activity, hence its own necessities.[102] Weber understands this activity, however, as historical: it is intelligible through a history in which the sovereign, self-legislating individual appropriates his own world. Science must affirm its "history" so construed. The final step in which scientific individuality appropriates its own world is the confrontation Weber frames in *Science as a Vocation,* a confrontation in which the individual must acknowledge the transience of the former ideals of science and prepare to draw new ones from his own breast. The practical historicist shares with theoretical historicism the awareness that ideals are mortal and contingent. What sets him apart is the turn away from theory. Seen from the practical standpoint, the dignity of science and its greatness, in this unique situation, depends on a practical resolution. Science is to assume responsibility for itself for the first time: full clarity about its own character, its relation to ideals and moralities, and hence its responsibility was not heretofore accessible to science.[103]

This precarious dignity is only visible in a history fully attuned to the pathos of our difficulty in affirming science today and in the future. Such a history must measure up to the fact that previous science and philosophy were not aware of the morally problematic character of their own initiatives. Only a historian attuned to the full practical implications of the fact that science has been a nihilistic force could make the moral predicament of contemporary science visible and thus pose to science the choice of responsibility for the ultimate meaning of its own conduct.[104] No previous science was completely autonomous in clarifying its own predicament: scholars were dependent upon the ideals of their time and were unaware of the nihilistic impact that science would have upon their ideals. No doubt some philosophers were aware, as Swammerdam was not, that science was a "specifically irreligious force."[105] But apparently no one grasped that it was potentially an immoral force as well.[106] With such arguments, Weber prepares science to take a new pride in its unprecedented moral seriousness, a pride enhanced by the spectacle of the moral irrationality of science. Weberian science disdains liberal inanities about peace and prosperity; it teaches that we are chained to progress as a fatality. We are enmeshed in a world brought into being by science; we all face the moral dilemmas of that world on the same terms. Science no longer overlooks the cruelty and the capacity to inflict suffering unleashed by its own remorseless advance.[107]

If these arguments could be sustained, the case for scientific autonomy would be formidable indeed. Intellectual probity would unite with a moral pathos of responsibility to oppose Nietzsche's philosophic leadership. To affirm itself, science would be obliged to take responsibility for its potential moral nihilism and curb that potential in the name of autonomy. Science would be divested of its debts to the liberal politics of progress and divorced from liberal ideology. Its connection to the original cause of modern philosophy would be of no significance. But having broken the connections between the liberal cause and the cause of science at the level of theory, Weber can nevertheless assert that the defense of liberal democratic institutions is a cause worthy of man as man. At the level of practice, there can be no doubt that a professional science resolved to take responsibility for itself along the lines we have sketched could do so energetically within the framework of the liberal commercial republic.[108] But the case Weber constructs depends on very dubious assertions about the history of science. I shall consider next the most crucial example in Weber's thumbnail history of science.

4. THE BACONIAN ROOTS OF WEBERIAN SCIENCE

Weber's sole statement on Bacon is

> to raise the experiment to a principle of research was the achievement of the Renaissance. They were the great innovators in *art,* who were the pioneers of experiment. Leonardo and his like and, above all, the sixteenth-century experimenters in music with their experimental pianos were characteristic. From these circles the experiment entered science, especially through Galileo, and it entered theory through Bacon. . . . What did science mean to these men who stood at the threshold of modern times? . . . science meant the way to *true* art, and that meant for them the path to true *nature*.[109]

This interpretation buttresses the wider claim that Weber is advancing in this section of *Science as a Vocation*: the understanding of nature which informed Baconian experimental natural philosophy is now irrelevant to modern science; the sciences have abandoned Bacon's understanding of art or *techne* as the key to nature's ways.[110] In contrast to the low expectations of science today, "during the period of the rise of the exact sciences one expected a great deal more."[111] Conspicuously absent from Weber's list of expectations are the hopes Bacon fostered through his writings on the promise of experimental science; Weber forgets that Bacon was "labouring to lay the foundation, not of any sect or doctrine, but of human utility and power."[112] Instead, the hopes featured by Weber are emphatically sectarian and doctrinal: they are religious and theological hopes.[113] Weber's assertion about what the modern scientific project meant "to these men who stood at the threshhold of modern times" is also designed to illustrate a more general truth. This is a truth about all action, but it holds with special force for the modern project for the relief of man's estate, the intention to remold political life through the politics of progress based upon scientific mastery of nature. It is a truth above all about political action.

Weber's account of Bacon illustrates the discrepancy between the original promises that moved men and the paradoxical, unforeseen, and unintended consequences of their activity. The truth that the result contradicts the initial purpose is exemplified in the history of science when we see how modern science renders quixotic the idea that science could bring man closer to true art and thereby to true nature. Bacon apparently failed to see that science is an enterprise in the world: a political economist like Weber can understand it as an integral part of a political economic system, whereas Bacon could not. Theorists like Bacon were blind to political economy and could not anticipate that the experimental enterprise would prove to be quite independent of the fanciful ends Bacon associated with experiment. On Weber's reading, art as the Baconian way to nature is the way to ridicule.

There is a moral to this story of unanticipated disillusionment. It is an example of the potential nihilistic consequence of modern experimental science. It indicates how that progressive enterprise destroys ideals or casts them into the dustbin of history. Weber strongly implies that Galileo and Bacon failed to perceive this nihilistic potential and therefore failed to take responsibility for the impact of science upon moral conduct and moral education, upon culture, or upon dedication to values and ideals in general. For Bacon and Galileo that responsibility was clouded because (like the piano-mongers) they were intoxicated with the promise of a well-tempered clavier.[114] The real burden of Weber's statement on Bacon is this implied accusation that early modern science was not really aware of the ultimate meaning of scientific progress. *Science as a Vocation* is Weber's attempt to put the individual scientist on the spot, forcing him to take responsibility for the ultimate consequences of his own actions insofar as he contributes to the distinctively modern, progressive scientific enterprise.[115] According to Weber, scientists did not confront such responsibilities in the past because they were distracted by various illusions or ideals. The Baconian chimera was one. Apparently what these former illusions denied to the scientist was that distinctive moral sobriety which Weber holds out for science today as the wellspring of its great dignity in the total ethical economy of human life. Only now does the full weight of responsibility fall upon the individual. Only now is it inescapably clear that each must find and obey the demon who holds the fibres of his very life.[116] Science can become nobly, even tragically aware of its obligations, and assume matter-of-fact responsibility for the routine scientific enterprise, precisely "now after all these former illusions, the 'way to true being,' the 'way to true art,' the 'way to true nature,' the 'way to true God,' the 'way to true happiness,' have been dispelled." [117]

But this morally high-toned historicism is won at a price. Both the moral and the story are jeopardized by the facts which Weber places before our eyes. The difficulty for Weber is to explain why the science that he describes throughout *Science as a Vocation* stands in a paradoxical and problematic relation to the Baconian project. No such paradox comes to light when we compare Weber's description with the Baconian project as it was understood by Kant, for example. [118] Nor is it evident when compared to Kuno Fischer's *Bacon,* one of the standard accounts of Weber's day. [119] The paradox is not apparent when one reads the maxims for which Bacon was most famous and with which his name was universally linked for centuries. One must recall certain elementary facts. In his writings on science, Bacon advocated the transformation of science into a specialized experimental enterprise such as Weber describes. He propounded the elaborate division of labor on which Weber dwells in the opening part of *Science as a Vocation* and attempted to persuade enlightened rulers to promote such scientific specialization. [120] The tasks Weber assigns to biology and physics are the Baconian tasks. [121] The turn away from cosmology, metaphysics, and theology, which Weber insists upon in *Science as a Vocation* (the turn away from the *vita contemplativa* toward critique and experiment), was persuasively urged by Bacon—a contribution for which Kant paid him eloquent tribute in his preface to *The Critique of Pure Reason.* [122] Weber's conception of empirical knowledge as the inversion of means/ends propositions is Baconian. [123] When Weber describes the vast project of transforming the world through science, he adopts unmistakably Baconian terms: "One need no longer have recourse to magical means in order to master or implore the spirits, as did the savage, for whom such mysterious powers existed. Technical means and calculations perform the service. That is above all what intellectualization means." [124] Weber's definition of science is straight from Bacon: it is "knowledge of the techniques by means of which one masters life, both external things and the action of men, through reckoning." [125] Science is not contemplative; its aim is "general knowledge of the conditions of life." [126] Its principle is that "there are no mysterious, unmeasurable powers, but that on the contrary one can master all things—in principle—through reckoning." [127] In the Weberian definition, science is necessarily interchangeable with "the technique of mastering life which rests upon science," because the science that

Weber has in view embodies the Baconian project for the mastery of nature by method and technique.[128]

That Weber incorporates Bacon's project in this respect should not surprise anyone. Hans Gerth and C. Wright Mills were referring to politics when they observed of Weber, "That knowledge is somehow power—this is the impulse behind this quest of a powerless man for knowledge."[129] But many readers of Weber would agree that this point can be extended to his scholarly enterprise as a whole. They have deferred to Weber as a reliable authority on rationalization because they are confident that he subsumed the conception of science inaugurated by Bacon and Descartes. They would not have found *Science as a Vocation* plausible if Weber had failed to exhibit the scientific movement evident to all observers of contemporary technology and did not mirror the scientific tradition that keeps that movement going, the tradition for which "the mastery of things through reckoning" is the guiding objective.[130] The subsuming of Bacon is also entirely consistent with Weber's effort to incorporate John Stuart Mill's logic of science, which was deeply indebted to Bacon.[131] What makes Weber's lecture so perplexing, however, and casts doubt upon its plausibility, is the attempt to combine a description which on its face seems to demonstrate that Bacon's plans for science have been amply realized and resoundingly successful, with an *interpretation* of Bacon's plans which makes this successful outcome seem unintended and unforeseen. If the aspiration to a "true art" revealing "true nature" is noble, the shattering of Bacon's illusions by his own enterprise is arguably tragic. At the very least there is a forlorn, pathetic side to Weber's Bacon. The relation between knowledge and power that shapes modern science throughout is a relation we are privileged to understand only in retrospect, through Weber's "empirical" history. Why this relation could become evident and intelligible only at the end of this episode in the history of science Weber does not explain. He presupposes that empirical science as a philosophic project planned in theory could not adequately clarify the equation of knowledge with power. Yet he offers no exposition or critique of Bacon's plans to prove their inadequacy. Nor could Bacon have conceived the methods by which modern science was instituted, executed, and brought to its completion. But again, Weber does not say why. Weber and his contemporaries appear uniquely situated to assume responsibility for science, to delimit it and measure up to the consequences of their activity, because these consequences (and indeed the activity itself) were essentially unforeseen. It would be pointless to look for architectonic plans in the founders of modern science, because its main features and its meaning were not understood "by these men who stood at the threshhold of modern times." Weber may have believed these assertions, but he did not even attempt to prove them.

Weber's account of the origin of modern science in *Science as a Vocation* seems to complete the project Weber undertook in *The Protestant Ethic*. The two accounts are clearly interdependent, parallel, and mutually reinforcing.[132] Just as the great scientists of the modern revolution in natural philosophy were seeking the way to true nature and true God, the rise of modern capitalism is to be understood through the sociology of religion. Calvinism gave a new meaning to routine economic activity, infusing it with extraordinary spiritual energy. Opposing the traditional evaluation of methodical labor in worldly callings, it made inner-worldly asceticism—the discipline of factory, office, and profession—into means for the subordination of natural or fallen man.[133] This too exemplifies Weber's "fundamental fact of all history," that the results of human action regularly stand in a completely inadequate, often even paradoxical relation to its original meaning.[134] The birth of capitalism was an unintended consequence of "the grandiose moral fervor of Christian ethics," but capitalism was the great engine behind the growth of modern science and its disenchantment of the world: capitalism drove religion from the public realm.[135] In *The Protestant Ethic*, Weber tried to show that great spiritual suffering and noble illusions stood at the origin of the modern division of labor. He concluded by describing the moral vacuum which must now be filled: "The idea of duty in one's calling prowls about in our lives like the ghost of dead religious beliefs."[136] The tragic self-knowledge which Weber sought to disclose was that today we are under the necessity to fill this moral vacuum by drawing our ideals from our own breasts.[137]

Weber consistently sought to exclude the possibility that philosophy could be the origin and cause of the regime most responsible for modern progress. His account of the origins of the modern vocational division of labor and of the liberal commercial republic is buttressed by his account of the origin of modern progress based upon the scientific conquest of nature. Both accounts preclude the possibility that reason could employ ignoble but constant human needs to create the necessary political structure and the commercial spirit of modern capitalism, or that science could be deliberately turned in this way to the relief of man's estate. Such a straightforward possibility would undercut Weber's convoluted and paradoxical explanation, for if Weber's history is to be credible, political philosophy cannot possibly have played a decisive, architectonic role in the origin of modern science and the liberal commercial republic.[138] In this respect, Weber's treatment of Bacon is not only consistent with his argument in *The Protestant Ethic*: it is positively required by that argument.

To appreciate the importance of Weber's moral argument for the dignity of contemporary science, one needs to reflect on the strengths of Nietzschean leadership of science. In several respects, Weber's argument does not meet Nietzsche's challenge. His case for scientific autonomy cannot take the form of an appeal to the *interests* of scientists, because Nietzsche's politics constitutes an uncompromising and ruthless defense of those interests. As we have shown, the strength of Nietzsche's philosophic leadership of science lies in its promise to preserve and protect science from the moralism and anti-intellectualism of popular government while extending scientific inquiries into morally problematic domains.[139] Nietzsche provides for the security of science but also promises to aggrandize it and lead it on imperial conquests of the forbidden unknown. While criticizing specialization, Nietzsche builds upon it, marshaling the regiments of modern science and leading them into new wars. Nietzsche's path to a new greatness for man is made possible by the prior scientific conquest of the natural and moral phenomena. As we have shown, Weber's argument undermines certain vulgar forms of Nietzscheanism that are hostile to science.[140] But it cannot marshal a consistent opposition to Nietzsche's philosophic politics on the basis of the enduring worldly interests of science. Weber wisely foregoes the attempt to do so. Such a defense would require him to show that Nietzsche's radical measures for securing science in the world were imprudent or that science is better secured by liberal democratic orders.[141] Such a defense would bind the worldly fortunes of science to the fate of the liberal democratic regime. But it would compel Weber to abandon his arguments for objectivity and the separation of science from politics by placing the interests of science or reason squarely on the side of a preferred regime. Weber could not disassociate science from the liberal cause, elevate the liberal cause as an object of ultimate value-commitment, and simultaneously combat Nietzschean nihilism by an appeal to the interests of science. Having banished political philosophy in order to reconstitute "the liberal cause," Weber could not logically call upon political philosophy against Nietzsche.

The preceding analysis of Weber's treatment of Bacon indicates why Weber was compelled to curtail empirical inquiry and to discourage scientific specialization in certain respects. It may help to explain why later Weberians have consistently imitated Weber's neglect of empirical inquiry into the origins of modern science.[142] Weber's credibility as an authority on the rise of Western rationalism to world dominance rests upon the most precarious foundation. The case of Bacon shows how easily and how irrevocably that foundation can be undermined. But Weber's entire argument for the autonomy of science stands or falls with the ethical doctrine conveyed by his treatment of Bacon, the doctrine of the unique predicament and responsibility of contemporary science. This historicist argument for the superior dignity of service to moral forces secures Weber's defense against Nietzschean leadership within science. But the "inconvenient facts" about Bacon's project are bound to come out through disinterested study of the history of philosophy and the role of philosophy in the rise of modern science.[143] Thus specialization in the history of philosophy as a branch of science potentially endangers Weber's entire argument for the autonomy of science. The result is a profoundly troubling ambivalence regarding the pursuit of truth. In order to "serve moral forces," Weberian science must insulate itself from the results of such inquiry; it must cultivate myths about its own history. Hagiography and legend-building about Weber himself is a sideshow of no scientific significance when compared with this myth-mongering about the nature and origins of modern science.[144]

Weber's unconvincing account of Bacon and of the origins of modern science is damaging because it strongly suggests that Weber was unable to meet Nietzsche's challenge at the level of reason and science. Weber's claim to have cleared the path toward a new self-knowledge founders and merges into a claimed prerogative for arbitrary self-assertion at precisely the point where further knowledge would undermine the will to scientific autonomy from Nietzschean philosophy. The exercise of such arbitrariness by Weber and lesser epigones of Weber provides the most convincing corroboration for Nietzsche's theorem that a science serving moral forces is a contradiction in terms or that science must become morally nihilistic in order to avoid a *sacrifizio dell'intelletto*.[145] One must therefore be clear about Weber's failure in order not to repeat it. Weber's failure need not demonstrate the dependence of science upon philosophic leadership or prove that science requires a tyrannical and illiberal politics. But so long as the failure is

not acknowledged, persistence in it makes Nietzsche's alternative almost irresistibly attractive. Weber's adherents should therefore reflect
on the experience of the many thoughtful students who have been unable to find in Weber a cogent response to Nietzsche or to Nietzsche's
most influential interpreter in Weimar, Martin Heidegger. The illusion
that Weber's rhetoric in *Science as a Vocation* rests upon a defensible
account of the rise of modern science is debilitating for social science
because it blinds one to the necessity for a more coherent defense of
the autonomy of science against Nietzschean politics.[146]

5. ANXIETY AND MORAL COMMUNITY IN THE LIBERAL DEMOCRATIC ORDER

The inadequacies of Weber's defense of the autonomy of science
at the level of reason and science jeopardize Weber's entire argument
for leadership just to the extent that *Science as a Vocation* is the foundation or rational substratum of Weber's argument. But however precarious Weber's defense may be, it does not claim to provide such a
rational foundation. The ultimate commitments, according to Weber,
are irrational. The irrational foundation of Weber's defense of liberal
democracy is introduced in *Science as a Vocation*. Weber employs science as a lens to focus and clarify the struggle between morality and
nihilism within the professions of the liberal democratic order. The distinction between science and politics is paradigmatic for Weber because it illuminates the practically significant distinction between private and public in the modern state, or between the political profession
and all other professions. *Science as a Vocation* culminates in the resolution that "We shall set to work to meet the 'demands of the day,' in
human relations as well as in our vocation. This, however, is plain and
simple, if each finds and obeys the demon who holds the fibers of his
very life."[147] The broad significance of this resolution is indicated by
Weber's preceding remarks on the statelessness of the Jews: a modern
nation-state like Germany does not depend upon politicians alone;
"the demands of the day" must be met in human relations as well as in
the non-political professions. *Science as a Vocation* culminates in
an appeal for moral sobriety and *Besonnenheit* or self-possession.
Weber's appeal is to the individual rather than to any principle of collective authority. If *Science as a Vocation* retains precisely its original
spoken form, Weber deliberately refused to invoke the authority of the

Wilhelmine Reich; if it was changed in the light of the revolutionary turmoil in 1918, the appeal to the individual makes sense because there was very little collective authority, and every reason to counter "sterile excitation" with sobriety.[148] In either case, it is a call for moral community, for resoluteness in affirming responsibility in human relations and daily work. Moral sobriety means sharing Weber's anxiety about the demands of the day in ordinary vocational work or sharing his concern to "serve moral forces" against nihilism. Because *Science as a Vocation* is Weber's fundamental statement on service to moral forces in professional work, our last topic in commenting upon it will be to distinguish Weber's interpretation of professions from several rival conceptions.

Sociologists have recently accentuated the "political" activities in which professional groups have increasingly engaged in their struggle to survive and prosper.[149] Weber had an acute eye for power and would not be one to overlook the pursuit of collective self-interest by organized professional groups. But he resisted both the "devaluation of politics" and the tendency in sociology to forget the distinctions between public and private upon which the liberal democratic order and the modern liberal state depends.[150] His most famous argument on the line between public and private, of course, was that the freedoms of the modern *Rechtsstaat* depend upon curbing the power of the state bureaucracy by juxtaposing against it the power of private enterprises (bureaucratically organized). That argument is not shaken by the discovery that "private" organizations engage in "political" activities such as lobbying. On the contrary, the argument is strengthened by such facts.[151] Weber also emphasizes precisely those features of professional work that elicit respect and deference. In interpreting the professions as a battleground of the struggle between nihilism and service to moral forces, Weber seems to join Durkheim and an earlier generation of sociologists who found professional norms to be a remedy to social evils. A brief attempt to distinguish Weber from those who regarded professions as the "sociological savior" of the modern welfare state is therefore in order.[152]

Weber and Durkheim do not attach the same moral significance to professional norms and discipline. Weber does not celebrate professions as collective authorities incorporating the individual, rescuing him from the anomic normlessness of a competitive liberal order, and teaching him the collective concepts of a social body. Weber argues that professional norms retain their moral authority only when they are affirmed as a "demonic" cause by the individual. He does not join Durkheim in smothering the demons of individualism with the weight of collective authority. Unlike Durkheim, Weber magnifies the crisis in the moral foundation of the modern division of labor. The disenchantment of the world by science culminates in the discovery that vocational morality was originally shaped by "the grandiose moral fervor of Christian ethics." [153] Hence it is not merely the scientist who must "find and obey the demon who holds the fibres of his very life." [154] So must every individual whose intellectual integrity prevents him from returning "to the bosom of the old churches." [155] The professions are not new churches. Weber sought to redirect the radical individualist away from Nietzsche's politics. To counter Nietzschean psychagogy, he construed the professions as a testing ground for the soul. Rather than sacrifice individualism for moral community, Weber attempted to attract demonic men into the professions and to make their anxieties about their own individuality into a force for the defense of the liberal democratic order. A closer look at his method will clarify the irrational foundation of his defense.

In *The Protestant Ethic,* Weber tried to show how Calvin's doctrinal reasoning had intensified Christian concern for salvation. He argued that the resulting spiritual tension and anxiety had given a powerful impetus to practical work and had transformed commerce into a profession for would-be saints. [156] This may be a fanciful interpretation of the rise of modern capitalism, but it is a sure reflection of Weber's own concerns. It showed Weber that the progress of science could be turned to the service of practical ethics. Calvin's theology, according to Weber, was a triumph of logic. By cutting off the escape routes toward superstition, Calvin's rationality drove Christians away from contemplation and prayer into more active proofs of faith. It finally drove them into professional commerce as a conquest of the fallen world. [157] Weber's own scientific and methodological efforts were modelled upon Calvin's accomplishment. Like Calvin, Weber began with a "given." Calvin began with the Christian desire to be saved or to be one of the elect. [158] Weber began with a secular equivalent of this Christian desire:

> The fruit of the tree of knowledge, which is distasteful to the complacent but which is, nonetheless, inescapable, consists in the insight that every single important activity and ultimately life as a whole, if it is not to be permitted to run on as an event in nature but is instead to be consciously guided, is

a series of ultimate decisions through which the soul—as in Plato—chooses its own fate, i.e., the meaning of its activity and existence.[159]

The individual's need to choose his own fate, the meaning of his activity and existence, and to distinguish his life from an event merely running on in nature, is the given with which Weber begins. Weber interprets that need for constancy through the ideal type of an "ethic of intentions" or *Gesinnungsethik*.[160] The "given" with which Weber begins comes very close to that root experience—the discovery of individuality—with which modernity begins.[161] However this may be, Weber's argument in *Science as a Vocation* places such acute emphasis upon service to moral forces that we are justified in understanding this given need for consistency in terms of conscience.[162] More specifically, I believe we can safely adopt Heidegger's terms and speak of the "given" to which Weber appeals as *Gewissenhabenwollen* or "wanting to have a conscience" in the existential sense.[163] The unity Weber seeks in his doctrine of science must be understood in ethical terms, as Dieter Henrich has argued.[164] Weber seeks to intensify the uncertainty and anxiety of the individual who wants to have a conscience by removing every escape route into superstition or ideology. That is a task not only for his doctrine of science but for his scholarship as a whole. Weber insists upon scientific determinism in method— the exclusion of every explanation based upon magical or mysterious forces—in order to compel the individual to assume responsibility for the ultimate meaning of his own conduct.[165] Although Weber did not articulate the implications of an existential analysis of *Gewissenhabenwollen* as resolutely and fully as Heidegger, he left a faint but traceable path. He himself drew out the parallel we have sketched between Calvinist rationalism and modern scientific determinism. In a passage we have quoted, he discussed the possibility that by taking the disenchantment of the world by science far enough, or by consistently applying scientific determinism to the moral phenomena, one could intensify the specific anxiety and shame of the individual who demands constancy in choosing his fate or the meaning of his existence, "regardless of the metaphysical basis" of his *Gesinnungsethik*.[166] The effect of determinist science upon the *Gesinnunsethiker*, or upon anyone who demands constancy of himself in choosing his fate, is directly parallel to the effect of Calvinist rationalism on the Christian who wished to be saved.[167] Because the effect of his work was to throw the individual back upon himself in this way, Weber could speak of his own science as service to moral forces and assert that it was inspired by hatred of intellectualism as the worst devil.[168]

The parallel between his Calvin and Weber provides a key to his rhetorical strategy in *Science as a Vocation*. Weber's rhetoric is powerful where it succeeds in joining the desire to have a conscience with devotion to professional work. Weber promises that to satisfy our noble desire for conscience and to endure the responsibilities of professional work can be a single unified task; thus work becomes a testing ground on which to prove that one has indeed found the demon who holds the fibers of one's very life. Weber conflates the demonic quest for authenticity, the quest for full actuation of the powers of the self, with the task of mastering a professional discipline and fulfilling its duties. Weber's rhetoric is appealing to those who experience the tension, anxiety, and shame of wanting to have a conscience in a world disenchanted by modern science. It persuades such men that there is no escape from their terrible psychic predicament; but by removing all intellectual solace it intensifies their practical determination to meet the demands of the day in human relations and in their vocations.[169] Weber insisted that this was the affair of a spiritual aristocracy, but it would be a mistake to dismiss the importance of such an "aristocracy" for the liberal democratic order or to exaggerate Weber's selectivity.[170] Regardless of Weber's weaknesses in meeting Nietzsche's challenge at the level of reason and science, his defense draws upon powerful irrational resources. It is not impractical to expect, as I believe Weber did, that a wide stratum of professionals in the liberal commercial republic, perhaps most of the leading professionals, would be cursed by doubts about their worth, haunted by a peculiar sense of shame, and unable to distinguish their ambitions from their anxieties. He expected a democratic age in which inner dignity would be required because external supports for dignity would be very weak indeed.[171] Because Weber appeals to anxieties common to a large cadre of professionals, his rhetoric and myth-making are bound to be effective against Nietzsche well beyond the merits of Weber's rational arguments.

Weber undertook to form liberal democracy as a regime and to defend it by tapping these constant experiences. Weber rejected Durkheim's view of moral community in the professions. To the extent that Weber would find it meaningful to speak of moral community in a liberal democracy, he would point to shared concern with meeting the demands of the day in human relations and the vocations. Because

Weber elevates this anxiety and throws the individual back upon himself in his desire to have a conscience, one might object that he opens liberal democracy to a politics of moral resentment and pious cruelty. But this is an objection, as I shall try to show, that Weber anticipated and met.[172]

Political scientists have stressed the trend toward close collaboration between professional groups and government agencies.[173] The prospect of a new corporatism in which public authority is farmed out to self-governing professions not directly accountable to the electorate, Lowi and others have argued, discredits interest-group liberalism. Lowi has advocated the reassertion of public authority through "juridical democracy,' a reassertion that he believes would require the abandonment of liberalism and the emergence of a successor. Lowi's writing is apparently a first essay in this new postliberal public philosophy.[174] He is aware that if political science is to provide the foundation for a new public philosophy, Weber's doctrine of science must be discarded.[175] More generally, Lowi provides an alternative in which political science could guide a new public interest journalism hostile to interest group liberalism. Weber's argument in *Science as a Vocation* consolidates the critique of opinion leadership discussed in chapter 1. It severs the connection between academic political science and journalism which Wilsonian liberalism had forged and which Lowi continues: science cannot discern a standard of the public interest or a public philosophy that political journalists could elaborate and bring to bear through the media. It represents, instead, a contrary intellectual fashion that may be relevant to American politics. Weber does not sever every link between university teaching and journalism. He relies upon academic education to inculcate certain politically relevant traits.

The most obvious is trained relentlessness in acknowledging facts that are inconvenient for one's partisan preferences. Less obvious is the way Weber would encourage responsibility and self-restraint.[176] A glance at Weber's unpublished "preliminary report on a projected investigation in the sociology of journalism" is therefore in order. Weber wrote that

A survey of journalism must in the last analysis conform to the great cultural problems of the present:
    1. It must delineate the characteristic formation of that apparatus of the means of psychological suggestion through which modern society continually tries to make individuals

adapt themselves to it and integrate themselves into it. The press is one of the means of imprinting the *subjective* individuality of modern *men!*

2. It must delineate the conditions created through public opinion (whose most important determinant today is the newspaper) for the establishment, maintenance, subversion, and reshaping of the components of culture: artistic, scientific, ethical, religious, political, social, and economic. The press is a constituent element of the *objective* individuality of modern *culture.* . . .

Such questions could easily be multiplied. It is in relation to them and similar questions that the truly great cultural questions of the significance of the press are to be discussed. What is in question is the influence of the press upon the sentiments and mental habits of modern men; their influence upon political, literary, and artistic enterprises; and upon the formation (or undermining) of the beliefs and judgments of the masses. That influence strives to become ever more ubiquitous, ever more uniform, and ever more impartially objective. Yet in so doing it becomes continuously emotionally colored.[177]

Let us begin with this last point. The press is the dominant determinant of public opinion; journalism as an independent profession apart from government would be what we have called "opinion leadership." Weber's critique was that opinion leadership places the polity at the mercy of undisciplined instincts and mass emotionality. The point is evident again in Weber's argument here. The press strives to make its influence "ever more ubiquitous, uniform, impartially objective," but its influence is thereby "continuously emotionally colored."[178] The press maintains the outward forms of impartial objectivity and claims to follow a uniform procedure which is routine and normal for all cases. But within these forms its influence is to follow the drift of popular sentiment, to amplify mass emotionality. The thrust of this fragment, as one might expect, is toward a science of journalism which would avoid Lowi's symbiosis of political science, public philosophy, and journalism, in order to make journalists take responsibility for the rationalized enterprise of modern journalism, or to make them aware of the distinctive means of journalism. The first question that arises from Weber's analysis is therefore how to separate the journalist as scholar from the enterprise in which he will be immersed. Academic political science must be a critique of opinion leadership as such in order to help or force the journalist to give himself an account of the ultimate meaning of his own conduct. Second, how is it possible for journalism to escape the vicious circle Weber describes, in which the ubiquitous impartial objectivity of journalistic forms makes the public increasingly prey to undisciplined sympathies and antipathies or mass emotionality?

Weber never conducted his projected investigation, but it foreshadows a very different relation between science and journalism than the relation Lowi cultivates. It suggests the possibility that journalists could learn scholarly matter-of-factness in the first instance through a sober study of the effect of the press on individuals and on the other institutions and activities of the liberal democratic order. By studying the price of slavery to intellectual fashion in journalism, political science might inculcate responsibility and self-restraint. Finally, Weber's delineation of "the conditions created through public opinion (whose most important determinant today is the newspaper) for the . . . subversion and reshaping of the components of culture" indicates that the scope of his sociology of journalism would be wide enough to encompass the problems we have discussed under the heading of Nietzsche's new opinion leadership.[179]

Science as a Vocation introduces journalists and politicians to a world thoroughly penetrated by modern science and technology. Weber shows laymen how modern science understands itself and its formative influence upon practical life. *Science as a Vocation* attempts to undermine the principal supports of the "media world" as an independent middle realm forming public opinion; it deprives opinion leadership of the dream of membership in a republic of letters and arts, forcing the journalist to choose between the probity of specialized science, on the one hand, and professional politics on the other.[180] It thus prepares us for Weber's account of journalism in *Politics as a Vocation,* where it appears exclusively as a political business or as professional demagogy.[181]

LEADING PROFESSIONS: *POLITICS AS A VOCATION*

> [T]he herd instinct is inherited best, and at the expense of the art of commanding. If we imagine this instinct progressing for once to its ultimate excesses, then those who command and are independent would eventually be lacking altogether; or they would secretly suffer from a bad conscience and would find it necessary to deceive themselves before they could command—as if they, too, merely obeyed. This state is actually encountered in Europe today: I call it the moral hypocrisy of those commanding. They know no other way to protect themselves against their bad conscience than to pose as the executors of more ancient or higher commands.
>
> Nietzsche, *Beyond Good and Evil*, No. 199

MEN do not enter politics in order to make themselves small. Nietzsche urged gifted and politically talented individuals to turn away from liberal democratic citizenship and to risk a more ennobling politics. His critique is plausible because the liberal delimitation of politics contracts its scope, making politics the handmaiden of administration and commerce and leaving the nobler tasks of forming men to "the gruesome dominion of accident and nonsense."[1] Consequently, democratic politics brutalizes the self and makes the heart small.[2] By contrast, Nietzsche awakens revolutionary hope for a politics more open to the higher tasks of premodern politics. He claims that the opportunity for power, for a new experiment in the exercise of force and fraud, is at hand and waiting to be seized; spiritual tyrants of every kind are still needed for the enhancement of man. He promises a higher politics practiced outside of the sphere delimited by the modern state and liberal electoral politics. That higher politics need not entail

174

"loss of *noblesse*" because it is insulated from the base means and brutalizing constraints of liberal democratic politics.[3] Nietzsche's appeal is seductive because the private institutions of the liberal commercial republic welcome and reward the talents of exceptional individuals and seldom put up determined resistance against a resourceful and sufficiently ruthless individualism. Nietzsche capitalizes upon the liberal concern for individuality in his interpretation of the self. Through this interpretation, he turns nongovernmental institutions toward the tasks of liberating the self from moral constraints.[4]

Politics as a Vocation was Weber's most eloquent attempt to counter Nietzsche's influence by making politics within the institutions of limited government once again choiceworthy for great-hearted men. Weber did not ignore the facts that make Nietzsche's critique plausible and his appeal seductive. But he blunted the impact of Nietzsche's arguments or deflected them into a case for heroic devotion to the political calling. One can discern the outlines of Weber's regime in *Politics as a Vocation*. In it, politics emerges as the leading profession within a division of labor organized by professions and based upon vocational morality. The lecture will enable us to understand more fully how Weber reconfigured liberal democracy as a regime without liberalism, and to distinguish his regime from Nietzsche's avowedly nihilistic experiment. My critical analysis of Weber's lecture will attempt to assess his resistance to Nietzsche's philosophic politics.

Weber's argument for the importance of political leadership is the crux both of his attempt to transcend liberalism and of his defense of liberal democratic institutions. To assess the significance of his policy for the future of American politics, we must ascend to principle and resist Weber's tendency to transmute questions of principle into empirical questions. No regime has yet succeeded in Weber's policy; we do not know "from experience" that liberal democracy can subsist without liberalism. We must evaluate Weber's project as a hypothesis or experiment and even assume that the weight of previous experience is against it. Weber's defense of liberal democracy would permit liberalism to perish, perhaps hastening its destruction. The current strength of "traditionalism" in the United States reminds us that the connection between liberalism and the preservation of "traditional morality" (as many Americans understand it) is a great topic of controversy.[5] Without going into the controversy or claiming to settle it, the questions I shall address to Weber admittedly reflect my judgment that until very recently American liberalism and traditional morality went hand in hand. Liberal opinions, strong devotion to habits of moderate self-government, and moral decency have been intertwined and mutually supporting in the American character. Many proponents of "liberation" from "bourgeois morality" have tried to modify liberal orthodoxies and to divide liberalism from "traditional" moral norms, in the hope that if the old liberal principles perished, a moral revolution would follow in train. It therefore seems reasonable to ask whether Weber's policy of allowing liberalism to perish would similarly entail a moral revolution. What is Weber's reply to the objection that his willing of leadership without liberalism would be no more than an overture to the Nietzschean alternative, willing leadership without moral limits? The question is whether Weber's doctrine paves the way for a more radical assault on the moral basis of liberal democratic politics.

Following his initial flirtation with Nietzschean rhetoric in the Freiburg Lecture, Weber developed two lines of reasoning that answer such objections; *Politics as a Vocation* is a compendium of both. The first is Weber's serious effort to incorporate and supersede liberal legislative science and reason of state. Weber's political economics is an effort to subsume all the mechanisms discovered by liberalism in theory and practice.[6] Weber denies that anything significant is lost when liberal dogmas and philosophical principles are transcended—that is to say, abolished—by social science: he does not diminish the rationality of modern liberal politics but enhances it by liberating it from indefensible principles.[7] On this view, the firmest possible footing that can be provided for politicians who wish to defend liberal democratic institutions, the foundation for their "rational orientation in the world," is provided by the empirical knowledge and ideal-typical constructs of Weberian social science: *Politics as a Vocation* is the best that science can do to educate a political leadership class.[8] By concentrating attention on the formation of a stratum of professional politicians, Weber completes the liberal political tradition and makes limited government defensible without recourse to liberal ideology.

The second line of reasoning comes at the objection from a very different angle. It is based upon Weber's sustained effort to incorporate and supersede the scientific insights of Marx and Nietzsche and to confront their most penetrating critiques of liberal democracy.[9] According to this line of reasoning, the task of defending liberal democracy is complex precisely because it is so interwoven with the fate of liberalism (and, more generally, with the fate of Western philosophy and of

"the grandiose moral fervor of Christian ethics.")[10] Nietzschean philosophy and Marxist revolution were not dangers that liberal thought
anticipated in framing the liberal democratic regime. These new
threats must be met with remedies that liberal policy does not provide
and that liberal principle might not countenance. In order to combat its
present enemies, liberal democracy must be reconfigured, and that undoubtedly entails a moral risk: "one has to see the devil's ways to the
end in order to realize his power and his limitations."[11]

These lines of argument are both cogent and persuasive. But they
work at cross purposes. The first represents Weber as the scion (or
Stammhalter) of modern liberal politics. It plays down the difficulty of
defending democracy in the absence of liberal beliefs and principles. It
reassures us that Weber was profoundly devoted to the method of democracy. The second celebrates Weber's profound break with the liberal tradition. It acknowledges that a modification of liberal democratic practice may be necessary when liberal beliefs and enthusiasms
cannot be relied upon. It admits that the democratic method cannot
cope with the challenge posed by Marx and Nietzsche and requires a
modification of the democratic method. Weber does not conceal these
contrarieties in his position. Through them he introduces the reader to
the practical problem of serving moral forces through political action
and to the ethical dilemmas of the political profession. Weber's method
requires him to avoid a definitive settlement of the most pressing questions we have raised. He attempts to inculcate or evoke an anxious solicitude for the outcome of the struggle between morality and nihilism.
Is Weberian political leadership a revanche against Nietzschean nihilism or a détente, even a surrender, to it? Does it defend moral forces
and exemplify devotion to ultimate moral values? Or does it foster
moral relativism, undermine devotion to absolutes, and contribute to
the relaxation of high standards of public morality? Weber compels or
helps us to raise these questions. In the end, one must judge whether
his final silence on them is a sublime prudence or a resolute folly.[12]

My commentary on *Politics as a Vocation* will mirror the twofold
reasoning just sketched. In the first section, I consider Weber's refor-
mulation of the liberal case for limited government. In the second, I
discuss some of the new difficulties to which Weber's defense re-
sponds. In the third and fourth, I treat his analysis of the relation between ethics and politics. In the course of the next chapter, I shall attempt to assess the adequacy of Weber's prudence.

1. LIMITED GOVERNMENT WITHOUT LIBERALISM

In *Politics as a Vocation*, Weber begins with a brief description of the politician as a charismatic leader, then turns abruptly to the administrative staffs on which such a leader must rely. The bulk of his history of the political vocation in the West is devoted to these staffs:

> [P]oliticians by virtue of a "calling" in the most genuine sense of the word, are of course nowhere the only decisive figures in the cross-currents of the political struggle for power. The sort of auxiliary means that are at their disposal is also highly decisive. How do the politically dominant powers manage to maintain their domination? . . . organized domination requires control of those material goods which in a given case are necessary for the use of physical violence. Thus, organized domination requires control of the personal executive staff and the material implements of administration. [13]

Weber concentrates upon the distinctive means of political action, the staffs of the party and the state apparatus. His history of politics as routine occupational work culminates in this alternative for Germany:

> [T]here is only the choice between leadership democracy with a "machine" and leaderless democracy, namely, the rule of professional politicians without a calling, without the inner charismatic qualities that make a leader, and this means what the party insurgents in the situation usually designate as "the rule of the clique." [14]

Weber's impressive historical summary seems to compel one to conclude that empirical inquiry reveals no other alternative under present conditions. No reasonable citizen would seriously consider Nietzsche's politics if this were so; it would be excluded on practical grounds, and the issue posed by Nietzschean nihilism would be disposed of without a principled argument. Such was not Weber's intention, as I shall demonstrate: his empirical account was designed to provoke rather than to settle the controversy over nihilistic politics.

Two-thirds of Weber's lecture is given over to the professional staff. The development of rational organizations for domination is a story of conflict that foreshadows the current struggle between leaders and staff. First come the princes, who built the modern state. Their work replaced the feudal estates with a permanent staff of professional counselors and civil servants. Then the princes fade from view, like Bismarck retiring into the forests of Saxony, leaving the administrative machine to grind on without them.[15] For a time, parties of notables governing in parliament dominate the public stage, but these give way to electoral armies under the leadership of party bosses and great orators, "generals of the electoral battlefields."[16] They inherit the legacy of two great historical battles, the first to defeat the barons, the second to defeat the *honoratiores* or notables. What they inherit is the task of disciplining the machinery that has emerged from these struggles. Weber's account seems to exhibit a "clear developmental tendency" extending into the indefinite future.[17]

As a basis for one's "rational orientation in the world," however, Weber's claim that the only choice is between leaderless democracy and democracy with leaders dominating a "machine" is clearly of limited utility. The "tendency" in question lasted little more than a decade in Germany. The Nazi alternative is not included among the two Weber describes: it was neither democratic nor "rule of the clique."[18] The possibility that the *Rechtsstaat* might be dismantled, that Germany might become a power organization without limited government, is not considered. Weber presupposes that the competition between parties will continue. These assumptions are interdependent because the modern parties complement the modern state; they are pacific electoral parties which presuppose the monopoly of legitimate violence by the state: "here we do not have to deal with such organizations for violence, but rather with professional politicians who strive for power through sober and 'peaceful' campaigns in the market of election votes."[19]

With this distinction, Weber excludes Hitler's movement; along with the Bolsheviks and Guelfs, he also excludes Nietzsche's new "party of life," a warfaring party which resembles the Ghibelline party of a united European Empire opposed to the Roman Church under the banner of the "antichrist," Friedrich II the Hohenstaufen.[20] One task of Nietzsche's party was explicitly the *Vermännlichung* of Europe, the restoration of its manly strength and military virtue, the task initiated a century earlier by Napoleon.[21] Pacific electoral parties will dominate the political stage in Europe only if democracy continues to be the main tendency: "The most modern forms of party organization are the children of democracy, of mass franchise, of the necessity to woo and organize the masses, and to develop the utmost unity of direction and the strictest discipline." [22] In assuming the permanence of democracy, Weber does not consider Nietzsche's insight into its vulnerability, his anticipation that it could be swept away by a European revolution and that the opportunity for a powerful antidemocratic politics was at hand. [23] This lack cannot be because Weber was unaware of the pathetic weakness of the democratic tendency in Germany, which worried him throughout his career. [24] One may, to be sure, insist that Weber was serious in staking his reputation as a realist on this statement of the alternatives. But one should then pass the same judgment on Weber that one passes on Carl Friedrich's realism in this prediction made in 1933: "Germany will remain a constitutional democratic state with strong socializing tendencies whose backbone will continue to be its professional civil service." [25] I do not think such a judgment does justice to Weber; his reliance upon the state and parties as "givens" deserves a closer inspection.

Weber defines politics initially as an attempt to influence the policy of a state. His reason for incorporating the state in his definition of politics seems to be that it is the main fact at the present time. But his subsequent definition of the state, which describes its means and its claim to monopolize all legitimate violence within its territory, is clearly an ideal type, and the place it occupies in Weber's science does not depend upon its empirical "givenness." The exclusion of warfaring parties is required by Weber's concept of the state, because such parties contradict the state's monopoly of legitimate violence. What is the logical necessity that leads Weber to his construct of the state?

From the beginning of his lecture, Weber emphasizes his adherence to the normal methods of political economy. One might therefore suppose that a methodological necessity explains his definition of the state in terms of its means. Because the state has served very different ends at different times, Weber asserts, one must define it by reference to means rather than ends. [26] This stipulation cannot be a reason for adopting Weber's procedure, however, because it simply restates the procedure. The multiplicity of ends that "the state" has served can only be conceived as ends separate from "the state" if one has previously defined the state in terms of means. The decision to treat the state as an assembly of means must therefore rest upon a conceptual choice prior to, and distinct from, the spurious "reason" that Weber adduces.

The basis for Weber's choice is not a methodological imperative specific to the state. It is his prior analysis of the proper relation between political science and "ultimate ends." It must be inferred from *Science as a Vocation* and Weber's other writings on this topic.[27] The 1919 lecture on politics is a model of specialized instruction according to the canons laid down in the lecture on science. As a compendium of Weber's political science, it fulfills the tasks outlined in *Science as a Vocation*. First, it is an introduction to reason of state for men of action: it provides a body of practical knowledge which can help the student to "bring home the groceries."[28] The most efficient mode of administration, for the purpose of bringing home the political groceries, is rational-legal bureaucracy: this is merely to restate Weber's principle in constructing the type. He sought the most efficient mode of administration he could conceive.[29] A similar point holds for the fully rationalized campaign machine as a means for winning elections.[30] Second, *Politics as a Vocation* is a presentation of "inconvenient facts" that the existing German parties would prefer not to face. The superior efficiency of the state and of the mass parties does not bode well for the German party system. Weber's analysis indicates why the multiparty system was vulnerable to Hitler's movement. The German parties were not mass electoral parties set up to exploit the means of modern campaigning. *Politics as a Vocation* would lead one to anticipate Hitler's victory, because his party came closest in practice to the American and English models of a "machine" dominated by a demagogue.[31] The analysis of the state is equally inconvenient. Following the collapse of the Hohenzollern dynasty, the parliamentary parties inherited a large measure of responsibility for maintaining strict discipline under rational-legal norms within the administrative apparatus.[32] The leniency of the courts toward the Nazis demonstrated that the parties were unable to shoulder this responsibility.[33] Third, Weber's lecture is designed to "serve moral forces" by making it possible for the student to attain clarity on the ultimate meaning of his own conduct—particularly in choosing or declining a career in politics.[34] The concept of the state as means follows from this task of clarification:

> If you take such and such a stand, then, according to all scientific experience, you have to use such and such a *means* in order to carry out your conviction practically. Now these means are perhaps such that you believe you must reject them. Then you simply must choose between the end and the inevitable means. Does the end "justify" the means? Or does

it not? The teacher can confront you with the necessity of this choice.[35]

There is a correspondence between the demand for rational control over means enforced by the state and parties and the demand of Weber's science for intelligibility with regard to means. For this reason it is irrelevant whether reality presents us with a situation in which the state is the prevailing form of organization. Even where the modern state and parties are of no practical significance, Weber's science is guided by these concepts; the Weberian ethic of service to moral forces would require them as standards of clarity with respect to means.[36] The monopoly of legitimate force concentrates responsibility for violence in the hands of the few officials who head the state. This concentration is paralleled in the political parties. Weber does not say what the parties claim to monopolize, but if the state is a machine of force, perhaps the parties are machines of "legitimate" fraud. Obviously the means of electioneering are in question. Weber's science is attuned to the specialization and concentration of the means of coercion and deception at a specific point in the division of labor, because this serves individual responsibility and accountability.[37]

Yet the task of clarification requires reflection on ends. Weber fails to fulfill his task of clarifying the relation between means and ends in his historical account because he tacitly rules out those ends that would justify the use of warfaring parties and mandate the relaxation of the state's monopoly of "legitimate" violence. Civil wars and revolutions are, after all, sometimes necessary and justified. While certain instrumentalities may promote responsibility in the routine or average case, responsibility might dictate other means in the exceptional case. As we have noted, Nietzsche thought his responsibilities to the cause of philosophy dictated extraordinary means.[38] We must therefore continue, and examine Weber's acount of the choice between ultimate commitments, for a clarification of his decision to limit his account of "means" to the state and the electoral parties.

The purpose of *Politics as a Vocation* is to bring professional politics to light as a possible object of a lifetime commitment. With Weber's aid, the student is to clarify for himself whether he has the calling for politics and the stance he is to take toward those who enter politics as their profession.[39] Weber leads the way toward the choice of a criterion, a standard of values, by which to judge, but as was the case in *Science as a Vocation,* Weber does not merely disclose a route to be retraced in thought. He poses a series of tests that one must surmount to attain an independent *Wertmaßstab* for ranking politics. There are principally two tests, of affirming a political vocation as one's personal fate and of affirming politics as such, from an "ultimate stance" toward life.[40] The impression Weber initially creates is therefore somewhat misleading: the state and the parties are not given a central place in *Politics as a Vocation* because they are unshakeable empirical facts, nor are the alternatives Weber describes in his history the only practical options. Weber emphasizes them in accordance with a moral purpose.

Weber conveys the impression that the modern state and electoral campaign organization are the culmination of a long historical development leading toward the most powerful forms of political organization. Although he makes no predictions, these institutions appear to be marching with accumulated momentum gathered over centuries toward greater triumphs over all alternative modes of political order. But upon closer inspection, these impressions dissolve and prove dispensable to Weber's argument. Like Gladstone, Weber had mastered the technique of apparently "letting sober facts speak for themselves."[41] There are several reasons for Weber's rhetorical design, corresponding to the different listeners he could expect to attend his lecture. For the Marxists, Weber's lecture is a means of turning historical materialism toward the understanding of political institutions, thereby curbing the rhetorical impact of vulgar Marxism, preventing Marxists from ignoring the independent force of political practices, and compelling them to face constitutional issues:

> We shall not be deceived about this by verbiage; the materialist interpretation of history is no cab to be taken at will; it does not stop short of the promoters of revolutions. Emotional revolutionism is followed by the traditionalist routine of everyday life; the crusading leader and the faith itself fade away, or, what is even more effective, the faith becomes part of the conventional phraseology of political Philistines and banausic technicians. This development is especially rapid with struggles of faith because they are usually led or inspired by genuine leaders, that is, prophets of revolution. . . . After coming to power the following of a crusader usually degenerates very easily into a quite common stratum of spoilsmen.[42]

Weber's remarks take into account the opportunist whose primary interest is to "bring home the groceries" for self-aggrandizement. Those who are looking for the main chance will be directed, by Weber's argument, toward a party on the model of Gladstone's. Weber attempts to deflect men of crude ambition toward responsible party politics and moral accountability. On the nobler end of the human spectrum lies the individual least given to what Weber despised as "an ethic of adaptation." [43] As I have suggested, Weber's account is framed so that such an individual can take it as a means of clarification, not as a picture of inevitable developments that cannot be opposed. For this listener, Weber's history is not so compelling as it must seem to the other two types. It is part of a larger argument on political ethics and the rationalization of the political domain. Although Weber treats the latter topic first, he tailors his treatment of political development to suit his subsequent account of political ethics. There is little in his history that is not preparatory to the discussion of the ethos of politics. In crucial respects the history is derivative from the ethical discussion and subordinate to it. [44]

The convoluted mode of argumentation that we have surveyed results from Weber's intention to fulfill an essential purpose of modern liberal politics without upholding liberal principles as a matter of right. Weber seeks to concentrate legitimate force and fraud in the institutions of the state and parties. That concentration had originally found its most persuasive ideal in the "humanity" of Montaigne and its most cogent rationale in the doctrines of modern natural right articulated by Hobbes, Spinoza, and Locke. [45] Weber's intention is to transcend liberalism; he is compelled to abandon that ideal and those principles. Yet he tries to transform the task of preserving limited government into a matter of ultimate commitment and to lend it a passionate intensity that makes the cool calculation of the liberal political philosophers seem insouciant by contrast.

The most sustained inquiry into Weber's politics and his abandonment of liberalism is Wolfgang Mommsen's political biography and his article on plebiscitary leader democracy. [46] These may help to focus our analysis of Weber's effort to defend limited government. Mommsen classes Weber's regime under the rubric of plebiscitary leader democracy because that term contains no reference to liberalism and implies no commitment to limited government. According to Mommsen, Weber's regime is neither simply democratic nor liberal in its modification of popular government: it does not refine democracy through the means of representative government, as (for example) *The Federalist* sought to do. Furthermore, Mommsen wished to forewarn the opinion leaders of the young Federal Republic of Germany that Weber's doctrine did not promote the public morality and right opinion favored by the proponents of liberal natural right. Nor was it consistent with the tenets of German Liberalism in the Idealist tradition.[47] Weber's break with earlier European liberalism and with natural right teachings was therefore a major concern for Mommsen. His final reason for adopting this rubric was to highlight the absence in Weber's regime of any firm resistance to the leader-principle that Hitler had drummed into the Hitler Youth and thus into a generation of Germans. In Weber's ideal type, "the dictatorship of Cromwell" and Napoleon are examples of "plebiscitary leader democracy."[48] Mommsen's work has been subjected to such wanton mistreatment and studied neglect that I am reluctant to belabor it. I consider it beyond comparison the finest study of Weber's politics and the most substantial work of historical scholarship on Weber yet written.[49] But the rubric Mommsen selects is not sufficiently discriminating. None of the distinctions we drew between Woodrow Wilson and Weber, for example, come to light through that rubric. (Were Mommsen to look more closely at Wilson, he would find that despite his celebration of democracy, Wilson too had abandoned natural right.) In concentrating our attention on Weber's recommendations for the office of the republican chief of state, Mommsen ignores Weber's lifelong concern with the development of a political leadership *stratum*. The argument on professional politics in *Politics as a Vocation* is disregarded in Mommsen's account.[50] The distinction between a defense of liberal democratic institutions and adherence to liberal principles is obscured by Mommsen: his claim that Weber was not sufficiently serious about the former rests on his abandonment of liberalism.[51] Weber's preoccupation with limited government and his attempt to secure it without relying upon liberal principles cannot be squared with Mommsen's interpretation. Finally, one can understand why Weber's admirers were so profoundly offended: the pathos of Weber's attempt, in *Politics as a Vocation,* to make the major institutions of the liberal democratic regime worthy of the heroic efforts of greathearted men, is transformed by Mommsen into an unintentional and misguided propaedeutic for Hitler's regime.[52]

Weber's attention to the means of political action replaces a traditional liberal argument for limited government. Weber tries to find a more vigorous and nobler drive to enforce the limits on which liberal democratic government depends. The moral pathos that he tries to elicit in *Politics as a Vocation* is a more constant and passionate form of sentiments that are familiar from American politics; hence his position is often mistaken for a novel style of liberalism. Accountability for the means of force and fraud is a major theme of representative government: Weber's stress on responsibility might well tempt one to conclude that Weber was four-square in the liberal tradition. Mommsen's critique alerts us against this temptation. But his account of liberal principles fails to clarify the main points on which Weber departs from liberal doctrine. What Weber tries to do without, as I shall try to explain, is the liberal principle that government is concerned only with the securing of rights, not with their exercise.[53] Because this distinction has been eroded and obscured as *The Federalist* and other classic expositions of modern liberal politics have lost favor, it requires some explication.

Let us recall the difficulty we found in Weber's Freiburg Lecture.[54] He sought to elevate political leadership by interpreting it as an assertion of a ranking of values. But the idea that politics should entail the assertion of a national way of life, we found, was at odds with liberal democratic institutions. This conflict was especially jarring in the Freiburg Lecture because Weber's rhetoric for describing the assertion of a ranking of values was Nietzschean rhetoric, and his rejection of liberalism was warlike and imperialistic.[55] The same conflict persists in *Politics as a Vocation* but in a form much less jarring to liberal sensibilities. Genuine leadership means devotion to a cause, hence the assertion of an independent ranking of values. Responsibility for the *means* of political action, however, is equally a matter of passionate concern for the genuine leader, and this responsibility holds the professional politician strictly to the methods of limited government. Weber's political leadership profession is to maintain the tension between these two requirements without relaxation. What was essential in liberal practice would thereby be subsumed into professional politics. The drive to control the means of power would somehow be bound to the assertion of a ranking of values. Through this chemistry or alchemy, Weber sought to provide for limited government without appealing to liberal principles. But from the standpoint of those principles strictly understood, Weber's alchemy can only be an attempt to combine irreconcilably opposed alternatives; his professional politicians are bound to be confused, because they must affirm politics as the exercise of right while defending a form of government based on the exclusion of precisely that kind of politics.

We may bring the liberal distinction into focus by discussing its most important instance: the exclusion of "the state" from the exercise of religious right. This distinction is closely linked, as we shall see, to Weber's definition of "the state" as a matter of means rather than ends.

Prior to Machiavelli, the "state" had been understood as a regime or *politeia*.[56] Regime politics cannot be defined in abstraction from ends. A regime is the rule of a certain quality of citizen; it is inseparable from the assertion of a standard of virtue. A regime is unintelligible apart from the ends it strives to live by: it is "a republic of virtue" or a Kingdom of God. As Machiavelli put it, political thought before him had been governed by "imaginary republics and principalities" which had oriented men toward how they ought to live.[57] Machiavelli's attempt to introduce new modes and orders meant a reorientation toward "the economy of violence."[58] His hints that religious politics fostered "pious cruelty" were taken by Montaigne and the *Politiques*. Montaigne argued that the rule of virtue fostered cruelty toward human nature and that the passions sanctioned by religious politics inevitably promoted the most destructive forms of war. Regime politics was bound to be inhumane politics. When right is a matter of duty according to eternal standards of virtue, righteousness must take the form of active justice. Regime politics knows only a right that must be exercised. A citizen's rights are essential to the fulfillment of his duties; any fall from virtue must entail a corresponding loss of right. A regime defines citizenship in terms of justice: if one does not exercise that virtue, one has no title to the privileges and immunities of citizens. Virtue is an invisible quality of soul that must become "morally visible" in civic life. Inevitably, a regime notices virtues by scrutinizing their most obvious manifestation, in opinions. In a regime, rights are inseparable from right thinking or right opinion. Government as the supervision of virtue is necessarily concerned with orthodoxy, for virtue comes to light in opinion or in right worship. The *Politiques* argued that the consequences of allowing government to be concerned with the exercise of right (and, in the first instance, with worship) were disastrous. Following Machiavelli and Montaigne, an illustrious line of liberal political philosophers sought to fashion a politics that would secure the right to worship without governing the exercise of that right. But to establish this distinction required a revolution in the understanding of rights. The founders of liberalism invented or discovered a kind of "right" that could be acquired and secured regardless of one's virtues or qualities of soul, a right wholly independent of righteousness. The original liberal principle was that such rights were anterior to human opinions about justice or virtue and more fundamental than the morals and manners of civil society. These were rights with which men were endowed by nature. They could be identified without reference to qualities of soul and provided a natural standard for judging political arrangements. Henceforth, political arrangements that secured these natural human rights were legitimate, and legitimate governments could be recognized because they alone limited themselves to the task of securing those rights.[59]

Weber's defense of liberal democracy is an attempt to preserve the institutions of state and party that arose upon the foundation of this new doctrine of right. His difficulty lies in combining the defense with an attempt to transcend that doctrine. Weber attempts to detach liberal democracy from a standard of human rights grounded in nature. Yet it is evident that he thought this could be done without endangering the *Rechtsstaat* or the liberties of subjects, which he knew to be indispensable.[60] Weber's desire to do without liberalism is not merely, however, a matter of his epistemic doubts about the possibility of grounding human rights in nature. He turns away from the liberal distinction because he is ambivalent about limited government. It makes politics subordinate to commerce and administration and rules out the assertion of a ranking of values by political means. Weber wishes to recover the nobler possibilities of "regime politics" without sacrificing limited government. While maintaining its limits, he wants a political leadership stratum that is preeminently concerned with *the quality of men* who are favored or harmed by legislation.[61] He is acutely aware that the founders of modern liberal politics did not provide adequately for his politician. Weber tries to modify their scheme to accommodate the political man who wishes to prove "what is humanly great and noble in [his] nature." Weber's politician is not a liberal statesman; he wants to rule directly, by virtue of his extraordinary qualities; his horizon is that of the Thucydidean *politikos* (although this horizon is "denuded of its inwardly genuine plasticity").[62] In further contrast to the classical liberal statesman, Weber's politician has no qualms about affirming the perpetual necessity for plebiscitary politics: his very métier is demagogy.[63] Weber, like Wilson, accepted the view that the form of representative government sought by *The Federalist* was ineligible: if one pursued it, one would only attain "leaderless democracy . . . the 'rule of the clique.'"[64] Weber abandoned the distinction between securing and exercising rights because that distinction ruled out the modification of representative government that he thought was most necessary to the defense of liberal democracy. (Whether he fully understood the distinction is a subtler question that does not affect the main point.)[65]

We will briefly outline Weber's modification and then turn to the new difficulties that made Weber's departure from liberal theory and practice necessary.

2. POLYARCHY AND THE CRISIS OF LIBERALISM

Weber's regime retains the rational-legal administration of the modern state and pacific parties competing in democratic elections. His regime is a species of plebiscitary leader democracy; this means that it legitimizes demagogy, contrary to the principles and recommended practice of liberal representation. It is emphatically not "leaderless government" along the lines of *The Federalist*.[66] But Weber qualifies and reshapes the plebiscitary elements of his regime in order to compel demagogy to serve the essential purposes of preserving limited government. The medium of this transformation of plebiscitary politics is the political profession. To understand Weber's regime, one must appreciate how plebiscitary modes of leadership selection are shaped by the action of a political profession and, conversely, how the necessities of plebiscitary politics shape the professionals.

These mutual dependencies should form something less mechanical than a "system of government" but more compelling than a mere standard of good political taste. The political profession is meant to be the bearer of the national political tradition. Weber's distinctive contribution to political thought after the Freiburg Lecture was his preoccupation with the forms of the political *Beruf:* the problem of creating the forms of liberal democratic politics is construed, in Weber's interpretation, as the task of forming a professional politics. The endeavor to unite the national cause with the liberal cause was no longer in the foreground in Weber's 1919 lectures. But that essential project was pursued less visibly in his attempt to delineate the forms of the calling for politics.[67]

Weber's profession is not an elite with expertise set against an incompetent mass; it is a profession within a division of labor made up of professions. The primary task of the politician is control of the party machinery and administrative staff. Those who are not professional politicians depend upon the leader precisely because they are not economically dispensable. Bureaucracy is objectified mind: an articulation of organized domination by means of knowledge separates the professionals. In any question that involves their corporate interests, the apparatchiki of the parties and state have the benefit of knowledge. The leader is dependent upon the people because their criteria of selection are different from those of the apparatchiki. Plebiscites provide an avenue to power that these staffs of the party and state would otherwise blockade. Through plebiscites, the leader can introduce criteria of policy that the staffs would otherwise suppress.[68] To translate this into the language of Weber's analysis of leadership classes in the 1895 address: plebiscites compel the professional politicians to will the national interest when it conflicts with their short-term institutional or economic interests.[69]

Conversely, professionalization imposes limits on plebiscitary politics. Although there is a constant tension between the "genuine leader" and his staffs, the thrust of *Politics as a Vocation* is to bring demagogy under the mantle of the political profession. The opportunity for revolutionary Caesarism provided by plebiscites requires supervision. Professional politics is Weber's counterweight against the danger that a temporary majority will coalesce behind a leader to overthrow the electoral system. The principle Weber adopts is that if the political profession acknowledges that demagogy is its métier, all the pressure of the routine interests of the staffs that live from politics can be brought to bear on testing talented demagogues for reliability and responsibility. The constant struggle with career politicians can be politically sterile, but Weber's purpose is to make it generate useful forms for liberal democratic politics. The combat can create customs and a bond. The machine bosses and career officeholders benefit from the glory and respect won by "genuine leaders." They have a corporate interest in the "routinization" of the "charisma" of the "true politician" insofar as his éclat gives their profession legitimacy and "class." Conversely, the politician has a utilitarian interest in customs that facilitate his control over his staffs.[70]

As I have suggested, a significant price must be paid for this modification of liberal democratic politics: it is not clear whether one can efface the original liberal distinction between securing rights and exercising rights without profound consequences for the institutions

grounded in that distinction. Weber was willing to risk these consequences, I believe, because he thought he confronted unprecedented
dangers. His break with liberal principles and his attempt to defend
limited government without them follow from his conviction that the
liberal cause could not be defended as a national cause, against Marx
and Nietzsche, unless liberalism and liberal political philosophy were
abandoned. I shall restrict my analysis to Nietzsche.[71]

Nietzsche stimulates an experimental interest in the power potential of activities that are not "political" according to the liberal delimitation of the public realm. Those (formerly "political") activities that
form the character of citizens, their desires and their hopes, are rele-
gated, under the liberal scheme, to the private sphere. We have
sketched the effect of Nietzsche's politics upon the capacity of private
institutions to nurture respect for the moral limits upon which liberal
democracy has depended.[72] We now turn to a problem that Nietzsche
did not discuss but on which Weber had reason to reflect. Recent
American experience with political parties suggests these reflections.
As private associations have become more political, parties in the
United States have suffered a steady decline. However this change is to
be explained, it is clear that private institutions no longer provide the
supports for parties that they once supplied. Strong party identification
was once transmitted by the family—not because the family was
highly political but apparently because it was not. It is doubtful that the
family will transmit partisan loyalties and sentiments when the family
itself, and the moral constraints it imposes, are reinterpreted in political terms, conceived as power relations, and evaluated in terms of the
opportunities for self-expression and self-assertion that they provide
(or fail to). Jury duty had long been a schooling for citizenship in the
United States, but as Tocqueville noted in his discussion of juries, this
education for self-government was conducted and formed by the
judge.[73] As a source of popular enlightenment and habituation to the
ways of constitutional government, public courts depend upon private
schools of law which shape the character and outlook of judges. Constitutional law was once the study of constitutional government;
through it, lawyers learned not only the procedures but also the necessary principles of a republican form of government. But few today
consider the schools of law responsible for continuing this tradition. If
they choose to neglect it and to adopt Nietzschean liberation from
moral limits as a mandate of the Constitution, they are free to do so.
Since most professional politicians receive a substantial part of their

education in law school, such a shift has great significance for political parties. If political parties cannot rely upon the legal profession to inculcate basic principles of constitutional democracy, their position is vexed by new difficulties. They must find new sources of strength to replace these valuable supports. They must form loyalties that were once formed in the family. Perhaps they must affirm or create limits which they previously were able to take for granted because private institutions upheld them so effectively.

This predicament is not wholly unlike the situation of the nascent parties of the Weimar Republic. Political leaders like Weber who sought to forge a national party knew that they could not assume the support of most social institutions. They certainly could not rely on the family. It swiftly became apparent that they could not rely upon the judges to transmit the principles and habits necessary for constitutional self-government.[74] Weber's concern with professional politics as a source of "forms" for democratic politics is appropriate to a liberal democratic order in which private institutions have ceased to nurture those forms, or (as in the German case) have never begun to nurture them.

But Weber's image of the permanent situation suggests a deeper problem.

> As Hellenic man at times sacrificed to Aphrodite and at other times to Apollo, and, above all, as everybody sacrificed to the gods of his city, so do we still nowadays. . . . Many old gods ascend from their graves; they are disenchanted and hence take the form of impersonal forces. They strive to gain power over our lives and again they resume their eternal struggle with one another.[75]

The political gods of the city are locked in a struggle with other gods for power over the lives of men. That struggle takes the form of a competition among impersonal forces, between the professions and organizations that compose the other spheres of human activity. This is an image that one might explicate by adapting Robert Dahl's term "polyarchy."[76] *Archein* is the Greek verb for rule: monarchy is the rule of one, oligarchy the rule of a few. In the light of our analysis of regime politics, one may say that polyarchy means a struggle among several different regimes, each asserting its title to rule and striving to exercise its "right" according to its own principle of rule. Dahl used the term to describe polities which permit contestation for governing offices. But the term is felicitous and especially apt to describe a liberal order in which the distinction between politics as the securing of rights and politics as the exercise of right has broken down or lost its authority. When that disintegration takes a Nietzschean direction, the struggle for power between the political "sphere" and the other "spheres" of activity begins to approximate a struggle between ultimate rankings of value (or between different "godheads"). Madisonian interest politics was not pluralist in this sense. Madison's plan was to fragment power among many factions and interests, while removing regime-politics. The Madisonian plan required factions to accept the principle that they could not aspire to dismantle the government or institute a new principle of rule. "Polyarchy," taken literally, describes a very different plurality, in which the political profession must assert its claims for sacrifice, against other professions ruled by other gods, without the mediation of a common framework of constitutional principles. The term "polyarchy" thus suits a liberal order undergoing a *crise de conscience* precipitated by Nietzsche's philosophic politics.

On Nietzsche's reading, there is no natural order or definition inherent in human nature, no ranking of values and virtues by nature. The self must be determined through self-assertion. The exercise and assertion of its "right" is crucial for the creation of the self: the only right the self can recognize is disclosed in self-assertion.[77] Nietzsche denies the existence of human rights: there are no natural rights that can be secured by government without regard to how (or whether) they are exercised.[78] Nietzsche's is a politics for individuals who know themselves to be needy because they are limitless and therefore seek a regime for themselves. Perhaps the closest approximation to Nietzsche's intention that a liberal order could attain would be a polyarchy of "discrete and insular minorities" preoccupied with the exercise of their rights and determined to overcome all the obstructions to self-assertion that are intrinsic to limited government. Nietzsche had reason to anticipate that such a liberal order would be merely an entr'acte on the way to an illiberal and inhumane regime.[79]

As I shall try to show in the balance of this chapter, Weber attempted to meet the dangers of this Nietzschean politics by conceding considerable ground to Nietzsche's creative and destructive nihilism. He chose to counter the form-seeking and form-giving drives of Nietzsche's demonic individualists by redirecting them into professional politics. Weber sought to harness the diabolical forces that

Nietzsche conjured up and to foster the belief that liberal democratic politics provided a field for the exertions of the demonic self. On Weber's reinterpretation, self-delimitation emerged as a possibility within the profession of politics. This implies that politics as the exercise of right would appear integral to the political calling in Weber's regime. An endangering of the boundaries of limited government—making human rights more precarious because government can no longer be relied upon to respect the principle that its task is solely the securing of rights—is inseparable from Weber's project. But Weber's intention was to strengthen rather than weaken the boundaries of limited government by thus endangering them. His purpose in bringing the struggle between morality and nihilism into the center of the political profession was to heighten anxiety and evoke solicitude for moral forces. Weber thought this modification was necessary in part because liberal beliefs and enthusiasms could not be relied upon to generate the constancy and resoluteness required for the defense of liberal democratic institutions against Nietzsche. But it is a modification that is bound to provoke the objection that it fosters moral relativism and contributes to the relaxation of strict standards of liberal public morality.[80]

3. WEBER'S ETHICAL DICHOTOMY: RESPONSIBILITY AND RES-SENTIMENT

We turn now to Weber's treatment of the relation between ethics and politics. He develops his dichotomy between an ethic of responsibility and an absolute ethic to illuminate a specific problem; his discussion is intended to distinguish "the kind of faith" that "must exist if action is to have inner strength."[81] This purpose gives a definite thrust to his "ethics." In contrast to the ancient political philosophers, who concentrated upon virtue, Weber approaches the relation between ethics and politics by attempting to clarify a kind of faith.[82] In order to clarify the faith proper to politics, Weber contrasts it with Christian faith and "the grandiose moral fervor of Christian ethics."[83] Fervor is a passion or pathos; faith as a matter of Christian love and suffering was more fundamental than the moral law or the virtues in Christian "ethics." This fervor "has blinded our eyes for a thousand years."[84] Christianity knew only one true form of faith; it precluded clarity about the varieties of faith and particularly about the distinctive character of political faith. This is not to say that Weber's account is limited to Christianity. His ideal type of an absolute ethic is general; Weber would contend that Kantian ethics obscured the faith proper to politics. The evident initial purpose of Weber's dichotomy is to undermine vulgar *Rechthaberei* or self-righteousness and to deprive politicians of the excuse that their intentions were good.[85] The indirect effect of his account is to make Nietzsche's attack upon Christianity, and Nietzsche's understanding of responsibility, superfluous.

Weber's characterization of political ethics as a matter of faith, a *Glaubensache,* complicates the task of distinguishing his alternative from Nietzsche's experiment. Like Weber, Nietzsche interprets the political as the noble and as a matter of faith.[86] In this section, I shall try to distinguish Weber from Nietzsche by comparing his dichotomy to its Nietzschean counterpart, the dichotomy between master morality and slave morality.

Neither Weber nor Nietzsche is concerned with "ethics" in the Aristotelian sense of the rational apprehension of and habituation to justice, moderation, *enkratia,* or prudence. Instead, their accounts are oriented toward the clarification of a pathos, a kind of psychological suffering. The pathos of chief concern to them is a "pathos of distance": "This is the decisive psychological quality of the politician: his ability to let realities work upon him with inner concentration and calmness. Hence his *distance* to things and men. 'Lack of distance' *per se* is one of the deadly sins of every politician."[87] The problem of the faith that gives action inner strength arises for Weber and Nietzsche primarily from the domination of man by man. The use of force and fraud, the imposition of the will of the master upon a subject or slave, entails a peculiar kind of suffering for both parties. That suffering is the result of a relation between different kinds of men, but the difference is largely a function of this relationship; it cannot be understood as the isolated psychological experience of either man alone. The problem of distance arises from their moral relatedness or from the moral conflict between them. Consequently, Weber and Nietzsche seek to clarify it by means of opposed "types" which occupy the logical extremes of the positions that may be taken by master and slave, ruler and ruled, politician and subject.

This mode of clarification is reminiscent of Aristotle's presentation of the conflict between oligarchic and democratic assertions about justice, in the *Politics.*[88] There the pathos of class struggle provided the background for a dispute over the nature of citizenship. The problem with which Weber and Nietzsche are concerned is similarly one of class struggle and of the opposed assertions of two different regimes or ways of life. But they differ from Aristotle in subordinating justice and citizenship to a matter of faith; they are concerned with what gives action "inner strength" in the context of such a conflict between moral claims. It is not the claims as such but the passions that inform them that occupy Weber and Nietzsche. Weber's distinction between the two ethics, like Nietzsche's contrast between master and slave morality, is intended to highlight the politics of *ressentiment*—the resentments not only of plebians but of declining patricians and beleaguered oligarchs as well. Neither Weber nor Nietzsche attempt to banish or uproot the desire for vengeance: the problem is to control the consequences of resentment, its political and cultural effects.[89]

Nietzsche sought a long-range policy toward resentment in order to prevent a repetition of the victory of Christian Rome over pagan Rome. He sought to insure that the higher men, or the natural aristocrats, would reject the moral evaluations of resentful slaves.[90] Weber is similarly concerned that the leading men will fail to recognize resentment as an affective reaction that provides no basis for policy. In particular, leaders must prevent standards of evaluation hostile to the power instincts from dictating policy. The task is to give resentment its due, or its day, without allowing it to determine policy.[91] Nietzsche and Weber provide their respective moral dichotomies in order to clarify these tasks. In *Parliament and Government,* Weber raised the issue "whether the emotional effect of the blind fury of the masses will activate the equally emotional and senseless cowardice of the bourgeoisie."

> The proud traditions of peoples which are politically mature and free from cowardice have always proved themselves in such situations in that they kept their nerve and a cool head, crushed force with force, but then tried to resolve soberly the tensions that had led to the outbreak—above all, in that they immediately restored the guarantees of civil liberties and in general did not let such events interfere with the manner of political decision-making.[92]

The same thought is reiterated in *Democracy and the Right to Vote* as a reason for stressing the importance of political leadership:

[W]hat matters is to increase the importance of the responsible leaders, the importance of political leadership *per se*. It is one of the strongest arguments for the creation of an orderly and responsible guidance of policy by a parliamentary leadership that thereby the efficacy of purely emotional motives . . . from below is weakened as far as possible . . . only the orderly guidance of the masses by responsible politicians can break the irregular rule of the street and the leadership of demagogues of the moment.[93]

The role of responsible leaders in "crushing force with force" is implied in Weber's emphasis upon violence as the decisive means of politics, in *Politics as a Vocation*. But a rather different task is also brought to the fore in the 1919 lecture: the task of controlling hatred and resentment by giving it a target, purging it by accepting its role in political struggle. Thus when Weber says that "A man who believes in an ethic of responsibility takes account of precisely the average deficiencies of people . . . he does not even have the right to presuppose their goodness and perfection,"[94] one should bear in mind how the party leader "takes account" of these deficiencies:

He must hold out the necessary internal and external premiums, heavenly or earthly reward, to his machine or else the machine will not function. Under the conditions of the modern class struggle, the internal premiums consist of the satisfying of hatred and the craving for revenge; above all, resentment and the need for pseudo-ethical self-righteousness: the opponents must be slandered and accused of heresy.[95]

It is not always possible to meet force with force and then resolve the tensions that led to the outbreak: some resentment must be vented. Weber's politician thus takes charge of the task Nietzsche had assigned, in the *Genealogy of Morals*, to the rabble-rousing priests and ministers.[96]

Nietzsche's dichotomy was intended to reinforce the class differences between democrats and oligarchs and to intensify the conflict between them. Nietzsche accentuated the moral extremes that those differences may take in order to precipitate a revolutionary political

conflict between the advocates of democratic politics and morality, on
the one hand, and his new aristocratic nihilism, on the other. In this
respect, Nietzsche sharpened from the Right a division that Marx
widened from the Left. Weber's dichotomy, by contrast, is intended to
cut across the lines of economic class in order to heighten the tension
between moral alternatives within each vocation and each class. This
was especially obvious in Weber's first public essay on the dichotomy,
"Between Two Laws." [97] The absolute ethic would preclude workers
from using the strike weapon in industrial conflicts: "He who wishes
to follow the ethic of the gospel should abstain from strikes, for strikes
mean compulsion; he may join the company unions." [98] Domination,
coercion, and exploitation are the natural targets of the politics of *ressentiment*. Granting the use of these weapons to the workers means
giving the workers an interest in affirming their use. The alternatives
are therefore either a sober conduct of economic conflicts, with strikes
as an ultimate resource, or class conflicts dominated by emotion. The
division between syndicalists and responsible politicians need not be a
division between classes or vocations; it can be a division within each.
Although the strike weapon may be an extreme case, Weber's discussion of politics and ethics clearly has an application far beyond the
public sphere delimited by the liberal scheme. Responsible leaders at
every level of the division of labor periodically face decisions comparable to those described in *Politics as a Vocation*. The means of the
state and the parties cannot be completely monopolized. The deliberate use of force "to resist evil," the removal of the causes of resentment, and the purging of resentments when their causes cannot be removed are tasks for leadership not only in the political vocation but in
every vocation. And the more "pacific" politics becomes, the more the
activities of leadership in the professions duplicate the features of political leadership.

The strike is an example of force. Responsibility for the consequences of fraud, as a means of action, would seem to be a more common or routine instance of this overlap between leadership in politics
and in the vocations (perhaps indeed in all social action). Weber's "responsible man" is not bound by duty or his conscience to tell the truth:
he is rather bound by both to take responsibility for the consequences.

> The politician will find that as a result [of the indiscriminate
> publication of truth] truth will not be furthered but certainly
> obscured through abuse and unleashing of passion; only an

all-round methodical investigation by non-partisans could bear fruit; any other procedure may have consequences for a nation that cannot be remedied for decades.[99]

The political decision to publish documents supporting the case for German guilt, in the context of the Versailles treaty deliberations, is for Weber a paradigm of the general problem of "truth" in politics: the responsible leader cannot fail to see that "as a result . . . *the peace will be discredited, not the war.*"[100] This is a grandiose instance of an everyday matter. The suppression of truth in the interest of truth, to prevent "vulgar *Rechthaberei*" and the unleashing of passion, is by no means the exclusive preserve of the politician.

This necessity for the extension of political ethics to most parts of "the total ethical economy of human life" is reinforced by other considerations. The transformation of the ancient struggle of the gods for control over man's life into a struggle between "impersonal forces" implies that every domain of human life can be (or has been) transformed by impersonal organization: the division of labor is refined within each profession or vocation. In particular, the tensions between leaders and staff are not peculiar to politics. A more subtle reason for considering the politics of resentment as a problem throughout the division of labor may be indicated by Nietzsche's Second Essay in *The Genealogy of Morals* and the corresponding analysis of conscience, guilt, and asceticism in Weber's *Protestant Ethic*.[101]

According to Weber, the vocational ethic that originally provided the foundation of the capitalist division of labor in its modern form was grounded in an *Absolutethik*; indeed, it was *the* case of "the grandiose moral fervor of Christian ethics," for Weber's purposes.[102] The free labor system, on his reading, removed the lash of the overseer and replaced it with the lash of conscience: Calvinism, or its residuum in the soul, drove men into the world of work with a compulsive sense of duty.[103] That compulsion generates a constant tension between "the idea of duty in a calling" and "the average deficiencies of people."[104] Souls under that tension are shadowed by anxiety, for work is a constant proof of their "inner strength" or faith, a test that they pass by strenuous effort only to find that the *certitudo salutis* has eluded them once again.[105] This vocational morality, even when its original impulse has been weakened, is an inexhaustible wellspring of resentment politics. Those who perform their duty may surmount the difficulty of the work itself and overcome their "average deficiencies." But they are subject to further suffering which they cannot control by working harder. They suffer at seeing others flout the standard of duty to which they hold themselves. That response appears to be inseparable from an ethic that makes universal demands. Backsliding threatens their morale; it undermines their confidence that they will continue to find the inner strength to overcome their average deficiencies. Thus there is a cleavage within the world of work, between those who are committed to the work "as a calling" and those who are not. For those who are conscientious, this must appear to be a cleavage between morality and immorality or, in the extreme case, between morality and nihilism.

Weber's ethic of responsibility, in the first instance, is an ethic for leaders who must confront *ressentiment* and select their course of action in anticipation of resentment as an "average deficiency" of people. The ethic of responsibility is an ethic of dignity and self-respect that applies to action in all moral relations and holds for "responsible men" in all professions. Precisely because a system of free labor rewards those who are driven by something like a Protestant Ethic, it is bound to be plagued by *ressentiment*. In every profession and in every large enterprise, the division of labor is bound to reflect the necessity of managing resentment: there will be a moral cleavage setting off those who assume responsibility for various forms of coercion and deception in order to prevent resentment from "discrediting the peace, not the war." [106]

The analogy we have explored between "master morality" and the ethic of responsibility was evidently clear to Weber. He knew that he was adapting a Nietzschean notion to counter the antidemocratic thrust of Nietzsche's politics. He had done so before *Politics as a Vocation* in several political writings. [107] During the war, the opponents of a more democratic electoral system, and the opponents of a strengthened parliament, had bandied about the Nietzschean term "master people." In *Parliament and Government,* Weber had turned that rhetoric to the service of the liberal cause, by defining a *Herrenvolk* as a self-commanding, self-governing nation, a people governing itself by an ethic of responsibility rather than the bureaucratic ethic of obedience. A nation of masters was the opposite of a nation of lackeys; in Weber's "newly ordered Germany" one would not dare invoke Nietzsche to defend the psychology of the *Untertan*. [108] The ethic of responsibility transforms Nietzsche's morality of mastery to suit Weber's purpose of asserting and defending liberal democratic institutions. In place of the choice between aristocratic and democratic regimes,

Weber's version yields the choice between leadership democracy and leaderless democracy. The tension between aristocrats and slaves is transformed into a tension between responsible leadership and *ressentiment* within the division of labor of the liberal commercial republic.

The risk that Weber runs in adopting this strategy is that he will become Nietzsche's most effective popularizer. In Nietzsche's works, there is little to attract democrats: his severity, his inhumanity and cruelty, his immoralism are eloquently proclaimed. There is no attempt to water them down or sweeten them with "solemn pomp-and-virtue names." [109] If an ethic of responsibility is essential in forming the distinctive "ethos" of Weber's political profession, it is not yet evident how Weber can rebut the objection that this "ethos" is a vulgate Nietzsche. We now turn to Weber's discussion of that "ethos."

4. SELF-DELIMITATION IN THE PROFESSION OF POLITICS

The ethic of responsibility is the ethic of matter-of-fact power politics. The responsible man is one who follows the maxim "thou shalt resist evil by force, or else you are responsible for the evil winning out." [110] It is evidently closely related to independence and "the art of command." If the absolute ethic resembles the Christian ethic and reminds one of Nietzsche's type of slave morality, the ethic of responsibility even more strongly parallels Nietzsche's master morality. However, the types of master and slave morality are merely the beginning of Nietzsche's *Genealogy*. They are preparatory to an ascent beyond the moral notions that constrain the masters and compel them to conform to a common type. Master morality does not know moral independence or conscience; it is a stranger to ascetic ideals. The path toward Nietzsche's philosophic politics leads through a critique of all common ideals dominated by a common moral type. As we saw in chapter 4, the higher task of cultural creation, for Nietzsche's "higher men," was to create a style by giving style to their own characters. Nietzsche presented that task as a revanche against the claims of universal morality, but it was also a counterweight to the demand for specialization and professionalization in the contemporary division of labor. [111] It is therefore no accident that the vulgar Nietzscheanism that settles out when ascetic ideals are exploded and a new greatness for man is proclaimed is an interpretation of the self which sanctions contempt for the bourgeois division of labor and for the moral restraints that support limited government and its "common good." Nietzsche's noble nihilism undermines the moral authority of the liberal common good but, more fundamentally, the authority of "common" moral standards as such.

In reply to Nietzsche's demonic individualism, Weber attempts to reform and breathe new life into the notion of a profession or calling. The difficulty of understanding his attempt to do so arises, I believe, from the fact that his notion of the *Beruf* both is and is not a common moral standard or common ideal. Weber does not directly combat Nietzsche's attempt to fortify a new individualism that asserts the sovereign right of the self to develop itself without acknowledging the reciprocal rights of others. Rather, he attempts to deflect the demonic self, toward professional work as a setting for self-delimitation. The consequence of the effort to give style to one's character within the professions is the creation of a common style, in this case the *forms* of professional politics.

Weber's project requires a profound transformation of vocational morality and of the notion of a *Beruf*. It requires that the absolute ethic that originally secured the modern capitalist division of labor must be replaced. Let us briefly consider what this entails for the themes Weber discussed in his piece "Religious Rejections of the World and Their Directions." [112] There he explored the tensions between the ascetic ideal undergirding modern vocational morality and the activities of art, science, and politics. [113] Prior to the Protestant Reformation, the "grandiose moral fervor of Christian ethics" had been relatively relaxed. "Faced with the realities of outer and inner life, Christianity has deemed it necessary to make those compromises and relative judgments, which we all know from its history." [114] The "realities of outer and inner life" most germane to Weber's primary theme of practical economic ethics were those that made art, science, and politics intractable to the Protestant Ethic of conscientious *duty* in a profession. Activities in which men do not normally act from motives of duty, but from the desire for glory, from inspiration, the will to truth, or the will to power, are difficult to subordinate to "the grandiose moral fervor of Christian ethics." The medieval papacy, to its glory and infamy, chose to protect art, science, and politics at the expense of that moral fervor. It brought these spheres of activity into the service of Christianity but relaxed or stretched the demands for ascetic discipline in Christian ethics in order to do so. Prior to "the Protestant Ethic," it seemed possible to subordinate esthetic and intellectual pursuits to a Christian *logos* without losing what was essential to Christianity. But the practical asceticism of urban tradesmen could not be elevated to the height it attained through the Reformation (on Weber's interpretation) without stripping the higher activities of this protective Christian mantle. The resentment that we have described as natural to a free labor system is not only directed at shirkers. Everyone who acts primarily from motives other than "duty in one's calling" is naturally suspect, even (or perhaps most of all) when they perform great and beautiful deeds.[115]

Nietzsche's appeal to the "higher men" to abandon liberalism is a claim to protect these higher activities from democratic resentment:

> Today . . . when only the herd animal receives and dispenses honors in Europe, when "equality of rights" could all too easily be changed into equality in violating rights— I mean, into a common war on all that is rare, strange, privileged, the higher man, the higher soul . . . today the concept of greatness entails being noble, wanting to be by oneself, being able to be different, standing alone and having to live independently.[116]

Weber's effort to interpret science and politics as "callings," to identify each with an "ethos," and to develop a notion of each as a profession, should be understood as an effort to protect these activities against the moral resentments that a free labor system is bound to generate. Weber seeks to accommodate the loss of a common religious framework by acknowledging the plurality of demons or gods. He argues that, at the heart of every profession, there is a god or demon. To put the point without metaphor: he regards each profession as a field of activity suited to an individual dominated by a specific drive or ruling passion. Giving style to one's character by finding and obeying one's ruling passion becomes a task within each profession. The ranking of values that results would replace Nietzsche's distinctions between the noble and the base, the great and the small, the master and the slave. Weber's ranking also relocates the problem of dealing with resentment against the "higher men" whose activities are not governed by duty. The resulting cleavage is between the "spiritual aristocracy" of genuinely inspired or "called" individuals in each of the professions; and the banausics, the "specialists without spirit or vision."[117] Weber's reinterpretation presupposes radical differences between the professions. Yet it also creates an analogy between the irrationally inspired activity of the artist, the "strange passion" of the scientist, the politician's craving for responsibility, and the "demonic" devotion of a businessman or union leader to his "calling."[118] What, then, is distinctive about politics that enables Weber to speak of its "ethos"?

Weber's attempt to isolate the political as a distinct sphere within "the total ethical economy of human life" seems to rest upon the empirical truth that "We are placed into various life spheres, each of which is governed by different laws."[119] Therefore politics can be rationalized, disenchanted, and made a routine profession. But in what sense is politics a distinct sphere? By whom are we placed in such "spheres"? What is the status of the "laws" that govern politics? Weber cites "the Indian ethic's quite unbroken treatment of politics by following politics' own laws and even radically enhancing this royal art."[120] The authority of the *Kautaliya Arthasastra* in this respect is reinforced by Catholic ethics, Luther, and Calvin.[121] Yet are these authorities for political science? Does Weber establish anything more than the fact that every tribe of priests has found it useful to circumscribe the use of force and fraud? What is the authority of the Indian caste system for the politics of the modern state? Unless Weber believes that there is a permanent natural order to which the wisdom of all the great religions has bowed—a belief of which there is not the faintest trace in Weber's scholarly writings—these "historical precedents" are not evidence; at best they may provide intimations. It would be extraordinary indeed if Weber, after turning his back resolutely upon political philosophy, suddenly saw the natural light of natural law in a blinding flash in 1919.

The traditional precept had been *Quem te Deus esse Jussit, et humana qua parte locatus es in re, Disce.*[122] God has placed you. But if Weberian politics can be delimited in a world disenchanted by science, the delimitation cannot be grounded in theology. It would be more accurate to say that the politician inherits the *formative* task of the priesthoods: he must circumscribe his own sphere and assume individual responsibility for this determination. The constituting of a life sphere depends upon the choice of a demon or god. But that choice is not merely a legislation of limits for the political sphere; it is a determination of the self. "*Quem te . . .*" was a precept for submission to the constraints upon individuality imposed by the division of labor; it was an appeal to the authority of a created, revealed, or discovered order. "Find and obey the demon," Weber's precept, is an appeal to individuality to curb itself. Weber's craft lies in making this self-delimitation a source of limits and form for the political life sphere.

The impression that empirical science delimits the alternatives is rhetorical: this is true of Weber's discussion of political ethics, just as it is true of his history of the external conditions of political work.[123] The history of political ethics in the world religions or in political philosophy cannot secure Weber's argument. While the criterion by which the politician asserts his distinctive domain can be illustrated by Weber's list of authorities, it cannot be derived from them. Weber begins from a premise that undermines their authority: the order of things, revealed to the sages or prophets, cannot support an ethos or ideal. The politician must "draw his ideals from his own breast."[124] The question is then one of individuality, of the peculiar self in which the political demon is nascent or there to be "found and obeyed." What kind of a breast must one have to "let oneself in for politics as a vocation"?[125]

Weber has shown that certain means can be singled out and organized into a distinctive life sphere for politics. This accomplishment was established as something more than a mere possibility by his history of entrepreneurial state-building. The man who has the calling for politics has a special disposition toward these means: what gives them coherence and welds them into a *Gebiet* or domain for a life work is the distinctive psychological drive of the politician. Weber denies from the outset that this drive can be reduced to mere power instinct or the vulgar will-to-power celebrated by "German drill-sergeants."[126] The typical inner collapse of the representatives of that mentality raised Weber's initial question as to what gave action inner strength. The politician cannot be a soulless Machiavellian prince, for if he were, Nietzsche's critique of the modern state, as an enterprise that makes the heart small, would apparently remain unanswered. Weber does cite Machiavelli in order to emphasize the distinctive character of the genuine political man. Like Machiavelli's citizen in the *Florentine Histories,* he makes his choice for "the genius or demon of politics" in full knowledge of what it means for his soul. That demon "lives in an inner tension with the god of love, as well as with the Christian God as expressed by the church. This tension can at any time lead to an irreconcilable conflict."[127] But if he is a prince without a soul, the politician's self-affirmation is of no great significance. If the calling for politics rests on a simple affirmation of the diabolical *virtú* which built the modern state, the possibility of moral grandeur, nobility, and magnanimity in politics would apparently be excluded. As one interpreter has put the problem,

> we would then be confronted with the paradoxical situation that the individual is at peace with himself while the world is ruled by war. The strife-torn world demands a strife-torn individual. . . . Weber had to combine the anguish bred by atheism (the absence of any redemption, of any solace) with the anguish bred by revealed religion (the oppressive sense of guilt). Without that combination, life would cease to be tragic and thus lose its depth.[128]

The political leader must not be beneath absolute ethics: he must sublimate the grandiose moral fervor of Christian ethics without being blinded by it. Otherwise Weber could not praise him as a hero comparable to Martin Luther:

> [I]t is immensely moving when a *mature* man . . . is aware of a responsibility for the consequences of his conduct and really feels such responsibility with heart and soul. He then acts by following an ethic of responsibility and somewhere he reaches the point where he says "Here I stand; I can do no other." That is something genuinely human and moving. And every one of us who is not spiritually dead must realize the possibility of finding himself at some time in that position. Insofar as this is true, an ethic of ultimate ends and an ethic of responsibility are not absolute contrasts but rather supplements, which only in unison constitute a genuine man—a man who *can* have the "calling for politics."[129]

We may restate Weber's difficulty by recalling the wider range of politics that Nietzsche affirmed in "What is Noble."[130] Weber and Nietzsche agree that reality is a chaos of particulars upon which meaning must be imposed through an assertion of values. But this implies that politics was spuriously delimited by all previous attempts to circumscribe the use of force and fraud. Why not then exploit the full diapason of political possibilities, capitalizing upon every kind of tyranny, "including the most spiritual," in order to enhance the type "man"? To oppose this Nietzschean orchestration of force and fraud, and to compress the range of political action within the scope of the modern state and parties, Weber requires an argument to deflect or weaken Nietzsche's claim that it is a violation of the noble or higher self to subject it to the limits of liberal democratic politics.[131]

Weber's solution to this difficulty is rather cunning. It reiterates his attempt to turn the tables on Nietzsche in *Science as a Vocation*.[132] The refinement of politics into a "long ladder of rank" culminating in philosophic soul-politics made possible Nietzsche's sequestration of the philosopher from base means. The philosopher is to rule but without loss of *noblesse*. Weber's handicap is that he requires the politician to descend into the state and the parties. Constant contact with "base means" places him in jeopardy of losing nobility. Weber must persuade the more gifted and politically talented individuals to descend into the morass. But he must hold out some promise that they will not be brutalized and wasted. Weber's stance recalls his appeal to Nietzschean toughness in *Science as a Vocation*:

> What is hard for modern man, and especially for the younger generation, is to measure up to *workaday* existence. The ubiquitous chase for "experience" stems from this weakness; for it is weakness not to be able to countenance the stern seriousness of our fateful times.[133]

Weber makes it a test of strength to overcome revulsion against base means and the fear of becoming degraded. The world that the politician affirms is the world of his staffs in the party and the state, a world of men of "average deficiencies." If he cannot find this affirmation in himself, if he does not have that unique psychological compulsion that causes him to affirm these psychically proletarianized tools as the very precondition of his own being, he does not have the calling for politics.

> Only he has the calling for politics who is sure that he shall not crumble when the world from his point of view is too stupid or too base for what he wants to offer. Only he who in the face of all this can say "In spite of all!" has the calling for politics.[134]

Weber makes the politician's conquest over his fears of loss of *noblesse* the final test of his greatness of heart. It is a nice twist that this conquest is framed as a Nietzschean affirmation of this world: the

Weberian citizen in these Weberian *Teutonic Histories* chooses his city and risks the loss of his Nietzschean self.

5. DISTINGUISHING WEBER'S REGIME

In order to comprehend Weber's regime, one must combine the teachings of *Politics as a Vocation* and *Science as a Vocation*. For the completion of the disenchantment of the world by science imposes limits independently of the politician's deeds. He may try to create institutions and laws to memorialize his career, but science is an obstacle to any reenchantment of the world or the public sphere: it is science that forces the ultimate and most sublime values into the private sphere.[135] At a deeper level, Weberian science intensifies the anxiety of conscientious men at every level of the division of labor. Despite the present connotations of the term "charisma," Weber's regime is at least by intention the antithesis of a leadership cult. The moral center of liberal democracy in Weber's reconfiguration is work in a calling. If the members of this regime can be said to share in a cult, it is the cult of devotion to a calling as one's cause or *Sache*. The followers of the Weberian leader (with the exception of the staff) need have no reverence for the person of the leader, as in Fascist and Communist regimes.[136] What they find "irresistible" is the man who approaches politics with matter-of-fact devotion. The forms engendered by professional politics are intended to have the effect that Weber admired in Anglo-Saxon politics:

> [T]he relative immunity of formerly Puritan peoples to Caesarism, and, in general, the subjectively free attitude of the English to their great statesmen as compared with many things which we have experienced since 1878 both positively and negatively. On the one hand, there is a greater willingness to give the great man his due, but, on the other, a repudiation of all hysterical idolization of him and of the naive idea that political obedience could be due anyone from thankfulness.[137]

It is impossible to be precise about the forms a Weberian regime would generate, for Weber was reticent about articulating them. His reserve was consistent with his elevation of the task of creating such forms as a task for professional politicians. It was a matter of principle.

> Democracy could perhaps . . . free the road for the development of valuable forms suitable to our civic, social, and economic structure, which therefore would be "genuine" and cultured values. One cannot invent such values, just as one cannot invent a style. Only this much (in an essentially negative and formal way) can be said, and it holds for all values of this nature: such forms can never be developed on any other basis than upon an attitude of personal distance and reserve. . . . "Distance," however, can by no means be gained exclusively on the "cothurnus" of snobbishly setting one's self off from the "far too many," as is maintained by the various and misconceived "prophecies" which go back to Nietzsche. On the contrary, when today it is in need of this inner support, distance is always spurious. Perhaps the necessity of maintaining one's inner dignity in the midst of a democratic world can serve as a test of the genuineness of dignity.[138]

Given Weber's reluctance to preempt the career politicians in creating these "forms," we shall confine ourselves to a comment on the significance of his attempt to make a "regime" (in the sense we have discussed) within the confines of liberal democracy.[139] To introduce regime politics Weber must efface the distinction between the securing of rights and their exercise as the just purpose of political action and government. By reinterpreting political leadership as passionate serving of a cause, Weber departs from the principles of representative government and makes the political profession a field for the exercise of a right to rule. But to some extent this relaxation of liberal principle is justified in Weber's eyes, as I have suggested, by the necessity to defend liberal democratic institutions. It is a response to a politics that makes formerly private institutions a battleground between democratic moralism and aristocratic nihilism, politicizing activities that were granted a certain immunity by virtue of their private status and placing them in competition with public institutions.[140] Weber's politics is an attempt to defend liberal democracy by a redefinition and reassertion of the political profession. His defense is made necessary by a philosophic politics that vitiates the restraining force of liberal principles.

The assertion of "the political" by professional politicians is Weber's remedy against cultural warfare or cultural subversion conducted in large measure outside the sphere of limited government and in antagonism to it. What is to be said for Weber's strategy is that he attempts to restrict the exercise of rights to those whose professional responsibility is for the concentration of force and fraud and who are most subject to the normal pressures of public accountability under liberal democratic procedures. One might also be willing to grant Weber considerable discretion to attract the best and most politically talented individuals to public service, given the contempt for liberal democratic politics that Marx and Nietzsche propagated. *Nondimanco,* as Machiavelli would say: there is a profound weakness in Weber's remedy. Consider the epigraph to this chapter. If Weber's professional politicians believe that they are truly serving a higher cause, then they are subject to Nietzsche's taunt of moral hypocrisy and lack of independence. If they are without illusions and see their cause as a self-generated ideal drawn from their own breasts, then there is nothing that binds them in principle to limited government. In this case a Nietzschean master class will have entered Troy through Weber's Odyssean strategem. This ambiguity is inseparable from Weber's indirection in defending moral forces against Nietzsche's nihilistic politics.

7. NIHILISM AND THE LIMITS OF LEADERSHIP

There he shall see the rise of opinions and find from what slight and sometimes shameful occasions some of them have taken their rise; which yet afterwards have had great authority and passed almost for sacred in the world, and borne down all before them. There also one may learn great and useful instructions of prudence and be warned against the cheats and rogueries of the world. . . .

John Locke[1]

1. THE CONVENTIONAL LIMITS OF OPINION LEADERSHIP

IT IS common knowledge that over several generations, reform liberals have effectively reshaped the milieu of American government and the intellectual context of political journalism. Many distinguished journalists have considered themselves reformers in the Wilsonian tradition; in political science, many influential teachers have carried forward the reform movement and have recruited political talents into public careers.[2] In chapter 1 of this study, I attempted to place the accomplishments of reform liberalism in perspective by elucidating a paradigm or leadership-convention from Wilson's writings. I delineated a notion of "opinion leadership" broad enough to account for the great variety of forums in which reform liberals have exercised leadership—including journalism, university teaching, and the courts, no less than the presidency and Congress. I attempted to account for the rise of opinion leaders in single-issue constituencies and for the ease with which conservatives have recently taken over Wilsonian methods. Though broad enough to embrace these disparate phenomena, the paradigm of Wilsonian opinion leadership I articulated was intended to be specific enough to account for the main legislative achievements of reform liberalism and particularly those which produced the current plebiscitary system of presidential selection.[3] My analysis of the "great movement of opinion" which Wilson tried to shape focused on the demoralizing discrepancy between the power that the Wilsonian movement achieved—a power by no means absolute but quite sufficient to transform American political institutions—and its evident inability to realize Wilson's principal goals. The power that reform liberalism wielded seemed paradoxically to contribute to the defeat of Wilson's purposes. In the first chapter, I sought to explain why reform did not eliminate private government but rather reintroduced it in novel and subtler forms; why, instead of removing suspicion of leadership, it intensified distrust of public government; why, instead of generating a national leadership cadre, it strengthened the leaders of single-issue constituencies. In that chapter, I thereby retraced the itinerary that many thoughtful friends of liberal democracy have taken in recent years: questioning the basic assumptions of reform liberalism, seeking critical distance on Wilsonian enthusiasms, and exploring the possibility that the Wilsonian project, despite the best intentions of reform liberals, is inherently destructive of constitutional democracy.[4]

> Reason and good sense absolutely prescribe . . . "whenever we are involved in difficulties from the measures we have pursued, that we should take a strict view of those measures" or that we should "enter into the most ample historical detail."[5]

Appropriate and timely though a critical and detached review of reform liberalism would be, it is unlikely that it would captivate public attention. American political arrangements now place a premium on motion and on urgent agendas. Hence it is predictable that many journalists and opinion leaders will respond to the malaise of reform by grasping for a paradigm that both accounts for what is wrong with the Wilsonian project and persuasively defines the current necessities of, and for, leadership. Weber's significance is best understood in the context of this predictable craving for a swift resolution of the crisis of reform liberalism. I displayed Weber's argument in this light in chapter 1 and made clear its attractiveness as a critique and alternative to "opinion leadership." Although Weber's reputation as a keen analyst is great, what he promises is more than a comprehensive and intellectually attractive interpretation of "politics as a profession." In the first chapter, I tried to indicate Weber's practical appeal at the level of *will*. Adopting his project would not require campaigners, or the electorate, to kick the leadership habits that they have formed but only to modify these habits of willing. Because he too advocates a form of plebiscitary leader democracy, Weber's project would retain considerable continuity with Wilsonian politics at the level of habit. Since such habits might be difficult or painful to shake, Weber's alternative has all the advantages of a program well adapted to established inclinations. I outlined in chapter 1 a project so convenient that it would have to be invented if Weber were not rediscovered to provide its ready articulation.

The likelihood that Weber will be overlooked, however, is remote. In the universities, he has long since displaced Wilson and other liberal lights in political science and sociology; his reputation is rivaled only by Marx. The academy is also far ahead of (or away from) the electorate in another respect. Academics have for the most part consciously turned away from classical Lockean liberalism.[6] Although they are for the moment partial toward Wilsonian opinion leadership, as I have suggested, it is not unreasonable to expect professors who have dabbled in Weber's scholarship to initiate and secure the shift toward Weber sketched in chapter 1. One might be inclined to welcome such a redirection of intellectual fashion because Weber's work centers upon serious political problems and might promote a sober professional politics. But every fashion has its price. Because the claims about Weber with which we began chapter 1 are widely accepted *as truisms* in American universities and schools of law, the professors are unlikely to provide critical foresight or foreknowledge of what is problematic in Weber's alternative to reform liberalism. Starting, then, from the hunch that Weber's teaching could supplant the Wilsonian leadership-convention, I have attempted in this study a critical analysis of Weber's argument on leadership. As a critique, it has been concentrated upon Weber's inability to prevent his initiative from developing into a frankly nihilistic politics.

In chapters 3 and 4, Nietzsche's novel uses for opinion leadership came into view. It became evident that reform liberalism could no longer be said to provide the complete context, or to define the horizon, of contemporary journalism. Journalists like George Will, Theodore H. White, and Thomas Sowell who still share Wilson's now-archaic enthusiasm for moderate self-government find themselves increasingly on the defensive in the "media world." That world now defines itself by a more aggressive reading of the importance of self-expression and self-assertion in public and private life, particularly with regard to the limits of media politics and the rights of the media.[7] In practice, therefore, the choice is not between Wilsonian liberalism and Weber's attempt to do without it. Opinion leadership is no longer confined within the boundaries of the Wilsonian leadership-convention. Weber's defense of liberal institutions is instructive because the tasks Weber undertook were in good measure posed by Nietzsche's unconventional politics. Henceforth every circumspect defense of liberal democracy must take the measure of Nietzsche's influence and anticipate the new forms of individualism that Nietzsche promoted.[8] Projecting the controversy between Weber and Nietzsche onto the screen of American politics proved, therefore, to be a less futuristic exercise than it at first appeared.

I demonstrated that Weber's argument for the importance of political leadership is more radical than Wilson's because it goes to the roots of Wilson's position and rejects its fundamental tenets. To reformulate this point: When the reform movement seeks to articulate what "the free unfolding of individuality" means in practical terms, it has two possibilities. It may either appeal to the enthusiasm for eudaemonistic progress and commercial prosperity—the promise of liberal political economy. Or it may appeal to theoretical historicism and seek to evoke awe, enthusiasm, or reverence for a collective identity or cultural whole—and in particular for those cultural wholes that have evolved historically rather than being planned or projected in advance.[9] In this latter vein, Wilson tried to interpret Anglo-Saxon political culture as the evolved and unplanned goal of historical development.[10] More recently, the historicist argument has been turned by opinion leadership to the service of ethnic and racial minorities or to the service of the various "subcultures."[11] Weber foresaw that the unification of the liberal cause with the national cause could not be based on either of these appeals, singly or in combination. He turned instead, as I have shown, toward a different fundamental experience, relying on political leadership to impose limits on the "free unfolding of individuality." The experience of ultimate commitment to a value-standard, on which Weber relies, is one of self-determination through self-imposed constraints, in which the passions are ranked and the self asserts its individuality by delimiting itself. I argued in chapter 1 that Weber sought to transcend liberalism by reinterpreting the national-liberal cause in the light of this root experience.

One might welcome a turn toward Weber because of his emphasis on responsibility and self-restraint. But we found upon closer inspection that Weber's emphasis requires a rejection of both liberal eudaemonism and theoretical historicism; the turn toward Weber means intepreting "individuality" in terms taken from atheoretical, practical historicism. This turn is more troubling and problematic for liberal democracy than the connotations of "responsibility" and "self-restraint" at first suggest. To demonstrate this, we explored the parallels between Weber's argument and Nietzsche's. For Nietzsche had also linked the liberal cause to the experience of self-determination through self-imposed constraint. In chapter 2 we considered Nietzsche's account of the philosophic discovery of "individuality" as the root of liberal institutions and the origin of modern science. According to Nietzsche, the liberal cause was originally an attempt by philosophers to create a world hospitable to experimental philosophy. It was a new, as yet untrodden path to human greatness. In chapters 2–4, we considered Nietzsche's philosophic politics as an expansion of this original modern project. The next stage of experimental science, according to Nietzsche, would require a scientific conquest of the domain of morality. He foresaw that the application of experiment and critique in moral matters was bound to encounter great resistance in regimes that rested upon popular consent, because the people or the herds have the greatest stake in morality.[12] The method of democracy was bound to promote resistance to the method of science. Nietzsche argued that philosophic leadership was imperative to protect science while it pursued morally dangerous questions and to overcome democratic resistance to the completion of experimental science. From the root experience of self-legislating individuality, Nietzsche thus deduced the original necessity for liberal institutions, the present necessity of destroying them, and the future necessity for an aristocratic politics subordinate to the rule of philosophers.[13] The fundamental experience on which Weber relied proved to be the matrix of a leadership that was defiantly nihilistic and destructive of the political forms and moral limits to which Weber was attached.

The upshot of the analysis of Nietzsche's political philosophy presented in chapters 2–4 may now be restated in the following terms. An aggressively nihilistic politics is latent in the experience of "the discovery of individuality" from which liberal democracy springs. Insofar as the liberal commercial way of life conserves, renews, and reasserts that root experience, it harbors its own nemesis.[14] I would not claim that this study has established the validity of this Nietzschean contention. For our purposes, it is sufficient that the contention should be plausible and attractive to those whom Nietzsche designated "the higher men." This is quite enough to provide the basis within liberal democracies for a new opinion leadership hostile to the liberal commercial republic and opposed to the limits of representative government. Moreover, the seductive and confusing resemblance between the liberal evaluation of individuality and Nietzsche's more radical evaluation opens liberal institutions to a politics of cultural subversion whether Nietzsche's contention is valid or not. Even if a strict scholarly investigation were to disprove Nietzsche's historical claim regarding the roots of liberal institutions, the rhetorical force of Nietzsche's promise of a further liberation and chaining up of the self might prove difficult to resist. Certainly the experience on which Weber relied is open to this Nietzschean interpretation. Perhaps we should say that it positively cries out for it.

Some of the novel problems posed for the defenders of liberal democracy by Nietzsche's doctrine of the self were indicated in chapters 4–6. I argued that the scope and character of Weber's defense of liberal democratic institutions were determined by Nietzsche's challenge or by Nietzsche's combining of experimental nihilism in science with an intrepid, power-conscious individualism directed toward political and cultural creativity. Weber's defense required science to become the bad conscience of a Nietzschean age and politics to become a profession on a new understanding of vocational or professional morality.[15] Weber found after 1895 that the experience on which he had based the argument of his *Antrittsrede* was capable of exploding his own project; his subsequent problem was to prevent it from doing so. Weber's solution was to locate the "demonic" experience of self-legislating individuality within the division of labor of the liberal commercial republic and to deflect its revolutionary potential into the creation of professions. His attempt to turn science and politics to the service of "moral forces," we concluded, was rhetorically powerful and promised to marshal formidable psychological resistance within the professions against Nietzschean politics. Yet Weber's indirection, in both *Science as a Vocation* and *Politics as a Vocation*, stymied our quest for a straightforward account of principles. This discrepancy between the force of the moral dispositions that Weber sought to tap and the flimsiness of his arguments compelled us to question Weber's indirection in order to decide whether it reflected a higher prudence for coping with Nietzsche or rather a compromise with his nihilism. To pursue this questioning further, I believe it will be helpful to restate our findings in somewhat more theoretical terms.

We discovered that Weber was more penetrating than Wilson in recognizing why opinion leadership could not be kept within the limits of Wilsonian liberalism. The limits on which Wilson relied were set by liberal political economy, on the one hand, and the theoretical historicism of the German Historical School, on the other. Wilson's project was stabilized (he thought) by the correspondence between the "great movement of opinion" that he initiated and the thoughts of the greatest minds or the progress of science. That correspondence cannot withstand the crisis of liberalism and the attacks of Marx and Nietzsche upon theoretical historicism, according to Weber. These attacks demonstrated that the limits to opinion leadership were never really fixed by knowledge. Those limits prove to be conventional or merely "ideological" and cannot withstand "the end of ideology." To put the matter bluntly: Weber is superior to Wilson because he adopts the principle that political philosophy is impossible. He supersedes Wilson's reliance upon conventional limits to opinion leadership, but not by ascending from opinion to knowledge or from mere convention to limits that are more than conventional. Weber rather transcends Wilsonian liberalism by recognizing that all limits are cultural or conventional: they depend upon an ultimate commitment. Reason cannot transcend merely conventional limits; hence no legislative science that combines normative and empirical discernment is possible. To avoid the confusions that flow from Wilson's reliance on the guidance of thinkers like Burke, Weber abandons the possibility of leadership based upon knowledge. There is no rational basis for holding to the liberal cause rather than any other cause as a matter of ultimate commitment. Knowing that knowledge is of no avail or that our opinions do not rest upon science, we must choose between our ultimate objects of loyalty.[16] This clarity makes Weberian political leadership more stable than opinion leadership because it cannot rationalize acquiesence in popular moods and trends of public opinion. It is alert for the misuse of social science to rationalize submission to fashion. Weber forewarns us that the appeal to knowledge is not only spurious but dangerous and that theoretical historicism in combination with popular sovereignty is inimical to constancy and firmness of purpose in politics. The question is whether Weber's attempted recovery of *Staatsraison* can restore constancy and firmness of purpose to the defense of liberal democratic institutions once the impossibility of political philosophy is taken seriously.[17]

Weber tries to arrest the motion of Nietzsche's attack upon political philosophy *in medias res*. He accepts Nietzsche's assertion that the limits discerned by previous political philosophy are merely ideological or conventional. But he denies the possibility of a comprehensive, architectonic imposition of limits. Weber rejects the possibility of a philosophic politics capable both of ranking values and of establishing its leadership over modern science. I do not see how Weber can resist the conclusion that the only limits that are constant and that impose rationality upon the flux of human affairs are, as Nietzsche said, essentially the creations of the most constant and determined will, or that values are the creations of philosophic commanders whose will to truth is will to power.[18]

Weberian leadership is rescued from certain illusions that produce inconstancy in action: the limiting principles are at war; one must choose between them and hold steadily to a cause. That steady responsibility to a cause will create and maintain a political community and a culture; Weber initially saw no reason why liberal democratic politicians could not create and maintain a national-liberal culture on this basis.[19] This enterprise proved more difficult and problematic to Weber after 1895, and he subsequently withdrew several steps from the possibility of a direct assertion of the national-liberal cause toward the indirection we found in his 1919 lectures.[20] Our analysis of *Politics as a Vocation* in particular indicated that Weber was reluctant, despite his emphasis upon empirical inquiry, to rest his argument upon facts. His confident assertion of the results of his empirical inquiries stood in perplexing contrast to his silence on matters of principle.[21] Upon close inspection, we found Weber curiously ambivalent about the empirical or "given" limits of political leadership. On the one hand, he wished to deny that anything so grandiose as Nietzschean leadership was empirically possible and asserted categorically that "the prophet for whom so many of our younger generation yearn simply does not exist."[22] The implication was that it *could not* exist. On the other hand, Weber wished to deny that science or reason could discern any stable or permanent limits for leadership; at best it could speak only of the reversals to which all action was subject or of the discrepancy between intentions and results.[23] The theoretical problem that Weber faced is reflected, I think, in this ambivalence toward the results of his empirical inquiries. His problem may be formulated in these terms: Weber must rely indirectly upon the founders of modern political philosophy in order to defend liberal democracy intelligently. This indirect reliance indicates that political philosophy is possible. Yet Weber accepted enough of Nietzsche's critique of political philosophy to be convinced that to admit the efficacy of Montaigne, Machiavelli, Bacon, or John Locke would be tantamount to abandoning the last defenses against Nietzschean leadership of science.[24]

Weber rules out Nietzsche's politics by appealing to the experiential regularities or *Erfahrungsregeln* that set limits to political action in modern states.[25] But his accounts of the origin of the modern state and modern science are unconvincing not only as arguments against Nietzsche's alternative but also against Whig historiography, in which Bacon, Locke, and the party of enlightened progress had figured as decisive causes.[26] By taking the *results* of the Baconian and Lockean initiatives as empirical givens, Weber relied indirectly upon political philosophy to make his case against Nietzsche. To defend limited government and the liberal commercial republic, Weber pointed to the strength and staying power of the institutions brought into being by the modern project, above all, rational-legal bureaucracy and capitalism applying scientific knowledge. Weber is dependent upon the achievements of modern liberal politics but unable to bring its *reasoning* to bear against Nietzsche. Weber is therefore consistent when he refuses to base his argument on empirical fact: the facts that serve his case are "constructed facts." They presuppose the intelligible plans of farsighted philosophers. Were Weber to admit that philosophy once played an architectonic and "creative" role, the case for Nietzsche's philosophic leaders, and for their primacy over mere political leaders, would be irresistible. It is hardly surprising that Weber sought to escape from this bind by means of impressive rhetoric: there is no escape from it by means of logic. One must either rely directly upon political philosophy, and defend liberal democratic institutions by recovering the legislative science of modern liberal politics, or give way before Nietzsche's alternative. In either case, Weber would have to surrender his doctrine that reason cannot rank ultimate values and that the endless struggle of the Weberian politician with irreconcilable gods cannot be judged by the measure of philosophic politics.[27]

The *locus classicus* of these difficulties is Weber's discussion of the relation between ethics and politics in *Politics as a Vocation*.[28] That account is also the key to Weber's treatment of the thematic questions with which our inquiry began: How does nihilism, as a term of blame or praise, square with the standard for approving or condemning political leaders that befits a free people? What is the standard that befits a free man and a citizen, or, better, "a gentleman and a scholar," or, best of all, a good man and citizen? This formulation asserts or presupposes that political philosophy is possible, implying that it is reasonable to pose and answer these questions more or less directly.[29] Weber's formulation rejects this possibility. He admits that the relation between ethics and politics depends on the relation between the good man and the political man.[30] But it is of the essence of Weber's indirection that he eschews a direct answer to our questions and indeed refuses to pose them directly.[31]

At this late stage in my study, I cannot, of course, undertake to investigate whether political philosophy is possible or to weigh Weber's arguments to the contrary. Instead, I shall merely remind the thoughtful reader of his own experience in ascending from opinions currently held in the course of the preceding chapters. My concern in this recapitulation is to complete the argument on political leadership and nihilism that underlaid these chapters.

In these chapters, I have tried to chart the rise of certain opinions, identifying the controversies in which they originated. I have argued that the assertions by Wilson and Weber of the importance and respectability of "political leadership" account for its present ascendancy in public discourse and the vocabulary of political science. In this last chapter I will review and bring to completion my argument on political leadership and nihilism. Because the currently held opinions with which the reader presumably began this study have been subjected to critique in the course of our inquiry, it should now be possible to state my argument more fully, without fear of running afoul of unquestioned preconceptions. I have tried to show how we have been induced to exempt the concept of "political leadership" from critical scrutiny. I have shown that Weber's polemical attempt to elevate the importance of political leadership informed his most comprehensive critique and analysis of it in his 1919 lectures. This demonstration should clear the path for a more intelligible account. It alerts us to the rhetorical dimensions of Weber's endeavor; it forewarns us that to attain critical distance on the problem of leadership we must treat Weber as an obstacle to clarity; and it should ready us to pursue the path that lies beyond him. To consolidate these results, I will retrace in the balance of this concluding chapter the path we have traversed, concentrating upon some of the principal landmarks and milestones along our ascent. By surveying the questions with which we began, from the vantage point now attained, I will attempt in sections 2 and 3 to conduct the reader a few steps beyond Weber, advancing my argument on political leadership and nihilism toward a concluding judgment on standards, which I outline in section 4. Having shown that Weber relied heavily upon indirection for his defense of liberal democratic institutions, I will emphasize that a more direct defense is both necessary and possible.

2. THE IRON CAVE

> Although philosophy seeks to replace opinions by truth, it cannot succeed unless it is able to make an accurate identification of opinions, past and present, and perhaps especially of past opinions presently masquerading as truths.
>
> Stanley Rosen, *Nihilism: A Philosophical Essay*

The path charted by the preceding inquiry passes through several experiences of perplexity. My own inquiry into Weber's politics became a study in political philosophy—or set forth on that path—when I realized that "political leadership" was not a transparent term that ostensively designated a set of facts, that it was rather the name for a fact constituted by conventions and opinions. For several years, I had labored under the assumption that Weber's distinctive contribution lay in the notion of "charisma," or perhaps his idea of the *Beruf* or calling. I adopted the practice still dominant in social science—and indeed in public discourse in general—of using "political leader" as a neutral term of description. Political leaders were the givens or things to which the term simply pointed. The discovery that the term itself might be problematic or, to use Wittgenstein's phrase, that here a picture held us captive came as a disquieting surprise. Newly skeptical, I found myself surrounded by uncertainties. Unwilling to trust this language, it was as if I had crushed my spectacles underfoot and had to grope around with my hands until my eyes became adjusted to their native powers. Subsequently, as I became more accustomed to seeing without it, the lens of the term no longer seemed at all transparent. Its former "look" of transparency struck me as more and more remarkable and troubling. If this study has succeeded in its minimal initial purpose, the reader should share this wonder and be aware that when he uses the term "political leader" ostensively he is accepting an alteration of his vision. As an initial turning point, the absence of this experience of perplexity sets off contemporary political science and sociology as precritical and therefore (in a certain sense) dogmatic with respect to "leadership." What one student has called "the burgeoning of interest in the study of political leadership per se" has not altered this situation but rather consolidates it.[32] Consider Dankwart Rustow's attempt to promote this burgeoning interest:

> In a field like political science, a focus on leadership may resolve some current methodological dilemmas. The generation that participated in the "successful revolt" waged against the older institutional-legal approach in favor of behaviorism has been engaged ever since in a wide search for a basic unit of analysis. Some have sought it in a "functional" vocabulary too abstruse to be applied in empirical research, some in the making of "decisions" that have proved difficult to isolate from the stream of reality, some in an elusive quantitative measure of power, and some in messages of communication so numerous as to defy inventory. The leader as a figure omnipresent in any political process, as the maker of decisions, originator and recipient of messages, performer of functions, wielder of power, and creator or operator of institutions, can bring these disparate elements into a single, visible focus. . . . In short, there may be the elements of a new theoretical view, both comprehensive and dynamic, of the political process as a whole.[33]

Any such attempt to supply a theoretical framework by appealing to common perceptions regarding the "givenness" of political leadership is more likely to obscure than to clarify the quest for comprehensive knowledge of politics. The seeming self-evidence of our current idioms constitutes a problem for theory, testifying to our acceptance of dogma rather than our capacity for science. Relying upon prevailing opinion will most assuredly not rid us of the confusion or dispel the theoretical darkness that beclouds the academic study of politics. The suggestion of this study is that "political leadership" is inexplicable if we take it ostensively and turn our attention to the things it putatively designates. The first task of critical reasoning is to look carefully at the pointer, which turns out to be far more than a neutral designator. I have tried to show that in "political leadership" the concept and its referent, or the pointer and its target, constitute a practical "whole," which is inexplicable in its own terms. A critique of the term and the states of fact that it helps to consolidate is both possible and necessary. To explicate this whole, I have argued that one must turn to the original arguments with which it was introduced into common usage and justified. When we do so, as I have tried to demonstrate for both Wilson and Weber, the term comes to light as an instrument in a strategy for rearranging the political agenda or for *shaping* "the political process as a whole." Theory begins in wonder at what appears self-evident and is not.

The second cause for perplexity that came to light in the course of our inquiry was the realization that political leadership, even in the mild form of liberal Wilsonian opinion leadership, might be problematic for liberal democracy. Here too the dawning of skepticism seems to leave us groping in the dark. Like most students of American politics, I find it almost torturous to think about the modern presidency, for example, without relying upon more or less Wilsonian notions of opinion leadership. In both the dream world of electoral technique and the daylight of the morning after, the American presidency has become "the rhetorical presidency." [34] It is equally difficult to understand the policy leadership of the imperial judiciary without thinking in terms of opinion leadership. Similarly, my conception of the highest possibilities of statesmanship in American party politics has been shaped by the idea of periodic party realignment in which a new "public philosophy" is forged that defines the agenda of public business for both parties for several subsequent decades. When the Weberian critique presented in chapter 1 compelled me to bracket this conception, along with every other identifiable element of the Wilsonian leadership-convention, I wondered whether I would ever regain my bearings within "the American political universe." [35]

To find one's bearings in such straits, it is always sound counsel to review *The Federalist*. But on this topic, the attempt to return to first principles by way of *The Federalist* gives rise to new and unexpected perplexities. It almost goes without saying that "a free man and citizen" will judge political leaders by his understanding of the republican way of life or, in the case of the United States, by his interpretation of the American form of government. When one studies *The Federalist*'s articulation of that standard, however, one is startled to find that "political leadership per se" is placed under a cloud of suspicion and opprobrium: integral to *The Federalist*'s standard of "a free man and citizen" is a certain principled resistance to the respectability of "political leadership." By what might be called "the strict construction" there is a distinction that makes a difference between the mere phenomenon of political leadership and the opinion that it is important and respectable. By examining how Wilson introduced political leadership into the American liberal tradition, we saw that only by overcoming and eliminating this distinction was Wilson able to make "political leader" a term of praise or even a neutral term of description.[36] Wilson remade the term, one might say, to form a crown for the republican way of life; *The Federalist* both anticipated and opposed that development.

Any attempt to recover this classical liberal distinction is bound to be unsettling precisely because the case for it remains strong and seems to contradict an equally strong case for ignoring the distinction. Let us consider the latter first. To most readers, my concentration upon Wilson's "leaderless government" must have seemed perverse because leadership seems self-evidently instrumental to socioeconomic change. The Progressive Movement succeeded in bringing socioeconomic questions of great importance onto the public agenda and compelled politicians to respond to them in closer proportion to their urgency in the minds of the laboring majority, the farmers and small businessmen, who could not buy the services of party politicians. For most of this century, thoughtful liberals have viewed "leadership" as an instrumental necessity in the light of this urgent agenda. They have adopted the Wilsonian conception of opinion leadership as the model for action in every branch of government, most recently in the courts, and have accordingly identified nice distinctions about leadership, or the concern with constitutional forms and respectability, as the counterinstruments of complacent conservatives who were callous about the social question and wished to remove it from the agenda. They conceived most of the political legislation of the reform movement, beginning with the primaries, the recall, and the referendum, as means to smash the private alliance between Wall Street and the party machines. They subsequently extended this instrumental thinking to reapportionment, the electoral college, the Voting Rights Act, and the rules governing party conventions and campaign financing. And a parallel understanding of the policy leadership of the judiciary captured the schools of law and the legal profession. For a long season of reform, the case for ignoring the constitutionalism of *The Federalist* and its distinctions regarding leadership eclipsed the counterargument in the minds of many liberals.[37]

This season is at an end because it is no longer possible for reform liberals to ignore their stake in the distinctions that secure constitutional democracy against vicious forms of popular leadership and potentially tyrannical majorities. Thoughtful citizens want to be able to call upon respectable opinion to suppress McCarthyism firmly and with energy. It is not clear whether respectable opinion will be forthcoming in the future if the distinctions of *The Federalist* continue to be suppressed. Having willed "leadership" on behalf of liberal values, in order to combat the legalism and private government that opposed the Square Deal, the New Freedom, the New Deal, and the Great Society, reform liberals find it disquieting to contemplate the possibility that the majority can now tyrannize them with the instrumentalities created by their own reforms.

In chapters 2–4 we opened an inquiry into Nietzsche's philosophy and thereby an inexhaustible wellspring of perplexity, for Nietzsche left almost no stone unturned in challenging the opinions of democratic egalitarians. As Wolfgang Müller-Lauter has remarked, it would be astonishing if Nietzsche did not excite our resistance on this score.

> Nietzsche's doctrine of domination-forms stands in unequivocal contradiction to the general consciousness of our time. Whoever speaks today of social equality as a phenomenon of decadence has the whole world against him, East, West, and in the North-South dialogue. Nothing is farther from us than the conviction which nourishes Nietzsche's vision of the future, the conviction about the necessity for "aristocratic societies."[38]

This stark contradiction, precisely because it is so unequivocal, would be less perplexing if Nietzsche's teaching were simply antithetical to opinions currently held. Instead, we discovered that Nietzsche's reassertion of slavery and tyranny as political possibilities was thoughtfully conceived as a continuation of principles to which "the general consciousness of our time" is vocally committed, and that Nietzsche's doctrine of the self was almost insufferably familiar, through its manifold popularizations.[39] It is both disconcerting and amazing to discover that an antidemocratic and anti-egalitarian teaching acceptable to *none* should be couched and propagated—as the subtitle of *Thus Spoke Zarathustra* implied—in terms acceptable to all.[40]

For students of Nietzsche, the combination of purposeful vulgarization and antidemocratic doctrine that we have emphasized is troubling because it calls into question an assumption that Nietzsche scholarship has generally shared: that since Nietzsche (and in order to understand Nietzsche), political philosophy is neither possible nor necessary. Nietzsche has attracted many intelligent readers because his philosophy has the charm of what is rare, excellent, difficult, and inaccessible. This study casts doubt upon the possibility of understanding the significance of Nietzsche without reflecting upon what is vulgar in his art. In this respect, the marketing and merchandising of the Nietzschean "self" is more unnerving than the uses to which his writings were put by the Nazis. So much intelligence has been invested in saving Nietzsche from the Nazi vulgarization that it is demoralizing to realize that Nietzsche intended a veritable jungle growth of such partial or mis-understandings to spring from the fertile soil of his writings. For this condemns those who love what is rare to a Sisyphean labor with what is not. By compelling the circumspect reader to pay the most careful attention to common opinions, and by reasserting the most untimely and repugnant dimensions of politics, Nietzsche forces those who would understand him to move closer to Socrates or to political philosophy in its original meaning. Why Socrates is the great antagonist—why Socratic political philosophy is impossible—is the greatest enigma and cause of perplexity that Nietzsche calls before us by his example.[41]

For the less specialized reader, Nietzsche raises the same problem in another way. The liberal delimitation of politics makes it fairly evident to everyone that politics is not the highest human activity and probably not even the most important practical activity: doctors and scientists who can eliminate disease are engaged in a practical activity, the importance of which is probably less controversial today than the importance of what politicians do. But despite this readiness to rank other activities above politics, "the general consciousness of the age" is obviously partial to Weber's position. The possibility of a higher form *of politics* by which mere "political leaders" could be measured or ranked, and to which they would be subordinate, runs counter to the notion that the people are sovereign and that their chosen leaders, who speak for them, are the highest authority. Nietzsche's historiography of the liberal cause is troubling in this connection because it points to the priority of political philosophy in framing the democratic regime of popular sovereignty. It reminds us that liberal democratic institutions are instrumentalities that set limits on leadership, and that to maintain these limits it is necessary to ascend to the governing reason and guiding intelligence of the philosophic founders of the modern project. Chapters 2–4 indicate, then, that the problem of ranking values and of articulating what is higher than mere political leadership is a permanent problem: liberal democracy does not eliminate philosopher-kings, it merely disguises their wisdom so that we accept it as our own enlightenment. Nietzsche strips away this mask and brings philosophy forward with his unequivocal claim that the limits to politics must be legislated or imposed *from above*. To compound his challenge to current opinion, Nietzsche exhibits the project of a higher politics whose task is in the first instance philosophical leadership of science.

A final reason for perplexity may be suggested. In Weber's account of the human possibilities, a spirit of gravity depresses reason. This depression is reflected in Weber's indirection: reason must fall silent, while each struggles "to find the demon who holds the fibres of his very life."[42] In order to be consistently silent, as Weber said, reason must abjure any attempt to solve the problem of ranking values. Reason can point to inconsistencies, wherever commitment to a given ultimate end is contradicted by the individual's choice of means. But so long as the choice of ultimate commitment is authentic, reason does not question it. If the Weberian rejects your demon, which you have authentically chosen, his ultimate ground for doing so must be equally demonic and hence of no higher status before the bar of reason. The two "ultimate commitments" must be granted precisely the same standing from the standpoint of reason. Weber claims, by means of this new self-denying ordinance, to have broken the grip of machinelike reason, thus releasing the authentic human possibilities, or "what is humanly great and noble in our nature."[43] Weber thinks that life only regains its inner plasticity and tragic indeterminacy when the "human possibility" of a reasonable critique of machinelike reason is foreclosed. At some point, one must wonder whether this is so, particularly because Weber's dogmatic foreknowledge, or his claim that there really are no alternatives for science and reason, is bound to vitiate or relax inquiry into the alternatives for reason. Is it so clear that Weber's position releases "the human possibilities" as such? Or is it not rather that he is defending certain privileged possibilities against others? Why does Weber join Nietzsche in presupposing or asserting that machinelike reason has definitively conquered "the pure mind and the good as such" within philosophy and science? Why is the *belief* that political philosophy, as Socrates understood it, is impossible so attractive to Weber? Why does Weber share Nietzsche's determination to defend life against machinelike reason and more generally against the authority of *unenforceable* values? Why does he share with Nietzsche the modern contempt for values that are not backed by "ultimate commitment," values that cannot be said "to hold the fibres of one's very life," or values that are aloof, transcendent, and serenely indifferent to "the world of concern to us"? This thought may intrude itself: the possibility that there may be intelligible, transcendent values, is repugnant to Weber and inspires his indignation and contempt, because it implies that reason could ascend to a height from which our tragic struggles with our "demons"—and the grave seriousness with which we surround these struggles—look comic. Weber's indignation is inseparable from the great passions, the contempt for pettiness, which Weber cherished: it is also our human, all-too-human response to irreverent laughter. That laughter reverberates through the works of political philosophy from Socrates to Machiavelli and Montaigne. Weber treats any reason or wisdom that lacks his all-too-human indignation as an inhuman possibility. For it is not human to join cheerfully in the laughter of the spheres. The contrast between Nietzsche's cheerful exuberance and Weber's indignation is instructive because Weber does not adequately meet Nietzsche at the level of reason; one may begin to doubt whether Weber can fulfill his gravest tasks if he is unable to shake this spirit of gravity. Perhaps the first step toward an insight into limits—the limits of limited government or the limits of human action more generally—is the recovery of a Socratic sense of humor and with it the Socratic sense of reason.[44]

However this may be, our study may at least teach us to laugh at one folly with which Weber's argument would saddle us. Erich Heller has observed that "We may well wonder how [Nietzsche] would react to the pious hopes of our day that the intelligence and moral conscience of politicians will save the world from the disastrous products of our scientific explorations and engineering skills."[45] Precisely because science generates unprecedented power, these pious hopes are comic. They are laughable because of the discrepancy between the gravity of the questions and consequences, on the one hand, and the kinds of politicians who are elevated by such hopes. I have argued that such hopes are intentionally promoted by Weber's teaching on science and politics. He found them necessary, I suggested, in order to combat Nietzsche's politics and, especially, philosophic leadership of science. They are essential to Weber's defense of liberal democracy because they enhance the importance of "political leadership per se," while relieving scientists as scientists of the primary responsibility for the consequences of scientific advance. These hopes allow scientists to continue their professional work while participating as politicians or citizens in calling for "responsible leadership." They supplant the Baconian promises and hopes regarding the beneficence of science, once the evidence that its consequences are horrific is impossible to ignore. What is comic in Weber's strategy is not that it takes seriously our anxieties that science has become a sorcerer's apprentice and has made human life precarious and dangerous as never before. It is the decision to focus these anxieties upon professional politicians whose primary business, by Weber's own analysis, is winning plebiscites. That decision makes it inevitable that these anxieties will be held over the heads of public officials in the form of heightened expectations. So far is this from likely to increase their capacity for responsible action on questions posed by technology and science that one might wonder whether a worse strategy could be found. Asking career demagogues to stretch their intelligence and moral conscience to encompass the questions raised by modern scientific progress is a request for a new quixotism, except that the windmills this time really are giants. Under Weber's strategy we are encouraged to hope that incompetence and ignorance combined with moral intuition and popular appeal will save us from knowledge combined with power. Weber surrounds these hopes with grave rhetoric and a great display of historical scholarship. Learning to laugh at Weber would be politically salutary if it gave us a clear view of the bizarre and groundless character of these hopes.

These observations on the path our inquiry has taken do not establish the possibility of political philosophy. But they may open the question whether a different way of reasoning with our anxieties, both about modern science and about political leadership, is worth undertaking. My recapitulation has stressed perplexities that might lead the thoughtful reader into inquiries that I have not pursued: it is in the nature of a journey of this kind that at each milestone there are vistas we cannot turn aside to explore. But I would like to consider the path we have taken an ascent that enables one to survey the questions with which we began in the perspective of political philosophy.

3. LEADERSHIP AND NIHILISM IN THE PERSPECTIVE OF POLITI-
CAL PHILOSOPHY

Why is political leadership problematic for liberal democracy? I
have indicated that the opinions that make "political leadership" respectable and important are part of a peculiar idiom of public discourse and political science which ought to be bracketed and subjected
to a comprehensive critique and analysis. I shall now turn briefly to the
phenomenon of leadership and sketch a phenomenology of one of our
familiar experiences: worrying about leadership.

For most of us, leadership is evidently an uncertain quantity about
which we worry fitfully: periodically, in elections, and during crises of
confidence or emergencies. For a smaller group more actively involved
in politics, worrying about leadership is a more constant preoccupation
and requires sustained attention to the institutions and laws that govern
campaigning for those periodic elections, and other institutions and
practices through which those crises of confidence and emergencies
are addressed. For a still smaller group, the weakness and irrationality
of these institutions and of the provisions we have made for leadership
are more or less constant anxieties: in this group, Max Weber and
Nietzsche stand out. But why should any of us worry? Why put up
with the anxieties and worries that make political leadership a problem
for us? Why not just solve the problem directly? The history of political philosophy is helpful here because it enables us to see what a direct
solution would entail. In the cities of Greece and Rome one can see the
problem directly solved, and in classical political philosophy the implications are reasoned through. With the advent of modern political
philosophy, one can see the rise of a critique of this direct solution and
an attempt to suppress ancient regime politics through modern representative institutions. But when the "problem" was approached directly, it was posed in very different terms from those we have used.
As the ancients saw it, the "problem" was that the city or public needs
a steady supply of men and women with certain definite habits and
qualities, the virtues most relevant to the right ordering and conduct of
public affairs. The direct solution is to acknowledge the problem and
use the laws to promote and shape citizen virtue or political virtue.
Law then becomes one with custom and political tradition. Instead of
worrying fitfully about leadership, the polity is permanently devoted to
the continuous task of evoking, disciplining, tempering, and perfecting certain virtues. Citizens who conceive the "problem" in this way

do not experience anxiety and worry about leadership: their preoccupations are rather associated with the inculcation of virtue. Guilt,
shame, indignation, and pride are the preoccupations of righteousness.
Political disputes turn primarily around the issue of virtue, and party
conflicts easily escalate into civil wars over conflicting conceptions of
virtue, when this direct approach is taken. Where the "problem" is
posed in terms of virtue, our familiar experiences of worry (or gnawing anxiety) about leadership are understood in a different light.
Shame and indignation are directed *against* the expression of such
worry, which is frowned upon because it may distract citizens from the
fulfillment of their duties or the law. Our experiences of anxiety about
leadership presuppose the rejection of the regime of virtue: we are both
unwilling and unable to rely upon the steady, customary disciplines
through which the ancient republics met their requirement for reliable
leadership. Our public law is not permitted to shape character.

The converse is that modern liberal democracies must keep alive
a certain animus against every attempt to pose the "problem" in the
direct way. The intolerance directed until recently against the Amish
reflected that animus, but the Amish were antinomian and posed no
political challenge.[46] In Nietzsche and Stefan George, Weber faced
such a challenge: when Stefan George gathered a coterie of aspiring
kalokagathoi, legislated for them a code of ruling discipline to govern
their aspirations and conduct, and created a poetry of piety and heroic
virtue resonant with political imagery, Weber's response was blunt:
"The aristocracy of Stefan George and his circle must be fought."[47]
That animus is necessary because liberal democratic institutions were
conceived in order to suppress regime politics. They ruled out the direct resolution of the problem of leadership by insuring that the principal institutions of political society could not undertake to form virtue.[48]

In this light, one can see why the experience of "worrying over
leadership" is problematic for liberal democracy: that worry is naturally "directed" or points toward "regime politics." It reveals a need
that liberal orders cannot reliably fulfill, a need that could be directly
addressed by a politics of virtue antithetical to representative government. The natural directedness of that need toward a constant provision for virtuous citizens constitutes a problem in itself. It reveals the
foundation in human nature of a revolution against the liberal commercial republic, a revolution that would also be a reaction against and
regress away from the achievements of limited government. The experience of "worrying over leadership" is dangerous and "atavistic" be-

cause it may flower into a full-blown politics of moral discipline at war with modern liberal institutions. Those who were willing to risk a regress to regime politics under the aegis of "participatory democracy" might be led to reconsider that risk by the resurgence of theocratic regime politics and potentially illiberal moral majorities. It is perplexing that the desire for virtue, for moral standards and respect for traditional forms, should be transvalued and become a revolutionary desire as a result of modern constitutionalism. But this paradox is the starting point for understanding how the "problem" of leadership arises.

One might ask why the liberal order cannot satisfy this "directed" need simply by filling public positions with paragons of civic virtue: certainly the law permits those who have such virtues to run for office, and it is just as certain that politics under limited government provides opportunity for the exercise of courage, moderation, justice, and prudence. Now it is indeed the case that most of the worries about leadership that attract attention today would be dispelled simply by a competent and matter-of-fact cadre of elected or career public servants—a cadre of professional politicians. But the natural "directedness" of worry about leadership remains a profound and permanent difficulty nevertheless. For if one may speak of a tropism toward the light of visible virtue, which makes every electorate potentially responsive to seeming "paragons of virtue," the problem of modern electorates is that this tropism cannot be perfected and cultivated. "Regime politics" approached the problem as a coherent whole; it was not incidental that the electorate of the ancient republics had to be profoundly attached to law, custom, and political tradition. Respect for virtue and for customary forms was integral to the direct approach. Anxiety about leadership had to be steadily disciplined by shame and indignation.[49] The same limits that prevent representative government from shaping clear and distinct political classes, which make liberal democracies tolerate a great diversity of ways of life and define a wide domain of private liberties, rule out any forceful discouragement of irrational fantasies about political leadership. The need for virtue is bound to be both a gnawing anxiety and an explosive force in modern electoral politics. As Montesquieu hinted (in his account of the paranoid style in English politics), liberal commercial republics must learn to tolerate an anxious electorate haunted by bizarre hopes and fears about leaders.[50] The tropism toward the radiance of visible virtue is seldom supportive of actual virtue in public office under liberal democratic institutions: instead it finds expression in abusive accusation, wild speculation, or support for political unknowns who cultivate the "look" of virtue which they think the anxious electorate is looking for. Hence even a liberal democracy well-supplied with capable officeholders must anticipate that "the politics of virtue" will remain a problem or that popular worry over leadership will never cease to vex even the best servants of moderate self-government.

Those who find satisfaction in the exercise of their political faculties and virtues in public office can of course tolerate a certain climate of madness in public affairs if they are sure of their own sanity and the soundness of their plans. But this tolerance presupposes that they understand that the formless worry about leadership to which we are prone is no guide to policy. They must have before them a standard independent of majority opinion, especially when the majority is worked up by such anxieties. Because an unavoidable task of public men under limited government is to work in the presence of such explosive anxieties without means of extirpating or quelling them, a firm standard is required in which they can repose confidence. Montesquieu taught, in *The Spirit of the Laws*, what he thought was the one thing needful in this context: a comprehensive liberal science of legislation. Public men must see clearly that the spirit of their laws is informed and guided by governing reason.[51]

The limits of leadership imposed by the modern plan for representative government cannot be upheld with confidence, then, without such an ascent to the governing reason of modern liberal politics. But to consider the obstacles to any such ascent today is to become aware of a third and subtler reason that leadership and liberal democracy are problematically related. For the project in which the liberal democracies are bound up, as we have seen, is a quest for knowledge. This quest into the unknown cannot be adequately explained as the inquiry of a scientific minority because it projects whole societies into the unknown. The enterprises in which almost every member of the liberal commercial republic is engaged are so entwined with science as to make everyone the perpetrators and patients in grandiose experiments. The practical consequences of these activities are in significant measure unforeseen precisely because the project as a whole is experimental. Whether or not Nietzsche was correct in claiming that modern science is bound to destroy all existing moral limits because it thrusts such experiments upon us, one can surely say this: from the beginning of the modern project it was probable, and now it is practically certain, that these precarious experiments are bound to stretch all the moral and political virtue that the citizens of the liberal democracies can muster. Surveying the last century of turmoil and global warfare, which has been essentially continuous since 1914, who can reasonably conclude that the opportunities for virtue and *virtú* have waned? The fields of action opened for the exercise of courage, moderation, justice, and prudence have been extraordinary, not least because the motion generated by modern science has been so erratic, unforeseeable, and dangerous.[52] Yet while we have had ample matter within living memory for the pen of a Plutarch or Thucydides *redivivus*, it is difficult today to share their confidence that the tests of virtue would remain essentially constant despite the endless variety of human affairs. The rational ground for that confidence was the refusal or inability of premodern science to breach the limits of political life or to merge politics with the systematic conquest of nature.[53] The merging of politics with the scientific conquest of nature has with good reason raised doubt as to the sufficiency of virtue as revealed in Plutarch and Thucydides. It is perhaps impossible for the most thoughtful citizens of contemporary polities to say what mix or balance of the virtues they require. This impossibility has not rendered ethics a less important subject for thought. But it has promoted a divorce between men of practical ability and what I have called the governing reason of modern liberal politics. This merging has also made it necessary to speak of leadership on a new plane or to distinguish philosophic leadership from political leadership along lines parallel to the division between Weber and Nietzsche. On this plane, what is in dispute is the "virtue" or qualities of soul now required to ride the tiger of our technology and science. In the last century, disputes have arisen in philosophy that are more than reminiscent of those wars over opinions about virtue that made the ancient republics so tumultuous. The rejection of ancient regime politics has in this respect neither ended the questioning about virtue nor diminished the conflict between opinions about human excellence with which Socratic political philosophy began. If anything, it has rather reopened that questioning with a new intensity and urgency. If "ethics" has become so unspeakably serious as to require Wittgenstein and Heidegger to fall silent, it is in part because they have taken as their distinctive task the governing of philosophy in the context of modern science.[54] When we attempt to ascend toward the governing reason of modern liberal politics, then, we are confronted with a bitter war for the high ground from which modern politics can be surveyed. One of the leading "causes" in that warfare is a philosophical nihilism. Reason must fall silent before ethics—not because moral matters and the nature of human excellence and practical virtue are trivial matters but, on the contrary, because the gravity of these matters outweighs reason.[55] Because the founders of modern liberal politics, including Montesquieu, seem not to have considered (much less come to terms with) such philosophical nihilism, no clear response has come forth from liberal political philosophy to meet Nietzsche's claim—repeated by Heidegger and substantially accepted by Weber—that the most stiff-necked obstacle to thinking is precisely that governing reason toward which one must ascend in order to defend liberal democracy with firmness and intelligence.[56]

Because we evidently require a prudence comprehensive enough to guide practical action in the presence of modern science and technology, philosophical nihilism concentered upon the practical turn where thought becomes action has held a profound appeal. And because neither liberal political philosophy nor liberal legislative science has seemed capable of meeting the challenge posed by Nietzsche and Heidegger, what began as an ascent toward governing reason has frequently found its terminus in the rejection of modern liberal politics—a rejection fired with the intensity of apostasy or conversion. There are grounds, therefore, for speaking of a separate phenomenon of worrying about leadership akin to Nietzsche's "anxieties and grounds for gloom." [57]

I have distinguished three ways of worrying about leadership. The first is familiar, or at least readily accessible, to everyone: the passive anxiety that makes contemporary electoral politics something like waiting for Godot. The second is a more active anxiety peculiar to those who have entered politics in order to exercise the politically relevant virtues and have recognized that the natural desire for a politics of virtue poses a constant problem for the liberal democratic polity. The third presupposes an understanding of the method by which the modern project merges politics and science by organizing society for the conquest over nature or over those weaknesses that flow from ignorance. This anxiety is chiefly directed toward philosophic leadership of science and the problems of action—or practical virtue—that philosophy discovers when it beholds the motion, the *kinesis*, generated by science. These three phenomena of worry about leadership are very different; they should be kept separate both in theory and in practice. Keeping separate things separate in theory is a matter for distinctions, and my argument has so far primarily concentrated upon such distinctions. In practice, it is a matter of upholding standards. The final stage of my argument will therefore attempt a judgment about limits.

4. STANDARDS OF LIMITED LEADERSHIP

Initially, we raised a threefold question: What is the standard of a free man and citizen or, better, "a gentleman and a scholar" or, best of all, a good man and citizen? As we have seen, Weber's division of science and politics prevented him from posing the question in this form. He raised a prior "epistemological" question about whether science could reach an intelligible standard on such questions. His answer to this methodological question was negative, in accordance with his premise that political philosophy is impossible. He then conflated our three into a single question concerning politics as a profession or genuine calling, but he knew in advance that his indirection would require tolerance of almost every answer: Weber cannot speak reasonably of *the* standard in answer to his interpretation of politics as a profession. In the absence of clear standards, however, Weber is left, and leaves us, without firm principles for defending liberal democratic institutions. In the light of the previous section, we can see that Weber collapses our initial threefold question and refuses to articulate it in its full complexity. That is why we were compelled to transcend the horizon or ceiling of Weber's argument in order to make sense of these forthright questions. My proposal is that the three questions should be kept separate. I shall briefly discuss the possibility that for the defense of liberal democracy and limited government, not one but three standards are required, in accordance with the different questions we originally posed. For these questions differentiate three kinds of citizens, the three most important kinds that constitute the liberal democratic regime and collaborate in it.[58] I shall treat the three in the sequence of the original questions.

Freeman and citizen.—Initially we said that "nihilism" had not as yet become a common term of praise or blame in American politics, and we attributed this to the Framers' success in providing for moderate self-government. It then became evident, in chapter 1, that their planning and provision for constitutional democracy included a subtle effort to keep "political leadership" under suspicion. The novel challenges to liberal democracy posed by Nietzsche's nihilist initiative support the conclusion that the Framers' reasoning should be reinforced rather than forgotten, because this suspicion remains a necessary resource of moderate self-government. The standard for the free man and citizen, then, should be the Constitution. At one time it would not have been necessary to explicate what this means, but our entire inquiry has demonstrated that there are powerful bodies of opinion supporting Wilson's argument for the abandonment of this standard as it applies to political leadership and that Weber's still more persuasive argument will have to be dealt with in the future. Adopting the Constitution as the standard means that worry over leadership should not be met by celebrating it or elevating it to new heights of respectability and importance. Instead, public concern should be focused as far as possible upon specific offices, translating diffuse popular anxiety into the strengthening of public, formal representation. Constitutionalist suspicion of "political leadership" should be sharpened and refined to apply to "opinion leadership," to prevent the erosion of the distinction between formal and informal representation and to maintain the distinctions between public and private on which limited government depends. Constitutionalist suspicion should therefore be directed toward a critique of popular leadership anticipating Weber's rhetoric and the attempt to professionalize demagogy. Restoring the Constitution to the center of public life and strengthening respect for the forms of limited government require a break with the dominant tendencies of social science and intellectual fashion because the trend of opinion leadership has been to reduce the Constitution to a merely procedural document and elevate informal representation by self-selecting opinion leaders. Adopting Weber's essentially instrumental view of constitutions would only intensify this drift. For the journalists and brain trusts of the left, my proposal would require a reconsideration of the assumption that the spirit of limited government and respect for forms is a conservative cause. Such a reconsideration would have to weigh the evidence—and there is a great deal—that such respect for forms has been the left's best defense against the tyranny of conservative majorities. There is good reason to think it will be their best defense against the Moral Majority or new threats of McCarthyism in the future. The right should reconsider its flirtation with populism and weigh the likelihood that the short-term gains to be won through opinion leadership and plebiscitary leader democracy, or by capturing the rhetorical presidency for their partisan purposes, will be more than canceled by the damage done to the American heritage of moderate self-government by the adoption of these methods.

Having proposed an unfashionably rigid standard and argued its necessity, I should stress my conviction that it is possible to uphold the strictness of *The Federalist* prudently. For reasons touched upon earlier in this chapter, general anxiety about leadership is something one must expect under limited government, along with the explosive behavior of the electorate under its stress. One might prudently view primary elections and other plebiscitary devices in this light, not so much as exercises of a right but as experiments in the venting and moderating of our anxieties. The standard for this experimentation should be whether it strengthens formal representation in constitutional offices and deepens respect for the forms on which limited government depends. I am well aware that a fig-leaf promise about such strengthening and deepening of moderate self-government has accompanied every weakening of formal representation passed into law since 1789. I am also aware that expert witnesses can be found to explain why such consequences will flow from every imaginable reform or refusal to reform. But these difficulties only strengthen my argument that additional standards are required to direct and limit the experts, who consider themselves to be among the gentlemen and the scholars. The first standard is addressed to a distinct problem. Having formed popular political habits through decades of experimentation with plebiscitary selection of presidential candidates (to mention only the most obtrusive case), upholding a strict constitutional standard is the necessary precondition for the long and difficult work of reforming those habits.

Gentlemen scholars.—The second standard should be the liberal cause critically understood. That means not as Weber conceived it, an irrational object of ultimate commitment, but rather as a philosophic project, a plan intelligible to reasonable men and subject like all plans to profound reservations. This rational understanding differs from the devotion to a cause around which Weber sought to build politics as a profession. He so feared the appeal of Nietzschean nobility and the threat that the gentlemen might withhold themselves from democratic citizenship that he insisted upon overwhelming their profound misgivings by making politics the object of a noble affirmation. Subsequently, Weber's lead in affirming "the political" has been followed by political theorists like Sheldon S. Wolin and Hannah Arendt, who have attempted to make politics an obsession or *idée fixe* for high-minded citizens.[59] As I believe Weber was aware, this affirmation requires the suppression of reasonable reservations about politics.[60] Once the habit of self-forgetfulness is cultivated, however, it swiftly leads toward the

inability to defend liberal democratic institutions which we have exam-
ined in Weber: any ascent to the governing reason of modern liberal
politics soon becomes unthinkable; and the high-minded "gentleman
and scholar" begins to forget that liberal democracy provides great
scope for the exercise of virtue.[61] It comes to be seen as a proving
ground of "ultimate commitment." For reasons I have explored, it is
somewhat perverse to defend the institutions of modern liberal politics
as such a proving ground.[62]

One path toward a critical understanding of the liberal cause was
traced by Montesquieu. In *The Spirit of the Laws*, he portrayed the
excellences and appeal of democracy, aristocracy, and monarchy before setting them aside in favor of the liberal commercial republic in
Books 11 and 12.[63] There is a basis for profound reservations; it is sobering to acknowledge that limited government stands in principled
tension with earlier regime politics and cannot give way before the noble aspirations that earlier forms of government had attempted to satisfy. In my judgment, such acknowledgment provides a sounder basis
for matter-of-factness, responsibility, and a sense of proportion in professional politics than the myths about ultimate commitment and devotion to a cause on which Weber relies. Once one acknowledges that the
turn toward governing reason has its price and disenchants politics
more fully than Weber could bear, one can take a cheerful look at the
grim differences between our situation and Montesquieu's. Montesquieu had intended to render the earth as a whole more peaceful
through the spread of a commercial way of life; he promised or hoped
for the triumph of the humanitarian ideal of Montaigne.[64] Instead, the
progress of science and the spread of technological power have made
the human future problematic as never before. Despite or because of
their preference for commerce and peaceful administration, the liberal
democracies find themselves face to face with an agenda of difficulties
in domestic and foreign policy that challenges all the politically relevant virtues. It is simply not true in fact that liberal democracy has no
place or cannot provide great scope for the exercise of prudence, courage, moderation, and justice. It is merely the case that one cannot demand that it do so as a matter of right.[65]

In one sense, my second standard is not overly taxing. It is well
within the capacities of an intelligent gentleman to understand the
Constitution in a supple manner, as a mode of planning for moderate self-government. The intellectual confusion that prevails in law
schools today on questions of public law shows how difficult it is to

speak intelligibly and consistently about the Constitution if one conceives of it as a merely procedural document. The standard I have proposed requires us to understand the Constitution as it was understood by the gentleman, scholar, and lawyer during the American Revolution and the Founding: as the framework of a political order responsive to the necessities and opportunities of political life, a framework based on a sober assessment of human nature, and an audacious acceptance of the capacity of science to disclose the politically relevant facts of human nature.[66]

A second path to the liberal cause critically understood lies in the study of the great modern liberal statesmen before Wilson and Weber. In this tradition, Lincoln's statesmanship merits special mention for its bearing upon our principal theme. We noted earlier that Nietzsche's nihilistic politics opened questions regarding slavery and tyranny that had been closed in American public life since the Civil War. We later observed that Montesquieu appears, at least on the surface, not to have come to terms with philosophical nihilism. What the gentleman scholar must acknowledge is the depth of the crisis of liberalism and the probability that nihilism springs from the same root as the liberal regime. Profound reservations are justified if nihilism lies latent within the political order framed by the Constitution. This ambiguity in the liberal regime might be likened to the ambiguities of the Union in Lincoln's day when slavery stood within the regime and indeed under the protection of the Constitution. Slavery had become sufficiently entwined with the commercial way of life of the United States that without political action this "shame of humanity" would have spread with the normal action of commerce.[67] That nihilism has emerged as a potential alternative for political action suggests that Lincoln's statesmanship may be particularly instructive for the defense of liberal democracy today. The root of an unlimited politics, if not indeed of a politics of limitless inhumanity, is immanent in the conflict between "the free unfolding of individuality," on the one hand, and the attempt to suppress that license by unleashing a "constraining individuality" in the name of the national liberal cause.[68] To consistently uproot Nietzschean nihilism may be impossible without tearing the liberal regime away from its roots in the "discovery of individuality." Lincoln provides a standard for acknowledging that great political evil can become intricately intertwined with the activities of a liberal commercial republic; for acknowledging that the American experiment could be transformed into an experiment with nihilism; and for finding in these possibilities the strongest possible motive for cleaving to the governing reason of modern liberal politics.

Acknowledging that nihilism may spring from the same root as the liberal regime does not require one to follow the lead of neoconservatives such as Irving Kristol and Alexander Bickel who have attempted in their writings to introduce "nihilism" as a political term of praise and blame.[69] It is unnecessary to do so if liberal legislative science can account for and provide institutional remedies against nihilist politics. My suggestion in the preceding pages was that it can be met by applying the original liberal critique of priestcraft, psychagogy, and domination, to this more radical and spiritual form of tyrannical politics.[70]

Good man and citizen.—Returning to the Constitution for limits to leadership, and to the liberal cause critically understood, is possible (if the foregoing arguments are sound) only if the ascent to governing reason or a recovery of modern liberal politics at the level of science and philosophy is possible. Limited government as such solves the comprehensive problem of limits only at the level of the public, as structured by liberal institutions and the modern state. We must consider the limits of philosophic leadership and how they may be discerned or secured.

The third standard should be the subject of a separate book, perhaps devoted primarily to Nietzsche. I shall limit myself here to some tentative assertions. First, Nietzsche has made the origins of the modern project more visible and more interesting. His hints that his soul mates were Machiavelli, Montaigne, Bacon, Spinoza, and Hobbes have helped to free philosophy from Hegel's imposing account of the history of philosophy. But deeper study provoked by Nietzsche has also weakened Nietzsche's Napoleonic hegemony over "free spirits." His literary brilliance no longer seems so singular when placed beside the works he has taught us to read or has encouraged us to see with fresh eyes. Scholars who have taken Nietzsche's "Journey to Hades," to converse with the minds he found "eternally alive," have also learned from them to question Nietzsche.[71] To mention only one problem: Nietzsche thought (as we have seen) that for Montaigne the liberal project was provisional rather than permanent. This claim is now subject to grave objections.[72] Nietzsche's genealogical account of the origins of modernity is now less the last word than an overture. Nietzsche has helped to reveal the depths of his modern soul mates. They, however, were more completely engaged with the tasks of political philosophy than Nietzsche. Thus inquiries prompted by Nietzsche have made the philosophical foundations of the liberal commercial republic more visible and the legislative science accompanying liberal humanitarianism more interesting.

They have also led to a reconsideration—inspired in part by Nietzsche's critique of the democratic enlightenment and dogmatic "free thinkers"—of the original strategy against "pious cruelty" propounded by Machiavelli, Montaigne, and Montesquieu.[73] This rediscovery helps one to question Nietzsche's project for a new cruelty. The difficulty is adumbrated, I believe, in a recent article by Gerd-Günther Grau.[74] Grau juxtaposed Walter Kaufmann's gloss on the Will to Power as a sublimation of political power drives into higher cultural activities, against Wolfgang Müller-Lauter's stress on the realization of Will to Power in politics, legislation, and action. Grau argued that this tension in Nietzsche generates a new practical "absolutism."[75] Although Nietzsche's politics incorporates a highly refined skepticism with regard to absolutes, this skepticism does not prevent Nietzsche from promoting the repression of ideological enemies or the inhumane measures of premodern absolutism.[76] Chapters 3 and 4 of this study support Grau's argument. Nietzsche risks not only the descent from bourgeois humanitarian ideals but the birth of a new persecution of philosophy by philosophers armed with sophisticated means of power. It may pose a threat to the freedom of philosophy no less serious than the "religious-ecclesiastical pressure of millenia" that Machiavelli and Montaigne overthrew.

This tension within Nietzsche's project means that in thinking about "the philosophy of the future," philosophers must ask which regime best equips philosophy to prevent the worst forms of practical absolutism generated by philosophy itself. These immanent problems within Nietzsche's project paradoxically make the liberal commercial republic once again a serious candidate—despite its obvious vices—as the best regime of the philosophers. This conclusion is independent of the practical considerations suggested by the fate of science and philosophy under communist regimes, though it is strongly reinforced by such observations.

There is also a less practical, more zetetic reason for philosophy to limit itself with respect to leadership. I have observed that the turn away from ancient regime politics initiated by modern philosophy has not terminated the questioning of human excellence or virtue, but that the indeterminacy in human affairs fostered by the merging of politics with the scientific conquest of nature has made the classic Socratic questions regarding excellence newly intriguing. The questioning that our political experience provokes, however, is endangered by the urgency of Nietzsche's overriding *practical* concern for philosophic leadership. This suspect tendency to foreclose questioning should lead one to question whether precisely Nietzsche's headlong and remorseless leadership, which claims to probe every prudential limit to the "experiment of the knowers," is not inherently limited, and limiting.

These observations point toward a standard of the good man in the ancient sense: the political philosopher who aspires to the most comprehensive and highest human excellence or to complete virtue. They suggest a standard that would make him embrace citizenship in the liberal democratic regime, not for reasons incidental to his philosophic quest but integral to his questioning of the value of truth.[77] They suggest that the philosophic inquiry into the conditions and highest possibility of philosophy is an inquiry into politics, which cannot henceforth be carried on without the liberal democratic regime. Perhaps they also point to the necessity for a nocturnal council within that regime to reopen periodically the argument on political leadership and nihilism and to deliberate what philosophy should do about its Alcibiades or Caesar.[78] In lieu of a more complete inquiry, then, my "best working hypothesis" would be that the proper standard for the good man and citizen is the liberal commercial republic as the practical foundation for the best life, the Socratic life.

For the purposes of practical collaboration, it should be evident that these three very different standards are in essential agreement about defending liberal democratic institutions.

5. CONCLUSION

In order to evaluate Weber's indirection in his most comprehensive argument for the importance of political leadership, I have attempted to sketch a more direct defense. In order to answer the claim that Weber holds out a higher prudence, I have tried to show what a higher prudence would entail. Such a showing was necessary because Weber's appeal to thoughtful citizens lies in the promise of a greater prudence which his rhetoric conveys. Weber seems to transcend the mechanical, institutional prudence upon which modern liberal politics relied. He seems to open political prudence once again to the ultimate or tragic questions about the highest values that are the touchstone of the most comprehensive practical wisdom. Weber's work beckons us toward "that knowledge of tragedy with which all action, but especially political action, is truly interwoven." [79] His discussion of the relations between ethics and politics seems to leap over the mechanical institutional science of Montesquieu and to reestablish contact with the great themes of Thucydides and Aristotle. [80] I have tried to show that these rhetorical gestures will not withstand critical scrutiny. Weber's framework does not widen the scope of prudence beyond Machiavellian reason of state. It does not open the way to practical wisdom in the ancient sense of *phronesis*. On the contrary, it forecloses any such ascent. It is not Weber but rather Nietzsche who comes close to Aristotle and Plato in this regard: Nietzsche's philosophic leader rivals Socrates and encompasses the *mere* politician or citizen. [81] In Weber's account, the "good man" has nothing whatever to do with complete excellence; there is no question of his encompassing the virtues and prudence of the political man. [82]

NOTES

NOTES TO THE INTRODUCTION

1. P. A. Kropotkin sought to deflect the polemical force of the term in an article he published in the English *Fortnightly Review* 31 (1882). "The Russian Revolutionary Party," he asserted, was "improperly called nihilist": Kropotkin, *Selected Writings on Anarchism and Revolution*, p. 135. See Adam Ulam, *In the Name of the People: Prophets and Conspirators in Prerevolutionary Russia*, pp. 115–38, 141–47; Daniel R. Brower, *Training the Nihilists: Education and Radicalism in Tsarist Russia*. The philosophical problem of nihilism is discussed in Dieter Arendt, ed., *Nihilismus. Die Anfänge von Jacobi bis Nietzsche;* Winfried Weier, *Nihilismus: Geschichte, System, Kritik;* and Stanley Rosen, *Nihilism: A Philosophical Essay*. See also Charles Irving Glicksberg, *The Literature of Nihilism;* Peter Heller, *Dialectics and Nihilism: Essays on Lessing, Nietzsche, Mann and Kafka;* Walter Hof, *Der Weg zum heroischen Realismus: Pessimismus und Nihilismus in der deutschen Literatur von Hamerling bis Benn*.

2. For example, the *International Encyclopedia of Social Sciences* (New York: Crowell, Collier and Macmillan, 1968), 11:175, where the entry on "Nihilism" reads: "See Alienation; Anarchism; Personality, Political." Under these headings, nothing is said about nihilism. Alexander M. Bickel did use the term, to describe the New Left of the sixties: "destructive nihilism is evil no matter how motivated": *The Morality of Consent*, p. 137.

3. For understanding the tradition of modern liberal politics to which the Founders had recourse, the most important political philosopher is Montesquieu. *The Federalist* Nos. 9, 10, and 14 (Hamilton et al.) recapitulate (with some delicacy) the movement of thought by which Montesquieu weans the reader from the allure of republics of virtue or conscience (republics prey to what Machiavelli called "pious cruelty") to the more sober gratifications of the liberal commercial republic and the politics of interest. This movement in the first twelve books of *The Spirit of the Laws* is elucidated in Thomas L. Pangle, *Montesquieu's Philosophy of Liberalism: A Commentary on "The Spirit of the Laws,"* pp. 48–161. The possibility that man could master his fortunes in this world and institute steady political progress, by giving ground to popular tumults and factional strife, was discovered by Machiavelli in opposition to spiritual authority and the rule of priests. See Harvey C. Mansfield, Jr., *Machiavelli's*

New Modes and Orders: A Study of the "Discourses on Livy," pp. 42–62, 160–64, 181–89.

4. "Nihilism as the disavowal of existing civilization was the only real belief of all truly educated people at the beginning of the twentieth century. Nihilism is not a result of the Great War but, on the contrary, its cause": Karl Löwith, "The Historical Background of European Nihilism," *Nature, History, and Existentialism,* p. 10.

5. For evidence of the current state of professorial opinion in the law schools, see the "Symposium: Judicial Review versus Democracy," *Ohio State Law Journal* 42, no. 1 (1981), particularly the remarks by Paul Brest, "The Substance of Process," pp. 131–42, and Richard Davies Parker, "The Past of Constitutional Theory—And Its Future," pp. 223–59. Consider Edward J. Erler, "Equal Protection and Personal Rights: The Regime of the 'Discrete and Insular Minority,'" and his forthcoming critical analysis, *The Supreme Court and the Fourteenth Amendment: A Study in Judicial Statesmanship.*

6. See *Voting Rights Act, Report together with Additional Views of the Subcommittee on the Constitution to the Committee on the Judiciary*; Walter Berns, "Voting Rights and Wrongs." Opponents and proponents agree that the constitutional standing of at-large elections for local government is called into question by the act. See Timothy G. O'Rourke, "Constitutional and Statutory Challenges to Local At-Large Elections." Max Weber's article on "Democracy and Voting Rights" (*Gesammelte politische Schriften,* pp. 233–79) was not addressed to the issue of proportional representation by race. The earlier controversy should not be forgotten by political scientists, however. See F. A. Hermens, *A Study of Proportional Representation,* pp. 147–300.

7. The dramatic contrast between the old mixed system of nominations and the new dominance of primaries is evident if one compares William R. Keech and Donald R. Matthews, *The Party's Choice,* with David Chagall's vivid description of the new plebiscitarian politics, *The New Kingmakers: An Inside Look at the Powerful Men behind America's Political Campaigns.* The dynamics of the new system are well described in John H. Aldrich, *Before the Convention: A Theory of Presidential Nominating Campaigns,* and its dangers are discussed in James W. Ceaser, *Presidential Selection: Theory and Development,* pp. 213–303.

8. See Regis A. Factor and Stephen P. Turner, "Weber, Morgenthau, and the Moral Basis of Foreign Policy." Morgenthau's knowledge of Weber was due to special circumstances: "After spending a year at the University of Berlin, I returned to Munich to take the first legal examination. While I prepared for it, I attended Professor Rothenbücher's seminar on Max Weber's political and social philosophy, based upon the latter's political writings. It was a great experience, on account of the subject matter as well as the teacher": Hans J. Morgenthau, "Fragment of an Intellectual Biography: 1904–1932."

9. Wolfgang J. Mommsen, *Max Weber und die deutsche Politik, 1890–1920,* 2d ed., is by far the best study of Weber's political writings to date. Mommsen's collection of essays in English, *The Age of Bureaucracy: Perspectives on the Political Sociology of Max Weber,* gives only a faint image of his accomplishment in the earlier German work. In English, the best account is David Beetham, *Max Weber and the Theory of Modern Politics.*

10. Joseph Kraft, "The Imperial Media," pp. 36–47; George F. Will, ed.,

Press, Politics, and Popular Government; Robert D. Novak, *The Mass Media and Modern Democracy,* ed. Harry M. Clor; "The Washington Press—Competing for Power with the Federal Government," *The National Journal* 14, no. 16 (April 17, 1982): 664–74. Slavery to intellectual fashion can result in the kind of injustice we have long associated with bigotry, as in the treatment of Thomas Sowell; see his "Media Smears: One Man's Experiences," pp. 17–20.

11. The malice test is from *N.Y. Times v. Sullivan,* 376 U.S. 254 (1964), at p. 280; see also *Herbert v. Lando,* 60 L.Ed.2d 115, especially note 6 (1979). Compare Hadley Arkes, "Political Discourse and the Defamation of Groups," in *The Philosopher in the City: The Moral Dimensions of Urban Politics,* pp. 23–55.

12. *The New Journalism, with an Anthology Edited by Tom Wolfe and E. Johnson.* Consider Weber's "Preliminary report on an investigation into the sociology of journalism," quoted toward the end of chap. 5, below. (His remarks, which have not otherwise been published, are quoted from Wilhelm Hennis, "Max Webers Fragestellung," p. 276.)

13. The phrase "The world of concern to us" is Nietzsche's term for what the Greeks of antiquity called the *pragmata;* he uses it to recover the horizon of the man of action, particularly as against the world revealed by modern science. See *Nietzsche, The Gay Science,* nos. 301, 340; *Beyond Good and Evil: A Prelude to the Philosophy and the Future,* no. 226. (For abbreviations to works used in this study, see the list at the beginning of the notes.)

14. See John Hollowell, *Fact and Fiction: The New Journalism and the Nonfiction Novel.*

15. Consider Joe McGuinniss, *The Selling of the President, 1968,* and Garry Wills, *The Kennedy Imprisonment: A Meditation on Power.*

16. Consider John Calhoun Merrill, *Existential Journalism,* pp. 97–138. Merrill dedicates his book to Daniel Schorr and Tom Wicker; his epigram on inner freedom from the lie is taken from Solzhenitsyn. His creed (p. 106) makes no mention of democracy. Journalistic style is understood as "revelation of self" (pp. 102–8); the existential journalist evidently knows nothing of representative government or democracy but a great deal about authenticity and Nietzsche.

17. This apt term is suggested by Ludwig Schajowicz, *Los nuevos sofistas: la subversion cultural de Nietzsche á Beckett.*

18. Friedrich Nietzsche, *EH,* "Why I Write Such Good Books" (on *BGE*), no. 2, p. 311.

19. See the remarks on Kaufmann's treatment of Nietzsche's politics in Werner J. Dannhauser, *Nietzsche's View of Socrates,* pp. 26–41. In keeping with the thrust of Kaufmann's interpretation, Richard Schacht denies that Nietzsche was a nihilist without troubling to consider his positions on political subjects. See Schacht's "Nietzsche and Nihilism," in *Hegel and After: Studies in Continental Philosophy Between Kant and Sartre,* pp. 175–203. He dedicates his book to Kaufmann, "who showed me how to see."

20. See chap. 4, sec. 1, below.

21. Werner J. Dannhauser, "The Trivialization of Friedrich Nietzsche"; Roberto Escobar, *Nietzsche e la filosofia politica del 19 secolo;* Gerd-Günther Grau, "Sublimierter oder realisierter Wille zur Macht?"; Pamela K. Jensen, "Nietzsche and Liberation: The Prelude to a Philosophy of the Future"; Wolfgang Müller-Lauter,

Nietzsche: Seine Philosophie der Gegensätze und die Gegensätze seiner Philosophie; Simone Goyard-Fabre, *Nietzsche et la question politique;* Harry Neumann, "Superman or Last Man? Nietzsche's Interpretation of Athens and Jerusalem"; Raymond Polin, "Nietzsche und der Staat oder die Politik eines Einsamen"; Tracy Burr Strong, *Friedrich Nietzsche and the Politics of Transfiguration.* For a survey of earlier works on Nietzsche's politics, see Hans Barth, *Wahrheit und Ideologie,* pp. 308–16.

22. One theme of chaps. 2–4, below, is how Nietzsche makes a fat faith pâté out of liberal democracy.

23. See Rosen, *Nihilism: A Philosophical Essay,* pp. 56–149.

24. See chap. 1, note 109, below.

25. Karl R. Popper, *The Poverty of Historicism;* see also *The Open Society and Its Enemies,* 2:76–79, 224–58.

26. I am indebted to William Shapiro's thoughtful study, "The Nietzschean Roots of Max Weber's Social Science." Many scholars have decried the tendency toward hagiography and legend-building in the sociological literature on Max Weber. See Hennis, "Max Webers Fragestellung," pp. 241–42; Helmut Fogt, "Max Weber und die deutsche Soziologie der Weimarer Republik: Aussenseiter oder Gründervater?" pp. 245–47, 258–61.

27. Robert C. Tucker, *Politics as Leadership,* p. 9.

28. Ibid.

29. Leo Strauss, *What Is Political Philosophy? And Other Studies,* p. 12. See Martin Diamond, "Teaching about Politics as a Vocation."

Chapter 1: Opinion Leadership and the Liberal Cause

1. The translations in the text are my own, from Weber, *Gesammelte politischen Schriften,* pp. 1–25. I have not used Keith Tribe's version, which appeared well after my work on this lecture had been completed: "The National State and Economic Policy (Freiburg Address), Freiburg May 1895," *Economy and Society* 9, no. 4 (November 1980): 428–49. The lecture draws upon Weber's contribution to a study of the land-labor situation in East Prussia. In 1890, a large-scale inquiry into agricultural conditions had been undertaken by the *Verein für Sozialpolitik,* an association of academics, government officials, and other experts concerned with social reform and the scientific analysis of social questions. Weber was responsible for evaluating the results of a questionnaire from the German provinces east of the Elbe River. His contribution established him as an expert in agricultural economics and led to his appointment to a chair in economics at Freiburg. The most complete exposition of the problems dealt with in the lecture is found in Wolfgang J. Mommsen, *Max Weber und die deutsche Politik, 1890–1920,* chaps. 1–4 (hereafter cited as *Weber und Politik*). See also Raymond Aron, "Max Weber and Power Politics," pp. 83–109, followed by Mommsen's remarks, pp. 109–16; Jacob Peter Mayer, *Max Weber and German Politics: A Study in Political Sociology,* pp. 31–36; Arnold Bergsträsser, "Max Webers Antrittsvorlesung in zeitgeschichtlicher Perspektive." Reinhard Bendix's useful précis, *Max Weber: An Intellectual Portrait,* does not recognize, or reflect upon, the fundamental importance of this early intellectual self-portrait.

2. See Jürgen Kocka, "Kontroversen über Max Weber." The controversy has a

long history, which is reviewed in Stephen Turner and Regis A. Factor, *Max Weber and the Dispute over Reason and Values: A Study in Philosophy, Ethics, and Politics.*

3. Alexander von Schelting, *Max Webers Wissenschaftslehre*, excursus on "Max Weber's 'liberalism,'" pp. 343–52. I have discussed these claims for Weber in "Doing without Liberalism: Weber's Regime Politics."

4. Further criticisms of these current views will be advanced in later chapters.

5. For an earlier, psychologistic comparison between the two, see Michael Rogin, "Max Weber and Woodrow Wilson: The Iron Cage in Germany and America." The emergence of the plebiscitary system is discussed in James W. Ceaser, *Presidential Selection: Theory and Development,* especially "Woodrow Wilson and the Origin of the Modern View of Presidential Selection," pp. 170–212. See also his essay "Political Change and Party Reform." For an excellent analysis of reform liberalism in action, see Ward E. Y. Elliott, *The Rise of Guardian Democracy: The Supreme Court's Role in Voting Rights Disputes, 1845–1969.* It is a bit odd, considering the title of his book, that Richard Hofstadter tells us so little in his chapter on Wilson about Wilson's reshaping of the American liberal tradition: *The American Political Tradition,* pp. 308–67. We shall return to Weber's concept of *plebiscitary leader-democracy.* It is discussed in Wolfgang J. Mommsen, "Zum Begriff der 'plebiszitären Führerdemokratie' bei Max Weber," and his *The Age of Bureaucracy.*

6. See William M. Sullivan's remarks on the contemporary crisis of liberal society and the resources of liberalism for meeting it: *Reconstructing Public Philosophy,* pp. 23–89. For a different account of Weber's significance for American politics, see Kathi V. Friedman, *Legitimation of Social Rights and the Western Welfare State: A Weberian Perspective.*

7. The immediate objects of Wilson's critique of "private government" were the party system and Van Buren's rationale for that system. See Ceaser, *Presidential Selection,* pp. 123–70. Ceaser shows that Van Buren's intention was to maintain the spirit of *The Federalist* by means of parties. On this problem prior to Van Buren, see Edward J. Erler, "The Problem of the Public Good in *The Federalist.*"

8. Wilson had studied law at the University of Virginia. See Henry W. Bragdon, *Woodrow Wilson: The Academic Years,* p. 87.

9. Woodrow Wilson, *College and State: Educational, Literary, and Political Papers (1875–1913) in Two Volumes,* 1:338 (hereafter cited as *Papers*).

10. Ibid.

11. The more explicit argument is developed by Walter Bagehot; see "The Practical Operation of the American Constitution at the Present Extreme Crisis" and "The American Constitution at the Present Crisis," in his *Collected Works,* 4:277–313. Bagehot holds that "The Constitution of the United States was framed upon a vicious principle" (4:281). "It appears that the constitution-makers of North America were not unnaturally misled by the political philosophy of their day" (4:309). Consider also "the function of public opinion . . . has been retarded by the unnatural influence of the artificial Constitution; and when found, it is long rendered useless by the same influence" (6:171).

12. Alexander Hamilton et al., *The Federalist,* pp. 125, 151; Robert K. Faulkner, "John Marshall."

13. Consider Harvey Flaumenhaft, "Hamilton's Administrative Republic and the American Presidency." The original plan for the gradual unfolding of the regime of

modern liberty—relying on no single founding—is one of the main themes of Harvey C. Mansfield, Jr., *Machiavelli's New Modes and Orders: A Study of the "Discourses on Livy."*

14. Wilson, *Papers*, 1:352.

15. Ibid., 1:338.

16. See John Collins, "Locke and Burke on Representative Government."

17. As Engeman points out, delimitation through checks and balances enabled the Founders to grant virtually absolute powers to both executive and legislative by balancing the right of the executive in an emergency against the right of the legislature to impeach: Thomas S. Engeman, "Presidential Statesmanship and the Constitution: The Limits of Presidential Studies," pp. 273–81. The American Founders had been too busy with the Revolution to read Rousseau's powerful critique of this system of popular enlightenment.

18. *The Federalist* No. 14, p. 154. See No. 10, p. 136.

19. Ibid., No. 62, p. 410, "seduced by factious leaders." In No. 66, speaking of impeachment, Publius suggests it for "the punishment of a few leading individuals in the Senate, who should have prostituted their influence in that body as the mercenary instruments of foreign corruption" (p. 426). In defending the decision to place the impeachment power in the Senate, Publius warns that "the delicacy and magnitude of a trust which so deeply concerns the political reputation and existence of every man engaged in the administration of public affairs, speak for themselves. The difficulty of placing it rightly, in a government resting entirely on the basis of periodical elections, will as readily be perceived, when it is considered that the most conspicuous characters in it will, from that circumstance, be too often the leaders or the tools of the most cunning or the most numerous faction, and on this account, can hardly be expected to possess the requisite neutrality towards those whose conduct may be the subject of scrutiny" (p. 426).

20. *The Federalist* pp. 91, 109, 112, 133, 136. Compare Hobbes on "popular men," *Leviathan,* chap. 30, pp. 380–81, 390, and Rousseau on "leading personages," *The First and Second Discourses,* p. 172.

21. *The Federalist*, No. 10, pp. 131, 136.

22. Wilson, *Papers,* 1:339.

23. As Walter Berns has argued, the Founders did not think it wise to rely exclusively on this indirection: *The First Amendment and the Future of American Democracy*, pp. 1–32.

24. *Œuvres Complètes de Montesquieu*, 2:70.

25. Woodrow Wilson, *Constitutional Government in the United States*, pp. 157–58, 170–71, 192–95; Daniel Yankelovich, Amitai Etzioni, et al., *Moral Leadership in Government: A Public Agenda Foundation Report, September 1976;* Hugh Heclo, "Issue Networks and the Executive Establishment," pp. 87–124, and Heclo, "Introduction: The Presidential Illusion," in *The Illusion of Presidential Government,* ed. Hugh Heclo and Lester M. Salamon, pp. 1–17.

26. Edward G. Bourne held up the warnings of Sir Henry Maine that Britain would not be able to absorb the democratic movement because it lacked the constitutional mechanisms of the American system: "Those parts of the English government which Mr. Wilson admires above our own are just those in which freer scope is given to democracy": *New England and Yale Review* 9 (March 1886): 284–88. A. Lawrence

Lowell argued that Wilson's program "would accustom us to seeing rapid and un-limited effect given to the opinions of the majority": *Atlantic Monthly* 57 (February 1886):187. He warned that "The Constitution of the United States depends . . . upon the fact that the people, with rare exceptions, care more about the Constitution than about any present issue" (ibid.).

27. *The Federalist* Nos. 1, 9.

28. *Atlantic Monthly* 57 (April 1886):542–53.

29. "If we are really attached to these principles [of constitutional separation of powers], the concentration of responsibility in government will doubly insure their preservation. If we are not, they are in danger of destruction in any case" (ibid., p. 553). This can hardly have been intended to reassure Lowell.

30. See note 29 above and p. 552, ibid.: "Popular governments need more than any other governments leaders so placed that . . . they shall see the problems of gov-ernment at first hand and shall at the same time be, not mere administrators, but also men of tact and eloquence, fitted to persuade masses of men, and to draw about them-selves a loyal following." The circularity reflects Wilson's reliance upon the orator's stock method of gaining trust by his testimonies of character.

31. Letter to Ellen Axson, February 24, 1885, in Bragdon, *Woodrow Wilson: The Academic Years*, p. 117.

32. Lincoln's development of the Declaration is exhibited best in Harry V. Jaffa, *The Crisis of the House Divided* (hereafter cited as *The House Divided*). See also Harvey C. Mansfield, Jr., *The Spirit of Liberalism*, pp. 72–88.

33. Bragdon, *Woodrow Wilson: The Academic Years*, pp. 52–53, 180–81, 184, 258–64. Burke's understanding of the British Constitution as popular government is treated in Harvey C. Mansfield, Jr., *Statesmanship and Party Government: A Study of Burke and Bolingbroke*, pp. 123–63.

34. The problem is brought out by Clor's observation that "Wilson can be said to have held the view that the fundamental standards of justice and duty are discoverable in man's historical *experience* which reveals a common awareness or sense of right. And the most decisive historical experience is the emergence and increasing . . . prev-alence in modern times of self-governing communities with the virtues of initiative, self-discipline and sociability required for their success" ("Woodrow Wilson," in *American Political Thought*, ed. Frisch and Stevens, p. 199).

35. Wilson, *Papers*, 1:338.

36. Wilson carried forward Burke's view of the importance of individuality as a concern of the sound political order and joined it with Mill's emphasis upon individu-ality, which was less radical than Nietzsche's. See Leo Strauss, *Natural Right and His-tory*, pp. 322–23. It could not be said of Wilson that he "himself was still too deeply imbued with the spirit of 'sound antiquity' to allow the concern with individuality to overpower the concern with virtue," as Strauss says of Burke (p. 323). In Wilson, Christianity and love resist the concern with individuality: see Wilson, *When a Man Comes to Himself*.

37. Bragdon, *Woodrow Wilson: The Academic Years*, pp. 15–26, 30–31, 43–45, 49–50, 76, 108, 114, 170–71, 193.

38. Ibid.; "Cabinet Government in the United States," in *Papers*, 1:37.

39. "Princeton in the Nation's Service," *Papers*, 2:259–85; "Princeton for the Nation's Service," ibid., 2:443–61. The maxim quoted is on p. 459.

40. Wilson, *The State*, Sections 1270, 1272–74, 1285 (pp. 659–61). "The case for society stands thus: the individual must be assured the best means, the best and fullest opportunities, for complete self-development" (p. 661).

41. Mansfield, *The Spirit of Liberalism*, pp. 8–14.

42. See the critique of Raoul Berger's argument against executive confidentiality by Gary J. Schmitt, "Executive Privilege: Presidential Power to Withhold Information from Congress," pp. 154–94. Schmitt quotes from the *Annals of Congress*, 4:150: "Because this Government is Republican, it will not be presented that it can have no secrets. The President of the United States is the depository of secret transactions, his duty may lead him to delegate those secrets to the members of the House, and the success, safety, and energy of the Government may depend on keeping those secrets inviolably. The people have a right to be well governed; they have interests as well as rights and it is the duty of the Legislature to take every possible measure to promote those interests" (Bessette and Tulis, p. 194).

43. "There ought to be no place where anything can be done that everybody does not know about": Woodrow Wilson, *The New Freedom: A Call for the Emancipation of the Generous Energies of a Free People*, p. 113; "If it is a public game, then why not come out into the open and play it in public?" (ibid., p. 115).

44. See "Non-elective Representation," in Harvey C. Mansfield, Jr., and Robert Scigliano, *Representation: The Perennial Issues*, pp. 57–62. See also Michael Malbin, *Unelected Representatives*; Harrison W. Fox, Jr., and Susan Webb Hammond, *Congressional Staffs: The Invisible Force in American Lawmaking;* and Mansfield's "The Media World and Democratic Representation." The difficulties entailed in such appeals are suggested by Jeffrey Tulis, "Public Policy and the Rhetorical Presidency." Wilson's fight for the League of Nations Treaty is one of Tulis's cases.

45. See the analysis of Van Buren's attempt to make parties serve this purpose, in Ceaser, *Presidential Selection*, pp. 123–69, and Erler, "The Problem of the Public Good in *The Federalist*."

46. This is especially true if one notes the stress on *leadership* and revolutionary change in the new opinion leaders. Consider these titles: *The New Right: We're Ready to Lead*, by Richard A. Viguerie; Charles L. Heatherly, ed., *Mandate for Leadership*; *The Reagan Revolution: An Inside Look at the Transformation of the United States Government*, by Rowland Evans and Robert Novak. It may be objected, of course, that the conservative nomenclature reflects a profound break with and animus toward the liberal tradition. But as Donald Maletz observes, the shift in terminology was a political gambit of the nonliberal left, which succeeded in making radical claims respectable under the new terminology: "The Neo-Conservatives and the Crisis of Liberalism."

47. See Harvey C. Mansfield, Jr., "The American Election: Towards Constitutional Democracy?"

48. Part of the sequel was not surprising: some of the reforms strengthened the authority of the leaders in both House and Senate, and the Republicans had traditionally shown more party discipline. Noting these points, Charles O. Jones could still justly conclude that "on balance, factionalism prospers, party does not. There is even less incentive than usual for members of Congress to be loyal to their political party in these times": "Can Our Parties Survive Our Politics?" p. 29. See William J. Crotty, *Political Reform and the American Experiment*; *The New Congress*, ed. Thomas E.

Mann and Norman J. Ornstein, pp. 39, 45, 53, 363–83. On the nominations, see Austin Ranney, ed., *The American Elections of 1980*, pp. 37–98.

49. There was no "new progressivism," despite Bruce N. Gyory and Thomas E. Riley, "Presidential Leadership and the New Progressivism: The Anderson Candidacy."

50. On the drooping of the liberal posture see Mansfield, *The Spirit of Liberalism*, pp. 89–125.

51. Weber, *ES*, 1:268–69, 3:1128–33; *From Max Weber*, pp. 95–96, 100–111. See Bessette et al., "The Rhetorical Presidency."

52. See "Politics as a Vocation," in *From Max Weber*, pp. 77–113.

53. *PS*, p. 7.

54. Ibid. Compare Nietzsche, *BGE*, no. 44.

55. *PS*, pp. 13, 25.

56. Ibid., p. 21.

57. Ibid.

58. Ibid., p. 13.

59. See Kent A. Kirwan, "Historicism and Statesmanship in the Reform Argument of Woodrow Wilson."

60. See Eugene F. Miller, "Positivism, Historicism, and Political Inquiry." On Weber and the Historical School, see Strauss, *Natural Right and History*, pp. 13–34, 36–80. Consider Clor's remarks in note 34, above.

61. *PS*, pp. 1–11; Bendix, *Max Weber: An Intellectual Portrait*, pp. 14–23, 30–42; Arthur Mitzman, *The Iron Cage: An Historical Interpretation of Max Weber*, pp. 75–147; Abraham Ascher, "Professors as Propagandists: The Politics of the *Kathedersozialisten*," pp. 282–302.

62. "It is not now fundamental matters of structure and franchise upon which we have to center our choice; but those general questions of policy upon which every nation has to exercise its discretion: foreign policy, our duty to our neighbors, customs, tariffs, coinage, currency, immigration, the law of corporations and of trusts, the regulation of railway traffic and of the great industries which supply the necessaries of life and the stuffs of manufacture. *These are questions of economic policy chiefly*; and how shall we settle questions of economic policy except upon grounds of interest? Who is to reconcile our interests and extract what is national and liberal out of what is sectional and selfish?": Wilson, "Leaderless Government," *Papers*, 1:354 (emphasis added). For further discussion of the primacy of politics over economics in Weber's Freiburg Lecture, see chap. 2, sec. 2, below. See also Donald R. Brand, "Progressivism and the New Deal."

63. *PS*, pp. 8–9, 18–23, 299–308; Mommsen, *Weber und Politik*, pp. 97–146, 176–86.

64. *PS*, pp. 8, 19–22.

65. Ibid., p. 24.

66. On instinct see ibid., pp. 1, 19, 22, 24, 25. See also "Political Leadership and Ultimate Values," in Robert Eden, "Political Leadership and Philosophic Praxis: A Study of Weber and Nietzsche," pp. 31–51. Weber's Freiburg Lecture joins the debate between Menger and Schmoller on the methods of political economy. See Dieter Lindenlaub, *Richtungskämpfe im Verein für Sozialpolitik. Vierteljahrschrift für Sozial-*

und Wirtschaftsgeschichte, Beiheft 52–53; Gerhard Ritzel, *Schmoller versus Menger: Eine Analyse des Methodenstreits im Hinblick auf den Historismus in der Nationalo- ekonomie.*

67. *PS,* pp. 11, 13.

68. Ibid., p. 1.

69. Ibid., p. 23.

70. Ibid., p. 20. Cf. *From Max Weber,* pp. 386–95; Mommsen, *Weber und Poli- tik,* pp. 97–107.

71. *PS,* pp. 20–21.

72. Ibid., p. 28.

73. Ibid., pp. 14–15. On the difference between modern liberal politics and re- gime politics, see Eden, "Doing without Liberalism: Weber's Regime Politics," pp. 380–85; see chap. 6, sec. 1, below.

74. Weber, *Methodology,* p. 67 (top); *From Max Weber,* pp. 279–81, 282–84. Compare *Methodology,* p. 27, with *PS,* p. 13.

75. *PS,* pp. 14–15, 274; *From Max Weber,* p. 394; *ES,* 1:266–71.

76. *PS,* p. 13.

77. Ibid., pp. 14–15, 18, 273; *From Max Weber,* p. 393.

78. *PS,* p. 16.

79. Ibid.

80. "Einem entsprechenden Vorsatze treu bleiben," ibid., p. 16.

81. Ibid., pp. 13–16.

82. Consider the remarks on liberal orthodoxy, notes 43–45, above. Recent dis- cussions worth consulting are Richard J. Bisherjian, *Public Philosophy Reader;* Sul- livan, *Reconstructing Public Philosophy;* Kenneth W. Thompson, *The President and the Public Philosophy;* and Samuel H. Beer's perceptive essay, "In Search of a New Public Philosophy." "Fundamental political change in the past . . . came through a few realigning elections in which one or the other of the parties, usually led by its presidential candidate, sought to implement policies reflecting a new public phi- losophy": James W. Ceaser, "Direct Participation in Politics," p. 134.

83. Joseph M. Bessette et al., "The Rhetorical Presidency."

84. Ceaser, *Presidential Selection,* pp. 213–59.

85. *PS,* p. 13.

86. Ibid., p. 29.

87. Ibid., pp. 13–15, 24–25. See Ascher, "Professors as Propagandists," p. 296. Adolf Wagner had come into conflict with the other members of the *Verein* be- cause he could not promote his fiercely nationalistic policies within their notions of professional objectivity. Weber's Freiburg Lecture reopens this issue.

88. Compare Elliot, *The Rise of Guardian Democracy,* pp. 1–33, 89–113, 265–74.

89. See Harry V. Jaffa, *The House Divided;* Don Edward Fehrenbacher, *The Dred Scott Case: Its Significance in American Law and Politics.*

90. *The Collected Works of Abraham Lincoln,* 4:168.

91. Harry V. Jaffa, "Expediency and Morality in the Lincoln-Douglas Debates."

92. *PS,* p. 23.

93. Fehrenbacher, *The Dred Scott Case;* Jaffa, *The House Divided,* pp. 275–301.

94. Jaffa, *The House Divided*, pp. 7–28.

95. See above, secs. 1–2.

96. Jaffa, *The House Divided*, pp. 226–27, 331–32, 355.

97. Ibid., pp. 330–46.

98. See above, sec. 2.

99. Ralph Lerner, "Commerce and Character: The Anglo-American as New-Model Man," pp. 3 ff.; Mansfield, *Machiavelli's New Modes and Orders: A Study of the "Discourses on Livy,"* pp. 30–34, 39–42, 110–16, 202–4. That the problem of individuality as insoluble for modern political philosophy is central to Strauss's understanding of the genesis of historicism is brought out by Richard Kennington's profound reading, "Strauss's Natural Right and History." For the Founders and Montesquieu, see especially William B. Allen, "Theory and Practice in the Founding of the Republic."

100. See Beer, "In Search of a New Public Philosophy," and "The National Idea in American Politics."

101. Strauss, *Natural Right and History,* pp. 252–94.

102. Richard M. Pious, ed., *The Power to Govern: Assessing Reform in the United States.* Cf. Hugh Heclo, "The Issue Networks and the Executive Establishment." See also James Sundquist, "The Crisis of Competence in Government," p. 531.

103. The multiplication of moral issues is remarked by Daniel Yankelovich: "The perspectives of the opinion leaders who participated in the study are rather different from those of the public. Church leaders, educators, philosophers, journalists, scientists, artists, jurists, writers, and community leaders stress many more new 'moral' imperatives than does the general public": Yankelovich, Amitai Etzioni, et al., *Moral Leadership in Government: A Public Agenda Foundation Report, September 1976.* The poignance of the question I have posed may be seen if one asks whether any appeal to our common humanity is possible, or has intelligible meaning, in the absence of such an order. When rights are asserted as human rights, is it not assumed that a bounded, intelligible human nature exists for us in common? Consider Clifford Orwin and Thomas L. Pangle, "Restoring the Human Rights Tradition," pp. 20–41.

104. Consider David Chagall, *The New Kingmakers: An Inside Look at the Powerful Men behind America's Political Campaigns,* p. 57: "More than ever before in U.S. history, as party loyalty wanes, smaller pockets of special-interest groups rush in to fill the power void. In place of the ward heelers who could fix a citizen's parking tickets or get him or her a twenty-five dollar check as an election official, we have a proliferation of groups who trade off votes for legislative backing of their cause. Surrounding themselves with halos of morality, such diverse cliques as the profeminist, anti-abortion, progun, antinuclear, and pro-ecology lobbies can deliver large blocs of adherents. They are available to the candidate who will do the most for their cause, regardless of party affiliation." Jeffrey M. Berry, *Lobbying for the People: The Political Behavior of Public Interest Groups,* finds that "the entrepreneurial theory of group origins has greater explanatory power for public interest organizations" (p. 25). But he does not consider the structural conditions that favor the existence of such organizations rather than parties. See also Jeffrey A. Ross et al., *The Mobilization of Collective Identity: Comparative Perspectives;* Arthur Mann, *The One and the Many: Reflections*

on the American Identity; Horace M. Kallen, *Cultural Pluralism and the American Idea: An Essay in Social Philosophy.*

105. Mansfield, "The American Election: Towards Constitutional Democracy?" pp. 11–14; Heclo, "The Issue Networks"; Malbin, *Unelected Representatives*; Edward J. Erler, "Equal Protection and Personal Rights: The Regime of the 'Discrete and Insular Minority'"; Thomas E. Mann and Norman J. Ornstein, eds., *The New Congress,* p. 49; S. J. Makielski, Jr., *Beleaguered Minorities: Cultural Politics in America,* pp. 139–53, 215–22; William R. Rosengren and Mark Lefton, *Organizations and Clients: Essays in the Sociology of Service,* pp. 71–91, 187–202; Bernard Rubin, *Small Voices and Great Trumpets: Minorities and the Media.*

106. *From Max Weber,* pp. 147–49; *Methodology of the Social Sciences,* pp. 81, 104–5, 111; see also p. 15.

107. No one has attempted to refute Strauss or Mommsen by proving that Weber was serious about Natural Right. See Strauss, *Natural Right and History,* pp. 35 ff.; Reinhard Bendix and Guenther Roth, *Scholarship and Partisanship: Essays on Max Weber,* pp. 62–69.

108. *Methodology,* pp. 18, 81; *PS,* pp. 1, 13, 25; Weber, *Gesammelte Aufsätze zur Soziologie und Sozialpolitik,* p. 420.

109. Strauss wrote, "The radical historicist . . . recognizes the absurdity of unqualified historicism as a theoretical thesis. He denies, therefore, the possibility of a theoretical or objective analysis, which as such would be trans-historical, of the various comprehensive views or 'historical worlds' or 'cultures.' This denial was decisively prepared by Nietzsche's attack on nineteenth-century historicism, which claimed to be a theoretical view. According to Nietzsche, the theoretical analysis of human life that realizes the relativity of all comprehensive views and thus depreciates them would make human life itself impossible, for it would destroy the protecting atmosphere within which life or culture or action is alone possible. Moreover, since the theoretical analysis has its basis outside of life, it will never be able to understand life. The theoretical analysis of life is noncommittal and fatal to commitment, but life means commitment": *Natural Right and History,* p. 26. The distinction between theoretical and practical historicism is fundamental to the study that follows. That Weber was aware of Nietzsche's more radical historicism is evidenced by his underlining of this passage from Georg Simmel's *Schopenhauer und Nietzsche:* "History as a whole displays perhaps no meaning, progress, or actual 'development.' But if these categories *do not connect the succession of moments, then there could be no history,* but rather only a happening. Nietzsche's deepest opposition to Schopenhauer is revealed in advance, in the fact that *historical representations form his entire thought.* The value concepts, whose rise and fall displays to him the meaning of the world process, insofar as men are their carriers, are of a specifically historical nature. . . . The need for redemption is satisfied in Nietzsche by the endless historical development of our species. . . . The contrast between the unique, accidental individual and the timeless, valuable, general idea, is sublimated (*aufhebt*) by Nietzsche" (p. 196, Weber's emphasis). On Weber's copy of this volume, see the remarks on translations and sources at the beginning of the notes, above.

110. Nietzsche, *Twilight of the Idols,* "Skirmishes of an Untimely Man," Nos. 38–39.

111. Ibid.; *BGE,,* Nos. 199, 202–3.

112. *TI,* "Skirmishes," Nos. 37, 39, 41; *BGE,,* Nos. 239 (p. 169, top), 257, 259.

113. *TI,* "Skirmishes," No. 38; *BGE,* Nos. 24–44, 268.

114. *GM,* Third Essay, Nos. 1, 28.

115. *BGE,* no. 23. It should be borne in mind that this introduces Nietzsche's thoughts on freedom in Part 2. In Weber's copy, Simmel's discussion of "Nietzsche the practical, preaching moralist" is underlined, and Weber has written *NB* (*nota bene,* note well) beside this passage: "Nietzsche alone has so strictly carried out the extremely dangerous association, *between the traditional content of morality* [*bisherigen Inhalt der Moral*] *and morality as a whole, that he designates his negation of that content as pure immoralism*" (Weber's emphasis). But Weber objected to the following passage, in which Simmel claimed that by making nicer distinctions, Nietzsche could have set himself apart from vulgar immoralism: "Nietzsche should have at least drawn out clearly the limits of his will to power *in contrast to the vulgar desire for possession,* in order to make clear that it was not mastery and power as outward actuality, but rather the character of the sovereign soul, *whose appearance and expression* in each sociological relation gives them their value" (Weber's emphasis). Beside the passage, Weber wrote, "That is however not at all Nietzsche's point of view!" See Weber's personal copy of Georg Simmel's *Schopenhauer und Nietzsche,* p. 231.

CHAPTER 2. PHILOSOPHY AND THE LIBERAL CAUSE

1. The benign stance sets the stage for a more aggressive doctrine by arguing that liberalism is to be jettisoned for the sake of "taking equality and liberty seriously," as Stephen Lukes put it in *Individualism,* pp. 148–57. The post-liberal politics would not "dispense with the need for consent, representation, and the protection of interests. But it would need to conceptualize these in a much more complex way [than had liberal politics], and take full account of the many degrees and modes of consent (and the acute problem of distinguishing true from false consensus), of different ways of implementing democracy than through legislative 'representatives' and different ways of conceiving 'representation' (e.g., of different social roles, or activities, or aspects of the individual), and finally of the need for such a democratic and representative government to take an ever more active role in shaping and controlling the natural and social environment if equality and liberty are to be enhanced" (p. 154). But representation through unelected and self-appointed opinion leaders will not, as Lukes clearly perceives, remain fully dedicated to equality and liberty unless it is bound to a certain understanding of individuality and self-development: "If, as I have argued, *the notion of self-development incorporates an irreducible teleological component, a belief in the existence of some determinate range of characteristic human excellences and the denial that what these consist in (and preclude) is open to irresolvable dispute,* then taking this central value of individualism seriously will require one to reject the extreme moral relativism or pluralism inherent in the doctrine of ethical individualism" (p. 156, emphasis added). Since a teleological conception of self-development is the keystone of Lukes's argument, his book should come to grips with the most resourceful opponent of that conception; yet Nietzsche's nihilistic individualism is not considered. The shift from a liberal to a Nietzschean understanding of self and hence of self-asser-

tion is remarked by Harvey C. Mansfield, Jr., *The Spirit of Liberalism*, pp. 24, 45, 90–91. The most prominent commentator to have sensed that the shift away from consent and majority rule was well under way was Alexander M. Bickel, especially in *The Morality of Consent*, pp. 11, 137. But Bickel's rejection of theory in favor of Burkean prudence seems to have prevented him from understanding the philosophical roots of the shift in Nietzsche's teaching: see Robert K. Faulkner, "Bickel's Constitution: The Problem of Moderate Liberalism," pp. 931–32.

2. This study retraces ground covered by Wolfgang J. Mommsen, who sought to demonstrate that Weber's argument on political leadership emerged from his analysis of the crisis of German liberalism and reflected his profound break with liberal principles: *Max Weber und die deutsche Politik*, pp. 1–22, 37–51, 147–205, 416 ff. See also Maurice Weyembergh, *Le Voluntarisme rationnel de Max Weber*, pp. 1–17, 32–45, 63–90, 395 ff. Neither Mommsen nor Weyembergh considered the connection between modern liberal politics and modern science, or the challenge of philosophic leadership within science, to be integral to the problem of Weber's doctrine of political leadership.

3. The study to follow will reopen the question raised by Georg Lukács in *Die Zerstörung der Vernunft*. Lukács argued that Nietzsche sought to rescue the liberal commercial republic with its capitalist economic institutions in the only way it could be rescued in the face of the higher rationality of Marxism: by a thoroughgoing destruction of reason. Lukács was compelled to minimize the extent of Nietzsche's projected destruction of "bourgeois culture"; nor did he think it necessary to explain how capitalism could survive without the other modes and orders of the liberal commercial republic. The gist of his argument was that Weber did not resist Nietzsche's projected philosophic leadership over the sciences and culture, in what he called "the imperialist epoch." See *Die Zerstörung der Vernunft*, pp. 270–350, 521–37. My reasons for rejecting Lukács's account will become evident in the next five chapters; they parallel the critical remarks by Werner J. Dannhauser, *Nietzsche's View of Socrates*, pp. 22–26.

4. It is remarkable how completely the problem of the origins of modern science has disappeared from sociology in the Weberian tradition; the project for a sociology of knowledge capable of explaining the development of rationalism and rationalization has been conceived in such a way as to exclude inquiry into the thoughts of the knowers. Thus the founders of modern philosophy and modern liberal politics—Hobbes, Locke, Spinoza—scarcely merit notice in Gunther Roth and Wolfgang Schluchter's *Max Weber's Vision of History: Ethics and Methods*. Schluchter's extended essay, *The Rise of Western Rationalism: Max Weber's Developmental History*, though conceived as a reconstruction and correction of Weber's work in the light of subsequent inquiry, minimizes the causal role of philosophy in initiating the modern project. For an analysis and critique of Weber's historiographical paradigm, see Hiram Caton, "World in Decay: Critiques of the Historiography of Progress." Caton's recovery of the problem that Weber suppressed is fundamental to the present inquiry: see his "Toward a Diagnosis of Progress" and "The Politics of Progress."

5. Horst Baier, "Die Gesellschaft—ein langer Schatten des toten Gottes. Friedrich Nietzsche und die Entstehung der Soziologie aus dem Geist der decadence," pp. 6–22 and passim; *From Max Weber: Essays in Sociology*, pp. 61–62; Reinhard Bendix and Guenther Roth, *Scholarship and Partisanship: Essays on Max Weber*, pp. 22–24.

6. Nietzsche, *The Genealogy of Morals*, Preface, no. 7.

7. Ibid.

8. Ibid.

9. *Beyond Good and Evil: A Prelude to the Philosophy of the Future*, no. 186.

10. *The Gay Science*, no. 345. Cf. *The Will to Power*, no. 263.

11. *GM*, Essay 1, nos. 11, 12.

12. *GS*, no. 345; *GM*, Essay 1, note to no. 17. Compare René Descartes, *Les Passions de l'âme*, Articles 153, 156, 159, 161; *Œuvres de Descartes*, 4:166, 168, 170–71, 174–75; Niccolo Machiavelli, *Discourses on the First Decade of Titus Livy*, Book 1, chap. 31; *GS*, nos. 183, 191, 293.

13. See Paul Valéry, "A Conquest by Method," in Valéry, *History and Politics*, pp. 52, 64–66; Francis Bacon, *Novum Organum*, nos. 90–98, *The Works of Francis Bacon*, 4:89–95; Hiram Caton, *The Origin of Subjectivity: An Essay on Descartes*, pp. 40–66. Compare Rousseau's irony in imitating the academic essay questions, *Discourse on the Origins of Inequality*, Preface and Note J, in *First and Second Discourses*, pp. 93, 203–13.

14. Nietzsche, *BGE*, nos. 1, 9, 23, 45.

15. *BGE*, no. 186; *GS*, nos. 7, 346.

16. *GM*, Essay 3, no. 27; *WP*, no. 674.

17. *BGE*, nos. 1, 6, 186; *GS*, no. 2.

18. Weber's *Einleitung* or "introduction" is known in English as "The Social Psychology of the World Religions": *From Max Weber*, pp. 267–301. One should compare Nietzsche's early statement, on the need for "knowledge of the conditions of culture" as "the enormous task of the great minds of the next century" (*Human, All-too-Human: A Book for Free Spirits*, vol. 1, no. 25), with Weber's parallel statement in *The Methodology of the Social Sciences*, pp. 67. Weber criticizes the theory of *ressentiment* at pp. 270 and 276–77. He then acknowledges, "But that the evaluation of *suffering* in religious ethics has been subject to a typical change is beyond doubt. If properly understood, this change carries a certain justification for the theory first worked out by Nietzsche" (p. 270). The ensuing discussion should be compared with *GM*, Essay 2, nos. 6–7, and Essay 3, no. 28. Weber addresses himself to Nietzsche's typification of master morality in speaking of the theodicy of good fortune (p. 271 and again on p. 276, bottom). Both Weber and Nietzsche use the notions of ascetic ideals and religious needs (pp. 270, 273–74, 276; compare *GS* no. 1). A list (by no means exhaustive) of the key topics on which Weber is indebted to Nietzsche would include *ressentiment* and pariah religiosity; the meaning of ascetic ideals; otherworldly versus innerworldly asceticism; warrior religiosity; the psychology of domination of the priests; the problem of theodicy of good fortune and theodicy of death and suffering conceived as problems of construing the world as a meaningful cosmos; the disenchantment of the world through a religious insistence upon truthfulness; prophetic revaluation of values as the key to the history of the human soul; the creation of conscience or of a human animal capable of keeping promises. The excursus on pariah peoples and *ressentiment* (Weber, *Economy and Society*, 2:492–99), is devoted to a critique of Nietzsche. See also Weber, *Gesammelte Aufsätze zur Religionssoziologie*, 3:168, 2:174; *From Max Weber*, p. 275, where Nietzsche is used almost verbatim; and compare the notes to chap. 4, sec. 1, and chap. 5, sec. 1, below, for references to Weber's copy of Simmel's *Schopenhauer und Nietzsche*.

19. Bendix and Roth, *Scholarship and Partisanship*, pp. 22–25, 272–81; Gerth and Mills, *From Max Weber*, pp. 61–62. See William Shapiro, "The Nietzschean Roots of Max Weber's Social Science"; Wolfgang J. Mommsen, "Universalgeschichtliches und politisches Denken bei Max Weber"; Eugène Fleischmann, "De Weber à Nietzsche." The Frankfurt School developed certain aspects of Weber's elaboration of Nietzsche; consider Günther Rohrmoser's formulation, "Modern society has today entered the phase in which it threatens to shatter itself on its contradictions, which it has embraced in the most essential form in the fundamental contradiction between technology and subjectivity": "Nietzsches Kritik der Moral," p. 332. See further Reinhart Klemens Maurer, "Nietzsche und die Kritische Theorie." But the Frankfurt School did not explore how Weber's historical studies came to terms with Nietzsche. Nor did what we may loosely term "mainstream sociology." This neglect led Horst Baier to remark that "Only in the last few years, after a long period during which those who knew Weber's work intimately had found no footholds, has Nietzsche been recognized as a source" (ibid., p. 26). Baier is incorrect, however, in attributing this to the supposed fact that "in Weber the influence does not often become evident [*liegt nicht offen zutage*]" (ibid.). As the last note may indicate, Weber's open references to Nietzsche are in fact more numerous than his citations to Marx; his use of Nietzschean terms and concepts is decidedly more evident than his use of Marx's. Ernst Behler is nearer the mark: "One perhaps wanted to avoid being identified with Nietzsche, and therefore did not say how much one had learned from him" (ibid., p. 24). Having appropriated Nietzsche for their own purposes, the Frankfurt School had little interest in identifying Weber with Nietzsche. And mainstream sociology had every reason to dissociate Weber from Nietzsche, since no science fathered by an ancestor of Nazism had any prospect of flourishing under the Allied Occupation or in the Anglo-Saxon academy during the postwar period.

20. Otto Stammer, ed., *Max Weber and Sociology Today*, pp. 83–132; Jürgen Kocka, "Kontroversen über Max Weber." By concentrating upon asceticism and eros, Arthur Mitzman reaches the conclusion that Weber became more Nietzschean and less moral as he matured; but to do so, Mitzman was compelled to abstract from Weber's defense of liberal democratic institutions: *The Iron Cage: An Historical Interpretation of Max Weber*, pp. 181 ff.

21. Eric Voegelin, *The New Science of Politics: An Introduction*, p. 22.

22. Roth and Schluchter, *Max Weber's Vision of History*, pp. 65–113; David Beetham, *Max Weber and the Theory of Modern Politics;* Maurice Weyembergh, *Le Voluntarisme rationnel de Max Weber*, pp. xxx, 144 note 8.

23. Compare Weyembergh's remark (ibid., p. 144 note 8) that if one identifies Weber's concept of rationalization with the "processus" that culminated in Nietzsche's concept of the will to power, one has failed to take account of Weber's political thought or his moral reflection.

24. Plato, *Phaedo*, 95e7–100a9; *The Works of Francis Bacon,*, 4:90 (*Novum Organum*, bk. I, no. 92). See Nietzsche, *WP*, no. 1051; Harvey C. Mansfield, Jr., *Machiavelli's New Modes and Orders: A Study of the "Discourses on Livy,"* pp. 35–41, 97, 187–189, 297–98. Hans Barth is on the right track in treating Nietzsche's "art of mistrust" as a radicalization of Bacon's doctrine of the idols. See his account of Nietzsche's "analysis of decadence," *Wahrheit und Ideologie*, 1:263–77.

25. Nietzsche, *The Birth of Tragedy and the Case of Wagner*, Preface. See Hiram Caton, "Toward a Diagnosis of Progress."

26. Nietzsche, *Ecce Homo*, "Why I Am So Wise," no. 2.

27. *Twilight of the Idols*, "The Problem of Socrates," no. 11.

28. Ibid., "Skirmishes of an Untimely Man," no. 35.

29. *WP*, no. 39.

30. Ibid., no. 41. See *EH*, Preface no. 2.

31. *WP*, no. 41.

32. Weber, *Gesammelte politische Schriften*, p. 24. A less warlike, more liberal stance was presented in Weber's American lecture, translated in *From Max Weber* as "Capitalism and Rural Society in Germany," pp. 363–85.

33. *PS*, pp. 14, 18–20.

34. Kenneth D. Barkin, *The Controversy over German Industrialization, 1890–1902*, passim; Mommsen, *Weber und Politik, 1890–1920*, pp. 97–107; "National Character and the Junkers," *From Max Weber*, pp. 386–95.

35. Ferdinand Tönnies, *Der Nietzsche-Kultus: Eine Kritik*. See also the reports in Richard Frank Krummel, *Nietzsche und der deutsche Geist. Ausbreitung und Wirkung des Nietzscheschen Werkes im deutschen Sprachraum bis zum Todesjahr des Philosophen: Ein Schrifttumsverzeichnis der Jahre, 1867–1900*, pp. 115, 183, 188. Not noted in Krummel's catalogue is Tönnies's pamphlet, *"Ethische Kultur" und ihre Geleite* (Berlin, 1892), a copy of which is held by the Robarts Library of the University of Toronto. From 1895 to 1899, Franz Wilhelm Förster, later mentioned by Weber in *Science as a Vocation*, headed the *Zeitschrift für "Ethische Kultur."* See Friedrich Pöggeler, *Die Pädagogik F. W. Försters*. Weber's letter to Alfred Weber of 17 May 1895 is quoted in Mommsen, *Max Weber und die deutsche Politik*, p. 39.

36. See Tönnies, *"Ethische Kultur" und ihre Geleite*, pp. 11–22. It was not only power-politics that was in question; Tönnies agreed with Franz Mehring (and hence with the position later elaborated by Georg Lukács) that Nietzsche could be called "the philosopher of capitalism" (Tönnies, ibid., p. 10).

37. See "Bismarck's Legacy," from *Parliament and Government in a Newly Ordered Germany*, in *ES*, 3:1385–92.

38. Weber quotes from Montesquieu's *The Spirit of the Laws*, Book 20, chap. 7, in *The Protestant Ethic and the Spirit of Capitalism*, p. 45. Book 20 follows Book 19, chap. 27, "How the laws can contribute to form the mores, the manners, and the character of a nation," and its theme is how manners are softened and made more humane by commerce. See Book 20, chaps. 1, 2, 5, 15, 22, 23. Kant's critique of the eudaemonistic form of liberalism which prevailed in Montesquieu (a critique on which Weber drew) was explicitly inspired by Rousseau. See William A. Galston, *Kant and the Problem of History*, pp. 64, 68, 93–102, 132, 240 ff.

39. Nietzsche, *The Case of Wagner*, Preface. See *GS*, no. 352.

40. *PS*, p. 12.

41. *TI*, "Skirmishes of an Untimely Man," no. 39. Compare *WP*, no. 65.

42. *TI*, ibid.

43. Ibid., no. 38.

44. *GM*, Essay 1, nos. 11–12.

45. *PS*, p. 23.

46. Ibid., pp. 24–25. Compare *BGE,* no. 208, discussed in chap. 3, sec. 4, below. Consider also chap. 1, note 109, above.

47. *PS,* p. 13.

48. Walter Kaufmann, *Nietzsche: Philosopher, Psychologist, Antichrist,* pp. 246–66; Kurt Rudolf Fischer, "Nazism as a Nietzschean Experiment," pp. 116–22.

49. Compare Leo Strauss, *Natural Right and History*, pp. 12–34, on the German Historical School. See also Baier, "Die Gesellschaft . . . Nietzsche und die Entstehung der Soziologie"; Hiram Caton, "Toward a Diagnosis of Progress"; Nietzsche, *Human, All-too-Human,* vol. 2, part 2, nos. 287, 289; vol. 1, no. 110; *The Dawn,* no. 159; *GS* nos. 370, 380 (end).

50. *WP,* no. 1, sec. 6; compare Baier, "Die Gesellschaft . . . Nietzsche und die Entstehung der Soziologie." *Human, All-too-Human,* vol. 1, nos. 24–25, 33, 224, 235, 450, 460, 463, 472–74; vol. 2, part 2, 218, 235, 275, 278, 279; *BGE,* nos. 199, 201–3, 208–9, 258, 259.

51. *TI,* "Skirmishes," nos. 37–39; *BGE,* no. 257.

52. *ES,* 3:1402. Compare *WP,* no. 888.

53. *BGE,* nos. 212, 223–27; *WP,* no. 970. See chap. 1, secs. 5, 7, above.

54. The issue is especially clear from *WP,* no. 679: "One must not let oneself be deceived; it is just the same with peoples and races: they constitute the 'body' for the production of isolated valuable individuals, who carry on the great process" (p. 360).

55. Compare Weber, *Methodology,* pp. 19, 27.

56. Compare chap. 1, sec. 8, above, and Caton, "Toward a Diagnosis of Progress."

57. See Charles E. Butterworth, "Frantz Fanon and Human Dignity."

58. *PS,* p. 20.

59. Ibid., p. 29. Compare the end of Nietzsche's *Twilight of the Idols.*

60. Compare Weber's letter to Adolf von Harnack, 5 February 1906: "The time for sects or anything similar is historically past. But the fact that our nation has never gone through the schooling of hard asceticism in *any* form, is on the other hand the source of everything which I find hateful in the nation *as in myself*!" Quoted in Mommsen, "Universalgeschichtliches und politisches Denken bei Max Weber," p. 292, note 48. See also Mommsen's account of *The Protestant Ethic* thesis, *Weber und Politik, 1890–1920,* pp. 417 ff.

61. Lest it be objected that Weber's explanation was not spiritualist or monocausal, I ask the reader's forebearance: it will become evident in the course of the analyses to follow that the dispute between Weber and Nietzsche concerns only the *exclusion* of a causal role for philosophy. The argument does not depend on reducing Weber's baroque structures of explanation to a monocausal caricature. The inquiry to follow pursues Weber's suggestion in *The Protestant Ethic* that "a foundational [*gründliche*], historically oriented conceptual analysis" of the terms *individuality* and *individualism* "would be precisely now once again of the highest value for science": *RS,* 1;95, note 3. See also *PE,* p. 222. The problem is that Weber never followed through on his claim that his account of the Protestant Ethic as a cause could be squared with an account giving due importance to the rise of modern science. His claim was advanced, obscurely enough, in his "Anticritical Last Word" on the debate over *The Protestant Ethic.* See Weber, *Die protestantische Ethik 2: Kritiken und Antikritiken,* p. 324.

62. That Weber was familiar with Nietzsche's use of "decadent" as a term of criticism directed against bourgeois civilization is evident from chapter 7 of Georg Simmel's *Schopenhauer und Nietzsche*, "The Value of Humanity and Decadence," pp. 195–232, on which Weber has written marginal comments in his copy. See Simmel's remarks on why a "social ethic" is thoroughly eudaemonistic, p. 214; and compare also p. 228.

63. *PE*, pp. 98–128, 155–83.

64. Ibid., p. 182. It is often said that this famous phrase, which Weber placed in quotes, came from Nietzsche. If so, no one has ever been able to locate the passage, including myself. For further discussion of Weber's causal explanation of the origins of modernity, see chap. 5, sec. 4, chap. 6, sec. 3, below.

65. *BGE* Preface. See Reinhart Klemens Maurer, "Das antiplatonisches Experiment Nietzsches. Zum Problem einer konsequenten Ideologiekritik"; Hans Peter Balner, *Freiheit statt Teleologie: eine Grundgedanke von Nietzsche*, pp. 68 ff. Weber marked "NB!" (*nota bene*) beside Georg Simmel's formulation: "The solution of the task by means of [Nietzsche's] life-concept depends on the possibility of ordaining a development that would not be dominated by an end-purpose" (Weber's copy of *Schopenhauer und Nietzsche*, p. 7).

66. *BGE*, Preface, and no. 204 on the war between theology and philosophy. See H. A. Rethy, "The Descartes Motto to the First Edition of *Menschliches, allzumenschliches*," pp. 292–93.

67. *BGE* Preface. Compare Rethy, ibid.: "What does seem certain is that *Menschliches, allzumenschliches*, as the motto from the 'father of modern philosophy's' first book testifies, represents the commencement of Nietzsche's retracing of the path of *modern* thought." Compare Descartes' aphorism: *Dii male perdeant/Antiquos, mea qui praeripuere mihi*—"Let the Gods cruelly destroy the Ancients, who snatched my things away from me beforehand," quoted in David R. Lachterman, "Descartes and the Philosophy of History," p. 6.

68. Maurer stresses Hobbes in this connection, "Das antiplatonisches Experiment Nietzsches," p. 105. Compare Machiavelli, *The Prince*, chap. 15; Spinoza, *Works*, trans. R. H. M. Elwes, pp. 287–89 (*Political Treatise*, chapter 1, sections 1–6). See Nietzsche's letter on Spinoza to Franz Overbeck, 30 July 1881, in *Werke*, ed. Karl Schlechta, 3: 1171–72.

69. See Mansfield, *Machiavelli's New Modes and Orders: A Study of the "Discourses on Livy*," pp. 182–85; Spinoza, ibid. Compare *Human, All-too-Human*, vol. 1, no. 472; *WP*, nos. 612, 674, 1051. "Truth, that is to say, the scientific method, was grasped and promoted by those who divined in it a weapon of war—an instrument of destruction" (ibid., no. 457).

70. *WP*, nos. 953, 260, 680, 759, 770, 1051. Note especially Nietzsche's interest in the enforcement-powers of the sexual drives, in no. 680. See Jean Granier's discussions of "Le Corps, fil directeur de l'interpretation ontologique," and "Le Corps, point de départ radical," *Le Problème de la Vérité dans la Philosophie de Nietzsche*, pp. 336–52. See also Hans Balner, *Freiheit statt Teleologie*, pp. 84–86.

71. *The Prince*, chap. 15. Cf. *Human, All-too-Human*, vol. 1, no. 224, and *WP*, no. 304 (a reflection upon or preliminary sketch for *GM*). Weber underlined and commented upon Simmel's remark: "*Das Vornehmheitsideal*, in dessen Dienst, vermöge des Verantwortlichkeitsmotivs, auch die Wiederkehr des Gleichen tritt, ist *absolut ir-*

disch-empirisch Natur, insofern es der Gipfel einer von der Tiefe her anhebenden Entwicklung ist, und der Weihe, freilich auch der Problematik aller von oben her, aus dem überempirischen stammenden Werte und Legitimierungen entbehrt" (*Schopenhauer und Nietzsche*, p. 259, Weber's emphasis). (Roughly translated: "Nietzsche's ideal of nobility—in whose service the Eternal Recurrence enters by way of the motif of responsibility—is of an absolutely earthly, empirical nature, insofar as it is the peak of a development instigated and rising from below. It lacks the sanctity, but also the difficulties, which attend all values and legitimations that descend from the supra-empirical downward.") Compare Martin Heidegger, *Nietzsche*, 1:27: "All values remain without force if the corresponding attitude of valuing and the corresponding manner of thinking do not accompany them."

72. *The Prince*, chap. 10. Compare *TI*, "Maxims and Arrows," no. 36: "Morality must be shot at." I do not see how Karl Löwith secures his view as to the necessity for a distinction between "the self-conscious I" and "the bodily 'self,'" a matter which he claims is not a matter for research but only for "experience": "Nietzsches Vollendung des Atheismus," p. 17.

73. *BGE*, no. 230. See *GS*, no. 2; *WP*, no. 659; and the Musarion Ausgabe of Nietzsche's *Werke* (Munich, 1922–29), 14:121: "4. Als Stoff haben wir alles Einverleibt, darin sind wir nicht mehr frei. Diesen Stoff *fassen*, begreifen (durch Wissenschaft). 5. Den Uebermenschen schaffen, nachdem wir die ganze Natur auf uns hin gedacht, *gemacht* haben." (4. "We have incorporated everything as matter: therein we are no longer free. To *grasp* this material, to conceive it (through science). 5. After we have thought, *made* the whole of nature leading up to ourselves, to create the superman.")

74. *GM*, Essay 1, no. 12 (end).

75. *TI* "The Problem of Socrates," nos. 1–12, and "The Four Errors," *WP*, nos. 973, 674. Compare Harry Neumann, "Superman or Last Man? Nietzsche's Interpretation of Athens and Jerusalem." See also this from the *Nachlass*: "Die Triebe *unterhalten* als Fundament alles Erkennens, aber wissen, wo sie Gegner des Erkennens werden: in summa *abwarten*, wie weit das Wissen und die Wahrheit sich *einverleiben* können–und in wiefern eine Umwandlung des Menschen eintritt, wenn er endlich nur noch lebt, um zu erkennen": *KGW*, vol. 5, no. 2, p. 393. ("To *maintain* the drives as the foundation of all knowing, but understanding where they become the enemy of knowing: in sum *to attend* to how far knowledge and truth can *embody* themselves/be embodied—and to what extent a transformation of man would commence, if he at last lived only in order to know.")

76. *GM*, Essay 1, no. 17 note; *WP*, nos. 975, 979, 1014. Gerd Günther Grau may be in agreement when he argues that "Nietzsche . . . stands entirely under the impress of a *Nötigungsmoral*," that is, a morality of need or necessitation: "Sublimierter oder realisierter Wille zur Macht?" p. 262. Weber objected to Simmel's statement comparing Nietzsche's emphasis (upon the extraordinary and exceptional) with a democratic morality emphasizing the everyday; Simmel suggested that reliance upon extraordinary performance or qualities of temperament "always had something accidental and external, could not come into being without some addition from the material world and fate"(*Schopenhauer und Nietzsche*, p. 221). As a political economist, Weber probably failed to see why the values of routine everydayness were less dependent upon things "accidental and external." To conquer chance or accident by modern science, technol-

ogy, and administration, as Bacon foresaw, we must submit to natural necessities or nature's ways.

77. *BGE*, no. 9; *GS*, no. 110; *WP*, no. 647. See Maurer, "Das antiplatonisches Experiment Nietzsches," pp. 117–18.

78. *BGE*, no. 203; *TI*, "The Four Errors"; *WP*, no. 972.

79. *BGE*, Preface, no. 9. Simmel remarks, "It is the same passion in Nietzsche and Spinoza: they cannot bear not to be God": *Schopenhauer und Nietzsche*, p. 204. For a more conservative reading of Descartes that eliminates his magnanimity, see Sheldon S. Wolin, "Political Theory as a Vocation," pp. 35–40.

80. *GM*, Essay 1, nos. 11–12; *WP*, nos. 767, 768, 783–84. This is not to overlook Nietzsche's critique of "ego" and "individual" in *WP*, nos. 379, 487. On the discovery of individuality, see Richard Kennington, "Strauss's Natural Right and History." Heidegger wrote, "For Nietzsche . . . subjectivity is not merely cut loose from the bounds of every limit or boundary; it henceforth declares and governs over every type of limitation or boundary": *Nietzsche*, 2:199; see also ibid., 2:35–36, 200.

81. *WP*, no. 767: "The individual is something quite new which creates new things, something absolute; all his acts are entirely his own. Ultimately, the individual derives the values of his acts from himself; because he has to interpret in a quite individual way even the words he has inherited. His interpretation of a formula at least is personal, even if he does not create a formula: as an interpreter he is still creative." Consider *KGW*, vol. 8, no. 1, p. 13: "*Advocatus diaboli*. New representations of God and Devil. Undetermined knowledge is an insanity of the virtue-period; life perishes from it. We must sanctify the lie, delusion and faith, injustice. We must liberate ourselves from morality *in order to be able to live morally*. My free *arbitrariness, my self-created ideal* desires this and that virtue of me. Which means: *going under as a consequence of virtue*. That is *heroism*." Compare "experimental morality" in *WP*, no. 260. Simmel's assertion that "the contrast between the unique, accidental individual and the timeless, valuable, general idea is sublimated by Nietzsche" (*Schopenhauer und Nietzsche*, p. 196), but without transcendence (p. 200), elicited from Weber the remark "Entirely right!" Compare ibid., p. 6. See also Jean Granier, *Le Problème de la Vérité dans la Philosophie de Nietzsche*, p. 628.

82. *From Max Weber*, pp. 117. Erich Heller's insightful and provocative book, *The Artist's Journey into the Interior and Other Essays*, promoted the misconception that Nietzsche's profound critique of modernity entailed a radical break with the modern scientific project. He ignored the depth of Nietzsche's affirmation of modernity's radical, audacious experiment with truth. The contrary view developed here owes much to George Parkin Grant, "Nietzsche and the Ancients: Philosophy and Scholarship." That Weber was well aware of Nietzsche's rejection of selfless devotion to a cause should be clear from Simmel: *Schopenhauer und Nietzsche*, p. 234.

83. *BGE*, no. 211. Compare *Human, All-too-Human*, vol. 1, no. 16: the greatest triumph of science would be "a *history of the origin of thought*." *BGE* seems to supply the necessary "historical philosophizing" demanded by this earlier work, vol. 1, no. 2.

84. *BGE*, no. 211.

85. Ibid.

86. Ibid., no. 212.

87. Ibid. "Das Ideal einer blöden entsagenden demütigen selbstlösen Men-

schlichkeit": *KGW,* vol. 6, no. 2, p. 150, lines 20–23. My translation differs from Walter Kaufmann's. Kaufmann has "the ideal of a dumb, renunciatory, humble, self-less humanity" (ibid., p. 137). This is a possible reading but leads the reader to think primarily of Luther and German Lutheranism. *Selbstlos* can mean selfless or disinterested; *blöden* can connote weaksightedness, coyness, or shyness, as well as imbecility and timidity. One should consider what an honor-loving aristocrat of the sixteenth century would see as abasement or humiliation, to catch the sense of *demütigen* here. Joseph Peter Stern was probably thinking of Luther when he mistranslated the phrase as "self-denial and mortification of the will for his ideal": *A Study of Nietzsche,* p. 78.

88. *BGE,* no. 212. What precisely is the *umgekehrte Lehre* (opposed teaching) that Nietzsche links to this new ideal? It is opposed to the ideal that Nietzsche begins to sketch. It must therefore *affirm* specialization, the modern division of labor, the collectivization of science as a cooperative social enterprise, and so forth. Since Nietzsche has just spoken of Hegel, it is not surprising that his next step entails a critique of the Hegelian, e.g., the fully modern, state. The origin of that state lies in the *umgekehrte Lehre* of modern liberal politics sketched in *BGE,* no. 212.

89. *Human, All-too-Human,* vol. 1, no. 472; *From Max Weber,* pp. 78, 88–90, 92–93; Lawrence Stone, *The Crisis of the Aristocracy, 1558–1641*; Hiram Caton, "On the Basis of Hobbes's Political Philosophy."

90. On the softening of manners, see *TI,* "Skirmishes of an Untimely Man," no. 37; J. W. Allen, *A History of Political Thought in the Sixteenth Century*, pp. 367–77; Thomas Hobbes, *English Works*, 2: ix–xiii, 93–95, 150–53, 163–64, 172; 3: 63–70, 85–86, 98–104, 140–41, 146–47, 203–4, 209; Spinoza, *Works*, pp. 3, 11, 245–66, 305–6. See also Caton, *The Politics of Progress,* chaps. 4–6.

91. I owe the idea for this section to David L. Schaefer, "The Good, the Beautiful, and the Useful: Montaigne's Transvaluation of Values," which led me to look more closely at *BGE,* no. 212. Heidegger ignores Nietzsche's account of Montaigne, tracing the discovery of individuality—or, in his terms, of subjectivity—only as far back as Descartes. See Heidegger, *Der Europäisches Nihilismus*, pp. 118–20. See also Charles Taylor, *Hegel,* p. 563.

92. See Schaefer, ibid.

93. Compare note 87, above.

94. As Ingeborg Heidemann puts it, for Nietzsche, "Philosophy itself is cause, origin of a forming of the world, and it is a necessity, insofar as man can live only in a world he comprehends": "Nietzsches Kritik der Metaphysik," p. 533.

If the preceding account is valid, a tradition of protecting Nietzsche from his own thought must be abandoned. It may be exemplified by Richard Wisser, "Nietzsches Lehre von der völligen Unverantwortlichkeit und Unschuld Jedermanns." In answer to Ernst Sandvoss, Wisser wrote that "He makes too light, not only of Nietzsche, but also of secular events which urgently need analysis and interpretation. Someone who drives away the golden plover (*Regenpfeifer,* rain-piper) does not ban the weather. Someone who smashes the seismograph does not make the earthquake surrender. Someone who slaughters a scapegoat, restores his own calm, not that of the gods" (p. 148). Wisser's problem is that Nietzsche himself treats philosophy as *the* moving and shaping force. It is not primarily Sandvoss but Nietzsche who speaks of his most comprehensive *responsibility*: *BGE,* nos. 61, 203.

95. *WP*, Preface, no. 1.

96. *From Max Weber*, p. 280.

97. *PE*, p. 182. Compare *ES*, 3: 1192, where philosophy is again deleted as a cause. See also the last citation in note 61, above.

98. See note 60, above. As Wilhelm Hennis has shown in a remarkable article, after 1910 Weber turned "humanity" into a resource of his own rhetoric: "Max Webers Fragestellung," pp. 257–58. Simmel had emphasized "humanity" as a resource of Nietzsche's rhetoric throughout his *Schopenhauer und Nietzsche*, but Weber's marginal comments indicate that he found Simmel's interpretation to be a sweetening of Nietzsche's politics. See chap. 1, note 115, above.

99. See note 35, above.

100. See chap. 1, secs. 5–6, above.

101. Mommsen describes Weber in these terms in "Universalgeschichtliches und politisches Denken bei Max Weber," p. 568.

102. *BGE*, no. 212.

103. *WP*, nos. 861; see also *WP*, nos. 51, 253, 748; *BGE*, no. 212; *EH*, "Why I Am a Destiny," no. 1.

104. The phrase "the ancient common law of Europe" is Edmund Burke's. Tocqueville argues in *The Old Regime and the French Revolution* that its destruction was the chief accomplishment of the French Revolution: "Burke did not see that what was taking place before his eyes was a revolution whose aim was precisely to abolish that 'ancient common law of Europe' and that there could be no question of turning the clock back" (Part I, chap. 5, p. 21). Cf. Nietzsche, *GM*, Essay 1, nos. 16–17.

105. *BGE*, nos. 228; compare nos. 212, 213; *GS*, no. 289, "A new justice is needed." Compare *TI*, "Skirmishes of an Untimely Man," no. 48.

106. *BGE*, nos. 219; see also no. 221: "Moralities must be forced to bow first of all before the *order of rank*." See Heidegger, *Nietzsche*, 2:197, 314 ff.

107. *BGE*, no. 213.

108. *BGE*, no. 39; *EH*, "Why I Am a Destiny," no. 3, Preface no. 3.

109. Nietzsche, *Thus Spake Zarathustra*, Part 4, "On the Higher Man," no. 8; *BGE*, no. 205.

110. *ASZ*, Part 2, "On Human Prudence."

111. *BGE*, nos. 61, 203, 212.

112. *WP*, nos. 999, 973. Compare Heidegger, *Nietzsche*, 2:40.

113. *WP*, no. 859; *GM*, Essay 2, no. 12.

114. *BGE*, no. 256; *WP*, nos. 26, 975; *GM*, Essay 2, no. 12.

115. *WP*, no. 1026; *GM*, Essay 1, no. 16; *GS*, no. 362.

116. *WP*, no. 1026.

117. *WP*, no. 983; *BGE*, nos. 199, 208.

118. *WP*, no. 978.

119. *WP*, no. 973; *BGE*, nos. 257, 262.

120. *WP*, no. 69, note (sketch for the fourth book), p. 46; *BGE*, no. 203.

121. *WP*, no. 862; no. 55, secs. 5, 6, 9, 10 (by Nietzsche's original enumeration); no. 56. See *EH*, "Why I Am a Destiny," no. 8.

122. *EH*, on "The Birth of Tragedy," no. 4; *WP*, 5, 7, 37, 55, 56, 114.

123. *WP*, nos. 55, 56.

124. Cf. note 71 above.

125. See chap. 3, sec. 6, below.

126. *BGE*, no. 61.

127. Ibid., Preface. On Weber's concern with the press and the formation of popular culture, see below, chap. 5, sec. 5, at note 177.

128. *From Max Weber*, p. 145.

129. *BGE*, nos. 241, 242, 247, 256. no. 251 is a parody of German anti-Semitic festival oratory which ends with a suggestion that through careful intermarriage the Prussian Junkers and the Jews could breed a new European ruling caste.

130. According to Nietzsche, "One gets a more correct picture of the basic character of Plato from the reports of his actions (for example, the political journeys) than one gets from his writings. We ought not to view him as a system-builder living in the shadows, but rather as a politician inclined to agitation [*agitorischen Politikern*], who intends to lift the whole world off its hinges, and who is also (among other things) an author for this purpose." See the introduction to the study of the Platonic dialogues, Nietzsche's lectures from winter 1871–72, 1873–74, and summer 1876, in *Nietzsches Gesammelte Werke*, Musarion Ausgabe (Munich, 1922), 4:369. What Nietzsche said of Plato's intention can be said of his own intention: it is to be conceived as his legislative mission. See ibid., 4:382.

131. A key figure in the subsequent vulgarization of Nietzsche was Georges Sorel, through whose teaching Nietzsche entered Spain and Italy. See Udo Rukser, *Nietzsche in der Hispania: Ein Beitrag zur hispanischen Kultur und Geistesgeschichte*, p. 334. For Germany, consult Armin Mohler, *Die konservative Revolution in Deutschland, 1918–1932. Ein Handbuch*, pp. 86–97. It would be useful to have more studies like Eva Kolinsky's *Engagiertes Expressionismus: Politik und Literatur zwischen Weltkrieg und Weimarer Republik*. Simone Goyard-Fabre has argued that "Nietzsche foresaw with frightening clairvoyance in his prophecy the dangers of propaganda and the mass media": *Nietzsche et la question politique*, p. 79. She asks, "In this climate of high spirituality, how could the 'politics' of Nietzsche be a will to proselytize, an intention to do ideological battle or an effort of propaganda? Such an interpretation of the 'politics' of Nietzsche could only proceed from a deformed Nietzscheism" (p. 166). This statement begs the question, or precludes it. The question is whether Nietzsche thought "high" spirituality required the promotion of a compatible lower politics: insulating the highest man from base means would not be necessary if such means were dispensable to Nietzsche's politics. Nietzsche wrote to Karl Knortz with enthusiasm, 21 June 1888, about the fact that Brandeis was lecturing on his work: "The thought of propaganda is entirely foreign to me for myself: I have not yet stirred a finger for that": *Werke*, ed. Schlechta, 3:1300. As the letter suggests, one can have it both ways; the problem of Nietzsche's politics is to combine the base and the noble, not to levitate above mass politics in stylized spiritual combat.

132. Hannah Arendt, *The Origins of Totalitarianism*, pp. 326–40.

Chapter 3. Leading Science: *Beyond Good and Evil*, Part 6: "We Scholars"

1. As Max Hammerton put it, "The fruits of science are declared to be bitter fruits; and attempts are made to limit enquiry in the name of new (but always self-

evident) religious truths": *Science under Siege*, p. 9. Gunther S. Stent speaks of the growing loss of will for the Baconian task of "The Effecting of All Things Possible," *Paradoxes of Progress*, p. 9. Nicholas Rescher notes "a great deal of defeatism and failure of nerve within the scientific community itself," which is "undergoing a crisis of confidence strongly reminiscent of that decline in the sense of legitimacy which enervated the French aristocracy in the closing decades of the old regime": *Scientific Progress: A Philosophical Essay on the Economics of Research in Natural Science*, p. xi. See also Kurt Hübner et al., *Die politische Herausforderung der Wissenschaft: gegen eine ideologisch verplante Forschung*; F. R. Jevons, *Knowledge and Power*, pp. 76–80, on the disillusionment with science; Raymond Aron, "For Progress."

2. The discrepancy between the methods of democracy and science becomes inescapable after Rousseau and because of his thought. See Leo Strauss, "On the Intention of Rousseau," pp. 254, 261, 264–65, 267–69, 274–76, 287–90. On Rousseau's importance in precipitating the crisis of liberal political philosophy, compare Strauss, *Natural Right and History*, pp. 252–94, with *Beyond Good and Evil*, no. 13. For recent attempts to reconcile the method of democracy with the method of science, see Milton R. Wessel, *Science and Conscience*; Mary E. Ames, *Outcome Uncertain: Science and the Political Process*; Guild K. Nichols, *Technology on Trial: Public Participation in Decision-Making Related to Science and Technology*; Richard P. Hiskes, "Science and Technology Policy Making in a Democratic Society"; Dorothy Nelkin, *Controversy: The Politics of Technical Decisions*.

3. See the symposium *Fear of Science, Trust in Science: Conditions for Change in the Climate of Opinion*, ed. Andrei S. Markovits and Karl W. Deutsch. Maurice N. Richter, Jr., warns that "We should avoid the creation of situations in which strong currents of public opinion find reason to interpret science as merely, or primarily, a weapon which the strong use against the weak, or which a few use in opposition to the interests of the majority": *The Autonomy of Science: A Historical and Comparative Analysis*, p. 172. Addressing an earlier wave of opinion leadership, William James Lyons spoke in 1940 of "the attack on the dominant positions which science, and the *scientific method*, have come to achieve, during the past 70 years, in the national philosophy of education. The most prominent and energetic leader of this thrust is, of course, Robert Maynard Hutchins . . . the neo-Thomist": "Science in an Unfriendly World," p. 377. Compare Paul Valéry, "The Crisis of the Mind," pp. 23–36; *From Max Weber*, p. 143; Nietzsche, *Human, All-too-Human*, vol. 1, no. 248.

4. *From Max Weber*, pp. 135, 155–56; Weber, *Methodology*, pp. 3, 6; *The Gay Science*, nos. 2, 107, 110, 335; *BGE*, nos. 8, 16, 227; *The Will to Power*, no. 458.

5. Weber, *Gesammelte Aufsätze zur Wissenschaftslehre*, 3d ed., p. 595 (*innerhalb des Gesamtlebens der Menschheit*); compare *Gesammelte politische Schriften*, 2d ed., p. 493 (*innerhalb der gesamten Lebensführung*); p. 536 (*innerhalb der sittlichen Gesamtökonomie der Lebensführung*). I take these to be interchangeable for Weber, with the last being the most complete formulation. It is no doubt intentional that Weber drops leadership (*Führung*) when speaking of science.

6. *PS*, p. 12; *From Max Weber*, p. 143.

7. *From Max Weber*, p. 143.

8. *Methodology*, pp. 4, 15–16, 23–25, 38, 46–47, and especially p. 14: "the possibility of, in principle, unbridgeably divergent ultimate evaluations." The example in "Science as a Vocation" is the impossibility of judging scientifically between

French and German culture—in 1917, this was a political example: *From Max Weber,* p. 148.

9. Wolfgang Schluchter, *Wertfreiheit und Verantwortungsethik: zum Verhältnis von Wissenschaft und Politik bei Max Weber*, pp. 34–48; Guenther Roth and Wolfgang Schluchter, *Max Weber's Vision of History: Ethics and Methods*, pp. 94–106.

10. Hans Henrik Bruun, *Science, Values, and Politics in Max Weber's Methodology*, pp. 184–90, 267–86. Bruun is, as we shall subsequently argue, too hasty in dismissing Dieter Henrich's inferences with regard to the existence of a normative theory of ethics in Weber's works. Weber does strive to create the impression that his thought is unified by a consistent normative concern. Bruun, pp. 189–90; Henrich, *Die Einheit der Wissenschaftslehre Max Webers*, pp. 114–18.

11. Compare *BGE*, no. 203, *The Genealogy of Morals*, Essay Two, no. 25, and Essay Three, nos. 25 and 27. Nicholas Rescher attempts to revive philosophic leadership in the classic Baconian mold, following Leibniz: "My main aim . . . is to vindicate in the face of this defeatism the Leibnizian vision of an open and hopeful future for scientific inquiry. For one cannot but feel that the end-to-progress theory has tragic implications for the human condition": *Scientific Progress: A Philosophical Essay,* p. xi. Rescher surveys a series of views "envisaging the approaching end of the scientific adventure" and then notes that "Indeed, this view seems at present . . . to have become an integral part of a more pervasive and widely diffused end-to-growth ethos. Our present discussion has as its prime aim the provision of an antidote to this currently pervasive tendency of thought" (ibid., p. 37). One shortcoming of most treatments of Nietzsche's politics is the absence of any consideration of Nietzsche's attempt to continue the forward motion of modern science; see, for example, Raymond Polin, "Nietzsche und der Staat oder Die Politik eines Einsamen"; Tracy Burr Strong, *Friedrich Nietzsche and the Politics of Transfiguration*. Strong finds in the Great Proletarian Cultural Revolution, which sent Chinese scientists into the fields, an attempt to induce the Baconian attitude—"that nature can be mastered by abstract thought"— in the Chinese people (p. 215); but the Baconian project itself receives scant attention in his account of Nietzsche's politics.

12. Karl Jaspers, *Three Essays: Leonardo, Descartes, Max Weber*, p. 227.

13. *BGE*, Preface, nos. 5, 6, 23, 199, 201–3. According to Rescher, the chief obstacles to further progress are economic. Science will slow down because society cannot afford the investments required. A counterpoint to Rescher which reminds us of the darker side of science is G.-A. Boutry, *La Connaissance et la puissance: essai sur l'envers de la recherche*. Boutry, who was in a position to know as president of the Laboratoires et de Physique appliquée, observes that "Two permanent wills define and govern the intelligence of those who know the things of research: The will to knowledge and the will to power" (p. 13).

Jean Granier's encyclopedic work does not come to grips with modern science as a practical problem for Nietzsche, perhaps because he denies that science is integral to the task of philosophy: "The chances for a philosophy of the future appear to him, then, to be incompatible with the deployment of a scientific imperialism": *Le Problème de la vérité dans la philosophie de Nietzsche*, p. 79. See also Stanley Rosen, *The Limits of Analysis*, pp. 153–54, 216–17, 256–60.

14. See the Preface to *The Dawn*, no. 3: morality is the real Circe of philosophy; *BGE*, no. 29. Consider Nietzsche's early resistance to any dependence upon "the lead-

ers of opinion": Ronald Hayman, *Nietzsche: A Critical Life*, p. 69. That Nietzsche absorbed Tocqueville's analysis earlier than his letter to Overbeck of 23 February 1887 (*Werke*, ed. Schlechta, 3:1249–50) seems evident from *Human, All-too-Human*, vol. 2, "The Wanderer and his Shadow," no. 287.

15. No. 204. Compare *WP*, nos. 437, 441–43.

16. *BGE*,, Preface; the "nonsense" mentioned in 203 surely includes the classical notion of the philosopher-king. See Harry Neumann, "Superman or Last Man? Nietzsche's Interpretation of Athens and Jerusalem," pp. 1–28; *Twilight of the Idols*, "The Problem of Socrates," nos. 1–12.

17. The problem for modern political philosophy may be summed up in a word: Rousseau. *TI*, "Skirmishes of an Untimely Man," no. 48; *Human, All-too-Human*, 1, no. 463. Compare *BGE*, no. 221; *The Dawn*, Preface, nos. 3, 48. On Nietzsche's relation to the modern philosophic movement, best is Hiram Caton, "Toward a Diagnosis of Progress."

18. Leo Strauss has argued that the first three parts are more substantial or deal with loftier matters than Parts 5–9, but this assertion does not seem to be borne out by his insights into Part 9: "Note on the Plan of Nietzsche's *Beyond Good and Evil*," pp. 98–99, 104, 106, 109, 112–13. As Werner J. Dannhauser remarks, "the book in all justice should be treated as a whole" because it is "marked by greater unity and perfection than Nietzsche's earlier aphoristic books": *Nietzsche's View of Socrates*, pp. 178–79. See *BGE*, nos. 1, 10, 24, 39, 45, 137, 186. See also Joseph Peter Stern's survey of *BGE*: *A Study of Nietzsche*, pp. 63–92.

19. *Ecce Homo*, "Why I Write Such Good Books," no. 1; *GS*, no. 381; *GM*, Preface, no. 8; *Thus Spake Zarathustra*, Part 4, "The Leech."

20. *KGW*, 6/2, p. 139, lines 10–15; p. 140, lines 13–15, 23–27.

21. Compare *GM*, Preface, no. 8, and consider the Third Essay, the "exegesis," as an assertion in the spirit of the first aphorism of that essay.

22. *TI*, "What the Germans Lack," no. 6.

23. *BGE*, no. 247; *EH*, "Why I Write Such Good Books," on *BGE*, no. 2.

24. *EH*, ibid.

25. Ibid.

26. *From Max Weber*, p. 134.

27. *KGW*, 8/2, p. 13, lines 5–6 (*Nachlass*, Autumn 1887). See *WP*, no. 864 (p. 462).

28. No. 204; *KGW*, 6/2, p. 133, lines 14–15.

29. Nietzsche's intention seems to be to set in motion "a sort of practical reflection on the conditions of our existence as men of knowledge": *WP*, no. 594.

30. Aristotle, *Politics*, 1310a2–13 (p. 435).

31. Compare the reversal of this rhetorical tack in *GM*, according to Nietzsche's account in *EH*, "Why I Write Such Good Books," on *GM*.

32. *KGW*, 6/2, p. 133, lines 22–24. Compare the Preface, ibid., p. 4, lines 30–35, and nos. 62, 63.

33. *WP*, no. 861; see also no. 51.

34. *KGW*, 6/2, p. 134, lines 27–35; p. 135, lines 14–27.

35. Ibid., p. 133, lines 4–5.

36. Ibid., lines 14–15.

37. An analysis Nietzsche reiterates, ibid., no. 258, pp. 216–17. See Alexis de Tocqueville, *The Old Regime and the French Revolution,* p. 30.

38. *KGW,* 6/2, p. 133, lines 20–22; p. 134, lines 2–6.

39. *KGW,* p. 135.

40. No. 205; *KGW,* 6/2, p. 136, lines 8–9.

41. Ibid.

42. Hegel, *The Phenomenology of Mind,* pp. 229–40, esp. p. 238.

43. *BGE,* nos. 1, 2, 4, 6, 19.

44. Hobbes, *Leviathan,* p. 83.

45. *KGW,* 6/2, p. 138 (no. 206).

46. Ibid., p. 5, lines 5–6.

47. Ibid., pp. 139–40.

48. Ibid., p. 272 (Essay 1, no. 1).

49. *GM,* Preface no. 8 (ibid., p. 267, lines 18–25). See also *BGE,* no. 270 (*KGW,* p. 236, lines 6–10).

50. One is led to expect this parallel by nos. 45, 46, 62, but above all by the observation that the struggle against Jesuitism and its relaxation of the tension in the European spirit—the struggle to which Nietzsche likens his own endeavor—was brilliantly carried on by Pascal with his *Lettres provinciales.* See Robert J. Nelson, *Pascal: Adversary and Advocate,* pp. 164–209.

51. See Henry Guerlac, "Vauban: The Impact of Science on War"; Charles Coulton Gillespie, *Science and Polity in France at the End of the Old Regime*; Kurt Mendelssohn, *The Secret of Western Domination.*

52. Compare chap. 2, sec. 1, above; *Human, All-too-Human,* vol. 1, no. 248; Hiram Caton, "The Politics of Progress," chap. 1; Timothy J. Paterson, "The Politics of Baconian Science: An Analysis of Bacon's *New Atlantis.*"

53. Jean-Jacques Rousseau, *On the Social Contract,* p. 69.

54. *BGE,* no. 203.

55. Ibid., and no. 199. See also Harvey Flaumenhaft, "Hamilton's Administrative Republic and the American Presidency."

56. *BGE,* no. 203. Machiavelli's conquest of accident and nonsense is discussed in Harvey C. Mansfield, Jr., *Machiavelli's New Modes and Orders: A Study of the "Discourses on Livy,"* pp. 30–40, 110–16, 164–66, 360–62. But Nietzsche's extension of Machiavellianism to the legislating of morality and tables of value inverts Machiavelli's purpose, which was to prevent such "pious cruelty" as was mentioned in *The Prince,* chap. 21. Compare *WP,* no. 304, with Harvey C. Mansfield, Jr., "Machiavelli's Political Science," pp. 293–305, esp. p. 305. A policy closer to Machiavelli's is voiced in *WP,* nos. 717, 729.

57. *BGE,* no. 203.

58. See chap. 2, secs. 2 and 3, above.

59. *BGE,* no. 203.

60. Ibid., no. 209.

61. *GS,* no. 1.

62. Compare *EH,* "Why I Am so Clever," no. 4.

63. *BGE,* no. 209; *KGW,* 6/2, p. 145.

64. *BGE,* no. 208.

65. That there is a certain simplicity to Frederick might be inferred from ibid., no. 200.

66. Chap. 7, p. 23.

67. *GS*, nos. 2, 12, 110, 113, 120, 319; *EH*, "Why I Am so Wise," nos. 1, 6; *The Birth of Tragedy and the Case of Wagner*, Preface; and compare *Human, All-too-Human*, "The Wanderer and His Shadow," no. 298, with *BGE*, no. 205 (end).

68. *BGE*, no. 210.

69. Kant is called "the great Chinese of Königsberg," but this invokes none of the adjectives just mentioned; *BGE*, no. 210, p. 135.

70. *BGE*, no. 211.

71. *KGW*, 6/2, p. 134, lines 5–30.

72. *BGE*, nos. 204, 213; *KGW* 6/2, p. 135, lines 20–25, p. 151, line 22.

73. Martin Heidegger, *Being and Time*, pp. 312–48; Mark Blitz, *Heidegger's Being and Time and the Possibility of Political Philosophy*, pp. 130–49; Weber, *The Protestant Ethic*, pp. 104–11, 221, 232; *Methodology*, p. 18; *Gesammelte Aufsätze zur Soziologie und Sozialpolitik*, p. 420. The Second Essay of *On the Genealogy of Morals* is the most celebrated writing by Nietzsche on this theme. It is considered by Catherine Held Zuckert, "Nietzsche on the Origin and Development of the Distinctively Human." See, further, Ingeborg Heidemann, "Nietzsches Kritik der Moral."

74. *WP*, no. 610: "muss *ebenso* wachsen" (Nietzsche's emphasis, deleted in Kaufmann's translation). Whether this is "conceiving" is questioned ibid., no. 624; see also no. 629.

75. *BGE*, no. 230. I have corrected Kaufmann's translation, which drops the word *schreckliche*, "horrific" or "terrible." Compare *KGW*, 6/2, p. 175, line 18. See also *GM*, Essay 3, no. 9.

76. Consider *WP*, no. 619, on the completion of the conquests of physics, and the famous aphorism No. 1067. This completion is an extension or refinement of scientific method; as such it is a conquest over "determinism" in its present forms, in which Nietzsche finds a residue of idealism or of the distinction between the world of appearances and the true world. See *WP*, nos. 95, 552, 618, 634, 638, 639, 667. To paraphrase the distinction in *BGE*, nos. 208–9, there seems to be a determinism of passivity and weakness, on the one hand, and a determinism of assertion and strength, on the other. Compare *BGE*, no. 36 with no. 39.

77. *BGE*, no. 22; *GS*, no. 346; *WP*, nos. 52, 400, 401, 403, 957. Reconsider chap. 2, sec. 3, above: if the original modern project made attendance to the needs of humanity a path to human greatness, then the nature disclosed by modern science from Bacon and Descartes forward must lend itself to human greatness. As Bacon emphasized, we become masters of nature only by obeying her: *Novum Organum*, book 1, no. 3; *The Works of Francis Bacon*, 4:47. The essential continuity between early modern philosophy and Nietzsche is suggested by his letter to Overbeck upon discovering Spinoza, 30 July 1881 (*Werke*, ed. Schlechta, 3:1171). It is brilliantly exhibited in Caton, "Toward a Diagnosis of Progress."

78. See Martin Heidegger, *An Introduction to Metaphysics*, pp. 52, 91, 126–38. One should not ignore *BGE*,, no. 230 or Nietzsche's emphasis on the experimental attitude of modern science when arguing, as Karl Löwith does, that access to human nature cannot be had through research but must come from experience and through the body: "Nietzsches Vollendung des Atheismus," p. 16.

79. *PE*, p. 232, note 66.

80. The translation is my own, from *WG*, p. 348. Roth translates the German word for "shame" (*Scham*) incorrectly as "guilt." See Weber, *Economy and Society*, 2:575–76. This is perhaps Weber's sole comment on the events preceding his nervous breakdown, in which biographers have been so interested.

81. *GS*, nos. 346, 357; compare Heidegger's "Letter on Humanism," beginning.

82. What inspires fervor is the conviction that prior evaluations and ways of thinking about conduct deprive human life of its grandeur or nobility. Consider Leo Strauss's restatement of the position of radical historicism: "Conflict would not be supreme if guilt could be escaped. The question of whether one can speak of guilt, if man is forced to become guilty, was no longer discussed by Weber: he needed the necessity of guilt. He had to combine the anguish bred by atheism (the absence of any redemption, of any solace) with the anguish bred by revealed religion (the oppressive sense of guilt). Without that combination, life would cease to be tragic and thus lose its depth": *Natural Right and History*, p. 66.

83. See chap. 2, secs. 3, 4, above.

84. *BGE*, no. 211. Here, as elsewhere, Nietzsche abstracts from the problem of the dependence of science upon prescientific common sense even as he asserts that dependence. See Jacob Klein, "Phenomenology and the History of Science." Compare *GS*, no. 76.

85. No. 211.

86. Ibid. See also no. 34, and *GS*, no. 301.

87. See *WP*, no. 673.

88. *BGE*, no. 203.

89. *GS*, no. 1. Consider Dannhauser, *Nietzsche's View of Socrates*, p. 182.

90. *BGE*, no. 203.

91. Ibid., nos. 25, 61, 211; *GS*, no. 76; *GM*, Note to Essay 1, no. 17.

92. *BGE*, no. 213.

93. Ibid., no. 204; *ASZ*, book 4, "On the Higher Men," no. 8.

94. *BGE*, no. 213; *GS*, no. 373.

95. Caton, *The Politics of Progress*, chap. 1, and "Toward a Diagnosis of Progress." Compare *BGE*, nos. 22, 36, 230; *GM*, Third Essay, no. 9, p. 113; *WP*, no. 405. See Nietzsche's early project of founding eternal works on scientific truths about the regimen of health: *Human, All-too-Human*, vol. 1, no. 22.

96. *BGE*, no. 208; *GS*, no. 283.

97. No. 213; *KGW*, 6/2, p. 151, lines 20–22, p. 152, lines 31–35; no. 44; and compare *WP*, nos. 770, 783.

98. *GS*, nos. 109, 269, 335; *GM*, Second Essay, no. 24. See Strong, *Friedrich Nietzsche and the Transfiguration of Politics*, pp. 108–34; and see especially Pamela K. Jensen, "Nietzsche and Liberation: The Prelude to a Philosophy of the Future"; Martin Heidegger, "The Truth as Justice," in Heidegger, *Nietzsche*, 1:632–48; Rosen, *The Limits of Analysis*, pp. 221–22.

99. "Two things my way of thinking unconditionally prohibits me: repentance, moral indignation": letter to Elisabeth Nietzsche, January 1882 (*Werke*, ed. Schlechta, 3:1188). Against remorse and repentance, see *WP*, nos. 41, 229–35. On enforcement, see chap. 2, sec. 3, above.

100. Chico Marx, in the Marx Brothers' film, *Night at the Opera*; compare *BGE*, nos. 201–3, 230; *GS*, nos. 76, 289.

101. *BGE*, Part 2, especially no. 30; *GS*, nos. 110, 324. This last is the epigraph for Heidegger's *Nietzsche*.

102. Nietzsche was quite frank about this; our difficulty in taking it seriously lies in the fact that what Nietzsche spoke of as a weakness of skepticism, or moral relativism, has become as dominant in educated opinion as it was in fin de siècle Europe— *BGE*, no. 208.

103. Hence, once again, "superstitions are indispensable and essential": *WP*, no. 238. See *Human, All-too-Human*, vol. 1, no. 438. Hence Nietzsche's rediscovery of religion, *BGE*, nos. 44, 61.

104. *BGE*, nos. 32, 98, 227; consider the shift in "bad conscience" through *GM*, Second Essay, nos. 11, 14, 15, 22, 24; *GS*, 291, 335, 343.

105. *KGW,* 6/2, p. 152, lines 15–29; *WP,* no. 405, on the new spell or charm of Nietzschean science.

106. See chap. 2, sec. 3, above.

107. "This book (1886) is in all essentials a *critique of modernity,* not excluding the modern sciences, modern arts, and even modern politics, along with pointers to a contrary type that is as little modern as possible—a noble, Yes-saying type. In the latter sense, the book is a school for the *gentilhomme,* taking this concept in a more spiritual and radical sense than has ever been done. One has to have guts merely to endure it; one must never have learned how to be afraid. All those things of which our age is proud are experienced as contradictions to this type, almost as bad manners; our famous 'objectivity,' for example; 'pity for all that suffers'; the 'historical sense' with its submission to foreign tastes, groveling on its belly before *petits faits,* and 'being scientific' ": *EH,* p. 311.

Chapter 4. Ennobling Nihilism: *Beyond Good and Evil,* Part 9: "What is Noble"

1. Niccolo Machiavelli, *Discourses on the First Decade of Titus Livy,* book 1, chaps. 33–34, 48, 52–54; Machiavelli, *Florentine Histories,* book 3, chaps. 13, 16, 17. See Harvey C. Mansfield, Jr., *Machiavelli's New Modes and Orders: A Study of the "Discourses on Livy,"* pp. 43, 47, 50–51, 74, 152–55, 188, 308; "Has not Machiavelli shown how a republic can thrive with many Caesars guarding each other, if it is willing to relax its moral restraints against Caesarism?" (p. 154). In addition to Weber's reference to the *Florentine Histories* in *Politics as a Vocation* (p. 126), Weber's familiarity with Machiavelli is indicated in his Machiavellian critique of Cicero's failure to deal firmly with Caesarism. See the letter to Fritz Baumgarten, 9 September 1878, in Eduard Baumgarten, ed., *Max Weber: Werk und Person*, pp. 6–8. The point is not simply that Weber was willing to risk Caesarism in order to domesticate it. He also thought that revolution "in the sense of the forceful creation of entirely new formations of authority" was rendered more and more impossible by the consolidation of rational-legal bureaucracy, and that the place of revolutions would be taken by coups d'états: *Economy and Society* , 3:989.

2. It is surprising that neither Mommsen nor Beetham has attempted to articu-

late Weber's understanding of plebiscitary leader democracy as a method of "occupying the way" of a potential Caesar and thereby averting revolution. See *PV,* p. 125, which should be compared with the passages cited in note 1, above.

3. Robert Coles, "The Politics of Ressentiment." Renewed attention to the career of Huey Long would be timely in the light of the new plebiscitary system.

4. Alan Bullock, *Hitler: A Study in Tyranny,* pp. 185, 195–201, and esp. p. 205. See Arnold Brecht, *The Political Education of Arnold Brecht: An Autobiography, 1884–1970,* pp. 331–68, 389–98.

5. Alexis de Tocqueville, *Democracy in America,* vol. 2, book 3, chap. 21; vol. 2, book 4, chap. 6. Tocqueville's argument needs to be reconsidered in view of Nietzsche's methods for overcoming bourgeois resistance to great revolutions. Alain Jouffroy, *De L'Individualisme revolutionnaire.*

6. The chief evidence that Weber was familiar with Nietzsche's politics is provided by the marginal notes and underlining in his copy of Georg Simmel's *Schopenhauer und Nietzsche,* esp. chap. 8, "Die Moral der Vornehmheit." Weber's copy is in the archive of the Max Weber Institute of the University of Munich. His underlinings and comments are a "crux of interpretation" because his handwriting is difficult to decipher, and one must make an informed guess as to what he had in mind when he wrote them. In these matters of judgment, I differ with Horst Baier, who argues as follows: "Nietzsche's metaphysic of power played an essential role in the constitution of German sociology. But two viewpoints essential to Nietzsche were thereby eliminated. The first shows itself in Max Weber's characterization of power as 'socially amorphous.' Only socially structured and organized power is the theme of sociology: namely, domination. The theme of power in its comprehensive bearing is thereby eliminated from sociology, despite Nietzsche's great influence on Max Weber. And secondly, there is no longer any discussion of *Machtgefühl* (feeling for power, or power-instinct). That here all the noise results from a misconceived psychologism is quite clear from Max Weber's marginal comments on Georg Simmel's lectures on *Schopenhauer und Nietzsche": Nietzsche-Studien* 10/11 (1982): 215. (This view is seconded by Volker Gerhardt, ibid., p. 218.) I believe both Baier's points are flatly contradicted by Weber's discussion of the personality of the power-politician in *Politics as a Vocation.* Nor do I see how they can withstand the evidence of Weber's reading of the Simmel study, which I present in the notes below.

One theme of Simmel's work that greatly interested Weber was Nietzsche's new individualism. Weber himself addresses the issue of "psychologism" raised by Baier, in a marginal note beside Simmel's comments on "the direction of modern *Individualisierung"* in Nietzsche (Simmel, ibid., p. 20). It is almost certain that Simmel had in mind Weber's portrait of the "disillusioned and pessimistically inclined individualism" promoted by Calvinism, in *The Protestant Ethic,* pp. 105 ff. Consider Simmel's comparisons between Calvin and Nietzsche, pp. 201–3. In Weber's *Protestant Ethic,* the antithesis of the Protestant *Berufsmensch* or man of the calling is the individualist, identified by Weber with the this-worldly interests of the individual ego and with Italian and French insistence on free will. See *PE,* 1:77–78, *Gesammelte Aufsätze zur Religionssoziologie,* 1:62, and Wilhelm Hennis, "Max Webers Fragestellung," p. 258. Conversely, Weber's marginal comments shed light on his lifelong preoccupation with Nietzsche's critique of the modern tendency to attach "bad conscience" to power politics as such—also a Christian tendency (p. 199).

7. "Citizen participation is currently being mandated as part of the decision-making process in most Federal agencies and programs and many state and local agencies": *Citizen Participation: Building a Constituency for Public Policy,* written by Nea Carrol Toner and Walter B. Toner, Jr., for the U.S. Department of Health, Education, and Welfare, Office of Education, 1979.

Consider Marshall Berman, *The Politics of Authenticity: Radical Individualism and the Emergence of Modern Society*: "The New Left's complaint against democratic capitalism was not that it was too individualistic, but that it was not individualistic enough" (p. x); "Our society is filled with people who are ardently yearning and consciously striving for authenticity . . . who are exploring the idea of 'self-realization' " (p. 325); "[T]hese new men could find their greatest happiness only through a direct, active engagement of their whole personalities . . . they demanded new forms of happiness which would enable them to enlarge and expand themselves" (p. 312). The possibilities of a new corporatist politics based upon a new individualism are discussed in Michael Novak, "The Communitarian Individual in America." These possibilities are criticized briefly in Michael Walzer, "Pluralism: A Political Perspective," p. 786. Because Hannah Arendt did much to revive interest in political participation, it is worth recalling how wary she was of the Nietzschean strain that swiftly revealed itself in the New Left. She was appalled by "the strange revival of the life-philosophies of Bergson and Nietzsche in their Sorelian version. We all know to what extent this old combination of violence, life, and creativity figures in the rebellious state of mind of the present generation. . . . Nothing, in my opinion, could be theoretically more dangerous than the tradition of organic thought in political matters by which power and violence are interpreted in biological terms. As these terms are understood today, life and life's alleged creativity are their common denominator, so that violence is justified on the ground of creativity" (*Crises of the Republic,* pp. 170–72).

8. See chap. 1, sec. 2, above. An instructive text is Woodrow Wilson's *When a Man Comes to Himself*. After adumbrating a tyrannic or demonic individualism, Wilson turned away from "the dream of the egotist" (p. 33); "It is for this reason that men are in love with power and greatness: it affords them so pleasurable an expansion of faculty, so large a run for their minds, an exercise of spirit so various and refreshing" (p. 13). In a passage of *Schopenhauer und Nietzsche* which is heavily marked and underlined by Weber, Simmel forcefully distinguished Nietzschean from liberal or bourgeois individualism (pp. 210–11).

9. Wilson Carey McWilliams, "Democracy and the Citizen: Community, Dignity, and the Crisis of Contemporary Politics in America."

10. Machiavelli, *Discourses on Livy,* book 1, chap. 40. The words are taken from the mouth of "King Ferdinand"—that virtuoso of pious cruelty (*The Prince,* chap. 21). Compare Simmel, *Schopenhauer und Nietzsche,* p. 221. On the predatory side: "for Nietzsche, *'to live' means 'to live more.'* Life thereby fulfills its deepest meaning first according to its form as 'development.' But this is only possible insofar as life (so to speak) lives at its own expense—indeed in a form that requires its height to be paid for at the expense of its breadth. . . . Nietzsche seems not to sense the unspeakable tragedy that is inherent in this approach, from the viewpoint of every other mode of perceiving: the tragedy in this logical necessity to let the social interest be destroyed by the interest of mankind; to bind the height of the individual, to the dis-

tance in which he stands over others, commanding, climbing over, and using them" (Weber's emphasis).

11. *Democracy in America,* vol. 2, book 2, chap. 2, p. 104. A similar distinction is drawn by Simmel between Stirner's solipsism and Nietzsche's more "objective" individualism, or between the Sophists and Nietzsche. With the Sophists, "the subject finds in himself only himself," whereas Nietzsche finds in the self a *Wertmassstab* by which to make demands both on the self and on society: *Schopenhauer und Nietzsche,* pp. 232–34 (marginalia and heavy underlining in the text by Weber).

12. *Democracy in America,* vol. 2, book 2, chap. 5, p. 117. Compare Harvey C. Mansfield, Jr., "The American Election: Towards Constitutional Democracy?" pp. 16–17. See Berman, *The Politics of Authenticity:* "All these seekers after authenticity are just beginning to learn . . . that whoever you are, or want to be, you may not be interested in politics, but politics is interested in you" (p. 325). Simmel draws a similar contrast between Nietzsche's more dynamic, expansive individualism and quiet bourgeois individualism: *Schopenhauer und Nietzsche,* pp. 220–21. In his marginal comments, Weber heartily approved of the comparison. See also Alain Jouffroy, *De L'Individualisme revolutionnaire.*

13. *Beyond Good and Evil,* nos. 257, 259. Compare the view of sex as power-expression, *The Will to Power,* no. 680, and the need for others as part of one's body, ibid., no. 679. Nietzsche did not think one could affirm the most refined and sublimated expressions of will to power without affirming its more vulgar and common forms. Most interpreters either cannot believe this is consistent with Nietzsche's excellence or wish to save him from such consistency. When Simmel took this tack, Weber resisted it; see the marginal comments, *Schopenhauer und Nietzsche,* p. 230. For dramatic examples of the vulgarization of Nietzsche, see John Calhoun Merrill, *Existential Journalism,* especially the remarks on individualism, commitment, and action, on individualism in pursuit of self, and on style as a revelation of self, pp. 97–117; Richard Grenier, "Why Herzog Differs."

14. *Democracy in America,* vol. 2, book 2, chap. 4, p. 112. Compare *KGW,* 7/1: "The shepherd is a gilded tool of the herd" (p. 112). See Tracy Burr Strong, *Friedrich Nietzsche and the Politics of Transfiguration,* pp. 87–107. Simmel argued that the Nietzschean individualist was as strongly fortified against the claims of society as the Calvinist was, on different grounds; and Weber concurred: *Schopenhauer und Nietzsche,* pp. 202, 223–24, 236. Tocqueville's concern is evidently shared by many who have written on participation. See Robert G. Lehnen, *American Institutions, Political Opinion, and Public Policy,* pp. 13–15; Sidney Verba and Norman H. Nie, *Participation in America: Political Democracy and Social Equality,* pp. 3–5, 11, 85–94. See also note 7, above.

15. "But the daemonic appears most fearfully, when it stands forth overwhelmingly in some man. During the course of my life, I have observed this at close range. . . . an unheard-of power radiates from such men, and they exercise an unbelievable influence over all creatures. . . . All the moral powers together are capable of doing nothing against such men; it is in vain that the more enlightened portion of mankind hold them in contempt as frauds or dupes; the masses will be led by them": Johann Wolfgang von Goethe, *Gedenkausgabe der Werke, Briefe und Gespräche,* 10:841 (from *Dichtung und Wahrheit,* chap. 20).

16. *BGE,* no. 230. On this text, see chap. 3 above, at note 75. Compare *KGW,*

7/1: "Liberation of selfishness, of evil, of the individual. The new good ('I will') and the old good ('I ought') . . . through all this liberation the excitation of life grows. Its inmost negation, the moralistic negation, is pushed aside.—Therewith the beginning of decline. The necessity of barbarism, to which, for example, religion belongs. Mankind must live in *cycles,* the *proper* form of duration. Not the longest possible culture, but rather the highest and shortest possible. . . . What defines the height of heights in the history of culture? The moment, where the stimulus is greatest. Measured thus: that the mightiest thought is endured, indeed loved" (pp. 42–43).

17. *BGE,* no. 9. See Merrill, *Existential Journalism,* pp. 118–38, "In Search of Authenticity." Simmel wrote: "Spinoza would sacrifice the individual and maintain God; Nietzsche would sacrifice God and rescue the personality": *Schopenhauer und Nietzsche,* p. 205.

18. *BGE,* no. 23. *Twilight of the Idols,* "Maxims," no. 36: "Morality must be shot at." Consider Karl Jaspers's view of the inherent benevolence of this shooting: "This danger is necessary and no one should be deprived of it, since it is impossible to tell in advance on whom it will act creatively and who will find it devastating": *Nietzsche: An Introduction to the Understanding of His Philosophical Activity,* p. 20. The accomplishment of nihilism is to detach the self from all prior moral relations. Moralities then become means which the self can adopt when necessary to its task of self-definition. This destruction of moral relations will usually result in moral shipwreck: hence Nietzsche must resist pity for the higher men. But on the whole, it will produce the precondition for philosophic leadership: it will free men for obedience to new tables of value. See note 16, above.

19. According to Jaspers, vulgarization too is benevolent: "It is through ambiguity that the truth is protected from appropriation by the unqualified. That is why Nietzsche enters the public forum where he is ostensibly audible to all. He wishes to encounter the one who is capable of facing up to his truth and to unmask the one who has no right to it, and of whose reaction to the misunderstood truth it might be said: '. . . a little fit of rage makes him expose his innermost and most ridiculous self'" (*Nietzsche*, p. 19). So even Hitler's tirades testify to the wisdom of Nietzsche's publication of "dangerous truths" (ibid., p. 20).

The latter books of *Beyond Good and Evil* consider means of discipline and the embodiment of values. The liberated self must accept discipline, using force and fraud even in the most unlikely places. In Part 7, marriage, sex, and reproduction; in Parts 6 and 8, science; in Part 8, the arts and what we would call "the media world"; and finally, in Part 9, aristocratic orders and religion, are taken up. Part 9 in particular is about the politics of the fully, or hypermodern, self, the expropriator who is alert to collective power and who therefore seeks political means to exploit and enhance his power. Paradoxically, this is possible only through a detachment from what is common.

20. *From Max Weber,* p. 156. See Sheldon S. Wolin, "Max Weber: Legitimation, Method, and the Politics of Theory," who argues that for Weber science was the only remaining stage in an otherwise bureaucratized world, for the life of "affirmation" (pp. 405, 411). On his reading, Weberian affirmation has the meaning of both Nietzschean affirmation and negation: it means the creation of meaning, a higher form of creativity. Wolin's Weber authorizes revolutionary politics within the profession of scholarship, a politics of theory (pp. 403, 409–10, 417, 419–20, 422). The inter-

pretation advanced in chap. 5, secs. 1−5, argues against this conflation of Weber with Nietzsche's philosophic politics.

21. "If one follows the origin and development of Nietzsche's thought, his work presents itself as perhaps the most radical attempt to think through the demands laid in the nature and principle of the modern world consistently to the end": Günther Rohrmoser, "Nietzsches Kritik der Moral," p. 331. Part 9 is Nietzsche's remedy to the disproportionate attention given by modern political economy and political science to commerce and administration. He remedies the squandering of commanding talent by disciplining the self for sustained self-assertion and adumbrates a regime concerned from first to last with the cultivation of will to power.

22. Simmel obscures this contrast (which was elaborated in chap. 2, sec. 3, above) by his promiscuous use of the term *Menschlichkeit* or "humanity." In his superior article on Weber's concern with *Menschlichkeit* (humaneness), Wilhelm Hennis does not, unfortunately, consider his relation to Nietzsche: "Max Webers Fragestellung."

23. *WP*, no. 304.

24. Raymond Polin, "Nietzsche und der Staat oder die Politik eines Einsamen," pp. 27−44. See chap. 6, sec. 1, below.

25. Leo Strauss, *What Is Political Philosophy? And Other Studies*, pp. 47, 49.

26. *BGE*, no. 257; compare *BGE*, nos. 1, 23, 45, 186, 204, 214, and *The Genealogy of Morals*, Essay 3, no. 1. On *BGE*, no. 204, see chap. 3, sec. 2, above. Compare Simmel, *Schopenhauer und Nietzsche*, p. 198. Nietzsche defines philosophy in Part 9: The grounding of philosophy by philosophy is a determination of the as-yet undetermined species, man. As our analysis in chap. 2, sec. 3, suggests, philosophy cannot determine itself without imposing form on the species through an ordering of rank.

27. *Human, All-too-Human*, vol. 2, part 2, no. 64.

28. Ibid., vol. 1, Preface, no. 6.

29. Bear in mind what is said about the transience of virtues in *BGE*, nos. 211−12. Compare chap. 2, sec. 3, above.

30. *WP*, nos. 635 (end), 255; *BGE*, no. 23.

31. This is inferred from *BGE*, nos. 23 (on morphology), 9, 211, 257.

32. This would be an articulation of the philosopher's task discussed in *BGE*, no. 212.

33. *BGE*, nos. 19, 22, 117, 132, 158, 188.

34. *GS*, no. 292; see also no. 317. Compare Aristotle, *The Nichomachean Ethics*, 1103a14−20, and on *pathos*, 1095a5. See the note to Simmel's *Schopenhauer und Nietzsche* on p. 220, where Weber wrote "nicht Ethik."

35. *Ecce Homo*, on *BGE*, no. 2.

36. Aristotle, *Politics*, 1282b14−1284a4, 1331b24−1333b3.

37. Ibid., and 1259b35; Aristotle, *Ethics*, 1123a34−1124a4.

38. *BGE*, nos. 257−59.

39. *Politics*, 1253a24−b15, 1253b14−1255b40; Aristotle, *Ethics*, 1095a2−12, 1094a18−b12.

40. Aristotle, *Ethics*, 1179b6−10.

41. Ibid., 1179b1−1180a35, 1160a36−b23; *Politics*, 1287b40−42, 1293b23−31, 1295a1−24, 1310a39−1313a17, 1313a34−1315b41.

42. *BGE*, nos. 257, 295.

43. Ibid.

44. *The Gay Science*, no. 292.

45. Aristotle, *Ethics*, 1095a10–12, 1103a14–b31.

46. *GS*, no. 317; *BGE*, no. 36; *GM*, entire Essay 2.

47. *BGE*, nos. 270, 287.

48. Ibid., nos. 3, 9, 13, 19, 36; *GS*, no. 26; Aristotle, *Politics*, 1252b28–1253a18; Aristotle, *Ethics*, 1103b32–34, 1144b17–25; Nietzsche, *WP*, no. 1067.

49. *BGE*, no. 257; *GS*, no. 301 (end); *TI*, "Skirmishes," no. 39.

50. *BGE*, nos. 202–3. See chap. 2, sec. 4, above.

51. *EH*, "Why I Write Such Good Books," no. 4; *BGE*, no. 28; *TI*, "What I Owe to the Ancients," no. 2.

52. *BGE*, no. 247; *GS*, no. 80. Compare *BGE*, no. 251 with *Human, All-too-Human*, vol. 4, no. 110.

53. Aristotle, *Ethics*, 1180b23 -1181b24; Thomas Hobbes, *English Works*, vol. 8: "Epistle Dedicatory," "To the Reader," and "On Thucydides." This standard is also implied in Socrates' critique of the sophists' reduction of politics to rhetoric: Plato, *Gorgias*, 503a3–b3, 504d1–e5, 515b7–517a7.

54. *The Birth of Tragedy*, nos. 3, 5, 8.

55. *GS*, no. 302.

56. Thucydides, *History of the Peloponnesian War*, book 1, chaps. 1, 3, 10–12, 21–22 (hereafter cited as *War*). Compare Nietzsche, "Homers Wettkampf," *Werke*, ed. Schlechta, 3:294–96. See Leo Strauss, *The City and Man*, pp. 155–62. Compare *Human, All-too-Human*, vol. 1, nos. 114, 154, 262; vol. 2, part 2, nos. 140, 199.

57. *War*, book 1, chaps. 10 (3–4), 21–22. Compare book 2, chap. 41 (4–5). See Strauss, *The City and Man*, pp. 163–74.

58. *War*, book 1, chaps. 21–22. See also book 1, chap. 3 (4), chap. 8 (3–4), chaps. 9–11.

59. *War*, book 2, chap. 41 (4–5); book 5, chaps. 50–51. See Strauss, *The City and Man*, pp. 158–60, 174–92; Seth Benardete, *Herodotean Inquiries*, pp. 149–50, 155–56, 160–63, 167–70.

60. *War*, book 1, chaps. 5–6. Compare Nietzsche, *WP*, no. 429; *GM*, Essay 1, no. 11; *Werke*, ed. Schlechta, 3:286–99. A Herodotean rebuttal is suggested by Marc Shell: "In his *Histories*, Herodotus himself spies on, or makes naked to the Greek people, *nomoi* different from their own": *The Economy of Literature*, p. 20.

61. *War*, book 1, chap. 22. Compare Hobbes, *English Works*, vol. 8: "Epistle Dedicatory," "To the Readers," and pp. viii, xx–xxi, xxx–xxxii. See Christopher Bruell, "Thucydides' View of Athenian Imperialism," p. 17; Nietzsche, *The Dawn*, no. 168.

62. *War*, book 1, chap. 22; Hobbes, *English Works*, pp. viii, xxii.

63. This is not to gainsay the possibility that Thucydides discloses necessity even more through his account of events than through the speeches themselves; *War*, book 1, chaps. 6, 8 (2–4), 11, 12 (4), 17, 19. See Strauss, *The City and Man*, pp. 163–74; Nietzsche, *Human, All-too-Human*, vol. 1, nos. 92, 474; vol. 4, no. 32; *The Dawn*, no. 168; *TI*, "What I Owe to the Ancients," no. 2; *WP*, nos. 428, 429, 443.

64. *War*, book 1, chaps. 1–23.

65. *War*, book 1, chap. 22; Nietzsche, *Human, All-too-Human*, vol. 4, no. 144.

66. Compare chap. 1, sec. 5, chap. 2, sec. 2, above.

67. See Michael Platt, "Joy and War: A Reading of *Ecce Homo*."

68. *War,* book 1, chap. 1; Strauss, *The City and Man,* pp. 155–57.

69. *BGE,* nos. 44, 62, 200–202, 208–9, 242–43, 251, 256; *GS,* nos. 23, 283, 362, 377; *WP,* nos. 954–57, 960. Compare chap. 2, sec. 4, chap. 3, sec. 1, above.

70. *EH,* "The Birth of Tragedy," no. 4, and "Why I Am a Destiny," nos. 1, 8; *GS,* nos. 283, 362; *WP,* nos. 126–27, 130, 133, 910. On this point I disagree with Jean Granier: see his *Le problème de la vérité dans la philosophie de Nietzsche,* pp. 73–92. See chap. 3, note 13, above.

71. *EH,* "Beyond Good and Evil," no. 2.

72. *BGE,* Preface.

73. *GM,* Essay 3, no. 27.

74. Schlechta and Kaufmann both reproduce the subtitle, though the latter only in his introduction (p. 3): "A Sequel to My Last Book . . . which it is meant to supplement and clarify." By some oversight, it is missing from the *Kritische Gesamtausgabe,* vol. 6, no. 1, p. 257.

75. *GS,* no. 381.

76. Similarly, *GM,* Preface, no. 2, recalls *BGE,* Part 5; Preface, no. 3 recalls *BGE,* no. 45; Preface, no. 5 points back to the treatment of pity, etc.

77. *GM,* Essay 2, no. 1. See Catherine Heldt Zuckert, "Nietzsche on the Origin and Development of the Distinctively Human."

78. *GM,* Essay 3, no. 1.

79. In the *KGW* edition, *GM,* Essay 3, is 72 pages long, almost the length of Essays 1 and 2 combined (76 pages): vol. 6, no. 2, pp. 357–430, 271–353.

80. *BGE,* no. 206; *GS,* no. 381 (end). Compare *BGE,* no. 260, with *GM,* Essay 1, nos. 4–11, 13, 15, and especially 16–17. Compare *BGE,* nos. 263–67, with *GM,* Essay 2, nos. 4–6, 8–15, 17–23.

81. Bruell, "Thucydides' View of Athenian Imperialism," p. 17; Nietzsche, *The Dawn,* no. 168.

82. Bruell, ibid., p. 17.

83. *War,* book 3, chaps. 82–84.

84. It is perhaps more difficult to interpret *BGE,* nos. 278–95, because there is no parallel in the *Genealogy* to rely upon.

85. *BGE* may indicate that Nietzsche provides scope for the expedient use of any of these appeals; see no. 61. But the rulers must not be taken in by them. Recall chap. 2, secs. 2, 4, above. On Nietzsche's hostility to the state and representative government, see *BGE,* no. 199; *WP,* nos. 69, 75, 280, 725, 750, 753, 762, 903.

86. *BGE,* nos. 257, 262.

87. Ibid., no. 257; *GS,* no. 18; *WP,* nos. 269, 356–58, 464, 660, 758, 954.

88. *BGE,* no. 284; *GS,* nos. 51, 283, 324, 370, 373.

89. *BGE,* no. 260; see also nos. 205, 211, 212.

90. Ibid., no. 261.

91. For a similar procedure, compare *BGE,* no. 241, with its oblique but unmistakable reference to the controversy over Bismarck in Germany, and no. 251, which parodies the anti-Semitic addresses of the Hohenzollerns' court preacher, Adolf Stöcker.

92. Thus nos. 258–62 comprise an alternative to Plato's account of the political

cycle in *The Republic*, books 8–9, culminating in Socrates' critique of the tyrannic soul. Compare the note from Nietzsche's *Nachlass* quoted in note 16 above.

93. Nos. 258–61 have no specific time reference. But there may be a necessary temporal order in the topics: monarchy is a threat to aristocratic rule from the outset, while vanity would be a typical problem for the ruling class toward the end of the political cycle. Compare Mansfield, *Machiavelli's New Modes and Orders*, pp. 32–41.

94. Jean-Jacques Rousseau, *On the Social Contract*, book 2, chap. 7; Nietzsche, *GM*, Essay 2; Zuckert, "Nietzsche on the Origin and Development of the Distinctively Human."

95. *BGE*, nos. 263, 265; *GM*, Essay 2, nos. 3, 11, 12, 14, 17. But see *GS*, no. 358 (end).

96. *BGE*, no. 263; *KGW*, 6/2, p. 228, lines 6–7.

97. *GM*, Essay 2, nos. 1–6, 14, 17, 24.

98. *BGE*, nos. 25 (end), 257; *GM*, Essay 2, nos. 4, 7, 16, 18, 19.

99. *GM*, Essay 2, nos. 2–5, 11, 20, 22. The importance of Rome and Christianity for the Second Essay may be brought into focus by comparing its topics with those of the principal work of traditional political philosophy which *The Genealogy of Morals* would supplant. As suggested (chap. 2, sec. 3, chap. 3, sec. 6), Nietzsche's philosophic politics must displace Hegel's philosophy of the state. The Second Essay's treatment of Rome and Christianity might be articulated, then, by comparing *The Philosophy of Right*, particularly part one, sec. 2 (contract) and sec. 3 (wrong); and part two (morality). Hegel had of course rejected a "genealogical" format in paragraph 32. Hegel's Introduction to *The Philosophy of Right* deals with many of the problems mentioned in chap. 2, sec. 3, as may be seen from the lucid essay by Donald J. Maletz, "The Meaning of 'Will' in Hegel's *Philosophy of Right*."

100. *BGE*, no. 262; *GM*, Essay 2, nos. 1, 24; *GS*, nos. 20, 23, 289 ("The moral earth too is round"); *WP*, no. 1019. Compare Plato, *The Republic*, 546a–547a5, and *GS*, nos. 292, 328, 356.

101. *BGE*, nos. 266–67; *GM*, Essay 1, no. 12.

102. *BGE*, nos. 275, 280, 290.

103. Ibid., nos. 268, 284; *GS*, nos. 3, 50, 76, 117, 301, 354; Plato, *Statesman*, 294a7–c8; *Laws*, 875; *Gorgias*, 483b4–d4; *Phaedrus*, 257e–258c7, 275c7–276b, 278c4–d2.

104. *BGE*, nos. 268, 273; *GS*, nos. 3, 55, 76, 290, 335; *Thus Spake Zarathustra*, part 3, "The Wanderer."

105. *GM*, Essay 3, no. 1; *GS*, nos. 290, 377; *BGE*, nos. 245, 254, 256; *WP*, nos. 966–67.

106. Simmel, *Schopenhauer und Nietzsche*, pp. 198–99; *BGE*, nos. 199, 273–74; *GS*, nos. 55, 277; *EH*, Preface, no. 4.

107. *BGE*, no. 265.

108. Ibid., nos. 269, 274, 276; *WP*, nos. 684–87; *ASZ*, part 4, "On the Higher Man," no. 15. See Laurence Lampert, "The End of *Thus Spoke Zarathustra*: Understanding Part 4."

109. *ASZ*, part 4, "On the Higher Man," nos. 6, 14, 15; *Human, All-too-Human*, vol. 4, no. 140. The problem of the relation between the forming of a style

and the forming of a people or nation was central to Nietzsche's preoccupations with the Germans and music, from *The Birth of Tragedy* through *The Case of Wagner.* See *BGE,* no. 240.

110. *BGE,* no. 269; *GM,* Essay 3. It is worth pondering why *The Antichrist* is so gentle with Jesus and so hard with Paul in this connection.

111. *BGE,* nos. 269, 270, 273–77, 293; *GS,* nos. 19, 48, 56, 277, 338; *ASZ,* part 4, "The Cry of Distress," "The Sign."

112. *BGE,* nos. 273, 274; *GS,* nos. 290, 294; *WP,* nos. 686–87, 933.

113. *GS,* no. 277; *BGE,* no. 213.

114. *BGE,* nos. 207, 292; *WP,* no. 544. For a different interpretation, see Lampert, "The End of *Thus Spake Zarathustra.*"

115. *GS,* no. 18.

116. *WP,* no. 1060; *TI,* "Skirmishes," no. 11; *The Antichrist,* no. 58.

117. *TI,* "What I Owe to the Ancients," no. 2.

118. Ibid., "Skirmishes," no. 11; *Human, All-too-Human,* vol. 4, no. 144; *The Dawn,* no. 168.

119. Marsilius of Padua, *The Defender of Peace,* part 1, chap. 1, secs. 3, 7; chap. 19, secs. 3–4, 11–13. See *GS,* no. 358.

120. Karl Löwith, *Nature, History, and Existentialism,* pp. 204–13.

121. *WP,* no. 916. This view is particularly clear in *BGE,* no. 287, and *GS,* no. 377: the essence of the noble is a "faith" (*Glaube*). Compare Machiavelli, *Discourses on Livy,* book 1, Preface; book 2, chap. 5.

122. Leo Strauss, *The City and Man,* pp. 142, 237–41.

123. *WP,* no. 443; *BGE,* Preface; *The Birth of Tragedy,* nos. 17, 23; *GS,* nos. 18, 149; *Human, All-too-Human,* vol. 1, no. 261, "The Tyrants of the Spirit."

124. *WP,* nos. 429, 443; *TI,* "What I Owe to the Ancients," no. 2.

125. See chap. 2, sec. 3, above, and Nietzsche, *Werke,* ed. Schlechta, 3:295.

126. Strauss, *The City and Man,* pp. 140–41, on Plato's *Timaeus* as a comparable challenge to Thucydides; *WP,* no. 427; *TI,* "The Problem of Socrates"; *The Birth of Tragedy,* "Attempt at Self-Criticism," nos. 1–7.

127. *The Dawn,* no. 168.

128. *BGE,* no. 200.

129. Plato, *Symposium,* 215a6–222c. See Stanley Rosen, *Plato's "Symposium,"* pp. 278 ff.

130. *TI,* "The Problem of Socrates," nos. 1–12; *GS,* no. 340.

131. The difficulty begins with Nietzsche's claim that Thucydides asserted through the Athenian ambassadors at Melos that justice had no meaning between unequal parties or that justice and necessity are the same: *Human, All-too Human,* vol. 1, no. 92, "The Origin of Justice." This Thucydides does not assert, nor is it self-evident that he believes it "between the lines." See Strauss, *The City and Man,* pp. 174–92, 236–41; Bruell, "Thucydides' View of Athenian Imperialism," pp. 11–17. Weber, however, clearly follows Nietzsche's interpretation of the Melian debate, without distinguishing between the ambassadors and the historian: *RS,* 1:146n9, 352; 2:145n1.

132. *TI,* "Skirmishes," no. 11; see also *WP,* nos. 341, 842, 1040.

133. *WP,* nos. 56, 417; *EH,* "Why I Am a Destiny," no. 2. Compare chap. 2, sec. 4, and chap. 3 on science, above.

134. *GS,* no. 1; *EH,* "Why I Am a Destiny," no. 1; *GM,* Essay 3, no. 27.

135. Plato, *Statesman*, 268d9–275b; compare Nietzsche's remarks on Plato as a would-be founder of new religions, *GS*, no. 149, and *WP*, no. 50.

136. *Statesman*, 270a–b, 271c, 272d7–273a4; see *WP*, no. 958.

137. *WP*, no. 877: "The Revolution made Napoleon possible: that is its justification. For the sake of a comparable prize one would have to desire the anarchical collapse of our entire civilization. . . . And why could not precisely that man who produced the most disastrous effects be the pinnacle of the whole species of man: so high, so superior that everything would perish from envy of him?"

138. *War*, book 2, chap. 41 (4–5).

139. *GM*, Essay 1, no. 11.

140. *EH*, on "The Birth of Tragedy," no. 4. On suffering in Thucydides, see Strauss, *The City and Man*, p. 217.

141. *WP*, no. 429; *BGE*, no. 265; *Human, All-too-Human*, vol. 1, no. 92.

142. *War*, book 5, chap. 117.

143. Ibid., book 2, chap. 41 (4–5).

144. Strauss, *The City and Man*, pp. 182–92.

145. Ibid.; Nietzsche, *WP*, no. 429; *The Dawn*, no. 168; Thucydides, *War*, book 5, chaps. 104, 112. See passages cited in note 140 above.

146. *War*, book 5, chaps. 112, 116.

147. *WP*, no. 1058.

148. Ibid., no. 1053.

149. Ibid., no. 1056.

150. Ibid., no. 429.

151. *War*, book 5, chap. 105.

152. The doctrine of the Athenian ambassadors at Melos covers all cases; only insofar as it is a general truth does it justify their tyranny over their colonies. At Melos this truth is spoken behind closed doors because the leaders of the Melians do not expect patriotism to outweigh this truth if it is told to the people in public. The Athenians teach it directly to their own people, and it does undermine Athenian discipline, if not patriotism. Being taught that they are tyrants abroad, they become more lawless and unrestrained at home in Athens: *War*, book 2, chap. 63 (2–3); book 3, chap. 37 (2–3); book 5, chap. 55. Thucydides calls attention to this declension by showing Cleon's effort to break down the sense of decency and limits in the parallel case of Mytilene; the Athenians refrain from the proposed massacre on Mytilene but carry it through on Melos: book 3, chap. 36 (2–3), chap. 69; book 5, chap. 116.

153. Compare Strauss, *The City and Man*, pp. 226–36.

154. *WP*, no. 1019.

155. Consider chap. 3, sec. 6, above.

156. *WP*, no. 1067; *BGE*, no. 257.

157. *BGE*, no. 263; *TI*, "Skirmishes," no. 39.

158. *BGE*, nos. 213, 265. See chap. 3, sec. 7, above.

159. Ibid., nos. 266–67.

160. Ibid., no. 265.

161. Ibid., nos. 2, 265.

162. See notes 131 and 152 above.

163. *BGE*, nos. 270, 273, 284.

164. Ibid., nos. 269 (end), 276; *GS*, no. 325; *GM*, Preface, no. 2.

165. *BGE*, no. 62; *ASZ*, part 3, "Wanderer," part 4, "On the Higher Man," no. 6.

166. *WP*, no. 1060.

167. *BGE*, no. 276.

168. *WP*, no. 996.

169. Ibid., nos. 895, 898, 907, 987; *GS*, nos. 54, 322, 337.

170. See chap. 2, sec. 3, above.

171. Nietzsche, *KGW*, 5/2, p. 392.

172. *GS*, no. 317.

173. Part 9 obeys strict laws of style, approximating a musical form. This is a natural outgrowth of Nietzsche's meditation upon music; it also reflects his concern to relate music and politics, as well as music and rhetoric, in Part 8 (*BGE*, nos. 240, 241, 247, 254–56). Part 9 is a series of speeches ordered within a sonata-like form, as follows:

The Armature

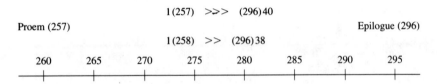

On this basic armature (units of five with the central aphorism in each unit receiving an accent or special emphasis), Nietzsche works these variations:

First Era: *Courage*. 258, 259, *260*, 261, 262
Second Era: *Justice*. 263, 264, *265*, 266, 267
Third Era: *Restraint*. ("What is common?")
   Part A. 268, 269, *270*, 271, 272
   Part B. 273, 274, *275*, 276, 277

Here Nietzsche introduces a new pattern, the double unit of two symmetrical groups. He also introduces a new accent, since the initial aphorism, bearing the question (268), marks a turn in his arguments. These new patterns are in turn the subject of new variations:

Fourth Era: *Wisdom*.
   Part A. (Two groups of aphorisms, but making only nine in toto)
      Subsection 1. 278, 279, *280*, 281, 282
      Subsection 2. 283, 284, *285*, 286
   Part B. ("What is Noble?")
      287, 288, 289, 290, *291*, 292, 293, 294, *295*

Thus the final recapitulation has all the formal features of the earlier sections, employing all the types of movement and rest introduced earlier but adding a new syncopation. A full analysis of Part 9 would convey the knowledge or insight that Nietzsche's accents point to, by making an aphorism central to its neighbors.

174. See Kaufmann's note, *BGE*, p. 234.

175. The speech in question is *Symposium,* 215a6–222c. See Rosen, *Plato's "Symposium,"* pp. 278ff. Plato's Alcibiades is obliged to praise no one but Socrates (214d2–9); Nietzsche's Alcibiades praises a god, Dionysus. The effect of Socrates on Plato's Alcibiades is to make him unprecedentedly ashamed (216b1–3, c3–5); the effect of Dionysus on Nietzsche's Alcibiades is to make him feel "richer, not having received grace . . . not as blessed and oppressed by alien goods but richer in himself, newer to himself than before, broken open," etc. (Compare *GS,* nos. 273–75.) The beauty of Plato's Alcibiades does not concern Socrates (216d9–10); Dionysus seeks to make man "more beautiful." Plato's Alcibiades wishes to get his revenge on Socrates (213d8, 214d10–12); Nietzsche's Alcibiades makes no mention of revenge. Plato's Alcibiades praises Socrates for virtues (216d6–e6); Nietzsche's Alcibiades does not follow human custom and praise Dionysus for virtues because "such a god has no use whatever for such venerable junk and pomp" or "solemn pomp-and-virtue names." Plato's Alcibiades is impressed by the fact that Socrates "conquers in discourse," and he is now moved by philosophic speeches (213e3–4, 218a7); Nietzsche's Alcibiades says nothing about *logos.* Plato's Alcibiades is turned into something worse than a wild fanatic by Socrates (215e); Dionysus teaches the soul of Nietzsche's Alcibiades "to lie still as a mirror."

176. *GS,* no. 302.

177. *BGE,* no. 257.

178. *WP,* no. 1018. Compare chap. 4, sec. 2, above.

179. *BGE,* no. 257.

180. *TI,* "What I Owe to the Ancients," no. 2; *BGE,* no. 28. The allusions to Machiavelli at the end of Essay 2 and in the aphorism to which Essay 3 is said to be the exegesis are unmistakable: wisdom replaces fortuna as the woman whose heart goes out to a warrior. Compare *GM,* Essay 2, no. 25, and Preface 8, with Machiavelli, *The Prince,* chap. 25. See the second section of this chapter, above.

181. *WP,* no. 1018.

182. *War,* book 1, chap. 17. Compare Plato, *Laches,* 194d9–196a4; Nietzsche, *GS,* no. 381, *WP,* no. 612. See Mark Blitz, "An Introduction to the Reading of Plato's *Laches,*" pp. 224–25. John H. Lomax has reached a very different conclusion in his commentary, "Nietzsche's New Nobility and the Eternal Return in *Beyond Good and Evil*: A Proemium." He regards Nietzsche's fear of death as the unsolved problem and governing motive of *Beyond Good and Evil.*

Chapter 5. Serving Moral Forces: *Science as a Vocation*

1. Weber, *Economy and Society,* 3:971–75, 980–83, 992–1000, 1155–56. See Gunther Roth and Wolfgang Schluchter, *Max Weber's Vision of History: Ethics and Methods,* pp. 45ff., 65–112, esp. 94: "The speech on *Science as a Vocation* is not only a political speech but also a speech on political education." For more recent elaboration, see Dean Schooler, Jr., *Science, Scientists, and Public Policy;* William R. Nelson, ed., *The Politics of Science: Readings in Science, Technology, and Government;* H. L. Nieburg, *In the Name of Science;* Sanford A. Lakoff, ed., *Knowledge and Power: Essays on Science and Government.* According to the 1974 *National Sample of*

Scientists and Engineers (Washington: National Science Foundation Publication 76–323, 1975), more than a fourth of the scientists and engineers in the United States are in management or administration (p. 7). Over 40 percent of the respondents in the sample reported that they were working in one of the areas included in the foundation's list of "problems of critical national interest" (p. 10).

Despite Weber's emphasis on science, David Beetham does not treat it as integral to "modern politics" in his concluding chapter of *Max Weber and the Theory of Modern Politics*, pp. 250–76.

2. Weber, *ES*, 3:973–75, 994–1001. See Hugh Heclo, "Issue Networks and the Executive Establishment"; Michael J. Malbin, ed., *Unelected Representatives*; James Warner Björkman, "Professionalism in the Welfare State: Sociological Savior or Political Pariah?" pp. 407–11, 415–22, 424–27.

3. See especially Hiram Caton, "The Politics of Progress," chaps. 4–6; Charles Frankel, *The Faith of Reason: The Idea of Progress in the French Enlightenment*; Henry Steele Commager, *The Empire of Reason: How Europe Imagined and America Realized the Enlightenment*; Thomas J. Schlereth, *The Cosmopolitan Ideal in Enlightenment Thought: Its Form and Function in the Ideas of Franklin, Hume, and Voltaire*; Peter Gay, *The Part of Humanity: Essays in the French Enlightenment*.

4. Weber was quite deliberate in turning away from "cultivation" in his prose. "Behind all the present discussions about the basic questions of the educational system there lurks decisively the struggle of the 'specialist' type of man against the older type of the 'cultivated man,' a struggle conditioned by the irresistibly expanding bureaucratization of all public and private relations of authority and specialised knowledge. This struggle affects the most intimate aspects of personal culture": *ES*, 3:1002. See *From Max Weber*, p. 74, and Fritz Ringer, *The Decline of the German Mandarins: The German Academic Community, 1890–1933*, pp. 34–35, 82, 176–80. Given Weber's pronounced affirmation of modernization and specialization, it requires critical distance from Weber to recover the older discussion of progress and to appreciate the depth of Weber's break with it. Consider Hiram Caton, "World in Decay: Critiques of the Historiography of Progress."

5. Leo Strauss, "On the Intention of Rousseau"; William A. Galston, *Kant and the Problem of History*, pp. 103–204; Susan Meld Shell, *The Rights of Reason: A Study of Kant's Philosophy and Politics*, pp. 20–32. The guiding question of Weber's pivotal essay on "Objectivity" is descended from Rousseau and Kant: "What is the meaning and purpose of the scientific criticism of ideals and value-judgments?" *Methodology*, p. 52.

6. *Science as a Vocation*, p. 148. Compare the remark on "Hellenic man, whose thinking was political throughout," ibid., p. 141.

7. Compare *Methodology*: "The highest ideals, which move us most forcefully, are always formed only in the struggle with other ideals which are just as sacred to others as ours are to us" (p. 57). *SV*, p. 148, suggests Antigone because her loyalty to her brother outweighs her loyalties to the city, which are decisive for Creon. Compare Hegel's famous remarks on Antigone, *The Phenomenology of Mind*, pp. 475–82. See also Wilhelm Hennis, "Max Webers Fragestellung," p. 272.

8. *Politics as a Vocation*, p. 115. See *Methodology*, pp. 4, 15–16, 23–25, 38, 46–47, 53, 56, and p. 57: "Nowhere are the interests of science served more poorly in

the long run than in those situations *where one refuses to see uncomfortable facts and the realities of life in all their starkness*" (emphasis added).

9. Marianne Weber, *Max Weber: A Biography,* p. 325. Weber's claims to have transcended relativism are questioned by William Shapiro, "Nietzsche, Weber, Human Nature, and Sociology." *PV,* pp. 128–29.

10. *PV,* p. 128. It is odd that Sheldon S. Wolin could place such emphasis upon "affirmation" in Weber's understanding of science yet omit the importance of "world-affirmation" in Weber's understanding of the politician, whose politics is not "the politics of theory": "Max Weber: Legitimation, Method, and the Politics of Theory," pp. 403, 405, 411, 417–22. For a critique of Wolin's interpretation, see Eden, "Bad Conscience for a Nietzschean Age."

11. *PV,* p. 118; see above, chap. 1, sec. 5. An awkward translation of *gesinnungsethische* as "principled" by Roth and Schluchter makes Weber appear to contradict the possibility of principled action which is also "worldly" in the Thucydidean sense: "Whatever may be the justification of principled action in politics, it detracts from the conditions of the present; it requires the sacrifice of the intellect or of empirical lessons or both. The principled deed polarizes: it turns the political follower into a disciple and the political opponent into an enemy. The principled deed cannot tolerate a critical empirical science as an independent agency": *Max Weber's Vision of History,* p. 92. They assert that "the principled deed . . . ultimately leads . . . to the destruction of structural pluralism and value antagonism" (p. 91). That the following of a modern political leader would consist largely of a "psychic proletariat" and that the political man is bound to have opponents who truly are his enemies seemed to Weber to be among those "harsh realities" that the Thucydidean *politikos*—and the scientist—simply had to face. See *PV,* p. 125, and compare pp. 117–24.

12. *SV,* p. 149. On the antithesis between *homo politicus* and *homo economicus,* see *ES,* 3:1354, and compare pp. 1266–1353. An adequate recovery of Weber's understanding of the ancient *homo politicus* would require a patient reading of Weber's most inaccessible work, *Agrärverhältnis in Altertums.* The existing translation by R. I. Frank, *The Agrarian Sociology of Ancient Civilizations,* bears only a remote resemblance to Weber's essay.

13. *Methodology,* pp. 111–12. In particular, the political problems of an age of mass politics and popular passion required Weber to move beyond the German classics, Kant, and Hegel, with "the light of the great cultural problems": *From Max Weber,* p. 394.

14. *SV,* p. 140; *PV,* pp. 122–23. Weber gave a narrow formulation of the problematic of his work as "the analysis of all the cultural problems which have arisen from the peculiar nature of the economic bases of our culture and which are, in that sense, specifically modern": *Methodology,* p. 67. But he then went on to present a wider formulation that was not thus tied to problems "specifically modern": "[T]he scientific investigation of the general cultural significance of the social-economic structures of the human community and its historical forms of organization is the central aim": (ibid.). The wider formulation was made possible by freeing political economy as a historical science from the necessity to study only what was causally relevant to the emergence of modern problems; see *Methodology,* pp. 155–57. Weber's teaching on value-relevance explained how political economy could study ancient political

culture (as Eduard Meyer did) despite the absence of any causal connection to modern problems. One could study ancient domination recognizing that it was the antithesis of modern economics and the modern state. Weber thought the ancient world was value-relevant; to describe our predicament with respect to ultimate values, he turned to the polis: "[W]e live today as did the ancients": *SV*, p. 148. But it was not causally significant in bringing modern institutions of political economy into existence. It might be worthwhile to reconsider the *value-relevance* of Weber's *The Protestant Ethic* in the light of Weber's understanding of ancient political man, instead of belaboring its attempt at causal explanation. As the discussion in chap. 2, sec. 3, should indicate, Weber's causal explanation is deeply flawed because it abstracts from the causal role of modern philosophy and science in the rise of modern capitalism. See Caton, "The Politics of Progress," chaps. 1–6.

15. Neither Hume nor J. S. Mill thought the fact/value dichotomy required anything like Weber's attempt to sever science from politics. To put the point more sharply: modern liberal politics was antithetical to the understanding of the "necessity" for "ultimate value-conflicts" in political life which Weber asserted. Weber's reinterpretation of the fact/value dichotomy was integral to his "expansion" of the horizon of political economy beyond classical liberalism; his attempt to establish the central importance of value-relevance in the logic of the cultural sciences was necessary for this expansion (see note 13, above). Compare Eden, "Doing Without Liberalism: Weber's Regime Politics," pp. 381–85.

16. Ibid.; *From Max Weber*, p. 394; *SV*, pp. 142–43; Leo Strauss, *Natural Right and History*, pp. 35–80. Weber seems to believe that the politics of progress was merely an ideology that *followed upon* (rather than *preceding* or *causing*) the *Entzauberung der Welt*. "The concept of 'progress' is required only when the religious significance of the human condition is destroyed and the need arises to ascribe to it a 'meaning' which is not only this-worldly but also objective": *Roscher and Knies, The Logical Problems of Historical Economics*, p. 229. That such a this-worldly and tangible meaning might be a powerful weapon that could destroy the religious meaning and thus accelerate the disenchantment of the world by science is a possibility Weber does not entertain. See Martin Heidegger, *Nietzsche*, 2:142–43.

17. *The Gay Science*, no. 12. See the introductory remarks to chap. 3, above. Paul Forman discusses the efforts of physicists to avoid guilt for the war and the world crisis in *Weimar Culture, Causality, and Quantum Theory, 1918–1927*.

18. See Jürgen Kocka, "Kontroversen über Max Weber"; Stephen Turner and Regis A. Factor, *Max Weber and the Dispute over Reason and Value: A Study in Philosophy, Ethics, and Politics*; Wolfgang J. Mommsen, *Weber und Politik*, pp. 442–54.

19. See chap. 2, secs. 2–4, chap. 3, secs. 6, 8, chap. 4, secs. 5, 7, above.

20. See chap. 1, sec. 8, chap. 2, sec. 3, above.

21. Nietzsche saw that tyrants and demagogues would no longer be restrained by higher standards once transcendent values began "to devalue themselves." The leveling potential is clearly stated in *Beyond Good and Evil*, no. 212. But as the preceding chapters have shown, Nietzsche sought a new hierarchy to impose philosophic leadership over mere "politicians." It is only with Weber that the political leader emerges from under the shadow of a higher ranking of values legislated by the philosopher, discerned by contemplation, or revealed to a prophet.

22. The evidence for reconstructing Weber's intellectual development after 1895 is notoriously scant. With regard to Nietzsche, an important document is Weber's copy of the book by Simmel, discussed in the notes to chapter 4. Wilhelm Hennis offers a contrary interpretation of Weber's development in his fine essay "Max Webers Fragestellung." Hennis denies the importance of Weber's nationalism although stressing the thematic significance of parts of the 1895 Antrittsrede. He also ignores Weber's relation to Nietzsche and exaggerates the continuity between Weber and the political philosophers of the tradition Weber rejected (pp. 266, 270, 272). Hennis likens Weber's concern to free himself from bourgeois ideas of progress with Nietzsche's critique of free spiritedness, conveying the impression that Weber rather easily digested Nietzsche. Although his valuable article is richly documented and sheds new light on Weber's evolution after 1910, Hennis's thesis could be strengthened and focused by closer attention to Weber's copy of Simmel's work.

23. *SV*, pp. 152, 156. See the remarks of Immanual Birnbaum in Rene König and Johannes Winkelmann, eds., *Max Weber zum Gedächtnis*, p. 21. The accuracy of Birnbaum's report is in doubt, especially as to dating. See Roth and Schluchter's excursus on the date of *Science as a Vocation* in *Max Weber's Vision of History*, pp. 113–16. After p. 152, Weber's talk becomes a confession of his personal stance, although (as Birnbaum remarks) the entire talk has a confessional—or, more precisely, pro-fessional—character.

24. *PE*, pp. 13–31; Karl Löwith, "Max Weber und Karl Marx." See also Hennis, "Max Webers Fragestellung," p. 253, and Eden, "Doing without Liberalism: Weber's Regime Politics," pp. 385–95.

25. See chap. 2, sec. 2, above.

26. *SV*, p. 152. To understand Weber's 1919 lectures in their full import it is useful to weigh what Weber's contemporaries found controversial in them. See Regis A. Factor and Stephen P. Turner, "Weber's Defenders in Weimar." Weber's animus is carried on in the polemic by his disciple Arthur Salz, *Für die Wissenschaft gegen die Gebildeten unter ihren Verächtern*, pp. 56, 58, 60. See, more recently, Helmut Fogt, "Max Weber und die deutsche Soziologie der Weimarer Republik: Aussenseiter oder Gründervater?"

27. See *From Max Weber*, pp. 74, 92–93, 176, 179, 268–69, 280–81, 353, 414–44, as well as the indirect reference to Nietzsche, p. 347. Compare Ringer, *The Decline of the German Mandarins*.

28. *SV*, p. 137; *Methodology*, pp. 3, 5.

29. *From Max Weber*, pp. 371–73.

30. See chap. 2, sec. 3, above. See the remark by G.-A. Boutry quoted above in chap. 3, note 13.

31. Ringer and others have placed almost exclusive emphasis upon Dilthey as the object of Rickert's attack: *Decline of the German Mandarins*, pp. 336–40; Rainer Prewo, *Max Webers Wissenschaftsprogram: Versuch einer methodischen Neuerschliessung*, pp. 185–91. This is a misreading both of Rickert and of the magnitude of Nietzsche's influence. For correctives consult the documentation in Richard Frank Krummel, *Nietzsche und der deutsche Geist*, and Ernst Troeltsch, "Die Revolution in der Wissenschaft," p. 68 ff.

32. Heinrich Rickert, *Die Philosophie des Lebens: Darstellung und Kritik der*

philosophischen Modeströmungen unserer Zeit. For Rickert, among the "thinkers who are distinctive for the life-philosophy of the most recent time, Nietzsche is to be named here above all" (pp. 18–19). "For with extraordinary rhetorical power he did more than anyone to give the word *Life* the radiance which it has today for many" (p. 19). "Most of all, the emphasis on life in our time was stimulated by Nietzsche's poem, *Thus Spake Zarathustra*" (p. 20).

33. Kurt Sontheimer, *Antidemokratisches Denken in der Weimarer Republic: die politischen Ideen des deutschen Nationalismus zwischen, 1918–1933*, pp. 48, 65. Nietzsche was Mann's model, prior to the twenties, of the "unpolitical German." See also Ernst Gundolf and Kurt Hildebrandt, *Nietzsche als Richter unsrer Zeit*. Published in 1923, this work was directed at Weber's lectures on politics and science as vocations (pp. 1–2). Compare Armin Mohler's account of nihilism and of Nietzsche's postwar influence, *Die konservative Revolution in Deutschland 1918–1932*, pp. 86–97.

34. *SV*, p. 137.

35. Ibid., p. 149.

36. Ibid., p. 152.

37. Ibid.

38. Ibid.

39. Ibid., p. 153.

40. Ibid., pp. 155–56. Weber similarly turns Nietzsche's animus toward moralism against Nietzsche in this passage from *The Religion of India: The Sociology of Hinduism and Buddhism*: "Nietzsche occasionally gives voice to the conception of the 'artist-god' with the negative moralistic pathos which often betrays an embarrassing residue of bourgeois philistinism even in some of his greatest passages. Its intention was to expressly renounce any 'meaning' of the empirical world. A powerful, and at the same time kind, God could not have created such a world. Only a villain could have done so" (p. 168).

41. Ibid., pp. 137, 152. Compare Max Hammerton's pithy characterization of the revolutionary promise of a new society "from which alienation has been dispelled, via the happy and sanctified murder of those who are sceptical of the new enlightenment": *Science under Siege*, p. 16. See also Guenther Roth's attempt at a Weberian critique of the demonic or charismatic sectarianism of the counterculture, in Roth and Schluchter, *Max Weber's Vision of History*, pp. 119–43.

42. Eduard Baumgarten, ed., *Max Weber: Werk und Person*, pp. 554–55. This passage should be read, as Gerhard Hufnagel suggests, in conjunction with Weber's portrait of Marx as a Nietzschean philosophic leader. "Dominating nature with boundless personal ambition devoid of impulses of feeling. Belief in his mission to domination over the intellects. This and not mastery over the masses in fact the goal. Contempt for his collaborators and for the masses": *Kritik als Beruf: der kritische Gehalt im Werk Max Webers*, p. 148, note 3.

43. Löwith, "Max Weber und Karl Marx," pp. 18, 30–37.

44. *SV*, p. 135.

45. Löwith, "Max Weber und Karl Marx," pp. 18, 30–37. One case that may be taken as a paradigm is Weber's effort with Roberto Michels. As Lawrence Scaff puts it, "These scientific and political divergences were reproduced in the interpersonal dynamics of this unique and stormy partnership. Weber's frank appraisal, 'You know you are something of a "ruthless personality" [*Gewaltmensch*] and somewhat touchy when

you run into opposition . . .' written to Michels concerning his request to join in the *Archiv* as co-editor—could have applied equally well to himself. In the end the clash of demonic personalities left too little room for continued cooperation: Michels chose to be a 'déclassé intellectual' and 'renegade,' Weber a 'bourgeois critic' and 'outsider.' . . . one might add that by insisting on enchantment, on a unity of 'vocation' and 'life,' Michels proved himself only a typical representative of the literati; whereas by attempting to demonstrate the practice of scientific and political vocations in a world without enchantment, Weber achieved a standing sui generis": "Max Weber and Robert Michels," p. 1284.

46. Walter Berns, *The First Amendment and the Future of American Democracy*, pp. 1–32. "In the past, individual citizens often felt the sting of moral pressure from neighbors and local community leaders forcing them to toe the line and to do what was expected of them. Moral conformity was enforced by the strength of social norms, all the more potent for being unspoken": Daniel Yankelovich, Amitai Etzioni, et al., *Moral Leadership in Government: A Public Agenda*, p. 19. The disintegration of the Victorian equivalent of this American practice is discussed in Stephen Yeo, *Religion and Voluntary Organizations in Crisis*.

47. See Wilson Carey McWilliams, *The Idea of Fraternity in America*, pp. 64–99. This confinement of politics has, of course, been the target of much eloquent criticism of modern liberal politics. See Sheldon S. Wolin, *Politics and Vision: Continuity and Innovation in Western Political Thought*, pp. 286–434.

48. Tocqueville, *Democracy in America*, vol. 1, chap. 14 (end).

49. David L. Schaefer, "Montaigne's Political Reformation"; "The Good, the Beautiful, and the Useful: Montaigne's Transvaluation of Values"; and "Of Cannibals and Kings: Montaigne's Egalitarianism"; Montesquieu, *The Spirit of the Laws*, book 12. See chap. 2, sec. 3, above.

50. Ralph Lerner, "Commerce and Character: The Anglo-American as New Model Man."

51. The Carter Administration sought legislation that would have greatly facilitated the movement within public broadcasting toward propaganda and "political education." The proposed Public Telecommunications Financing Act of 1978 (H.R. 9620) would have weakened the authority of the Corporation of Public Broadcasting over local programing so that accountability for political bias would be unclear. "The President believes that this will decentralize creative decisions and place them further away from potential political control," wrote Larry Rothstein in *New Directions in Mass Communications Policy: Implications for Citizen Education and Participation*, p. 14. "In addition, the President calls on public broadcasters to make available for minorities and women Government funds appropriated for national programming as well as funds from the pooled resources of the stations. The President also proposes that the Public Broadcasting Act should be amended to allow non-governmental licensees to advocate positions on public issues, thereby eliminating the current ban on editorializing" (ibid., p. 1). Although this legislation died in Congress, "creative decisions" in "citizen education" employing public revenues for propaganda did not fall off.

52. Baumgarten, ed., *Max Weber: Werk und Person*, pp. 554–55; Harvey C. Mansfield, Jr., *The Spirit of Liberalism*, pp. 27, 48, 50. See also John Calhoun Merrill, *Existential Journalism*, for a forceful exposition of the new creed.

53. See chap. 4, sec. 1, above. Alisdair MacIntyre has responded sharply to

these recent developments by counseling a return to the cultivation of moral virtue in small circles opposed to the main tendencies within modern liberal democracies today. MacIntyre's target, it seems to me, is in part the strain of demonic individualism that I have traced to Nietzsche (chap. 4, sec. 1). An insightful account of MacIntyre which highlights this point is Michael A. Mosher's "After Virtue: The 'Vices' of a Juridical Society." William A. Galston's critique may enable us to see what separates MacIntyre's response to moral nihilism from Weber's: Weber makes the Nietzschean threat a new incentive and problem for the defense of liberal democratic institutions, while MacIntyre's argument has the same effect as Nietzsche's, persuading us to withdraw from liberal democratic citizenship. See Galston, "Aristotelian Morality and Liberal Society: A Critique of Alisdair MacIntyre's *After Virtue*."

54. "Rome meanwhile grows on the ruins of Alba" (Machiavelli, *Discourses*, book 2, chap. 3).

55. *BGE*, nos. 200, 242, 262.

56. Compare Hans Heinz Holz, *Die abenteuerliche Rebellion Bürgerliche Protestbewegungen in der Philosophie: Stirner, Nietzsche, Sartre, Marcuse, Neue Linke*; *BGE*, no. 44. For illustrations from the cinema, see Richard Grenier, "Bolshevism for the 80's"; "Why Herzog Differs."

57. Consider H. David Kirk, *The Friendly Perversion. Quakers as Reconcilers: Good People and Dirty Work*. See Harvey C. Mansfield, Jr., "Party and Sect in Machiavelli's *Florentine Histories*."

58. David Knoke and James R. Wood, *Organized for Action: Commitment in Voluntary Organizations*; Jeffrey M. Berry, *Lobbying for the People: The Political Behavior of Public Interest Groups*. Consider Michael Walzer's warnings about a new corporatism: "But now, it is said, pluralism cannot survive unless ethnic groups, as well as individuals, share directly in the benefits of state power. . . . The world they point to is a corporatist world, where ethnic groups no longer organize themselves like voluntary associations but have instead some political standing and some political rights": "Pluralism: A Political Perspective," p. 785.

59. This points to the flaw in the argument made by Garry Wills in *The Kennedy Imprisonment: A Meditation on Power*. Wills argues that Martin Luther King, Jr., was of a higher stature than John F. Kennedy. But he also uses King to elevate opinion leadership *qua* moral suasion over power politics, forgetting that opinion leadership is subject to precisely the same organizational power-imperatives that come into play in political parties and in formal governing institutions. He overlooks the high price that private associations pay when they become heavily politicized. Wills prefers a church to a state and a saint to a politician but he forgets what politics has done to the moral quality of previous churches, a lesson the Scottish Enlightenment might have taught him. By putting moral suasion forward not only as the antithesis of power-politics, but as a substitute for it, Wills advocates the politicization of formerly private associations and forgets the work those institutions can accomplish in a liberal order.

60. Thucydides, *History of the Peloponnesian War*, book 3, chaps. 82–84.

61. See Edward J. Erler, "Equal Protection and Personal Rights: The Regime of the 'Discrete and Insular Minority'"; Hadley Arkes, *The Philosopher in the City: The Moral Dimensions of Urban Politics*, pp. 27–28, 34–36, 83–86; Alexander I. Solzhenitsyn, on "Legalistic Life," *Solzhenitsyn at Harvard: The Address, Twelve Early Responses, and Six Later Reflections*, p. 7.

62. A comparison of recent American developments with the problems that were on Weber's mind in his 1919 lectures may strike the reader as anachronistic. One should bear in mind Karl Löwith's observation that "Nihilism as the disavowal of existing civilization was the only real belief of all truly educated people at the beginning of the twentieth century. Nihilism is not a result of the Great War, but on the contrary, its cause": *Nature, History, and Existentialism*, p. 10. The danger that private associations would undermine rather than promote the moral habits necessary for liberal democratic civility was very much on Weber's mind. He was also concerned with combating the demoralizing effects of the war by fostering youth-associations based upon American models. See Weber's letter to Crusius, 24 November 1918, in Marianne Weber, *Max Weber: A Biography*, pp. 635–37.

63. Joseph Peter Stern speaks of "a pervasive limitation of Nietzsche's thinking: it is his consistent neglect of, and his indiscriminate bias against, what I shall call *the sphere of association*": *A Study of Nietzsche*, p. 116. He argues that "His consistent rejection of the sphere of association forms the most important and the most disturbing limitation of his philosophical thinking" (p. 121). But, as I have tried to show, Nietzsche does not ignore the associative part of our world; he adopts a ruthlessly instrumental attitude toward it in order to subordinate it to his practical purposes.

64. Recall chap. 1, sec. 8, chap. 2, secs. 1–2, and the introductory remarks to chap. 3, above.

65. *SV*, pp. 129–34; *PV*, pp. 77–114; *Methodology*, p. 66.

66. *SV*, pp. 134–40; *PV*, pp. 114–17.

67. *SV*, pp. 140–52; *PV*, pp. 117–27.

68. *SV*, pp. 155–56; *PV*, pp. 128–29.

69. *SV*, pp. 129, 134.

70. Inquiry No. 2 (*SV*, pp. 134–38): question on p. 138; Inquiry No. 9 (*SV*, p. 152).

71. *SV*, pp. 129, 134. Compare *PV*, p. 115; *Methodology*, pp. 3, 5; Roth and Schluchter, *Max Weber's Vision of History*, pp. 65–76. See also Marianne Weber, *Max Weber: A Biography*, p. 663.

72. Löwith, *Max Weber und Karl Marx*; Ringer, *Decline of the German Mandarins*, pp. 336–40; Factor and Turner, "Weber's Defenders in Weimar."

73. *PV*, p. 128.

74. *Methodology*, p. 68.

75. See Factor and Turner, "Weber's Defenders in Weimar." Compare note 83, below, and text.

76. *SV*, p. 134.

77. Ibid., pp. 138–39.

78. Ibid., pp. 139–40.

79. Ibid., p. 135.

80. Weber, *The Religion of China: Confucianism and Taoism*, p. 119. On the modern discovery of individuality, see chap. 1, sec. 7, chap. 2, sec. 3, chap. 4, sec. 1, above.

81. *SV*, pp. 142–43.

82. Nietzsche, *BGE*, no. 211, and see also nos. 9, 22, 36, 56; *The Will to Power*, no. 1067; *GS*, no. 343.

83. *PV*, pp. 119–20, 122, 125, 128; Marianne Weber, *Max Weber: A Biography*, pp. 620–33.

84. Nietzsche, *GS*, no. 12; *BGE*, no. 23. Note the rhetorical character of *The Genealogy of Morals*, emphasized in *EH*, "The Genealogy of Morals."

85. *PV*, p. 115.

86. Löwith, "Max Weber und Karl Marx."

87. *SV*, pp. 138–39. Weber underlined this sentence on Socrates, but I cannot decipher his remark in the margin: "[Nietzsche] is the most extreme opposite to the Socratic conception, according to which there is only one virtue which is the same for all": Georg Simmel, *Schopenhauer und Nietzsche*, p. 211. Compare Weber, *ES*, 2:445.

88. *SV*, p. 140.

89. Ibid., pp. 152–56.

90. Ibid., p. 152.

91. Ibid., pp. 140–43.

92. Ibid., p. 143.

93. Ibid., p. 141.

94. Ibid., p. 152. This was the crux of the controversy over *Wissenschaft als Beruf*, as Factor and Turner show in "Weber's Defenders in Weimar."

95. See the discussion of the Preface to *BGE*, chap. 2, sec. 3, above.

96. See chap. 3, above. Stanley Rosen, *Nihilism: A Philosophical Essay*, pp. 56–197; and consider also Rosen, *The Limits of Analysis*, pp. 156–75, 190–215.

97. *SV*, pp. 140–43. Compare Eden, "Doing Without Liberalism," pp. 397–400.

98. *SV*, pp. 153.

99. Ibid., p. 152.

100. Ibid., pp. 141, 152, 153. Consider Rickert's remarks on *ASZ*, in note 32, above.

101. See chap. 1, sec. 7, especially note 109, and chap. 2, sec. 3, above.

102. Löwith, "Max Weber und Karl Marx," pp. 30–37.

103. *SV*, p. 152. Compare Weber, *Gesammelte Aufsätze zur Soziologie und Sozialpolitik*, p. 420; *Methodology*, pp. 18, 52, 111–12. See also Erik Wolf, "Max Webers ethischer Kritizismus und das Problem der Metaphysik."

104. Nevertheless, it cannot be said that Weber made any inquiry into the "practical ethics" of the founders of modern science (that is, into their political philosophy), comparable to his study of the practical ethics of the world religions. Compare Weber, *Die protestantische Ethik 2: Kritiken und Antikritiken*, p. 324.

105. *SV*, p. 142.

106. Weber ridicules Wilhelm Förster for ignoring the ethical irrationality of the world that Indian philosophy had recognized for millenia; he indicates that Machiavelli's understanding of political power was child's play compared to the *Kautilya Arthasastra;* but Weber does not explain how the diabolical dimension of power and its immoral or soul-destroying possibilities escaped the notice of the early modern philosophers who equated knowledge with the acquisition of power. See *PV*, pp. 122–26.

107. See chap. 3, introductory remarks, above. Weber's attempt to attain critical distance on the various forms of "rationalization"—especially those which "revolutionize from without" (*ES*, 3:1116)—is meant to exemplify this new moral responsibility. Compare the remarks on his radicalization of the problematic of Rousseau and Kant, at note 5, above.

108. Roth and Schluchter, *Max Weber's Vision of History,* pp. 92–106; Wolfgang J. Mommsen, *The Age of Bureaucracy: Perspectives on the Political Sociology of Max Weber*, pp. 98–100, 103–7, 111–12.

109. *SV*, p. 141.

110. Ibid., pp. 129, 141, 142.

111. Ibid., p. 142.

112. Preface to *The Great Instauration, The Works of Francis Bacon,* 4:21.

113. *SV*, p. 142.

114. Ibid., pp. 141–43, 149, 155.

115. Ibid., pp. 140, 151–52.

116. Ibid., p. 152, 155–56; *Methodology,* p. 18; *Gesammelte Aufsätze zur Soziologie und Sozialpolitik,* p. 420.

117. *SV*, p. 143. See Löwith, "Max Weber und Karl Marx," pp. 18, 37.

118. Immanuel Kant, *The Critique of Pure Reason,* pp. 4, 20. The epigraph left in Latin in the Norman Kemp Smith translation is from the preface to Bacon's *The Great Instauration*: "Of myself I say nothing; but in behalf of the business which is in hand I entreat men to believe that it is not an opinion to be held, but a work to be done, and to be well assured that I am labouring to lay the foundation, not of any sect or doctrine, but of human utility and power. Next, I ask them to deal fairly by their own interests . . . and join in consultation for the common good. . . . Moreover, to be of good hope, nor to imagine that this Instauration of mine is a thing infinite and beyond the power of man, when it is in fact the true end and termination of infinite error": *The Works of Francis Bacon,* 4:21.

119. Weber took Kuno Fischer's course on logic in the spring semester of 1882, when he was eighteen, and then took his course on the history of philosophy. One of Fischer's first works was *Baco von Verulam: Realistische Philosophie und seine Zeitalter* (1856). He later published an expanded version as volume 10 of his *Geschichte der neuern Philosophie* (1903). Weber read this history as early as 1882.

Weber also took Frederick A. Lange's course, from which we have Lange's famous *The History of Materialism.* Lange opposed Fischer, and attacked Bacon as a dubious materialist, but after quoting from the crucial passage of Descartes's *Discourse on Method,* culminating in "render ourselves the lords and possessors of nature," Lange was emphatic that "all this had already been more forcibly said by Bacon": *History of Materialism,* p. 276. He also notes that J. S. Mill considered Bacon the father of his method, a point not to be forgotten in light of Weber's careful study of Mill's writings on logic and political economy.

But Kuno Fischer stated the importance of Bacon most eloquently: "The method of invention is the instrument with which Bacon would equip science, and render it capable of conquering the world" (p. 53, Oxenford translation). "This, then, was the problem apprehended by Bacon, and proposed to his age: the subjection of science to the spirit of invention, and the liberation of this spirit from the chance by which human inventions had previously been governed" (ibid., p. 47). Fischer gives the *regnum hominis,* the project for rendering men the lords and possessors of nature, its proper place in Bacon's project. After a competent summary of the obvious main parts of Bacon's program, he concludes: "That Bacon thought through his perspectives in such coherence and bound them together so consequentially, made him a *great* thinker. That from these standpoints he opened the widest perspectives in the realm of science, as well as in the whole of human cultivation; that everywhere he designated goals, set tasks, raised problems, and never finished the edifice of his teaching or closed it off dogmatically, made him not only a great thinker, but an *epoch-creating* one. For it is the authentic distinction of epoch-making minds, that they open upon the future. Bacon wanted to create no finished system, but rather a living work, that should progressively unfold with the ages. He sowed the seed for a future harvest, that would ripen slowly and be complete only in centuries. Bacon was well aware of this. It sufficed him to be the sower and to begin the work which only the ages could complete. His sense of himself was the just consciousness of his task [*Sache*], no more and no less. In the Preface to the *Novum Organum* he said in conclusion: 'Of myself I say nothing. But about the task of which I treat . . . I desire to find new foundations for the needs and the greatness of humanity' " (my translation from the 1856 edition). In the 1903 edition of Fischer's *Geschichte der neuern Philosophie*, the passage appears in somewhat different form (vol. 10, p. 104). Compare this last passage from Bacon with Nietzsche's account, chap. 2, sec. 3, above. For the biographical information cited above, see Eduard Baumgarten, *Max Weber: Werk und Person*, pp. 15–16.

120. See *The Works of Francis Bacon*, 3:261 ff., 302–3, 4:11–12, 14, 17, 23, 27, 29, 31, 32, 40–42, 79–81, 86–87, 89–93, 98–100, 101, 109, 247–48, 252, 283–91, 372–73.

121. On medicine and biology, compare Weber, *SV*, p. 144, with Bacon, *Works*, 4:379, 383–84, 387, 390. On physics, compare Weber, *SV*, p. 144, with the paper by Timothy J. Paterson on the difference between Epicurean and Baconian physics, "Ancients and Moderns: The Case of Bacon and Lucretius."

122. Kant, *The Critique of Pure Reason*, pp. 4, 20, 22, 23 (and see note 118, above); Weber, *SV*, pp. 152, 154 (and compare Fischer's observations in note 119, above).

123. Compare *SV*, pp. 152, 154, with the observations by Fischer in note 119, above.

124. *SV*, p. 139.

125. Ibid., p. 150. The translation is my own, from Weber, *Wissenschaftslehre*, p. 607. *Berechnung* usually means calculation, but it can also mean accounting; I have used *reckoning* with a view to Weber's own instance, musical instrument making. Bacon's failure to grasp the power of mathematics for the mastery project was corrected by Descartes, but Descartes fell short in appreciating instrumentation and technology, which was Bacon's strength. Despite Weber's emphasis upon statistics and calculations (*SV*, p. 135), mathematics played a relatively minor part in his ideal-typical method. *Berechnung* as "reckoning" is a proper term to describe the judgment of the distance between an ideal-type and the phenomena that was central to Weber's logic of the cultural sciences.

126. *SV*, p. 139; compare p. 152.

127. Weber, *Wissenschaftslehre*, p. 594. See the remarks in note 122 above. For Gerth's translation, see *SV*, p. 139.

128. *SV*, p. 143.

129. *From Max Weber*, p. 44. Compare Marianne Weber, *Max Weber: A Biography*, p. 663.

130. Rolf Gruner, *Theory and Power: On the Character of Modern Sciences*; Richard Kennington, "Descartes and Mastery of Nature." Gruner underestimates

Weber when he says that he "did not see the problematic character of the modern conception" of "rationality conceived in terms of power" (pp. 5–6).

131. See Regis A. Factor and Stephen P. Turner, "Objective Possibility and Adequate Causation in Weber's Methodological Writings," pp. 6–8.

132. Weber acknowledged this link in concluding his reply to his critics, *Die protestantische Ethik 2: Kritiken und Antikritiken, p. 324.*

133. *PE,* pp. 117–27, 153–54, 155–83.

134. *PV,* pp. 117, 123; *SV,* pp. 148–49; *From Max Weber,* pp. 323–59.

135. *SV,* p. 149; *PE,* pp. 24, 180–83; *ES,* 1:138–39.

136. *PE,* p. 182.

137. *SV,* pp. 152, 156; *PE,* p. 182; *Gesammelte Aufsätze zur Soziologie und Sozialpolitik,* p. 420.

138. Hence Weber's thesis is undermined by the investigations of C. B. Macpherson, to mention only one prominent case. See the critique of *The Protestant Ethic* in Caton, "World in Decay: Critiques of the Historiography of Progress." See also Robert K. Faulkner, "Empire Humane and Economic: Bacon, Machiavelli, and the Politics of Progress."

139. See chap. 3, secs. 1, 6, 8, above.

140. See sec. 1 of this chapter.

141. See chap. 3, above; see also Leo Strauss, *On Tyranny,* pp. 21–27, 223–26.

142. As an instance, see Wolfgang Schluchter, *The Rise of Western Rationalism: Max Weber's Developmental History,* which follows Weber in omitting science and ignoring early modern philosophy. Compare chap. 2, sec. 3, above.

143. *SV,* p. 147.

144. See Hennis, "Max Webers Fragestellung," pp. 241–43; Fogt, "Max Weber und die deutsche Soziologie der Weimarer Republik: Aussenseiter oder Gründervater?"

145. *BGE,* nos. 23, 29–30, 186, 198, 227, 230; *GM,* Essay 3, no. 27.

146. Guy Oakes reaches a complementary conclusion in "Methodological Ambivalence: The Case of Max Weber," p. 615.

147. *SV,* p. 156.

148. See Schluchter's excursus on the dating of *Science as a Vocation*: Roth and Schluchter, *Max Weber's Vision of History,* pp. 113–16. Compare *PV,* pp. 115, 127.

149. Björkman, "Professionalism in the Welfare State," pp. 407, 412–13.

150. An attempt to associate Weber with the devaluation of politics may be found in Bryan S. Turner, "Nietzsche, Weber, and the Devaluation of Politics: The Problem of State Legitimacy." See chap. 6, sec. 1, below, and the problems discussed in sec. 2 of this chapter.

151. Mommsen, *The Age of Bureaucracy,* pp. 47–71; Beetham, *Max Weber and the Theory of Modern Politics,* pp. 63–89; Eden, "Doing without Liberalism: Weber's Regime Politics," p. 382.

152. Björkman, "Professionalism in the Welfare State," pp. 410–11, 415, 422–24; Burkart Holzner and John H. Marx, *Knowledge Application: The Knowledge System in Society,* pp. 141–55, 196–207, 257–59, 284–87, 306–7, 333–38.

153. *SV,* p. 149.

154. Ibid., p. 156.

155. Ibid., p. 155.

156. *PE*, pp. 97–98, 102–4, 105–6, 108, 114–15, 117–19, 232 note 66.
157. Ibid., p. 232 note 66.
158. Ibid., pp. 97, 109–10.
159. *Methodology*, p. 18.
160. *PV*, pp. 120–22, 127.
161. See chap. 1, note 99, and chap. 2, note 80, above.
162. As Strauss observed, Weber conveys the impression that moral values are not only distinct from cultural values but are superior to them; that impression dissolves, however, upon closer inspection. See Strauss, *Natural Right and History,* pp. 43–44, 48. Compare Strauss's remarks on Weber's insistence upon the necessity of guilt and his belief that without a combination of the anguish bred by atheism and the anguish bred by revealed religion, life would lose its tragic depth (ibid., p. 66). The passage is quoted in chap. 6, sec. 4, at note 128, above.
163. Compare Martin Heidegger, *Being and Time,* pp. 314, 316–22, 324–25, 334–35, 342; Mark Blitz, *Heidegger's* Being and Time *and the Possibility of Political Philosophy,* pp. 130–40.
164. Dieter Henrich, *Die Einheit der Wissenschaftslehre Max Webers,* pp. 2–3, 16–19, 105–22, 131.
165. *SV*, pp. 147, 151–52; *PV*, p. 115.
166. *ES,* 2:576; *WG,* p. 348. The passage is quoted in chap. 3, sec. 6 at note 80, above.
167. Ibid.
168. *SV*, p. 152.
169. Compare note 162, above.
170. *ES,* 2:575–76; *WG,* p. 348.
171. From Max Weber, p. 393.
172. See chap. 6, sec. 3, below. I have discussed Weber's attempt to form the liberal democratic order into a coherent regime in "Doing Without Liberalism: Weber's Regime Politics."
173. Björkman, "Professionalism in the Welfare State," pp. 415, 422–24.
174. Theodore J. Lowi, *The End of Liberalism: The Second Republic of the United States,* pp. 3–21, 42–63, 295–313.
175. "The separation of facts from values is apologetic. . . . Juridical democracy can be scientific even while working toward a fusion of facts and values. . . . Above all else, the juridical principle would demand constantly that political science look to itself as part of the very political process it presumes to study": ibid., p. 312.
176. *PV*, pp. 126–27; *SV*, p. 152. See Introduction at note 11, above.
177. Quoted from manuscript sources in Hennis, "Max Webers Fragestellung," p. 276.
178. Ibid. See chap. 1, sec. 5, at notes 78–81, above.
179. Hennis, p. 276; compare chap. 2, sec. 5, chap. 3, secs. 1, 8, chap. 4, sec. 1, above.
180. See the beginnning of chap. 5, above.
181. *PV*, pp. 96–97.

CHAPTER 6. LEADING PROFESSIONS: *POLITICS AS A VOCATION*

1. *Beyond Good and Evil*, no. 203. Compare chap. 2, secs. 2, 4, above. See also Werner J. Dannhauser, *Nietzsche's View of Socrates*, pp. 31–32.

2. *BGE*, nos. 267–68. Compare Georg Simmel, *Schopenhauer und Nietzsche*, pp. 196–99 (lightly marked by Weber). For particulars on Weber's copy of this volume, see the note on abbreviations and translations, above.

3. *BGE*, nos. 242, 257. See chap. 2, sec. 4, chap. 4, secs. 7–8, above.

4. See chap. 2, sec. 5, chap. 3, secs. 6, 8, chap. 4, sec. 1, chap. 5, sec. 2, above. See also Tracy Burr Strong, *Friedrich Nietzsche and the Politics of Transfiguration*, pp. x–xi, 105–7, 189, 197, 198–202, 273, 280, 336; Pamela K. Jensen, "Nietzsche and Liberation: The Prelude to a Philosophy of the Future," pp. 89–91.

5. See chap. 1, sec. 8, above. These questions were raised by Wolfgang J. Mommsen in his early writings on Weber, but he seems to have been at a loss to articulate their full implications because his understanding of modern political philosophy before Weber was essentially historicist, and because he hoped to employ historicist arguments against Weber. His work is punctuated by claims that Weber was bound by the nationalist prejudices of his age, that he was incapable of criticizing such prejudices, and that events rather than arguments prove Weber to have been wrong (*Weber und Politik*, pp. 51–53, 55, 57, 64, 67–68, 72, 85, 90, 95, 100, 110, 112, 169, 202, 332, 441, 445). Mommsen's indignation against Weber for abandoning the principles of natural right was bound to terminate in silence, one might say, because he did not have rational grounds for defending those principles. (See Stanley Rosen, *Nihilism: A Philosophical Essay*, pp. xiii–xvii.) It does not follow, however, that Mommsen's questions were irrelevant; and Weber's defenders have certainly not measured up to them. Guenther Roth's effort, "Political Critiques," in Reinhard Bendix and Guenther Roth, *Scholarship and Partisanship: Essays on Max Weber*, pp. 62–69, may be taken as exhibiting the vulnerability of Weber's defenders: Roth evidently presupposes that social scientists will not trouble to read the works criticized and require no more than a convenient excuse for ignoring them. Schluchter's defense of Weber is more selective, abandoning what he calls Weber's "ethical fundamentalism" and attempting to "bring Weber's model closer to the pragmatic one even on the institutional level." See Guenther Roth and Wolfgang Schluchter, *Max Weber's Vision of History*, pp. 111–12. These qualifications, urged by Hans Albert and Niklaus Luhmann, bring Weber closer to the original principles of modern liberal politics, but only at the price of abandoning what was distinctive and essential to Weber's position. They excise the doctrines in which Weber came to grips with Nietzschean nihilism by his own lights.

6. Hence Mommsen could assert (though in contradiction to his main claim about liberal principles) that Weber was "the last great representative of classical liberalism": "Universalgeschichtliches und politisches Denken bei Max Weber," p. 568. Compare Reinhard Bendix, *Max Weber: An Intellectual Portrait*, p. 494.

7. "The constructs of the natural right and organic theories of the state have exactly the same function, and, to recall an ideal type in *our* sense, so does Benjamin Constant's theory of the ancient state: it serves to a certain extent as an emergency harbor until one has learned to navigate safely in the vast sea of empirical facts": *Methodology*, p. 106. (I have slightly altered the Shils/Finch translation to bring it into closer agreement with the German; compare Weber, *Wissenschaftslehre*, p. 206.)

8. Lawrence A. Scaff, "Max Weber's Politics and Political Education," pp. 138–40; Roth and Schluchter, *Max Weber's Vision of History*, pp. 65–116 (with the provisos mentioned in note 5, above).

9. Eduard Baumgarten, ed., *Max Weber: Werk und Person*, p. 554. See Karl Jaspers as quoted in chap. 3 at note 12, above. See also Bendix and Roth, *Scholarship and Partisanship: Essays on Max Weber*, pp. 22–25, 84 ff., 227–45.

10. *Science as a Vocation*, p. 149.

11. Ibid., p. 152; *Politics as a Vocation*, pp. 23–26; *From Max Weber*, pp. 13, 25, 46–51, 61–66.

12. Compare the debate over Weber on this point between Martin Diamond, "Teaching about Politics as a Vocation," pp. 4–6, and Charles Frankel, "Facts, Values, and Responsible Choice," p. 26.

13. *PV*, p. 80.

14. Ibid., p. 113.

15. Ibid., pp. 80–84, 88–90, 92; *Economy and Society*, 3:1386; *PS*, p. 20.

16. *PV*, p. 106; see also pp. 90–113.

17. Ibid., pp. 2–84, 94–96, 100–103, 118; *Methodology*, p. 23.

18. See Hannah Arendt, *The Origins of Totalitarianism*, pp. 318–22.

19. *PV*, pp. 99–100.

20. *Ecce Homo*, "Birth of Tragedy," no. 4; *BGE*, no. 200; *EH*, "Why I Am a Destiny," nos. 1–9. See the most politically insightful work to emerge from the *Georgekreis:* Ernst Kantorowicz, *Frederick the Second, 1194–1250*.

21. *The Gay Science*, no. 362.

22. *PV*, p. 102.

23. *BGE*, nos. 251, 256; *The Will to Power*, no. 898.

24. Mommsen, *Weber und Politik*, pp. 145, 176–205, 326–27; David Beetham, *Max Weber and the Theory of Modern Politics*, pp. 44–49, 95–115, 164–70.

25. Carl Joachim Friedrich, "The Development of the Executive Power in Germany," p. 203.

26. *PV*, pp. 77–78; *Methodology*, pp. 50–52, 98–99.

27. *Methodology*, pp. 50–52, 98–99; *SV*, pp. 47–52; Hans Henrik Bruun, *Science, Values, and Politics in Max Weber's Methodology*, pp. 213–45.

28. *SV*, pp. 50–139, 145, 150–51; *Gesammelte politische Schriften*, p. 14.

29. *ES*, 1:223–25.

30. *PV*, pp. 102, 113.

31. *SV*, p. 147; *PV*, pp. 11–14.

32. Prior to the collapse of the Wilhelmine dynasty, Weber had advocated a strengthened parliament to fortify the monarchic executive and consolidate his control over the bureaucratic staffs. Without the weapon of parliamentary inquiry, he argued, the head of state could not possibly bring his own administrative staff to heel: *PS*, pp. 308–38, 357–70; *ES*, 3:1394–95, 1400–1407, 1408–10; see Mommsen, *Weber und Politik*, pp. 176–86. Until the dynasty collapsed, Weber's consistent policy was designed to transform the Wilhelmine Reich into a constitutional monarchy essentially along British lines. This would preserve traditional loyalty to the Kaiser as a lever for subordinating all administration officers, but especially the military, to the constitutional regime. It would also curb the excesses of political ambition by removing the highest office from electoral politics, which Weber thought would have a sobering

effect on professional politicians. See *From Max Weber*, pp. 368–70; *ES*, pp. 1405–7; *Politische Schriften*, pp. 325–28. It is against this background that one must see Weber's effort to transfer to the Weimar Executive all the powers that had been exercised by Bismarck at his height and to make the new executive something of a Kaiser (Mommsen, *Weber und Politik*, pp. 356–96). Mommsen's account focuses exclusively on Weber's prescriptions for the highest executive office, conveying the impression that these prescriptions represent the logical terminus of his thinking on plebiscitary leader-democracy, rather than a desperate emergency measure that he was compelled to adopt. Throughout his interpretation, Mommsen minimizes and deemphasizes Weber's argument for constitutional monarchy and leads the reader to forget Weber's foremost preoccupation in *Politics as a Vocation*, the concern for the professionalization of German politics and the promotion of a leadership class or stratum of professional politicians. Hence Mommsen concludes that Weber's conception is subject to criticism on pragmatic grounds because it fails to provide for professional statesmen skilled in interest politics (p. 454). Mommsen does not come to terms with what Weber regarded as the distinctive problem posed by rational-legal bureaucracy in a liberal democratic regime, namely, how to coordinate a cadre of professional politicians in order to make the administrative machine accountable to elected representatives.

33. See Otto Kirchheimer, *Political Justice: The Use of Legal Procedure for Political Ends*, pp. 213–17, and see also pp. 10, 139. Compare Alan Bullock, *Hitler: A Study in Tyranny*, pp. 72, 98, 114–20, 127, 131.

34. *SV*, p. 152; *PV*, pp. 14, 125, 127–28.

35. *SV*, p. 151.

36. *PV*, p. 112; *SV*, p. 152.

37. *PV*, pp. 8, 94–95, 108, 120; *SV*, p. 152.

38. See chap. 2, secs. 3–4, chap. 4, secs. 4, 7, 8, above.

39. *PV*, pp. 14–15, 125, 127–28.

40. Ibid., pp. 114, 117.

41. *ES*, 3:1132–33; *Methodology*, pp. 2, 9–10.

42. *PV*, p. 125.

43. *Methodology*, pp. 23–25; *PV*, pp. 106–7.

44. One might ask how the syndicalist discussed in *Methodology*, pp. 24–25, would read *Politics as a Vocation*, to say nothing of the patriotic officer who goes down with guns blazing.

45. See Harvey C. Mansfield, Jr., *The Spirit of Liberalism*, pp. 8–15, 43–46; Hiram Caton, "On the Basis of Hobbes's Political Philosophy," pp. 418–23; Stanley Rosen, "Benedict Spinoza," pp. 432–34. On Montaigne's humanitarian ideal, see chap. 2, sec. 3, notes 87–90, above; David L. Schaefer, "Montaigne's Political Reformation"; and Schaefer, "Of Cannibals and Kings: Montaigne's Egalitarianism."

46. Mommsen, *Weber und Politik*, pp. 199–205, 363–66, 380, 407–9, 411, 416–41, 450, 454; Mommsen, "Zum Begriff der 'plebiszitären Führerdemokratie' bei Max Weber," and his *The Age of Bureaucracy*.

47. Mommsen, *Weber und Politik*, pp. xi, 201, 365, 378, 416–41, 454, 465.

48. Ibid., pp. xi–xx, and "Plebiszitäre Führerdemokratie," pp. 296–97, 308–13; Weber, *ES*, 1:267–68.

49. The polemical literature is listed in Mommsen, *Weber und Politik,* pp. 442–48.

50. Ibid., pp. 396–441.

51. Ibid., pp. 418–20.

52. Ibid., pp. 407–15.

53. Since the distinction is asserted in *BGE,* no. 199 (the epigraph to this chapter) and is restated by Simmel, *Schopenhauer und Nietzsche,* p. 199, in a passage marked by Weber in his copy, we can be confident that it was a distinction he understood. It was a familiar theme of public policy and political economy from the debate over laissez-faire doctrines. Is it the province of government to do more than secure the right to acquire property? Should it also be concerned with the exercise of property rights, for example by legislating maximum interest rates (laws against usury)?

Kathi V. Friedman has attempted to develop a Weberian rationale for the redistributive policies of the modern welfare state, according to which welfare legislation would not constitute state intervention in the exercise of property rights. It would instead be justified exclusively as a legitimate effort to secure citizens' rights; the welfare state would thus become a more rational and inclusive form of the liberal state based on natural rights: *Legitimation of Social Rights and the Western Welfare State: A Weberian Perspective,* pp. xii, 35–61. But Friedman does not discuss political leadership or Weber's interpretation of professional politics and therefore does not confront the question of how Weber's insistence on politics as devotion to an (irrational) god or cause can be reconciled with the principles of impartiality and limited government (government limited to the securing of rights).

54. See chap. 2, sec. 2, above.

55. Ibid.

56. See Eden, "Doing Without Liberalism: Weber's Regime Politics," pp. 380–84, 395–96.

57. Machiavelli, *The Prince,* chap. 15, p. 127: "many have imagined republics and principalities that have never been seen or known to exist in reality."

58. Sheldon S. Wolin, *Politics and Vision: Continuity and Innovation in Western Political Thought,* pp. 195–238.

59. J. W. Allen, *A History of Political Thought in the Sixteenth Century,* pp. 370–77, 492–94; Joseph Cropsey, "Hobbes and the Transition to Modernity," in Cropsey, *Political Philosophy and the Issues of Politics,* pp. 291–314; Thomas L. Pangle, *Montesquieu's Philosophy of Liberalism: A Commentary on "The Spirit of the Laws,"* pp. 107–61.

60. "After all, it is a gross self-deception to believe that without the achievements of the age of the Rights of Man any one of us . . . can go on living": "Parliament and Government in a Newly Ordered Germany," in *ES,* 3:1403. It is Weber's emphasis on conserving limited government as the securing of rights that makes the title of Mommsen's tenth chapter, "From the Liberal Constitutional State to Plebiscitary Leader-Democracy," so disquieting: *Weber und Politik,* p. 416. The historicist form of Weber's assertion here should give one pause: today we are factually dependent on the achievements of an age that believed in principles we can no longer reasonably defend. Compare *ES,* 2:868–74.

61. See chap. 1, sec. 5, above; *Methodology,* pp. 25–26; *PS,* p. 18. Compare Eden, "Doing Without Liberalism: Weber's Regime Politics," pp. 380–85, 397–401.

62. *SV*, p. 148. See the introduction to chap. 5, above.

63. *PV*, pp. 80, 96, 104, 125.

64. Ibid., p. 113.

65. Weber looks most like a liberal when he asserts that the main "question about the future forms of political organization" can be posed only as the question of how to preserve "the achievements of the Rights of Man" against "the irresistible advance of bureaucratization": *ES*, 3:1403. The question here seems to be how to keep government limited in purpose and specifically to the purpose of securing rights. Since the question is raised in the context of a debate over state socialism, it would seem that the distinction between securing and exercising rights was crystal clear to Weber (see note 53, above). But even in this passage, Weber introduces an ambiguity: in the German text, the Rights of Man are placed in quotations, as if to emphasize that what were once thought to be permanent natural rights of all men are now "so-called" rights, the products of historically transient earthly ideals. (Compare *PS*, p. 321 with p. 1.) The root of the difficulty is that passionate devotion to a cause, or charisma as the specifically revolutionary force in history, is creative, perhaps even creating its own revolutionary right. What this entails may be suggested by the following: "Plekhanov took the French Revolution as an example of a Nietzschean truth. The revolutionaries were forced to go 'beyond good and evil' to take the Bastille. The Revolution was justified in going beyond 'good and evil' because it forced the evil in French society to yield to the good. To be beyond good and evil, Plekhanov argues, means 'to do such a great historical deed that the judgment of it cannot be placed in the framework of the given concepts of good and evil which arose on the soil of a given social order' ": Ann Marie Lane, "Nietzsche in Russian Thought, 1890–1917," p. 499. Compare chap, 3, sec. 6, above, and note 136, below.

66. See chap. 1, sec. 1, above.

67. See chap. 1, sec. 5, chap. 2, sec. 2, above. The most explicit statement on the importance of "forms" in Weber's political thought is from "Wahlrecht und Demokratie in Deutschland," *PS*, pp. 270–74, translated in *From Max Weber*, pp. 392–94. Compare Harvey C. Mansfield, Jr., "The Forms and Formalities of Liberty," pp. 121–31.

68. *ES*, 1:266–67.

69. See chap. 1, sec. 5, above.

70. Consider *ES*, 3:1140.

71. For some analysis of Weber's response to Marx, see Eden, "Doing Without Liberalism: Weber's Regime Politics," pp. 384–96.

72. See chap. 4, sec. 1, chap. 5, sec. 2, above.

73. Tocqueville, *Democracy in America,* vol. 1, part 1, chap. 6; chap. 16, pp. 283–97.

74. See Kirchheimer, *Political Justice*, pp. 213–15.

75. *SV*, p. 148.

76. Robert A. Dahl apparently chose the term in order to drive home the point "that differences in national regime" matter a great deal, while maintaining a safe distance from classical liberalism, which asserted a normative political science: "polyarchy" is meant to describe democratic representation without committing political science to liberal principles: *Polyarchy: Participation and Opposition*, p. 17. That the term is meant to denote liberal democracy is most clearly shown in this definition:

"Regimes that impose the fewest restraints on the expression, organization, and representation of political preferences and on the opportunities available to opponents of government. Most individuals are effectively protected in their right to express, privately or publicly, their opposition to the government, to organize, to form parties, and to compete in elections where voting is secret, unintimidated, and honestly counted and where the results of elections are binding according to well-established rules. Ordinarily, the use of violent means is forbidden, and in some cases it is punishable to advocate the use of violence for political purposes. I shall call such systems *polyarchies*": Dahl, ed., *Regimes and Oppositions*, p. 3. I have chosen a more literal use of the term in light of the difficulties in Dahl's usage pointed out in Mansfield, *The Spirit of Liberalism*, pp. 69–71.

77. Jensen, "Nietzsche and Liberation: The Prelude to a Philosophy of the Future."

78. Ibid., p. 96.

79. See Strong, *Friedrich Nietzsche and the Politics of Transfiguration*, pp. 208–16. Strong's selection of China and Cuba to illustrate Nietzsche's intention suggests more about their inhumanity or cruelty than Strong admits.

80. Compare chap. 3, sec. 6, above; Leo Strauss, "Comments on Carl Schmitt's *Der Begriff des Politischen*"; Preface to *Spinoza's Critique of Religion*, pp. 10–11.

81. *PV*, p. 117. Compare *Methodology*, p. 55.

82. Plato, *Meno*, 97a–100a9; Aristotle, *The Nichomachean Ethics*, 1140a24–b30, 1141b8–1143b16.

83. *SV*, p. 149; *PV*, pp. 19, 124, 126.

84. *SV*, p. 149.

85. *PV*, pp. 19–21. Thus Weber begins, as Hans-Martin Schmolz insists, by rejecting the idea that any intention can justify the use of power or that the aim can justify the means: "Das Dilemma der politischen Ethik bei Max Weber" (p. 480). Weber's initial emphasis upon an ethic of responsibility need not lead one to the erroneous conclusion that Weber does without an ethic of intentions, a conclusion that Schmolz draws (p. 493) despite *PV*, p. 127.

86. See chap. 4, sec. 7, above. Nietzsche seeks to divide two stances that tend to converge, in practice, because of the psychological pressure inherent in moral relatedness. One curious result, to which Werner Dannhauser has called attention, is that to endure the pathos of distance in slavery over one's equal or superior becomes a test of heroism for Nietzsche. Jorge Luis Borges attempted to reveal the psychology of this inversion in his story "Deutsches Requiem."

87. *PV*, p. 115; Nietzsche, *BGE*, no. 260; *The Genealogy of Morals*, Essay 1. Compare Weber, *Methodology*, p. 97, and also Simmel, *Schopenhauer und Nietzsche*, p. 211. See also Weber, *Gesammelte Aufsätze zur Soziologie und Sozialpolitik*, p. 445.

88. Aristotle, *Politics*, 1274b30–1276b15; 1301b1–5, 1302a8–16, 1304b19–1306b21, 1307a20–27, 1308a4–1310a38. Unlike Aristotle, Weber treats these opposed perspectives as ultimate standpoints from which science or reason cannot ascend. Compare Weber, *Methodology*, pp. 15–16, which essentially repeats the point made by Simmel, *Schopenhauer und Nietzsche*, p. 223: "Between these modes of evaluating there is clearly no understanding and agreement, because their opposition does not simply concern the value of this or that fact, but rather the yardstick itself, by

which all values are measured." Weber drew a line in the margin to highlight this passage. See Leo Strauss, *Natural Right and History*, pp. 68–69.

89. *PV*, p. 125; *GM*, Essay 3, no. 15.

90. *GM*, Essay 1, no. 16; *The Antichrist*, nos. 58–61.

91. *From Max Weber*, p. 394; *ES*, 3:1461.

92. *ES*, ibid.

93. *From Max Weber*, p. 394.

94. *PV*, p. 121.

95. Ibid., p. 125.

96. *GM*, Essay 3, nos. 20, 13–18.

97. *PV*, pp. 39–42. Compare *ES*, 3:1391, on solidarity, with *From Max Weber*, p. 335. Weber's critique of Bismarck laid special emphasis upon his policy toward trade unionism. Bismarck did not appreciate the link between union solidarity—an ethic of responsibility toward one's union brothers, exercised in industrial class conflict during peace—and solidarity in war, e.g., an ethic of responsibility exercised in conflict between nations. Corroboration for Weber's argument is supplied by Erich Eyck, who noted that the German workers voluntarily avoided military service under the Weimar Republic—despite the strength of the SDP in the government—thereby greatly strengthening the hold of conservatives in military affairs: *A History of the Weimar Republic*, 1:153.

98. *PV*, p. 120; *PS*, pp. 138–42.

99. *PV*, p. 120.

100. Ibid.

101. *The Protestant Ethic*, pp. 68–69, 109–12, 117–22, 232n66. Compare chap. 2, sec. 1, chap. 3, sec. 6, above.

102. *SV*, p. 149.

103. *PE*, pp. 21–23, 108, 117–27, 153–55, 224n30.

104. Ibid., p. 182; *PV*, p. 121.

105. *PV*, pp. 109–112, 114–15.

106. Ibid., pp. 120, 125.

107. For Weber's use of "master nation" (*Herrenvolk*), see *From Max Weber*, pp. 24, 391; *PS*, pp. 139–42, 429–30. Compare chap. 2, sec. 1, note 18, above.

108. *PS*, pp. 429–30.

109. *BGE*, no. 295; see also no. 39.

110. *PV*, pp. 119–20.

111. *BGE*, nos. 199, 212, 268, 284, 287.

112. *From Max Weber*, pp. 323–59.

113. Ibid., pp. 326, 336–40, 342–43, 353.

114. *SV*, p. 149.

115. *From Max Weber*, pp. 284–86, 326, 331, 336, 339–40, 342, 350–51, 355. Compare Simmel, *Schopenhauer und Nietzsche*, pp. 206–8.

116. *BGE*, no. 212. Compare no. 199.

117. *From Max Weber*, p. 355; *PE*, p. 182; *SV*, p. 156; *PV*, pp. 127–28. Talcott Parsons translates the phrase *Fachmenschen ohne Geist* as "specialists without spirit": *PE*, p. 182. *Geist* has an emphatically intellectual connotation; hence I render it here as "spirit" or "vision." Compare *RS* 1:204.

118. *SV*, pp. 135–36; *PV*, pp. 15–16.
119. *PV*, p. 123.
120. Ibid. Compare *The Religion of India*, pp. 144–46.
121. *PV*, pp. 123, 124.
122. Persius, *Satires*, 3, lines 71–72: "Learn whom God has ordered you to be, and in what part of human affairs you have been placed." See Jean-Jacques Rousseau, *Discourse on the Origins of Inequality*, pp. 97, 234n17.
123. See sec. 1. at notes 41–44, above.
124. Weber, *Gesammelte Aufsätze zur Soziologie und Sozialpolitik*, p. 420.
125. *PV*, pp. 115, 125.
126. Ibid., pp. 116–17. See Simmel, *Schopenhauer und Nietzsche*, p. 230, where Weber has written in the margin, "But that is just not Nietzsche's view! He was himself precisely on this point a German drill sergeant." Compare chap. 4, note 13, above.
127. *PV*, p. 126. Machiavelli does not use the word "soul" in *The Prince* or *The Discourses*.
128. Strauss, *Natural Right and History*, pp. 65–66.
129. *PV*, p. 127.
130. Compare chap. 4, secs. 5–8, above.
131. *BGE*, no. 212. See chap. 2, secs. 3–4, chap. 4, sec. 7, above.
132. See chap. 5, secs. 1, 3, 5, above.
133. *SV*, p. 149.
134. *PV*, p. 128. Although Maurice Merleau-Ponty grasped the importance of this "affirmation" in Weber, he makes the politician seem selfless: "The Crisis of the Understanding," pp. 209–10. Weber's ambivalent place in Merleau-Ponty's thought is clarified in Barry Cooper, *Merleau-Ponty and Marxism: From Terror to Reform*, pp. 110–13.
135. *SV*, p. 155.
136. *PV*, p. 125. The need for the psychic proletarianization of the campaign staff is particularly troubling in view of the quasi-religious cravings for a theodicy of suffering which Weber traced in modern mass politics; when Weber spoke of letting oneself in for a diabolical politics, he was not exaggerating. Merleau-Ponty seems far off the mark in describing Weber's political leader as "loving the political apparatus" ("The Crisis of Understanding," p. 210). He does not distinguish between the elevation of party rule (as in Lenin and Trotsky) and Weber's affirmation of demagogic party leaders, whose responsibility imposes a pathos of distance between them and the party apparatus. Hence the ravages of "partyness" as a new form of political conscience, documented by Lev Kopelev, are foreign to Weber's politics. See Kopelev, *To Be Preserved Forever*, pp. 11–14.
137. *PE*, pp. 224–25, note 30; *PV*, p. 115; *From Max Weber*, p. 391.
138. *From Max Weber*, p. 393.
139. See note 65, above. I have discussed Weber's regime politics from a somewhat different angle in "Doing without Liberalism: Weber's Regime Politics," pp. 393–96.
140. See chap. 4, sec. 1, chap. 5, sec. 2, chap. 6, sec. 2, above.

CHAPTER 7: NIHILISM AND THE LIMITS OF LEADERSHIP

1. Manuscript f.2, folio 139 from the Bodleian Library; quoted in Richard H. Cox, *Locke on War and Peace*, p. 193.

2. Paul B. Cook, *Academicians in Government from Roosevelt to Roosevelt*, pp. 44–93, 115–50; Ward E. Y. Elliott, *The Rise of Guardian Democracy: The Supreme Court's Role in Voting Rights Disputes, 1845–1969*, pp. 89–236; Steven A. Kesselman, *The Modernization of American Reform: Structures and Perceptions*, pp. 334–511.

3. See chap. 1, secs. 1–3, 5 (beginning), 6 (end), 7, above. Compare Harvey C. Mansfield, Jr., "The Media World and Democratic Representation"; James W. Ceaser, *Presidential Selection: Theory and Development*, pp. 170–303; Ceaser, *Reforming the Reforms: A Critical Analysis of the Presidential Selection Process*; Richard Hofstadter, *The Age of Reform: From Bryan to F.D.R.*, pp. 186–214; Bernard Crick, *The American Science of Politics: Its Origins and Conditions*, pp. 73–175; Kesselman, *The Modernization of American Reform*, ; Elliott, *The Rise of Guardian Democracy*, pp. 1–33, 55–113, 237–64; Cook, *Academicians in Government*, pp. 115–71.

4. See chap. 1, secs. 3, 7, above. See Donald J. Maletz, "The Neo-Conservatives and the Debate about Liberalism"; Norman Podhoretz, *Breaking Ranks: A Political Memoir*; Theodore H. White, *America in Search of Itself: The Making of the President, 1956–1980*; and Robert K. Faulkner, "Bickel's Constitution: The Problem of Moderate Liberalism," pp. 925–40.

5. The statements are Burke's, quoted in Leo Strauss, *Natural Right and History*, p. 306.

6. See Fred J. Evans, "Toward a Theory of Academic Liberalism," and chap. 1, secs. 3–6, above. As academics have turned away from the Lockean politics of progress, they have become increasingly hungry for commitment in a cause. This hunger is, of course, not cultivated only in academia: "The perspectives of the opinion leaders who participated in the study are rather different from those of the public. Church leaders, educators, philosophers, journalists, scientists, artists, jurists, writers, and community leaders stress many more new 'moral' imperatives than does the general public": Daniel Yankelovich, Amitai Etzioni, et al., *Moral Leadership in Government: A Public Agenda Foundation Report*, September 1976, p. 16.

7. See introduction; chap. 1, introduction; chap. 2, introduction, sec. 5; chap. 3, sec. 8; chap. 4, sec. 1, above. See also Mansfield, "The Media World and Democratic Representation"; Mansfield, "The American Election of 1980: Towards Constitutional Democracy?"; John Calhoun Merrill, *Existential Journalism*; James Neuchterlein, "Liberalism and Theodore H. White"; Thomas Sowell, "Media Smears: One Man's Experiences."

8. See chap. 4, sec. 1, above. See also David L. Norton, *Personal Destinies: A Philosophy of Ethical Individualism*, pp. 79–121; Marvin Zetterbaum, "Self and Subjectivity in Political Theory"; Alisdair MacIntyre, *After Virtue: A Study in Moral Theory*; Michael A. Mosher, "After Virtue: The 'Vices' of a Juridical Society."

9. The most recent popular celebration of the promise of liberal political economy is George Gilder's *Wealth and Poverty*. The superiority of evolved over planned cultural "wholes" is a theme of Burke's which was adopted by the German Historical

School. See Strauss, *Natural Right and History,* pp. 16–26, 303–16, 319–23, and chap. 1, sec. 5, above.

10. Woodrow Wilson, *Constitutional Government in the United States,* pp. 4–9, 12, 14–15, 22–23, 35–40, 49, 51–53. See Kent A. Kirwan, "Historicism and Statesmanship in the Reform Argument of Woodrow Wilson."

11. One of the curiosities of public policy has been the contradiction between the unwillingness of civil libertarians to support the doctrine of group libel in order to limit or punish injustices done through speech and their willingness to apply retroactive correctives after such injustices have been committed. Compare Michael D. Bayles, "Reparations to Wronged Groups," pp. 301–5, with Hadley Arkes, "Political Discourse and the Defamation of Groups", in *The Philosopher in the City: The Moral Dimensions of Urban Politics,* pp. 23–55. For an argument on behalf of affirmative action which relies heavily upon historicist doctrines, see William Chafe, "Affirmative Action," unpublished paper, Department of History, Duke University, 1981. See also George Sher, "Ancient Wrongs and Modern Rights."

12. See chap. 1, sec. 8; chap. 2, sec. 4; chap. 3, secs. 1, 7, 8; chap. 4, secs. 1–2, 8, above.

13. See chap. 2, sec. 4; chap. 3, sec. 6; chap. 4, secs. 2, 5–8, above.

14. As Maletz remarks, the left has been more inclined to see immanent nihilism in liberal modes and orders than to recognize virulent nihilism within the left: "The Neo-Conservatives and the Debate about Liberalism," pp. 31–32.

15. See chap. 2, secs. 2, 5; chap. 3, secs. 6–8; chap. 4, secs. 1, 8; chap. 5, secs. 1–2; chap. 6, secs. 2, 5, above.

16. See chap. 1, secs. 5–7; chap. 2, sec. 1; chap. 3, introduction; chap. 5, introduction and sec. 3, above. See also William Shapiro, "The Nietzschean Roots of Max Weber's Social Science," pp. 30–33, 51–65, 76–80, 147–50, and Stephen Turner and Regis A. Factor, *Max Weber and the Dispute over Reason and Values: A Study in Philosophy, Ethics, and Politics.*

17. See chap. 1, secs. 5–6; chap. 6, secs. 1, 4, above. On Weber's argument for the impossibility of political philosophy, see Strauss, *Natural Right and History,* pp. 36 ff.

18. See chap. 2, secs. 3–4; chap. 5, sec. 4, above.

19. See chap. 1, secs. 3, 5, 6; chap. 2, sec. 2, above.

20. See chap. 2, sec. 1 (end); chap. 5, secs. 1, 3; chap. 6, secs. 3–4, above.

21. See chap. 6, secs. 1, 4–5, above.

22. "Science as a Vocation," p. 153.

23. Ibid., p. 152; "Politics as a Vocation," pp. 117, 122–123, 125.

24. See chap. 2, secs. 1, 3; chap. 3, secs. 1, 6, above. Compare Eden, "Doing Without Liberalism: Weber's Regime Politics," pp. 380–85, 397–400. Wilhelm Hennis overlooks this problem in his effort to assimilate Weber into the great tradition of political philosophy: "Max Webers Fragestellung," pp. 277, 279.

25. See chap. 6, sec. 1, above.

26. See chap. 2, sec. 3; chap. 5, sec. 4; chap. 6, sec. 1, above. See Eden, "Doing Without Liberalism: Weber's Regime Politics," pp. 399–400; Hiram Caton, "World in Decay: Critiques of the Historiography of Progress"; Caton, "The Politics of Progress," chaps. 1, 4–6, 8.

27. See chap. 5, secs. 4–5; chap. 6, sec. 1, above. For a neo-Weberian history of

rationality without reference to the reasoning of the rationalists, consult Wolfgang Schluchter, *The Rise of Western Rationalism: Max Weber's Developmental History.* Schluchter's neglect of the historiographic problem of the rise of modern science (and of the causal role of philosophy) is instructive because he regards Weber's work as defective on other counts and because he has no particular animus against philosophy, having studied Weber with Dieter Henrich.

28. See Schluchter's essay on value neutrality and the ethic of responsibility, in Guenther Roth and Wolfgang Schluchter, *Max Weber's Vision of History: Ethics and Methods,* pp. 65–116. Also compare Hans-Martin Schmolz, "Das Dilemma der politischen Ethik bei Max Weber," pp. 476–95.

29. Weber's indirection would seem to be a more radical form of the indirection discovered by Hobbes and Machiavelli. See Harvey C. Mansfield, Jr., "Hobbes and the Science of Indirect Government," and Mansfield, "Machiavelli's Political Science," pp. 293, 305.

30. *PV,* pp. 118–24. Weber identifies the good man with the ethic of intentions, the politician with an ethic of consequences, though a genuine man who has the calling for politics would reconcile these two ethics or prove them complementary (pp. 127–28).

31. In place of the direct question we find the remarkably antiteleological question "What calling can politics fulfill *quite independently of its goals* within the total ethical economy of human conduct?" (*PV,* p. 117; emphasis added).

32. Thomas V. Baylis, "Collegial Leadership in Advanced Industrial Societies: The Relevance of the Swiss Experience," p. 34. See also Glenn D. Paige, *The Scientific Study of Political Leadership,* and Donald D. Searing, "Models and Images of Man and Society in Leadership Theory." Searing does not consider the possibility that "leadership" is itself a concept with a conceptual history or that in adopting it he has already ruled out significant alternatives; the choice he examines and attempts to supersede is between mechanistic and organic models (pp. 8–10, 26–31). For Wittgenstein's suggestive remarks, consult his *Philosophical Investigations,* nos. 104, 107, 115, 123, 140.

33. Dankwart A. Rustow, "Introduction" to *Philosophers and Kings: Studies in Leadership.* The title of this volume is misleading, since neither kings nor philosophers are discussed—unless one mistakes Mill the elder for a philosopher. For a more sustained attempt to reshape the study of politics as the study of leadership, see Robert C. Tucker, *Politics as Leadership.*

34. Joseph M. Bessette et al., "The Rise of the Rhetorical Presidency." For efforts to understand the presidency without giving way to the rhetorical fashion now dominant, consider Joseph M. Bessette and Jeffrey Tulis, eds., *The Presidency in the Constitutional Order;* Thomas S. Engeman, "Presidential Statesmanship and the Constitution: The Limits of Presidential Studies."

35. The phrase is from Walter Dean Burnham's fine article, "The Changing Shape of the American Political Universe." See Samuel H. Beer, "In Search of a New Public Philosophy," p. 5; Bruce A. Campbell and Richard J. Trilling, eds., *Realignment in American Politics: Toward a Theory,* pp. 3–21.

36. See chap. 1, sec. 1, above.

37. Donald R. Brand, "Progressivism and the New Deal"; Hofstadter, *The Age*

of Reform; Elliott, *The Rise of Guardian Democracy*; Martin Shapiro, "The Supreme Court: From Warren to Burger."

38. Wolfgang Müller-Lauter, in *Nietzsche-Studien* 10/11 (1982):31.

39. See chap. 2, sec. 5; chap. 4, sec. 1, above. Consider the very sanguine portrait of Nietzsche by a capable student of the psychologist Abraham Maslow: David L. Norton, *Personal Destinies: A Philosophy of Ethical Individualism*, pp. 79–94. Maletz remarks the influence in American politics and law of "the combination of Mill's libertarianism with a popularized interpretation of Freud (as for example in H. L. A. Hart, *Law, Liberty. and Morality*): "The Neo-Conservatives and the Debate about Liberalism," p. 43.

40. *KGW*, 6/1 title page: "A Book for All and None."

41. Werner J. Dannhauser, *Nietzsche's View of Socrates*; Harry Neumann, "Superman or Last Man? Nietzsche's Interpretation of Athens and Jerusalem"; Neumann, "Socrates and History: A Nietzschean Interpretation of Philosophy."

42. *SV*, p. 156.

43. See chap. 2, sec. 3, above. See also Weber, *PS*, p. 13; *SV*, pp. 148–49, 150–52; *PV*, pp. 127–28.

44. See chap. 2, sec. 3; chap. 3, sec. 6; chap. 5, sec. 4, above.

45. Erich Heller, *The Artist's Journey into the Interior and Other Essays*, p. 188.

46. John A. Hostetler, *Amish Society*.

47. Friedrich Wolters, *Stefan George und die Blätter für die Kunst*, p. 477. See also *From Max Weber*, p. 393, and Ernst Troeltsch, "Die Revolution in der Wissenschaft"; Stanley J. Antosik, *The Question of Elites: An Essay on the Cultural Elitism of Nietzsche, George and Hesse*.

48. Eden, "Doing Without Liberalism: Weber's Regime Politics." See chap. 2, secs. 2–3; chap. 4, sec. 3; chap. 5, sec. 2; chap. 6, secs. 1–2, above.

49. An echo of this policy still resonates in Tory politics. See Samuel H. Beer, *Modern British Politics: Parties and Pressure Groups in the Collectivist Age*, pp. 91–102. Compare Shakespeare's *Julius Caesar*, Act 1, Scene 1, lines 66–67.

50. Montesquieu, *The Spirit of the Laws*, bk. 19, chap. 27; Thomas L. Pangle, *Montesquieu's Philosophy of Liberalism: A Commentary on "The Spirit of the Laws,"* pp. 125–30, 145–60, 197–99.

51. *The Spirit of the Laws*, Preface and bk. 1, chap. 3.

52. William Stevenson, *A Man Called Intrepid: The Secret War*.

53. Leo Strauss, *Thoughts on Machiavelli*, pp. 198–99; Strauss, *On Tyranny*, pp. 22, 27, 190, 199. 226; Richard Kennington, "Descartes and Mastery of Nature," pp. 201–5.

54. Richard Rorty, "Philosophy in America Today," pp. 183–90, 198–200; Tibor R. Machan, "'Ein besserer und gescheiterer Mensch': Eine Wittgensteinsche Idee menschlicher Vortrefflichkeit?" pp. 359–64. Compare Ludwig Wittgenstein, *Tractatus Logico-Philosophicus*, 6.42–6.421 with 4.113 and 6.13. Consider also his remark in the "Lecture on Ethics" that "if a man could write a book on Ethics which really was a book on Ethics, this book would, with an explosion, destroy all the other books in the world" (p. 7). As the context makes clear, the books in question are scientific books. See Stanley Rosen, *Nihilism: A Philosophical Essay*, pp. xiii–xvii, 23–27, 119–39; Mark Blitz, *Heidegger's Being and Time and the Possibility of Political Philosophy*, pp. 13–15, 169–80, 210–20. Compare chap. 3, sec. 6, above.

55. Rosen, *Nihilism,* pp. xiii–xvii.

56. Martin Heidegger, "Nietzsches Wort, 'Gott ist Tot,'" p. 267. Some readers will doubtless object that Rawls has come forward on behalf of liberal political philosophy to defend reason against Nietzsche's claim. For several reasons I do not believe this objection can be sustained in the light of my preceding analysis of Nietzsche: it cannot be said that Rawls has understood or presented Nietzsche's claim as I have developed it. Rawls's comprehension of Nietzsche would have to be sufficient to sustain his contention that Nietzsche's doctrine is "teleological doctrine." On the grounds for doubting that Rawls defends the governing reason of modern liberal politics, see William A. Galston, "Defending Liberalism," pp. 621–22, 627–29, and Galston, "Moral Personality and Liberal Theory: John Rawls's 'Dewey Lectures,'" pp. 492–517.

57. *BGE,* no. 203. It is perhaps not surprising that Ortega y Gasset's students almost all became Falangists, despite his defense of the Spanish Republic but consistent with his teaching of Nietzsche. See Udo Rukser, *Nietzsche in der Hispania: Ein Beitrag zur hispanischen Kultur und Geistesgeschichte,* pp. 341–43. Compare Sheldon S. Wolin, "Hannah Arendt and the Ordinance of Time," pp. 104–5.

58. Harvey C. Mansfield, Jr., *The Spirit of Liberalism,* pp. 1–15; Joseph Cropsey, "The United States as Regime and the Sources of the American Way of Life," in Cropsey, *Political Philosophy and the Issues of Politics,* pp. 1–15.

59. Sheldon S. Wolin, "Max Weber: Legitimation, Method, and the Politics of Theory," pp. 402–4, 406, 416, 421–22; Hannah Arendt, *The Human Condition,* pp. 22–57, 175–235. Compare Benjamin I. Schwartz, "The Religion of Politics: Reflections on the Thought of Hannah Arendt."

60. "Only timely problems of a concrete inner-worldly conduct could emerge and demand answers. All other problems were precluded. One must fully realize the tremendous economy of psychic resources conditioned thereby, to assess the importance of this state of affairs. For Bismarck the exclusion of all metaphysical rumination and in its stead the psalter on his night table was one of the preconditions for conduct unbroken by philosophy": *Ancient Judaism,* p. 317.

61. On the self-forgetfulness of recent liberal thought, see Mansfield, *The Spirit of Liberalism,* pp. 89–114.

62. See chap. 2, secs. 2–3; chap. 5, sec. 2, above.

63. The development of Montesquieu's argument is made almost insultingly clear (as Nietzsche said of J. S. Mill) in Pangle, *Montesquieu's Philosophy of Liberalism: A Commentary on "The Spirit of the Laws,"* pp. 48–160. The arc of Montesquieu's argument is more cryptically brought out by Hamilton in *The Federalist,* No. 9.

64. See chap. 2, sec. 3, above, on Montaigne. Montesquieu, *The Spirit of the Laws,* bk. 12, chap. 2; bk. 20, "Invocation to the Muses"; bk. 25, chap. 13.

65. Tucker, *Politics as Leadership,* pp. 114–57. As the preceding analysis indicates, I think that Tucker's understanding of statesmanship would be more accurately formulated if he subjected the leadership idiom to critical scrutiny and abandoned it.

66. Gordon S. Wood's account of the "Whig Science of Politics" attempts to diminish the Whig interest in human nature to the level of a "common belief of the age" while abstracting their interest in "scientific principles about the historical process" from its foundation in scientific principles about human nature: *The Creation of the*

314 NOTES TO PAGES 240-44

American Republic, 1776–1787, p. 29. For a corrective, consult Caton, *The Politics of Progress.*

67. Harry V. Jaffa, *The Crisis of the House Divided: An Interpretation of the Lincoln-Douglas Debates,* pp. 275–301.

68. See chap. 1, secs. 7–8; chap. 2, secs. 3–4; chap. 3, secs. 6 and 8; chap. 4, entire, above.

69. Alexander M. Bickel, *The Morality of Consent,* p. 137.

70. See chap. 5, secs. 1–2; chap. 6, sec. 2, above.

71. Nietzsche, *Human, All-too-Human,* vol. 2, bk. 1, no. 480. See chap. 2, sec. 3, above.

72. See chap. 2, sec. 3, above. Compare David L. Schaefer, "Science and Skepticism in Montaigne's *Essays.*" The foundation of a permanent new civilization would have to be provided by an adequate biology disclosing a permanent human nature. See Hiram Caton, "Biosocial Science: Knowledge for Enlightened Leadership."

73. Consider Schaefer's application of Nietzsche's notion of transvaluation of values to Montaigne: "The Good, the Beautiful, and the Useful: Montaigne's Transvaluation of Values." See Pangle, *Montesquieu's Philosophy of Liberalism: A Commentary on "The Spirit of the Laws,"* pp. 162–64, 221–23, 243–59. The most sustained attempt to follow up Nietzsche's suggestions that Machiavelli was one of his kind is found in chapter 4 of Strauss's *Thoughts on Machiavelli,* pp. 232–52, 255, 265, 284–88, 291. See also these works by Harvey C. Mansfield, Jr.: "Machiavelli's Political Science," p. 305; "Party and Sect in Machiavelli's *Florentine Histories,*" pp. 219–26, 238, 244–46; 266; *Machiavelli's New Modes and Orders: A Study of the "Discourses on Livy,"* pp. 373–74. Compare chap. 4, sec. 2, above.

74. Gerd Günther Grau, "Sublimierter oder realisierter Wille zur Macht?" Some of the problems treated by Grau are covered in Jean Granier, *La problème de la vérité dans la philosophie de Nietzsche,* pp. 369–461, 557–602.

75. Grau refers to Wolfgang Müller-Lauter's study, *Nietzsche: Seine Philosophie der Gegensätze und die Gegensätze seiner Philosophie.* See Grau, ibid., pp. 223–24, 237–39, 244–47, 251–52. Grau does not have in view the articulation of Nietzsche's politics of rank order which we exhibited in chap. 4, secs. 2–8, above. It is not clear to me why Grau believes that to "translate" the Will to Power "into politics" "would denature" Nietzsche's project (p. 247).

76. Grau, *ibid.,* pp. 244, 246. Simmel does not speak of Nietzsche in terms of absolutism or pious cruelty, though he calls him "a fanatic for development": *Schopenhauer und Nietzsche,* p. 216.

77. It may be, as Harry Neumann has argued, that the precondition of ancient political philosophy was a form of political community that cannot be resuscitated today. If the preceding reasoning is sound, however, the permanent problems toward which Socrates directed his gaze preside no less over our affairs than over the classical polis or people. See Neumann, "Political Philosophy or Nihilist Science? Education's Only Important Question."

78. *The Laws of Plato,* trans. Thomas L. Pangle, Books 10–12, and pp. 496 ff.; Strauss, *On Tyranny,* pp. 198–226. See chap. 4, sec. 7, above.

79. *PV,* p. 117.

80. See chap. 5, introduction, above.

81. Compare Leo Strauss, *Thoughts on Machiavelli,* pp. 234–35, 237, 243–47, 249, 251–52, 254, 257–58, 265, 269, 290–92.

82. See chap. 6, sec. 3, above. In Weber's defense, it might be objected that the tests we have posed are improper tests of his practical prudence. A proper test would require a study of Weber's political writings; it would weigh his deeds and speeches, applying the criteria of rationality that Weber articulated sketchily in his methodological writings: *Methodology,* pp. 120–21, 124–25, 164–66; see also p. 21. Mommsen has attempted a critique along these lines in *Max Weber und die deutsche Politik, 1890–1920.* I would not deny the force of this objection, and for several reasons I believe that Mommsen's critique does not fully meet it. Mommsen's analysis suffers from three serious shortcomings. The first, as I have indicated, is due to its strength as a political biography: The analysis is so closely bound to the specifics of Wilhelmine politics as to defy application to other situations. The second (discussed in chap. 6, sec. 1, above) is that Mommsen's account obscures Weber's defense of limited government and liberal institutions, making that defense inapplicable to American politics. Third, Mommsen artificially limits the application of Weber's thought by historicizing it. Mommsen seems to hold that all thought is bound to historical context and that Weber's political thought in particular was uncritically determined by the prejudices of his age. As a result of this historicist dogma, Mommsen is eager to find Weber's politics outdated or superseded by events. This blunts the edge of his analysis by making Weber's present and future relevance obscure. For these reasons, Mommsen's account of the relation between domestic and foreign policy in Weber's politics needs to be reconsidered in the light of my remarks on Weber's domestic policy in chaps. 5 and 6.

In this study, I have implicitly distinguished between Weber's personal prudence and his doctrine or his interpretation of his prudence. I have assumed—not unreasonably—that it is Weber's doctrine rather than his precise example that is likely to influence American politics. But I will admit that the objection raised points to a limitation of my study. Weber's political writings are largely concerned with foreign policy. I have simplified my task by concentrating on what Machiavelli called "public counsel on domestic policy" (*Discourses on Livy,* bk. 1, chap. 1, end). Although I mentioned several reasons for expecting that Weber could be a formidable influence on American politics, I withheld what is probably the strongest reason. Weber unites two concerns that have traditionally been articulated in mutually estranged schools of American political thought and have worked at cross-purposes in American politics. Weber is unique in joining an argument for democratization and plebiscitary leadership with "the primacy of foreign policy" (Mommsen, *Weber und Politik,* pp. 85, 95, 205; "Zum Begriff der plebiszitären Führerdemokratie bei Max Weber"). In the United States, the reform movement made leadership selection through primaries a matter almost entirely for domestic policy (see Ceaser, *Presidential Selection,* pp. 170–353). A separate tradition that attempts to rationalize executive control over foreign policy has unfolded in almost complete isolation from the movement to reform electoral law and campaign practice (see I. M. Destler, *Presidents, Bureaucrats, and Foreign Policy: The Politics of Organizational Reform*). I believe that the considerations advanced in this study become more rather than less significant when one adds to them the urgent need to correlate the procedure for selecting presidents and senators with the functions they must perform once elected, foreign policy being the function for which American politicians are commonly least prepared.

Bisherjian, Richard J. *A Public Philosophy Reader.* New Rochelle, N.Y.: Arlington House, 1978.

Björkman, James Warner. "Professionalism in the Welfare State: Sociological Savior or Political Pariah?" *European Journal of Political Research* 10 (1982):407–28.

Blitz, Mark. *Heidegger's* Being and Time *and the Possibility of Political Philosophy.* Ithaca: Cornell University Press, 1981.

_____. "An Introduction to the Reading of Plato's *Laches.*" *Interpretation* 5 (Winter 1975):185–225.

Böhme, Gernot, et al. *Experimentielle Philosophie: Ursprünge autonomer Wissenschaftsentwicklung.* Frankfurt am Main: Suhrkamp, 1977.

Boutry, G.-A. (President des Laboratoires et de physique appliquée.) *La connaissance et la puissance: essai sur l'envers de la recherche.* Paris: Editions Albin Michel, 1974.

Bragdon, Henry W. *Woodrow Wilson: The Academic Years.* Cambridge: Harvard University Press, 1967.

Brand, Donald R. "Progressivism and the New Deal." Paper presented at the annual meeting of the American Political Science Association, Denver, Colorado, September 1982.

Braybrooke, David. "Work: A Cultural Ideal Ever More in Jeopardy." *Midwest Studies in Philosophy* 7 (1982):321–41.

Brecht, Arnold. *The Political Education of Arnold Brecht: An Autobiography, 1884–1970.* Princeton: Princeton University Press, 1970.

_____. *Political Theory: The Foundations of Twentieth Century Political Thought.* Princeton: Princeton University Press, 1959.

Brower, Daniel R. *Training the Nihilists: Education and Radicalism in Tsarist Russia.* Ithaca: Cornell University Press, 1975.

Bruell, Christopher. "Thucydides' View of Athenian Imperialism." *American Political Science Review* 67 (March 1974):11–17.

Bruun, Hans Henrik. *Science, Values, and Politics in Max Weber's Methodology.* Copenhagen: Muunksgaard, 1972.

Bullock, Alan. *Hitler: A Study in Tyranny.* New York: Harper and Row, 1962.

Burnham, Walter Dean. "The Changing Shape of the American Political Universe." *American Political Science Review* 59 (March 1964):7–28.

Butterworth, Charles E. "Frantz Fanon and Human Dignity." *Political Science Reviewer* 10 (1980):257–327.

Campbell, Bruce A., and Trilling, Richard J., eds. *Realignment in American Politics: Toward a Theory.* Austin: University of Texas Press, 1979.

Caton, Hiram. "Biosocial Science: Knowledge for Enlightened Leadership." Paper presented to the annual meeting of the American Political Science Association, Denver, Colorado, September 1982.

_____. "Marx's Sublation of Philosophy into Praxis." *Review of Metaphysics* 26 (December 1972):233–59.

_____. "On the Basis of Hobbes's Political Philosophy." *Political Studies* 22 (1974):414–31.

_____. *The Origin of Subjectivity: An Essay on Descartes.* New Haven: Yale University Press, 1973.

_____. "Toward a Diagnosis of Progress." *Independent Journal of Philosophy* 5 (1983): in press.

_____. "World in Decay: Critiques of the Historiography of Progress." *Canadian Journal of Political and Social Theory* (1983): in press.

Ceaser, James W. "Direct Participation in Politics." In *The Power to Govern: Assessing Reform in the United States,* edited by Richard M. Pious. New York: The Academy of Political Science, 1981.

_____. "Political Change and Party Reform." In *Political Parties in the Eighties,* edited by Robert A. Goldwin, pp. 97–115. Washington: American Enterprise Institute, 1980.

_____. *Presidential Selection: Theory and Development.* Princeton: Princeton University Press, 1979.

_____. *Reforming the Reforms: A Critical Analysis of the Presidential Selection Process.* Cambridge, Mass.: Ballinger Publishing Co., 1982.

Chagall, David. *The New Kingmakers: An Inside Look at the Powerful Men behind America's Political Campaigns.* New York: Harcourt Brace Jovanovich, 1981.

Clor, Harry. "Woodrow Wilson." In *American Political Thought: The Philosophical Dimension of American Statesmanship,* edited by Morton J. Frisch and Richard A. Stevens, pp. 191–218. New York: Scribner's, 1971.

Cohn, Jonas. "Die Erkenntnis der Werte und das Vorrecht der Bejahung. Betrachtungen, angeknüpft an Max Webers Lehre von der Wertfreiheit der Wissenschaft." *Logos* 10 (1921–22):195–226.

Coles, Robert. "The Politics of Ressentiment." *The New Republic,* August 2, 1982, pp. 32–34.

Collins, John. "Locke and Burke on Representative Government." Paper presented at the annual meeting of the American Political Science Association, New York City, September 1981.

Commager, Henry Steele. *The Empire of Reason: How Europe Imagined and America Realized the Enlightenment.* Garden City, N.Y.: Anchor, 1977.

Cook, Paul B. *Academicians in Government from Roosevelt to Roosevelt.* New York: Garland, 1982.

Cooper, Barry. *Merleau-Ponty and Marxism: From Terror to Reform.* Toronto: University of Toronto Press, 1979.

Cox, Richard H. *Locke on War and Peace.* Oxford: Clarendon Press, 1960.

Crick, Bernard. *The American Science of Politics: Its Origins and Conditions.* Berkeley: University of California Press, 1959.

Cropsey, Joseph. *Political Philosophy and the Issues of Politics.* Chicago: University of Chicago Press, 1977.

Crotty, William J. *Political Reform and the American Experiment.* New York: Thomas Y. Crowell, 1977.

Dahl, Robert A. *Polyarchy: Participation and Opposition.* New Haven: Yale University Press, 1971.

_____, ed. *Regimes and Oppositions.* New Haven: Yale University Press, 1973.

Dannhauser, Werner J. "Nietzsche in his Letters." *Commentary* 48 (December 1969):86–93.

_____. *Nietzsche's View of Socrates.* Ithaca: Cornell University Press, 1974.

_____. "The Trivialization of Friedrich Nietzsche." *The American Spectator* 15 (May 1982):7–13.

Descartes, René. *Œuvres de Descartes*. Edited by Victor Cousin. 11 vols. Paris: Levrault, 1824.

Destler, I. M. *Presidents, Bureaucrats, and Foreign Policy: The Politics of Organizational Reform*. Princeton: Princeton University Press, 1974.

Diamond, Martin. "The Federalist." In *American Political Thought: The Philosophical Dimensions of American Statesmanship*, edited by Morton J. Frisch and Richard A. Stevens, pp. 51–70. New York: Scribner's, 1971.

_____. "Teaching about Politics as a Vocation." In *The Ethics of Teaching and Scientific Research*, edited by Sidney Hook et al., pp. 3–22. Buffalo: Prometheus Books, 1977.

Durkheim, Emile. *Durkheim's Essays on Morals and Education*. Edited by W. S. F. Pickering. Translated by H. L. Sutcliffe. London: Routledge and Kegan Paul, 1979.

_____. *Professional Ethics and Civic Morals*. Translated by Cornelia Brookfield. London: Routledge and Kegan Paul, 1957.

Eden, Robert. "Bad Conscience for a Nietzschean Age: Weber's Calling for Science." *Review of Politics* 45 (1983): in press.

_____. "Doing Without Liberalism: Weber's Regime Politics." *Political Theory* 10 (August 1982):379–407.

_____. "Political Leadership and Philosophic Praxis: A Study of Weber and Nietzsche." Ph.D. dissertation, Harvard University, 1974.

Elkin, Stephen L. "State and Regime in the American Republic." Paper presented at the annual meeting of the American Political Science Assocation, New York City, September 1981.

Elliott, Ward E. Y. *The Rise of Guardian Democracy: The Supreme Court's Role in Voting Rights Disputes, 1845–1969*. Cambridge, Mass.: Harvard University Press, 1974.

Engeman, Thomas S. "Presidential Statesmanship and the Constitution: The Limits of Presidential Studies." *The Review of Politics* 44 (April 1982):266–81.

Erler, Edward J. "Equal Protection and Personal Rights: The Regime of the 'Discrete and Insular Minority.'" *Georgia Law Review* 16 (Winter 1982):407–44.

_____. "The Problem of the Public Good in *The Federalist*." *Polity* 13 (Summer 1981):650–67.

_____. "Statement on the Voting Rights Act for the Senate Committee on the Judiciary Subcommittee on the Constitution, 28 January 1982."

_____. "The Supreme Court and Equality: A Case Study in Judicial Statesmanship." Manuscript, Department of Political Science, San Bernardino State University, San Bernardino, California.

Escobar, Roberto. *Nietzsche e la filosofia politica del 19 secolo*. Milan: Formichiere, 1978.

Evans, Fred J. "Toward a Theory of Academic Liberalism." *Journal of Politics* 42 (November 1980):993–1030.

Evans, Rowland, and Robert Novak. *The Reagan Revolution: An Inside Look at the Transformation of the United States Government*. New York: Dutton, 1981.

Everson, David H. *Public Opinion and Interest Groups in American Politics*. New York: Franklin Watts, 1982.

Eyck, Erich. *A History of the Weimar Republic*. 2 vols. Translated by Harlan P.

Hanson and Robert G. L. Waite. Cambridge, Mass.: Harvard University Press, 1967.

Factor, Regis A. "The Notion of 'Leader' in the Writings of Stefan George." Paper presented to the annual meeting of the Western Association of German Studies, October 1981.

_____, and Stephen P. Turner. "The Limits of Reason and Some Limitations of Weber's Morality." *Human Studies* 2 (1979):301–4.

_____, and Stephen P. Turner. "Objective Possibility and Adequate Causation in Weber's Methodological Writings." *Sociological Review* 29 (February 1981): 5–28.

_____, and Stephen P. Turner. "Weber, Morgenthau, and the Moral Basis of Foreign Policy." Paper presented at the annual meeting of the Walter Bagehot Council, 1978.

_____, and Stephen P. Turner. "Weber's Defenders in Weimar." Paper presented to the annual meeting of the Southern Political Science Association, March 1978.

_____, and Stephen P. Turner. "Weber's Influence in Weimar Germany." *Journal of the History of the Behavioral Sciences* 18 (1982):147–56.

Faulkner, Robert K. "Bickel's Constitution: The Problem of Moderate Liberalism." *American Political Science Review* 72 (1978):925–40.

_____. "Empire Humane and Economic: Bacon, Machiavelli, and the Politics of Progress." Paper presented at the annual meeting of the Northeastern Political Science Assocation, Newark, N.J., November 1981.

_____. "John Marshall." In *American Political Thought: The Philosophic Dimensions of American Statesmanship,* edited by Morton J. Frisch and Richard G. Stevens, pp. 71–98. New York: Scribner's, 1971.

Fehrenbacher, Don Edward. *The Dred Scott Case: Its Significance in American Law and Politics.* New York: Oxford University Press, 1978.

Fischer, Kuno. *Francis Bacon: Realistic Philosophy and its Age.* Translated by John Oxenford. London: Brown, Green, Longmans & Roberts, 1857.

_____. *Franz Bacon von Verulam: Realistische Philosophie und seine Zeitalter.* Leipzig: F.A. Brockhaus, 1856.

_____. *Geschichte der neuern Philosophie Bd. 10. Francis Bacon und seine Schule. Entwicklungsgeschichte der Erfahrungsphilosophie.* 3d ed. Heidelberg: C. Winter, 1904.

Fischer, Kurt Rudolph. "Nazism as a Nietzschean Experiment." *Nietzsche-Studien* 6 (1977):116–22.

Flaumenhaft, Harvey. "Hamilton's Administrative Republic and the American Presidency." In *The Presidency in the Constitutional Order,* edited by Joseph M. Bessette and Jeffrey Tulis, pp. 65–112. Baton Rouge: Louisiana State University Press, 1981.

Fleischmann, Eugène. "De Weber à Nietzsche." *Archives européennes sociologiques* 5 (1964):190–238.

Fogt, Helmut. "Max Weber und die deutsche Soziologie der Weimarer Republik: Aussenseiter oder Gründervater?" In *Soziologie in Deutschland und Österreich, 1918–1945: Materialien zur Entwicklung, Emigration und Wirkungsgeschichte,* edited by M. Rainer Lepsius, pp. 245–61. Cologne: Westdeutscher Verlag, 1981.

Forman, Paul. *Weimar Culture, Causality, and Quantum Theory, 1918–1927.* Historical Studies in the Physical Sciences, no. 3, edited by R. McCormach. Philadelphia: University of Pennsylvania Press, 1971.

Fox, Harrison W., Jr., and Susan Webb Hammond. *Congressional Staffs: The Invisible Force in American Lawmaking*. New York: The Free Press, 1977.

Frankel, Charles. "Facts, Values, and Responsible Choice." In *The Ethics of Teaching and Scientific Research,* edited by Sidney Hook et al., pp. 23–28. Buffalo: Prometheus Books, 1977.

_____. *The Faith of Reason: The Idea of Progress in the French Enlightenment*. New York: King's Crown Press, 1948.

Friedman, Kathi V. *Legitimation of Social Rights and the Western Welfare State: A Weberian Perspective*. Chapel Hill: University of North Carolina Press, 1981.

Friedrich, Carl Joachim. "The Development of the Executive Power in Germany." *American Political Science Review* 27 (1933):185–203.

Galston, William A. "Aristotelian Morality and Liberal Society: A Critique of Alisdair MacIntyre's *After Virtue.*" Paper presented at the annual meeting of the American Political Science Association, Denver, Colorado, September 1982.

_____. "Defending Liberalism." *American Political Science Review* 76 (September 1982):621–29.

_____. *Kant and the Problem of History*. Chicago: University of Chicago Press, 1975.

_____. "Moral Personality and Liberal Theory: John Rawls's 'Dewey Lectures.'" *Political Theory* 10 (November 1982):492–519.

Gay, Peter. *The Party of Humanity: Essays in the French Enlightenment*. New York: Knopf, 1964.

Gilbert, Alan. "Social Science and the Common Good in Weber and Lenin." Paper presented at the annual meeting of the American Political Science Association, New York City, September 1981.

Gilder, George. *Wealth and Poverty*. New York: Basic Books, 1981.

Gillespie, Charles Coulton. *Science and Polity in France at the End of the Old Regime*. Princeton: Princeton University Press, 1980.

Glicksberg, Charles Irving. *The Literature of Nihilism*. Lewisburg: Bucknell University Press, 1975.

Goethe, Johann Wolfgang von. *Gedenkausgabe der Werke, Briefe und Gespräche*. Edited by Ernst Beutler. Zürich: Artemis Verlag, 1948–54.

Goyard-Fabre, Simone. *Nietzsche et la question politique*. Paris: Sirey, 1977.

Granier, Jean. *Le Problème de la vérité dans la philosophie de Nietzsche*. Paris: Editions du Seuil, 1966.

Grant, George Parkin. "Nietzsche and the Ancients: Philosophy and Scholarship." *Dionysius* 3 (December 1979):5–16.

Grau, Gerd Günter. "Sublimierter oder realisierter Wille zur Macht?" *Nietzsche-Studien* 10–11 (1982):222–53.

Graubard, Stephen R., ed. *Philosophers and Kings: Studies in Leadership*. Introduction by Dankwart A. Rustow. *Daedalus* (Summer 1968).

Grenier, Richard. "Bolshevism for the 80's." *Commentary* 73 (March 1982):56–63.

_____. "Why Herzog Differs." *Commentary* 74 (December 1982):59–67.

Gruner, Rolf. *Theory and Power: On the Character of Modern Sciences*. Amsterdam: B.R. Gruner Verlag, 1977.

Guerlac, Henry. "Vauban: The Impact of Science on War." In *Essays and Papers in the History of Modern Science,* pp. 413–39. Baltimore: Johns Hopkins University Press, 1977.

Gundolf, Ernst, and Kurt Hildebrandt. *Nietzsche als Richter unsrer Zeit.* Breslau: Ferdinand Hirt, 1923.

Gyory, Bruce N., and Thomas E. Riley. "Presidential Leadership and the New Progressivism: The Anderson Candidacy." *Presidential Studies Quarterly* 10 (Summer 1980):492–96.

Hamilton, Alexander, et al. *The Federalist.* Edited by Benjamin F. Wright. Cambridge, Mass.: Harvard University Press, 1966.

Hammerton, Max. *Science under Siege.* Kendal, England: University of Newcastle upon Tyne, 1974.

Hart, H. L. A. *Law, Liberty, and Morality.* Stanford, Calif.: Stanford University Press, 1963.

Hartz, Louis. *The Liberal Tradition in America.* New York: Harcourt Brace Jovanovich, 1955.

Hayman, Ronald. *Nietzsche: A Critical Life.* New York: Oxford University Press, 1980.

Heatherly, Charles L., ed. *Mandate for Leadership.* Washington: Heritage Foundation, 1981.

Heclo, Hugh. "Issue Networks and the Executive Establishment." In *The New American Political System,* edited by Anthony King, pp. 87–124. Washington: American Enterprise Institute, 1976.

————, and Lester M. Salamon. *The Illusion of Presidential Government.* Boulder, Colo.: Westview Press, 1981.

Hegel, G. W. F. *Lectures on the History of Philosophy.* Edited and translated by E. S. Haldane and Frances H. Simson. 3 vols. London: Routledge and Kegan Paul, 1955.

————. *The Phenomenology of Mind.* Translated by J. B. Baillie. 2d ed. London: Allen and Unwin, 1949.

————. *The Philosophy of Right.* Translated by T. M. Knox. Oxford: Oxford University Press, 1952.

Heidegger, Martin. *Being and Time.* Translated by John Macquarrie and Edward Robinson. New York: Harper and Row, 1962.

————. "Brief über den 'Humanismus.'" *Wegmarken,* pp. 145–94. Frankfurt am Main: Klostermann, 1967.

————. *Der Europäische Nihilismus.* Pfullingen: Neske, 1967.

————. *Introduction to Metaphysics.* Garden City, N.Y.: Anchor, 1961.

————. *Nietzsche.* 2 vols. Pfullingen: Neske, 1961.

————. "Nietzsches Wort 'Gott ist tot.'" *Holzwege,* pp. 209–67. Frankfurt am Main: Klostermann, 1977.

————. "Wer ist Nietzsches Zarathustra?" *Vorträge und Aufsätze,* pp. 101–26. Pfullingen: Neske, 1954.

————. *What Is Called Thinking?* New York: Harper and Row, 1972.

Heidemann, Ingeborg. "Der Antagonismus der Ideale und das Problem der Sinneinheit in Nietzsches Entwurf der Moralkritik von 1886 und 1887." *Kant-Studien* 62 (1971):427–45.

_____. "Nietzsches Kritik der Metaphysik." *Kant-Studien* 53 (1962):507–43.

_____. "Nietzsches Kritik der Moral." *Nietzsche-Studien* 1 (1972):95–137.

Heller, Erich. *The Artist's Journey into the Interior and Other Essays.* New York: Vintage, 1968.

Heller, Peter. *Dialectics and Nihilism: Essays on Lessing, Nietzsche, Mann and Kafka.* Amherst: University of Massachusetts Press, 1966.

Hennis, Wilhelm. "Max Webers Fragestellung." *Zeitschrift für Politik* 29 (August 1982):241–81.

Henrich, Dieter. *Die Einheit der Wissenschaftslehre Max Webers.* Tübingen: J.C.B. Mohr, 1952.

Hermens, F. A. *A Study of Proportional Representation.* Notre Dame, Ind.: Review of Politics, 1945.

Herschfeld, John Milton. *The Academie Royale des Sciences 1666–1683.* New York: Arno Press, 1981.

Hiskes, Richard P. "Science and Technology Policy Making in a Democratic Society." Paper presented to the annual meeting of the American Political Science Association, Denver, Colorado, September 1982.

Hobbes, Thomas. *The English Works of Thomas Hobbes of Malmesbury.* Edited by William Molesworth. 11 vols. London: J. Bohn, 1839–1845. Reprinted Aalen, Germany: Scientia, 1966.

_____. *Leviathan.* Edited by C. B. Macpherson. Baltimore: Penguin Books, 1968.

Hof, Walter. *Der Weg zum heroischen Realismus: Pessimismus und Nihilismus in der deutschen Literatur von Hamerling bis Benn.* Bebenhausen: Rotsch, 1974.

Hofstadter, Richard. *The Age of Reform: From Bryan to F. D. R.* New York: Vintage, 1955.

_____. *The American Political Tradition.* New York: Vintage, 1973.

Hohn, Hans Peter. *Die metaphysische und anthropologische Voraussetzungen der Politik bei Friedrich Nietzsche.* Inaugural dissertation, University of Bonn, 1959.

Hollowell, John. *Fact and Fiction: The New Journalism and the Nonfiction Novel.* Chapel Hill: University of North Carolina Press, 1977.

Holz, Hans Heinz. *Die abenteurliche Rebellion. Bürgerliche Protestbewegungen in der Philosophie: Stirner, Nietzsche, Sartre, Marcuse, Neue Linke.* Darmstadt: Luchterhand, 1976.

Holzner, Burkart, and John H. Marx. *Knowledge Application: The Knowledge System in Society.* Boston: Allyn and Bacon, 1979.

Honigsheim, Paul. *On Max Weber.* Translated by Joan Rytina. New York: Free Press, 1968.

Hostetler, John A. *Amish Society.* Baltimore: Johns Hopkins University Press, 1968.

Hübner, Kurt, et al. *Die politische Herausforderung der Wissenschaft: gegen eine ideologisch verplante Forschung.* Hamburg: Hoffmann und Campe, 1976.

Hufnagel, Gerhard. *Kritik als Beruf: der kritische Gehalt im Werk Max Webers.* Frankfurt am Main: Verlag Ullstein, 1971.

Jaffa, Harry V. *The Crisis of the House Divided: An Interpretation of the Lincoln-Douglas Debates.* Seattle: University of Washington Press, 1973.

_____. "Expediency and Morality in the Lincoln-Douglas Debates." *The Anchor Review* 2 (1957):177–204.

Jaspers, Karl. *Nietzsche: An Introduction to the Understanding of His Philosophical Activity.* Translated by Charles F. Wallraff and Frederick J. Schmitz. Chicago: Regnery, 1965.

_____. *Three Essays: Leonardo, Descartes, Max Weber.* Translated by Ralph Mann-heim. New York: Harcourt Brace Jovanovich, 1964.

Jensen, Pamela K. "Nietzsche and Liberation: The Prelude to a Philosophy of the Future." *Interpretation* 6 (May 1977):79–106.

Jevons, F. R. *Knowledge and Power.* Canberra: The Australian National University Advisory Committee on Science and Technology Research, 1977.

Jones, Charles O. "Can Our Parties Survive Our Politics?" In *The Role of the Legislature in Western Democracies,* edited by Norman J. Ornstein. Washington: American Enterprise Institute, 1981.

Jouffroy, Alain. *De l'Individualisme revolutionnaire.* Paris: Union générale d'éditions, 1975.

Kallen, Horace M. *Cultural Pluralism and the American Idea: An Essay in Social Philosophy.* Philadelphia: University of Pennsylvania Press, 1956.

Kant, Immanuel. *Critique of Pure Reason.* Translated by Norman Kemp Smith. New York: St. Martin's, 1965.

Kantorowicz, Ernst. *Frederick the Second, 1194–1250.* Translated by E. O. Lorimer. London: Constable and Co., 1931.

Kargon, Robert H. *Science in Victorian Manchester: Enterprise and Expertise.* Baltimore: Johns Hopkins University Press, 1977.

Kaufmann, Walter. *Nietzsche: Philosopher, Psychologist, Antichrist.* Cleveland: Meridian, 1964.

Kaulbach, Friedrich. *Nietzsches Idee einer Experimentalphilosophie.* Cologne: Bohlan Verlag, 1980.

_____. "Nietzsches Interpretation der Natur." *Nietzsche-Studien* 10–11 (1982): 442–64.

Keech, William R., and Donald R. Matthews. *The Party's Choice.* Washington: The Brookings Institution, 1976.

Kennington, Richard. "Descartes and Mastery of Nature." In *Organism, Medicine, and Metaphysics,* edited by S. F. Spicker. Dordrecht: D. Reidel, 1978.

_____. "Strauss's Natural Right and History." *Review of Metaphysics* 35 (September 1981):57–86.

Kesselman, Steven A. *The Modernization of American Reform: Structures and Perceptions.* New York: Garland, 1979.

Kirchheimer, Otto. *Political Justice: The Use of Legal Procedure for Political Ends.* Princeton: Princeton University Press, 1961.

Kirk, H. David. *The Friendly Perversion. Quakers as Reconcilers: Good People and Dirty Work.* New York: Americans for a Safe Israel, 1979.

Kirwan, Kent A. "The Crisis of Identity in Public Administration: Woodrow Wilson." *Polity* 9 (Spring 1977):321–43.

_____. "Historicism and Statesmanship in the Reform Argument of Woodrow Wilson." *Interpretation* 9 (September 1981):339–51.

Klein, Jacob. "Phenomenology and the History of Science." In *Philosophical Essays in Memory of Edmund Husserl,* edited by Marvin Farber, pp. 143–63. Cambridge, Mass.: Harvard University Press, 1940.

Klossowski, Pierre. *Nietzsche et le cercle vicieux.* Paris: Mercure de France, 1975.

Knoke, David, and James R. Wood. *Organized for Action: Commitment in Voluntary Organizations.* New Brunswick, N.J.: Rutgers University Press, 1981.

Kocka, Jürgen. "Kontroversen über Max Weber." *Neue politische Literatur* 21 (1976):281–301.

Koellreutter, Otto. "Die staatspolitischen Anschauungen Max Webers und Oswald Spenglers." *Zeitschrift für Politik* 14 (1924):481–500.

Kolinsky, Eva. *Engagiertes Expressionismus: Politik und Literatur zwischen Weltkrieg und Weimarer Republik.* Stuttgart: Poeschel und Metzler, 1970.

König, René, and Johannes Winckelmann, eds. *Max Weber zum Gedächtnis.* Cologne: Westdeutscher Verlag, 1963.

Kopolev, Lev. *To Be Preserved Forever.* Translated by Anthony Austin. Philadelphia: J.B. Lippincott, 1977.

Kraft, Joseph. "The Imperial Media." *Commentary* 71 (May 1981):36–47.

Kristol, Irving. "Capitalism, Socialism, and Nihilism." *The Public Interest* 31 (Spring 1973):3–16.

Kropotkin, P. A. *Selected Writings on Anarchism and Revolution.* Edited and with an Introduction by Martin A. Miller. Cambridge, Mass.: M.I.T. Press, 1970.

Krummel, Richard Frank. *Nietzsche und der deutsche Geist. Ausbreitung und Wirkung des Nietzscheschen Werkes im deutschen Sprachraum bis zum Todesjahr des Philosophen: Ein Schrifttumsverzeichnis der Jahre 1867–1900.* New York: De Gruyter, 1974.

Künzler, Gottfried. "Unbekannte Quellen der Religionssoziologie Max Webers." *Zeitschrift für Soziologie* 8 (August 1978):215–27.

Lachterman, David R. "Descartes and the Philosophy of History." *Independent Journal of Philosophy* 5 (1983), in press.

Lakoff, Sanford A., ed. *Knowledge and Power: Essays on Science and Government.* New York: Free Press, 1966.

Lampert, Laurence. "The End of *Thus Spoke Zarathustra*: Understanding Part 4." Paper presented at the annual meeting of the American Political Science Association, New York City, September 1981.

Lane, Ann Marie. "Nietzsche in Russian Thought, 1890–1917." Ph.D. dissertation, University of Wisconsin, Madison, 1976.

Lange, Frederick A. *The History of Materialism.* Translated by Ernest Chester Thomas. New York: Arno Press, 1974. Reprint of the 1879–81 edition.

Lehnen, Robert G. *American Institutions, Political Opinion, and Public Policy.* Hinsdale, Ill.: Dryden, 1976.

Leibnitz, Heinz Maier. *An der Grenze zum Neuen: Rollenverteilung zwischen Forschern und Politikern in der Gesellschaft.* Zürich: Edition Interfrom AG, 1977.

Lerner, Ralph. "Commerce and Character: The Anglo-American as New-Model Man." *William and Mary Quarterly* 36 (January 1979):3–26.

Lincoln, Abraham. *The Collected Works of Abraham Lincoln.* Edited by Roy P. Basler. 9 vols. New Brunswick, N.J.: Rutgers University Press, 1953.

Lindenlaub, Dieter. *Richtungskämpfe im Verein für Sozialpolitik. Vierteljahrschrift für Sozial- und Wirtschaftsgeschichte,* Beiheft 52–53. Wiesbaden, 1967.

Lomax, John H. "Nietzsche's New Nobility and the Eternal Return in *Beyond Good and Evil*: A Proemium." Manuscript, Department of Political Science, Memphis State University, Memphis, Tennessee.

Lowi, Theodore J. *The End of Liberalism: The Second Republic of the United States.* 2d ed. New York: W.W. Norton, 1979.

Löwith, Karl. "Die Entzauberung der Welt durch Wissenschaft." *Merkur* 18 (June 1964):501–19.

_____. "Max Weber und Karl Marx." In *Gesammelte Abhandlungen: Zur Kritik der geschichtlichen Existenz*, pp. 1–67. Stuttgart: W. Kohlhammer Verlag, 1960.

_____. *Nature, History, and Existentialism*. Evanston, Ill.: Northwestern University Press, 1966.

_____. "Nietzsches Vollendung des Atheismus." In *Nietzsche: Werk und Wirkungen*, edited by Hans Steffen, pp. 7–18. Göttingen: Vandenhoeck und Ruprecht, 1971.

Lukács, Georg. *Die Zerstörung der Vernunft*. 2d ed. Berlin: Luchterhand, 1962.

Lukes, Stephen. *Individualism*. Oxford: Blackwell, 1973.

Lyons, William James. "Science in an Unfriendly World." In *Science in America: Historical Selections*, edited by John C. Burnham, pp. 377–84. New York: Holt, Rinehart and Winston, 1971.

McGinniss, Joe. *The Selling of the President, 1968*. New York: Trident Press, 1969.

Machan, Tibor R. "'Ein besserer und gescheiterer Mensch': Eine Wittgensteinsche Idee menschlicher Vortrefflichkeit?" In *Ethics: Foundations, Problems, and Applications. Proceedings of the Fifth International Wittgenstein Symposium*, edited by Edgar Morscher and Rudolf Stranzinger, pp. 359–64. Vienna: Holder-Pichler-Tempsky, 1981.

Machiavelli, Niccolò. *The Discourses*. Edited by Bernard Crick. Baltimore: Penguin Books, 1970.

_____. *The History of Florence*. Vol. 3 of *Machiavelli: The Chief Works and Others*. Translated by Alan Gilbert. Durham, N.C.: Duke University Press, 1965.

_____. *The Prince*. Translated and edited by Mark Musa. New York: St. Martin's, 1964.

MacIntyre, Alisdair. *After Virtue: A Study in Moral Theory*. Notre Dame, Ind.: University of Notre Dame Press, 1981.

Macpherson, C. B. *The Political Theory of Possessive Individualism: Hobbes to Locke*. Oxford: Clarendon, 1962.

McWilliams, Wilson Carey. "Democracy and the Citizen: Community, Dignity, and the Crisis of Contemporary Politics in America." In *How Democratic is the Constitution?*, edited by Robert A. Goldwin and William A. Schambra, pp. 79–101. Washington: American Enterprise Institute, 1980.

_____. *The Idea of Fraternity in America*. Berkeley: University of California Press, 1973.

Makielski, S. J., Jr. *Beleaguered Minorities: Cultural Politics in America*. San Francisco: W.H. Freeman, 1973.

Malbin, Michael J., ed. *Parties, Interest Groups, and Campaign Finance Laws*. Washington: American Enterprise Institute, 1980.

_____.*Unelected Representatives*. New York: Basic Books, 1980.

Maletz, Donald J. "An Introduction to the 'Introduction' to Hegel's *Philosophy of Right*." Paper presented to the annual meeting of the American Political Science Association, New York City, September 1981.

_____. "The Meaning of 'Will' in Hegel's *Philosophy of Right*." Paper presented at the annual meeting of the American Political Science Association, Denver, Colorado, September 1982.

_____. "The Neo-Conservatives and the Debate about Liberalism." Paper presented to the annual meeting of the Southern Political Science Association, Knoxville, Tennessee, November 1980.

Mann, Arthur. *The One and the Many: Reflections on the American Identity*. Chicago: University of Chicago Press, 1979.

Mann, Thomas E., and Norman J. Ornstein. *The New Congress*. Washington: American Enterprise Institute, 1981.

Mansfield, Harvey C., Jr. "The American Election of 1980: Toward Constitutional Democracy?" *Government and Opposition* 16 (Winter 1981):3–18.

_____. "The Forms and Formalities of Liberty." *The Public Interest* 70 (Winter 1983):121–31.

_____."Hobbes and the Science of Indirect Government." *American Political Science Review* 65 (March 1971):97–110.

_____. *Machiavelli's New Modes and Orders: A Study of the "Discourses on Livy."* Ithaca: Cornell University Press, 1979.

_____. "Machiavelli's Political Science." *American Political Science Review* 75 (June 1981):293–305.

_____. "The Media World and Democratic Representation." *Government and Opposition* 16 (Summer 1982).

_____. "Party and Sect in Machiavelli's *Florentine Histories*." In *Machiavelli and the Nature of Political Thought,* edited by Martin Fleisher, pp. 209–66. New York: Atheneum, 1972.

_____. *The Spirit of Liberalism*. Cambridge, Mass.: Harvard University Press, 1978.

_____. *Statesmanship and Party Government: A Study of Burke and Bolingbroke*. Chicago: University of Chicago Press, 1967.

_____, and Robert Scigliano. *Representation: The Perennial Issues*. Washington: The American Political Science Association Division of Educational Affairs, 1978.

Markovits, Andrei S., and Karl W. Deutsch. *Fear of Science, Trust in Science: Conditions for Change in the Climate of Opinion*. Publications of the Science Center Berlin, vol. 19. Cambridge, Mass.: Oelgeschlager, Gunn and Hain, 1980.

Marsilius of Padua. *The Defender of Peace*. Translated by Alan Gewirth. New York: Harper and Row, 1956.

Maurer, Reinhart Klemens. "Das antiplatonisches Experiment Nietzsches: Zum Problem einer Konsequenten Ideologiekritik." *Nietzsche-Studien* 8 (1979):104–26.

_____. "Nietzsche und die kritische Theorie." *Nietzsche-Studien* 10–11 (1982): 34–58.

Mayer, Jacob Peter. *Max Weber and German Politics: A Study in Political Sociology*. 2d ed. London: Faber and Faber, 1956.

Mendelssohn, Kurt. *The Secret of Western Domination*. New York: Praeger, 1976.

Merleau-Ponty, Maurice. "The Crisis of the Understanding." In *The Primacy of Perception and Other Essays,* edited by James M. Edie, pp. 193–210. Evanston, Ill.: Northwestern University Press, 1964.

Merrill, John Calhoun. *Existential Journalism*. New York: Hastings House, 1977.

Miller, Eugene F. "Positivism, Historicism, and Political Inquiry." *American Political Science Review* 66 (September 1972):796–817.

Mitzman, Arthur. *The Iron Cage: An Historical Interpretation of Max Weber*. New York: Grosset, 1969.

Mohler, Armin. *Die konservative Revolution in Deutschland 1918–1932. Ein Handbuch*. 2d ed. Darmstadt: Wissenschaftliche Buchgesellschaft, 1972.

Mohr, Jürgen. "Nietzsches Deutung des Gewissens." *Nietzsche-Studien* 6 (1977): 1–17.

Mommsen, Wolfgang J. *The Age of Bureaucracy: Perspectives on the Political Sociology of Max Weber.* Oxford: Blackwell, 1974.

———. "Max Weber." In *Deutsche Historiker*, vol. 3, edited by Hans-Ulrich Wehler. Göttingen: Vandenhoeck und Ruprecht, 1972.

———. *Max Weber und die deutsche Politik, 1890–1920.* 2d ed. Tübingen: J.C.B. Mohr, 1974.

———. "Universalgeschichtliches und politisches Denken bei Max Weber." *Historische Zeitschrift* 201 (1965):557–612.

———."Die Vereinigten Staaten von Amerika im politischen Denken Max Webers." *Historische Zeitschrift* 213 (1971):358–81.

———. "Zum Begriff der 'plebiszitären Führerdemokratie' bei Max Weber." *Kölner Zeitschrift für Soziologie und Sozialpsychologie* 15 (1963):295–322.

Montaigne, Michel de. *The Complete Essays of Montaigne.* Translated by Donald M. Frame. Stanford: Stanford University Press, 1943.

Montesquieu, Charles Secondat, Baron de. *Œuvres complètes de Montesquieu.* Edited by Roger Callois. Paris: Gallimard, 1961.

———. *The Spirit of the Laws.* Translated by Thomas Nugent. New York: Hafner, 1966.

Morgenthau, Hans J. "Fragment of an Intellectual Biography: 1904–1932." In *Truth and Tragedy: A Tribute to Hans J. Morgenthau,*, edited by Kenneth Thompson and Robert J. Myers, pp. 1–17. Washington: New Republic Book Co., 1977.

Morrell, Jack, and Arnold Thackray. *Gentlemen of Science: Early Years of the British Association for the Advancement of Science.* Oxford: Clarendon Press, 1981.

Mosher, Michael A. "After Virtue: The 'Vices' of a Juridical Society." Paper presented at the annual meeting of the American Political Science Association, Denver, Colorado, September 1982.

Müller-Lauter, Wolfgang. *Nietzsche: Seine Philosophie der Gegensätze und die Gegensätze seiner Philosophie.* Berlin: de Gruyter, 1971.

National Science Foundation. *Characteristics of the National Sample of Scientists and Engineers.* No. 76-323. Washington: U.S. Government Printing Office, 1975.

Nelkin, Dorothy. *Controversy: The Politics of Technical Decisions.* Beverly Hills, Calif.: Sage Publications, 1979.

Nelson, Allan D. "John Stuart Mill: The Reformer Reformed." Unpublished paper, University of Waterloo, Waterloo, Ontario.

———. "'Science' and 'Values': Arnold Brecht's *Political Theory* Revisited." *The Political Science Reviewer* 10 (1980):139–88.

Nelson, Benjamin. *On the Roads to Modernity: Conscience, Science, and Civilizations.* Edited by Toby H. Huff. Totowa, N.J.: Roman and Littlefield, 1981.

Nelson, Robert J. *Pascal: Adversary and Advocate.* Cambridge, Mass.: Harvard University Press, 1981.

Nelson, William R., ed. *The Politics of Science: Readings in Science, Technology, and Government.* New York: Oxford University Press, 1968.

Neuchterlein, James. "Liberalism and Theodore H. White." *Commentary* 74 (September 1982):32–38.

Neumann, Harry. "Political Philosophy or Nihilist Science? Education's Only Serious Question." Paper presented at the annual meeting of the American Political Science Association, Denver, Colorado, September 1982.

_____. "Socrates and History: A Nietzschean Interpretation of Philosophy." *Nietzsche-Studien* 6 (1977):64–74.

_____. "Superman or Last Man? Nietzsche's Interpretation of Athens and Jerusalem." *Nietzsche-Studien* 5 (1976):1–28.

Nichols, Guild K. *Technology on Trial: Public Participation in Decision- Making Related to Science and Technology.* Paris: OECD, 1979.

Nieburg, H. L. *In the Name of Science.* Chicago: Quadrangle Books, 1966.

Nietzsche, Friedrich. *The Birth of Tragedy and The Case of Wagner.* Translated, with Commentary, by Walter Kaufmann. New York: Vintage, 1967.

_____. *Beyond Good and Evil: A Prelude to a Philosophy of the Future.* Translated, with Commentary by Walter Kaufmann. New York: Vintage, 1966.

_____. *The Dawn of Day.* Translated by J. M. Kennedy. New York: Russell and Russell, 1964; originally published 1911, reprinted 1924.

_____. *The Gay Science. With a Prelude in Rhymes and an Appendix of Songs.* Translated, with Commentary, by Walter Kaufmann. New York: Vintage, 1974.

_____. *On the Genealogy of Morals and Ecce Homo.* Translated by Walter Kaufmann and R. J. Hollingdale. New York: Vintage, 1967.

_____. *Gesammelte Werke.* Edited by R. Oehler, M. Oehler, and F. Würzbach. Munich: Musarion Verlag, 1920–.

_____. *Human, All-too-Human: A Book for Free Spirits.* Translated by Paul V. Cohn. New York: Russell and Russell, 1964.

_____. *Nietzsche Werke. Kritische Gesamtausgabe.* Edited by Giorgio Colli and Mazzino Montinari. Berlin: Walter de Gruyter, 1968–.

_____. *Philosophy and Truth: Selections from Nietzsche's Notebooks of the Early 1870's.* Translated by Daniel Breazeale. Atlantic Highlands, N.J.: Humanities Press, 1977.

_____. *The Portable Nietzsche.* Translated by Walter Kaufmann. (Contains translations of *The Antichrist, The Twilight of the Idols,* and *Thus Spake Zarathustra.*) New York: Vintage, 1954.

_____. *Werke in Drei Bänden.* Edited by Karl Schlechta. 3 vols. Munich: Carl Hanser Verlag, 1966.

_____. *The Will to Power.* Translated by Walter Kaufmann and R. J. Hollingdale. Edited by Walter Kaufmann. New York: Vintage, 1968.

Norton, David L. *Personal Destinies: A Philosophy of Ethical Individualism.* Princeton: Princeton University Press, 1976.

Novak, Michael. "The Communitarian Individual in America." *The Public Interest* 68 (Summer 1982):3–20.

Novak, Robert D. *The Mass Media and Modern Democracy.* Edited by Harry M. Clor. Chicago: Rand McNally, 1974.

Oakes, Guy. "Methodological Ambivalence: The Case of Max Weber." *Social Research* 49 (Autumn 1982):589–615.

O'Rourke, Timothy G. "Constitutional and Statutory Challenges to Local At-Large Elections." Paper presented at the annual meeting of the American Political Science Association, Denver, Colorado, September 1982.

Orwin, Clifford, and Pangle, Thomas L. "Restoring the Human Rights Tradition." In *Human Rights: Theory, History, Policy—Essays in Memory of Victor Baras,* edited by Marc F. Plattner. Boulder, Col.: Westview Press, forthcoming.

Paige, Glenn D. *Political Leadership: Readings for an Emerging Field*. New York: Free Press, 1972.

———. *The Scientific Study of Political Leadership*. New York: Free Press, 1977.

Pangle, Thomas L. *Montesquieu's Philosophy of Liberalism: A Commentary on "The Spirit of the Laws."* Chicago: University of Chicago Press, 1973.

———. "The Roots of Contemporary Nihilism and its Political Consequences According to Nietzsche." *Review of Politics* 75 (January 1983):45–70.

Paterson, Timothy J. "Ancients and Moderns: The Case of Bacon and Lucretius." Paper presented at the annual meeting of the American Political Science Association, Denver, Colorado, September 1982.

———. "The Politics of Baconian Science: An Analysis of Bacon's *New Atlantis*." Ph.D. dissertation, Yale University, 1982.

Pious, Richard M., ed. *The Power to Govern: Assessing Reform in the United States*. New York: The Academy of Political Science, 1981.

Plato. *Charmides, Alcibiades 1, Hipparchus, The Lovers, Theages, Minos, Epinomis*. Translated by W. R. M. Lamb. Cambridge, Mass.: Loeb Classics, Harvard University Press, 1927.

———. *Euthyphro, Apology, Crito, Phaedo, Phaedrus*. Translated by H. N. Fowler. Cambridge, Mass.: Loeb Classics, Harvard University Press, 1914.

———. *Laches, Protagoras, Meno, Euthydemus*. Translated by W. R. M. Lamb. Cambridge, Mass.: Loeb Classics, Harvard University Press, 1924.

———. *The Laws*. Translated, with notes and an interpretive essay, by Thomas L., Pangle. New York: Basic Books, 1979.

———. *Lysis, Symposium, Gorgias*. Translated by W. R. M. Lamb. Cambridge, Mass.: Loeb Classics, Harvard University Press, 1925.

———. *The Republic of Plato*. Translated by Allan Bloom. New York: Basic Books, 1968.

———. *The Statesman. Philebus*. Translated by Harold N. Fowler. *Ion*. Translated by W. R. M. Lamb. Cambridge: Loeb editions, Harvard University Press, 1925.

———. *Timaeus, Critias, Cleitophon, Menexenus, Epistles*. Translated by R. G. Bury. Cambridge: Loeb editions, Harvard University Press, 1929.

Platt, Michael. "Joy and War: A Reading of *Ecce Homo*." Paper presented at the annual meeting of the American Political Science Association, New York City, September 1981.

Podhoretz, Norman. *Breaking Ranks: A Political Memoir*. New York: Harper and Row, 1979.

Pöggeler, Franz. *Die Padagogik Friedrich Wilhelm Försters*. Freiburg: Herder, 1957.

Polin, Raymond. "Nietzsche und der Staat oder die Politik eines Einsamen." *Nietzsche: Werk und Wirkungen*. Göttingen: Vandenhoeck und Ruprecht, 1974.

Popper, Karl R. *The Open Society and Its Enemies*. 2 vols. New York: Harper and Row, 1962.

———. *The Poverty of Historicism*. 2d ed. London: Routledge and Kegan Paul, 1960.

Prewo, Rainer. *Max Webers Wissenschaftsprogram: Versuch einer methodischen Neuerschliessung*. Frankfurt am Main: Suhrkamp, 1979.

Ranney, Austin, ed. *The American Elections of 1980*. Washington: American Enterprise Institute, 1980.

Rauschning, Herman. *The Revolution of Nihilism. Warning to the West*. New York: Alliance Book Corporation, 1939.

Rawls, John. *A Theory of Justice*. Cambridge, Mass.: Harvard University Press, 1971.

Rescher, Nicholas. *Scientific Progress: A Philosophical Essay on the Economics of Research in Natural Science*. Oxford: Blackwell, 1978.

Rethy, H. A. "The Descartes Motto to the First Edition of *Menschliches, alzumenschliches.*" *Nietzsche-Studien* 5 (1976):289–95.

Richter, Maurice N., Jr. *The Autonomy of Science: A Historical and Comparative Analysis*. Cambridge, Mass.: Schenkman Publishing Co., 1980.

Rickert, Heinrich. *Die Philosophie des Lebens; Darstellung und Kritik der philosophischen Modeströmungen unserer Zeit*. Tübingen: J.C.B. Mohr, 1922.

_____. "Max Weber und seine Stellung zur Wissenschaft." *Logos* 15 (1926): 222–37.

Ringer, Fritz K. *The Decline of the German Mandarins: The German Academic Community, 1890–1933*. Cambridge, Mass.: Harvard University Press, 1969.

Ritzel, Gerhard. *Schmoller versus Menger: Eine Analyse des Methodenstreits im Hinblick auf den Historismus in der Nationaloekonomie*. Offenbach: Bollwerk Verlag, 1951.

Rogin, Michael. "Max Weber and Woodrow Wilson: The Iron Cage in Germany and America." *Polity* 3 (1972):557–75.

Rohrmoser, Günter. "Nietzsches Kritik der Moral." *Nietzsche-Studien* 10–11 (1982):328–51.

Rorty, Richard. "Philosophy in America Today." *The American Scholar* 51 (Spring 1982):183–200.

Rosen, Stanley. "Benedict Spinoza." In *History of Political Philosophy*, edited by Leo Strauss and Joseph Cropsey. 2d ed. Chicago: Rand McNally, 1972.

_____. *The Limits of Analysis*. New York: Basic Books, 1980.

_____. *Nihilism: A Philosophical Essay*. New Haven: Yale University Press, 1969.

_____. *Plato's "Symposium."* New Haven: Yale University Press, 1968.

Rosengren, William R., and Mark Lefton. *Organizations and Clients: Essays in the Sociology of Service*. Columbus, Ohio: Charles E. Merrill, 1970.

Ross, Jeffrey A., et al. *The Mobilization of Collective Identity: Comparative Perspectives*. Lanham, Md.: University Presses of America, 1980.

Roth, Guenther, and Wolfgang Schluchter. *Max Weber's Vision of History: Ethics and Methods*. Berkeley: University of California Press, 1979.

Rothstein, Larry. *New Directions in Mass Communications Policy: Implications for Citizen Education and Participation*. Washington: Department of Health, Education, and Welfare, 1978.

Rousseau, Jean-Jacques. *The First and Second Discourses*. Edited by Roger D. Masters. Translated by Roger D. Masters and Judith R. Masters. New York: St. Martin's, 1964.

_____. *On the Social Contract with Geneva Manuscript and Political Economy*. Edited by Roger D. Masters. Translated by Judith R. Masters. New York: St. Martin's, 1978.

Rubin, Bernard. *Small Voices and Great Trumpets: Minorities and the Media*. New York: Praeger, 1980.

Rukser, Udo. *Nietzsche in der Hispania: Ein Beitrag zur hispanischen Kultur und Geistesgeschichte*. Bern: Francke, 1962.

Runciman, W.G. *A Critique of Max Weber's Philosophy of Social Science*. Cambridge: Cambridge University Press, 1972.

Rustow, Dankwart A. *See* Graubard.

Salz, Arthur. *Für die Wissenschaft, Gegen die Gebildeten unter ihren Verächtern*. Munich: Drei Masken, 1921.

_____. "Zur Geschichte der Berufsidee." *Archiv für Sozialwissenschaft und Sozialpolitik* 37 (1913):380–423.

Scaff, Lawrence A. "Max Weber and Robert Michels." *American Journal of Sociology* 86 (1981):1269–85.

_____. "Max Weber's Political Theory." Paper for the Colloquia and Symposia on Max Weber, University of Wisconsin, Milwaukee, February 24, 1977.

_____. "Max Weber's Politics and Political Education." *American Political Science Review* 67 (March 1973):128–41.

_____. "Social Science and Democratic Practice: Max Weber's Revisionism." Paper presented at the annual meeting of the Midwest Political Science Association, Chicago, Illinois, April 1980.

Schacht, Richard. *Hegel and After: Studies in Continental Philosophy between Kant and Sartre*. Pittsburgh: University of Pittsburgh Press, 1975.

Schaefer, David L. "The Good, the Beautiful, and the Useful: Montaigne's Transvaluation of Values." *American Political Science Review* 73 (March 1979): 139–53.

_____. "Montaigne's Political Reformation." *Journal of Politics* 42 (August 1980):766–91.

_____. "Montaigne's Political Skepticism." *Polity* 11 (Summer 1979):512–41.

_____. "Of Cannibals and Kings: Montaigne's Egalitarianism." *Review of Politics* 43 (January 1981):43–74.

_____. "Science and Skepticism in Montaigne's *Essays*." Paper presented at the annual meeting of the American Political Science Association, Denver, Colorado, September 1982.

Schajowicz, Ludwig. *Los nuevos sofistas: la subversion cultural de Nietzsche à Beckett*. Rio Piedras, Puerto Rico: Editiones Universitarias, 1979.

Schambra, William A. "The Roots of the American Public Philosophy." *The Public Interest* 67 (Spring 1982):36–48.

von Schelting, Alexander. *Max Webers Wissenschaftslehre*. Tübingen: J.C.B. Mohr, 1935.

Schlereth, Thomas J. *The Cosmopolitan Ideal in Enlightenment Thought: Its Form and Function in the Ideas of Franklin, Hume and Voltaire*. Notre Dame, Ind.: University of Notre Dame, 1977.

Schluchter, Wolfgang. *The Rise of Western Rationalism: Max Weber's Developmental History*. Translated with an Introduction by Guenther Roth. Berkeley: University of California Press, 1981.

_____. *Wertfreiheit und Verantwortungsethik: zum Verhältnis von Wissenschaft und Politik bei Max Weber*. Tübingen: J.C.B. Mohr, 1971.

Schmidt, Gustav. *Deutscher Historismus und der Übergang zur parlamentarischen Demokratie*. Lübeck: Mathiesen Verlag, 1964.

Schmitt, Gary J. "Executive Privilege: Presidential Power to Withhold Information from Congress." In *The Presidency in the Constitutional Order*, edited by Joseph M. Bessette and Jeffrey Tulis, pp. 154–94. Baton Rouge: Louisiana State University Press, 1981.

Schmolz, Hans-Martin. "Das Dilemma der politischen Ethik bei Max Weber." In *Politische Ordnung und menschliche Existenz: Festgabe für Eric Voegelin*, edited by Alois Dempf et al., pp. 476–96. Munich: Beck, 1962.

Schooler, Dean, Jr. *Science, Scientists, and Public Policy*. New York: Free Press, 1971.

Schwartz, Benjamin I. "The Religion of Politics: Reflections on the Thought of Hannah Arendt." *Dissent* (March 1970):144–61.

Searing, Donald D. "Models and Images of Man and Society in Leadership Theory." *Journal of Politics* 31 (February 1969):3–31.

Shapiro, Martin. "The Supreme Court: From Warren to Burger." In *The New American Political System*, edited by Anthony King, pp. 179–211. Washington: American Enterprise Institute, 1976.

Shapiro, William. "Nietzsche, Weber, and the Foundations of Political Science." Paper presented at the annual meeting of the American Political Science Association, Washington, D.C., August 1980.

_____. "Nietzsche, Weber, Human Nature, and Sociology." Paper presented at the annual meeting of the Southern Sociological Society, Knoxville, Tennessee, March 1980.

_____. "The Nietzschean Roots of Max Weber's Social Science." Ph.D. dissertation, Cornell University, 1978.

Shell, Susan Meld. *The Rights of Reason: A Study of Kant's Philosophy and Politics*. Toronto: University of Toronto Press, 1980.

Shell, Marc. *The Economy of Literature*. Baltimore: Johns Hopkins University Press, 1978.

Sher, George. "Ancient Wrongs and Modern Rights." *Philosophy and Public Affairs* 10 (Winter 1981):3–17.

Simmel, Georg. *Schopenhauer und Nietzsche*. Leipzig: Duncker und Humblot, 1907.

Solzhenitsyn, Alexander I. *Solzhenitsyn at Harvard: The Address, Twelve Early Responses, and Six Later Reflections*. Edited by Ronald Berman. Washington: Ethics and Public Policy Center, 1980.

Sontheimer, Kurt. *Antidemokratisches Denken in der Weimarer Republik: die politischen Ideen des deutschen Nationalismus zwischen 1918–1933*. Munich: Nymphenberger, 1968.

Sowell, Thomas. "Media Smears: One Man's Experiences." *The American Spectator* 15 (May 1982):17–20.

Spinoza, Benedict. *Works of Spinoza*. Vol. 1, *Theological-Political Treatise and Political Treatise*. Translated by R. H. M. Elwes. New York: Dover, 1951.

Stammer, Otto, ed. *Max Weber and Sociology Today*. New York: Harper, 1971.

Stent, Gunther S. *Paradoxes of Progress*. San Francisco: W.H. Freeman, 1978.

Stern, Joseph Peter. *A Study of Nietzsche*. Cambridge: Cambridge University Press, 1979.

Stevenson, William. *A Man Called Intrepid: The Secret War*. New York: Harcourt Brace Jovanovich, 1976.

Stone, Lawrence. *The Crisis of the Aristocracy, 1558–1641.* New York: Oxford University Press, 1965.

Strauss, Leo. *The City and Man.* Chicago: Rand McNally, 1964.

_____."Comments on Carl Schmitt's *Der Begriff des Politischen.*" In *Spinoza's Critique of Religion,* translated by E. M. Sinclair, pp. 331–51. New York: Schocken Books, 1965.

_____. *Natural Right and History.* Chicago: University of Chicago Press, 1953.

_____. "Note on the Plan of Nietzsche's *Beyond Good and Evil.*" *Interpretation* 3 (Winter 1973):97–113.

_____. "On the Intention of Rousseau." In *Hobbes and Rousseau: A Collection of Critical Essays,* edited by Maurice Cranston and Richard S. Peters. Garden City, N.Y.: Anchor, 1972.

_____. *On Tyranny.* Ithaca: Cornell University Press, 1969.

_____. "Philosophy as Rigorous Science and Political Philosophy." *Interpretation* 2 (Summer 1971):1–9.

_____. *Thoughts on Machiavelli.* Seattle: University of Washington Press, 1969.

_____. *What Is Political Philosophy? And Other Studies.* New York: Free Press, 1959.

Strong, Tracy Burr. *Friedrich Nietzsche and the Politics of Transfiguration.* Berkeley: University of California Press, 1975.

Sullivan, William M. *Reconstructing Public Philosophy.* Berkeley: University of California Press, 1982.

Sundquist, James. "The Crisis of Competence in Government." In *Setting National Priorities: Agenda for the 1980's,* pp. 531–63. Washington: Brookings Institution, 1980.

"Symposium: Judicial Review Versus Democracy." *Ohio State Law Journal* 42 (1981).

Taubes, Jacob. "Die Entstehung des jüdischen Pariavolkes: Ideologiekritische Noten." In *Max Weber Gedächtnisschrift* , edited by Karl Engisch et al. Berlin: Duncker und Humblot, 1966.

Taylor, Charles. *Hegel.* Cambridge: Cambridge University Press, 1975.

Thernstrom, Abigail M. "The Odd Evolution of the Voting Rights Act." *The Public Interest* 55 (Spring 1979):49–76.

Thompson, Kenneth W. *The President and the Public Philosophy.* Baton Rouge: Louisiana State University Press, 1981.

Thucydides. *History of the Peloponnesian War.* With an English translation by Charles Foster Smith. 4 vols. Cambridge, Mass.: Loeb Classics, Harvard University Press, 1919.

de Tocqueville, Alexis. *Democracy in America.* Translated by Phillips Bradley. 2 vols. New York: Knopf, 1945.

_____. *The Old Regime and the French Revolution.* Translated by Stuart Gilbert. Garden City, N.Y.: Anchor, 1955.

Toner, Nea Carrol, and Walter B. Toner, Jr. *Citizen Participation: Building a Constituency for Public Policy.* Washington: Health, Education, and Welfare, 1979.

Tönnies, Ferdinand. *Der Nietzsche-Kultus: Eine Kritik.* Leipzig: O.R. Riesland, 1897.

_____. *"Ethische Kultur" und ihre Geleite.* Berlin: F.Dümmler, 1892.

Troeltsch, Ernst. "Die Revolution in der Wissenschaften." *Gesammelte Schriften,* vol. 4, pp. 653–77. Tübingen: J.C.B. Mohr, 1921.

Tucker, Robert C. *Politics as Leadership.* Columbia: University of Missouri Press, 1981.

Tulis, Jeffrey. "Public Policy and the Rhetorical Presidency." Paper presented to the annual meeting of the American Political Science Association, New York City, September 1981.

Turner, Bryan S. "Nietzsche, Weber, and the Devaluation of Politics: The Problem of State Legitimacy." *The Sociological Review,* n.s. 30 (August 1982):367–91.

Turner, Stephen, and Regis A. Factor. *Max Weber and the Dispute over Reason and Values: A Study in Philosophy, Ethics, and Politics.* London: Routledge and Kegan Paul, forthcoming.

Ulam, Adam. *In the Name of the People: Prophets and Conspirators in Prerevolutionary Russia.* New York: Viking, 1977.

Valéry, Paul. *History and Politics.* Translated by Denise Folliot and Jackson Mathews. New York: Pantheon, 1962.

Verba, Sidney, and Norman H. Nie. *Participation in America: Political Democracy and Social Equality.* New York: Harper and Row, 1972.

Viguerie, Richard A. *The New Right: We're Ready to Lead.* Falls Church, Va.: The Viguerie Co., 1980.

Voting Rights Act. Report together with Additional Views of the Subcommittee on the Constitution to the Committee on the Judiciary. United States Senate, 97th Cong., 2d sess., on S.1992, April 1982. Washington: U.S. Government Printing Office, 1982.

Voegelin, Eric. *The New Science of Politics: An Introduction.* Chicago: University of Chicago Press, 1952.

Walzer, Michael. "Pluralism: A Political Perspective." In *Harvard Encyclopedia of American Ethnic Groups,* edited by Stephen Thernstrom et al.,pp. 781–87. Cambridge, Mass.: Harvard University Press, 1980.

Weber, Marianne. *Max Weber: A Biography.* Translated and edited by Harry Zohn. New York: Wiley, 1975.

———. *Max Weber: Ein Lebensbild.* Tübingen: J.C.B. Mohr, 1926.

Weber, Max. *The Agrarian Sociology of Ancient Civilizations.* Translated by R. I. Frank. London: NLB, 1976.

———. *Ancient Judaism.* Translated and edited by Hans H. Gerth and Don Martindale. New York: Free Press, 1952.

———. *Critique of Stammler.* Translated, with an introductory essay, by Guy Oakes. New York: Free Press, 1977.

———. *Economy and Society: An Outline of Interpretive Sociology.* Edited by Guenther Roth and Claus Wittich. 3 vols. New York: Bedminster, 1968.

———. *From Max Weber: Essays in Sociology.* Translated and edited by Hans H. Gerth and C. Wright Mills. New York: Oxford University Press, 1958.

———. *Gesammelte Aufsätze zur Religionssoziologie.* 3 vols. Tübingen: J.C.B. Mohr, 1963.

———. *Gesammelte Aufsätze zur Soziologie und Sozialpolitik.* Tübingen: J.C.B. Mohr, 1924.

_____. *Gesammelte Aufsätze zur Wissenschaftslehre*. 3d ed. Tübingen: J.C.B. Mohr, 1968.

_____. *Gesammelte politische Schriften*. 2d ed. Tübingen: J.C.B. Mohr, 1958.

_____. *Max Weber: Werk und Person*. Edited by Eduard Baumgarten. Tübingen: J.C.B. Mohr, 1964.

_____. *Max Weber on Universities: The Power of the State and the Dignity of the Academic Calling in Imperial Germany*. Translated and edited by Edward Shils. Chicago: University of Chicago Press, 1976.

_____. *The Methodology of the Social Sciences*. Translated and edited by Edward A. Shils and Henry A. Shils. New York: Free Press, 1949.

_____. "The National State and Economic Policy (Freiburg Address), Freiburg, May 1895." Translated by Keith Tribe. *Economy and Society* 9 (November 1980): 428–49.

_____. *The Protestant Ethic and the Spirit of Capitalism*. Translated by Talcott Parsons. New York: Scribner's, 1958.

_____. *Die protestantischen Ethik 2: Kritiken und Antikritiken*. Edited by Johannes Winckelmann. Munich and Hamburg: Siebenstern Taschenbuch Verlag, 1968.

_____. *The Religion of China: Confucianism and Taoism*. Translated and edited by Hans H. Gerth. New York: Free Press, 1951.

_____. *The Religion of India: The Sociology of Hinduism and Buddhism*. Translated and edited by Hans H. Gerth and Don Martindale. New York: Free Press, 1958.

_____. *Roscher and Knies: The Logical Problems of Historical Economics*. Translated by Guy Oakes. New York: Free Press, 1975.

_____. *Wirtschaft und Gesellschaft: Grundriss der verstehenden Soziologie*. 5th ed. Edited by Johannes Winckelmann. Tübingen: J.C.B. Mohr, 1972.

Weier, Winfried. *Nihilismus: Geschichte, System, Kritik*. Paderborn: F. Schöningh, 1980.

Wessel, Milton R. *Science and Conscience*. New York: Columbia University Press, 1980.

Weyembergh, Maurice. *Friedrich Nietzsche et Eduard von Hartmann*. Brussels: Publications of the University of Brussels, 1977.

_____. *Le voluntarisme rationnel de Max Weber*. Brussels: J. Duculot, 1971.

White, Theodore H. *America in Search of Itself: The Making of the President, 1956–1980*. New York: Harper and Row, 1982.

Will, George F. *Press, Politics, and Popular Government*. Washington: American Enterprise Institute, 1972.

Wills, Garry. *The Kennedy Imprisonment: A Meditation on Power*. Boston: Little, Brown and Co., 1981.

Wilson, Woodrow. *College and State: Educational, Literary, and Political Papers (1875–1913) in Two Volumes*. New York: Harper, 1925.

_____. *Constitutional Government in the United States*. New York: Columbia University Press, 1908.

_____. *The New Freedom: A Call for the Emancipation of the Generous Energies of a Free People*. With an introduction and notes by William E. Leuchtenberg. Englewood Cliffs, N.J.: Prentice-Hall, 1961.

_____. *The State*. Boston: D.C. Heath, 1892.

_____. *When a Man Comes to Himself.* New York: Harper, 1901.

Wisser, Richard. "Nietzsches Lehre von der völligen Unverantwortlichkeit und Unschuld Jedermanns." *Nietzsche-Studien* 1 (1972):146–72.

Wittenberg, Erich. "Die Wissenschaftskrisis in Deutschland im Jahre 1919. Ein Beitrag zur Wissenschaftsgeschichte." *Theoria* 4 (1938):235–64.

Wittgenstein, Ludwig. *Philosophical Investigations.* 3d ed. Translated by G. E. M. Anscombe. New York: Macmillan, 1953.

_____. *Tractatus Logico-Philosophicus.* Atlantic Highlands, N.J.: Humanities Press, 1963.

_____. "Wittgenstein's Lecture on Ethics." *The Philosophical Review* 74 (January 1965):3–12.

Wolf, Erik. "Max Webers ethischer Kritizismus und das Problem der Metaphysik." *Logos* 19 (1930):359–75.

Wolfe, Christopher. "How the Constitution Was Taken Out of Constitutional Law." Paper presented at the annual meeting of the American Political Science Association, New York City, September 1981.

_____. "John Marshall and Constitutional Law." *Polity* 15 (Fall 1982):5–25.

Wolfe, Tom. *The New Journalism, with an Anthology Edited by Tom Wolfe and E.Johnson.* New York: Harper and Row, 1973.

Wolin, Sheldon S. "Hannah Arendt and the Ordinance of Time." *Social Research* 44 (Spring 1977):91–105.

_____. "Max Weber: Legitimation, Method, and the Politics of Theory." *Political Theory* 9 (August 1981):401–42.

_____. "Political Theory as a Vocation." In *Machiavelli and the Nature of Political Thought,* edited by Martin Fleisher, pp. 23–75. New York: Atheneum, 1972.

_____. *Politics and Vision: Continuity and Innovation in Western Political Thought.* Boston: Little, Brown and Co., 1960.

_____. "The Politics of the Study of Revolution." *Comparative Politics* 5 (April 1973):343–58.

Wolters, Friedrich. *Stefan George und die Blätter für die Kunst.* Berlin: Georg Bondi, 1930.

Wood, Gordon S. *The Creation of the American Republic, 1776–1789.* Chapel Hill: University of North Carolina Press, 1969.

Yankelovich, Daniel; Amitai Etzioni; et al. *Moral Leadership in Government: A Public Agenda Foundation Report, New York, September 1976.*

Yeo, Stephen. *Religion and Voluntary Organizations in Crisis.* London: Croom Helm, 1976.

Zetterbaum, Marvin. "Self and Subjectivity in Political Theory." *Review of Politics* 44 (January 1982):59–82.

Zuckert, Catherine Held. "Nature, History, and the Self: Friedrich Nietzsche's Untimely Considerations." *Nietzsche-Studien* 5 (1976):55–82.

_____. "Nietzsche on the Origin and Development of the Distinctively Human." Paper presented at the annual meeting of the American Political Science Association, New York City, September 1981.

Zvesper, John. "Ethnicity and Liberal Democracy." Paper presented to the annual meeting of the American Political Science Association, Denver, Colorado, September 1982.

INDEX

Accident: of birth, 128; Caesarism as, 98, 275n1; conquest of, 272n56; creation of conscience as, 92; and everydayness, 264n76, 265n81, 266n109; forming of men as, 174; highest man as greatest, 129; mastery and release of, 130; popular morality as, 75, 86; popular tumults as, xiv, 245n3; science and release of, 94–95
Accountability, 11
Alcibiades, 123, 126, 131, 243, 287n175
Aldritch, John, 246n7
Allen, J. W., 266n90, 304n59
Allen, William B., 255n99
Ames, Mary E., 269n2
Antosik, Stanley J., 312n47
Arendt, Dieter, 245n1
Arendt, Hannah, 70, 238, 313n59
Aristocracy, 105, 107–9, 121, 127–28, 131–32; absurdity of, 127; as acorn, 105, 121, 127; brutality of, 107–8; as collective willing, 117–19; Montaigne's persuasion of, 60–61; nausea and, 118; Nietzsche's resuscitation of, 49–52, 64–67; as slavery for aristocrats, 121; work of, 109
Aristotle, 20, 55, 79, 106–9, 122, 195–96, 244, 306n88
Arkes, Hadley, 247n11, 310n11
Aron, Raymond, 248n1, 269n1
Asceticism, 259n18; as what is common, 118–20; destruction of, 201–2; and eros, 260n2; of the heroic bourgeoisie, 52–53; needed as historical cause, 163–64; not needed as historical cause, 61–62; as punishment of man's original nature, 117; and resentment against higher callings, 202–3; and resentment politics today, 199–200; and voluntary associations, 144–46; of Weberian science, 157–58, 160–61; and Weber's self-esteem, 262n60
Ascher, Abraham, 253n61
Axson, Ellen, 251n31

Bacon, Francis, 40, 72–73, 85–86, 89, 95–96, 155–56, 159–66, 219, 229, 241, 297n119
Bagehot, Walter, 9, 249n11, 258n5, 260n19, 276n6
Baier, Horst, 258n5, 260n19, 276n6
Balner, Hans Peter, 263nn65, 70
Barkin, Kenneth D., 261n34
Barth, Hans, 248n12
Bayles, Michael D., 310n11
Baylis, Thomas V., 311n32
Beer, Samuel H., ix, 254n82, 303n35, 304n49
Beetham, David, 246n9, 275n2, 288n2
Behler, Ernst, 260n19
Benardete, Seth, 281n59
Bendix, Reinhard, 41, 248n1, 256n106, 258n5
Bergstraesser, Arnold, 248n1
Berman, Marshall, 277n7, 278n12
Berns, Walter, 246n6, 250n23
Berry, Jeffrey M., 255n104
Bessette, Joseph M., 254n83, 311n34
Bickel, Alexander, 241, 245n2, 258n1, 314n69
Bisherjian, Richard J., 254n82
Bismarck, Otto von, 45, 282n91, 307n97
Björkman, James Warner, 288n2, 299n149
Blitz, Mark, 273n73, 312n54
Borges, Jorge Luis, 306n86
Bourne, Edward, 6–7
Boutry, G.-A., 270n13
Bragdon, Henry W., 249n8
Brand, Donald R., 245n1
Brecht, Arnold, 276n4
Brest, Paul, 246n5
Bright, John, 8–9
Brower, Daniel R., 245n1
Bruell, Christopher, 281n61, 282n81, 284n131
Bruun, Hans Henrik, 270n10

339

Eudaemonism, 59; flabby, 21, 46, 54, 60–61, 63
Evans, Fred J., 309n6
Evans, Rowland, 252n46
Eyck, Erich, 307n97

Faction, xiv, 5, 29, 31–32; Nietzsche's, 67, 70; and polyarchy, 145–47, 189–93; sixteenth-century religious, 60, 179; Weber's, 53, 63. See also Political parties
Factor, Regis A., 246n8, 250n2, 310n16
Faith, 8, 9, 93, 120, 126, 128–29, 152, 155; of politician, 194–95
Fatalism, 142, 152–53; affirming, 169, 183; and crisis of liberalism, 176–77; constancy in, 169; not science, 136; requires experimentalism, 129
Faulkner, Robert K., 249n12, 258n1, 309n4
Federalist, The, xix, 2, 3–12, 18, 28, 37, 186–89, 223–25, 238, 245n7, 252nn17–21, 313n66
Fehrenbacher, Don Edward, 254n89
Fischer, Kuno, 297n119
Fischer, Kurt Rudolf, 262n48
Flaumenhaft, Harvey, 249n13
Fleischmann, Eugene, 260n19
Fogt, Helmut, 248n26, 291n26
Force and fraud, 265n81, 268n131, 285n52; accountable, 186; affirmed, 278n13, 279nn16, 20; circumscribed by priests, 204; circumscribed by professional politics, 206–7; diapason of, 131–32; in enforcing values, 103–5; exercised by self against the self, 120–21; legitimate, 182; and life philosophy, 277n7; in obscuring terms of political discourse, xviii–xix; pathos of, 195–96; in politics of science, 94–97; in private associations, 144–46; in reshaping men, 117–18; responsible, 198–99
Forman, Paul, 289n17
Förster, Friedrich Wilhelm, 261n35
Founders of the American Republic, xiii–xv, 3–6, 11, 18, 30, 245n3, 249nn11, 13, 250n23, 252n42, 258n4, 313n66
Fox, Harrison W., Jr., 252n44
Frankel, Charles, 288n3, 302n12
Friedman, Kathi V., 249n6, 304n53
Friedrich, Carl Joachim, 180
Friedrich the Great, 85–87
Friedrich II the Hohenstaufen, 179
Friedrich Wilhelm I (Hohenzollern), 86
Frisch, Morton J., 249n12

Galileo, Galilei, 159–60
Galston, William A., 261n38, 289n5, 294n53, 313n56
Gay, Peter, 288n3
Generosité, 40, 175; not cursed, 58. See also Magnanimity
Gentleman, 65–66; bourgeois gentilhomme, 60, 62; Christian?, 112; kalokagathia, 107,

231; and scholar, xiv, 236–41; school for, 110–13, 124; as slave, 121; warlike, 132–33; Weberian suspicion of, 141; works on the, 109; written for, 78
George, Stefan, 231
Gerhardt, Volker, 276n6
Gilder, George, 309n9
Gillespie, Charles Coulton, 272n51
Gladstone, William, 183, 184
Glicksberg, Charles Irving, 245n1
Godot, waiting for, 235
Goethe, Johann Wolfgang von, 102, 118, 278n15
Good Man and Citizen, xiv, 220, 236, 241–44, 311n30; Aristotle on, 106–8, 244
Goyard-Fabre, Simone, 248n21, 268n131
Granier, Jean, 263n70, 270n13, 282n70, 314n74
Grant, George Parkin, 265n82
Grau, Gerd Gunter, 242, 247n21, 264n76, 314nn74, 76
Great politics, 48, 66–67, 103. See also Nietzsche
Grenier, Richard, 278n13, 294n56
Gruner, Rolf, 298n130
Guerlac, Henry, 272n51
Gundolf, Ernst, 292n33
Gyory, Bruce N., 253n49

Hamilton, Alexander, 85, 249n12, 313n63
Hammerton, Max, 268n1, 292n41
Harnack, Adolf von, 262n60
Hart, H. L. A., 312n39
Hartz, Louis, xviii
Hayman, Ronald, 271n14
Heatherly, Charles L., 252n46
Heclo, Hugh, 6, 250n25, 255n102
Hegel, G.W. F., xix, 58–59, 82, 88, 91–92, 97, 241, 283n99, 288n7
Heidegger, Martin, xiii, 89–91, 132, 166, 169, 234–35, 265n80, 266n91, 312n54, 313n56
Heidemann, Ingeborg, 266n94, 273n73
Heller, Erich, 265n82, 312n45
Heller, Peter, 245n1
Hennis, Wilhelm, 247n12, 267n98, 288n7, 291n22, 310n24
Henrich, Dieter, 169, 270n10
Hermens, F. A., 276n6
Hiskes, Richard P., 269n2
Historical school, xix, 18–19, 21–22, 24, 28, 32–33, 49, 51, 59, 63, 217
Historicism, xiii–xv; Nietzsche's practical, 110–21, 125–31, 215; premise of, 17–18; snakeskin, 18; theoretical, 18, 59, 214–15, 217; in Weber's account of science, 156–57; Weber's practical, 32–33, 35, 51, 62–63, 157–58, 215, 217
Hitler, Adolf, 98, 179, 181, 185, 279n19
Hobbes, Thomas, 82, 84, 85, 184, 241
Hof, Walter, 245n1